THE CAMBRIDGE COMPANION TO
ADAM SMITH

Adam Smith is best known as the founder of scientific economics and as an early proponent of the modern market economy. Political economy, however, was only one part of Smith's comprehensive intellectual system. Consisting of a theory of mind and its functions in language, arts, science, and social intercourse, Smith's system was a towering contribution to the Scottish Enlightenment. His ideas on social intercourse, in fact, also served as the basis for a moral theory that provided both historical and theoretical accounts of law, politics, and economics. This companion volume provides an up-to-date examination of all aspects of Smith's thought. Collectively, the essays take into account Smith's multiple contexts – Scottish, British, European, Atlantic; biographical, institutional, political, philosophical – and they draw on all his works, including student notes from his lectures. Pluralistic in approach, the volume provides a contextualist history of Smith, as well as direct philosophical engagement with his ideas.

Knud Haakonssen is Professor of Intellectual History in the Department of History at the University of Sussex. A Fellow of the Royal Society of Edinburgh and the Academy of Social Sciences in Australia, and Foreign Member of the Royal Danish Academy of Sciences and Letters, he is the author and editor of numerous books and texts, most recently, *Natural Law and Moral Philosophy: From Grotius to the Scottish Enlightenment* and *The Cambridge History of Eighteenth-Century Philosophy*.

CAMBRIDGE COMPANIONS TO PHILOSOPHY

OTHER VOLUMES IN THE SERIES OF CAMBRIDGE
COMPANIONS:

ABELARD *Edited by* JEFFREY E. BROWER *and*
  KEVIN GUILFOY
ADORNO *Edited by* TOM HUNN
AQUINAS *Edited by* NORMAN KRETZMANN *and*
  ELEONORE STUMP
HANNAH ARENDT *Edited by* DANA VILLA
ARISTOTLE *Edited by* JONATHAN BARNES
AUGUSTINE *Edited by* ELEONORE STUMP *and*
  NORMAN KRETZMANN
BACON *Edited by* MARKKU PELTONEN
SIMONE DE BEAUVOIR *Edited by* CLAUDIA CARD
DARWIN *Edited by* JONATHAN HODGE *and*
  GREGORY RADICK
DESCARTES *Edited by* JOHN COTTINGHAM
DUNS SCOTUS *Edited by* THOMAS WILLIAMS
EARLY GREEK PHILOSOPHY *Edited by* A. A. LONG
FEMINISM IN PHILOSOPHY *Edited by* MIRANDA
  FRICKER *and* JENNIFER HORNSBY
FOUCAULT *Edited by* GARY GUTTING
FREUD *Edited by* JEROME NEU
GADAMER *Edited by* ROBERT J. DOSTAL
GALILEO *Edited by* PETER MACHAMER
GERMAN IDEALISM *Edited by* KARL AMERIKS
GREEK AND ROMAN PHILOSOPHY *Edited by*
  DAVID SEDLEY
HABERMAS *Edited by* STEPHEN K. WHITE
HEGEL *Edited by* FREDERICK BEISER
HEIDEGGER *Edited by* CHARLES GUIGNON
HOBBES *Edited by* TOM SORELL
HUME *Edited by* DAVID FATE NORTON
HUSSERL *Edited by* BARRY SMITH *and*
  DAVID WOODRUFF SMITH
WILLIAM JAMES *Edited by* RUTH ANNA PUTNAM
KANT *Edited by* PAUL GUYER

KIERKEGAARD *Edited by* ALASTAIR HANNAY *and*
    GORDON MARINO
LEIBNIZ *Edited by* NICHOLAS JOLLEY
LEVINAS *Edited by* SIMON CRITCHLEY *and*
    ROBERT BERNASCONI
LOCKE *Edited by* VERE CHAPPELL
MALEBRANCHE *Edited by* STEVEN NADLER
MARX *Edited by* TERRELL CARVER
MEDIEVAL PHILOSOPHY *Edited by* A. S. MCGRADE
MEDIEVAL JEWISH PHILOSOPHY *Edited by*
    DANIEL H. FRANK *and* OLIVER LEAMAN
MILL *Edited by* JOHN SKORUPSKI
NEWTON *Edited by* I. BERNARD COHEN *and*
    GEORGE E. SMITH
NIETZSCHE *Edited by* BERND MAGNUS *and*
    KATHLEEN HIGGINS
OCKHAM *Edited by* PAUL VINCENT SPADE
PASCAL *Edited by* NICHOLAS HAMMOND
PEIRCE *Edited by* CHERI MISAK
PLATO *Edited by* RICHARD KRAUT
PLOTINUS *Edited by* LLOYD P. GERSON
QUINE *Edited by* ROGER F. GIBSON
RAWLS *Edited by* SAMUEL FREEMAN
THOMAS REID *Edited by* TERENCE CUNEO *and*
    RENÉ VAN WOUDENBERG
ROUSSEAU *Edited by* PATRICK RILEY
BERTRAND RUSSELL *Edited by* NICHOLAS GRIFFIN
SARTRE *Edited by* CHRISTINA HOWELLS
SCHOPENHAUER *Edited by* CHRISTOPHER JANAWAY
THE SCOTTISH ENLIGHTENMENT *Edited by*
    ALEXANDER BROADIE
SPINOZA *Edited by* DON GARRETT
THE STOICS *Edited by* BRAD INWOOD
WITTGENSTEIN *Edited by* KANS SLUGA *and*
    DAVID STERN

The Cambridge Companion to

ADAM SMITH

Edited by

Knud Haakonssen
University of Sussex

CAMBRIDGE
UNIVERSITY PRESS

CAMBRIDGE UNIVERSITY PRESS
Cambridge, New York, Melbourne, Madrid, Cape Town, Singapore, São Paulo

Cambridge University Press
40 West 20th Street, New York, NY 10011-4211, USA

www.cambridge.org
Information on this title: www.cambridge.org/9780521770590

First published 2006

A catalog record for this publication is available from the British Library

Library of Congress Cataloguing in Publication data

The Cambridge companion to Adam Smith / edited by Knud Haakonssen.
  p. cm.
Includes bibliographical references and index.
ISBN-13: 978-0-521-77059-0 (hardcover)
ISBN-10: 0-521-77059-9 (hardcover)
ISBN-13: 978-0-521-77924-1 (pbk.)
ISBN-10: 0-521-77924-3 (pbk.)
1. Smith, Adam, 1723–1790.   I. Haakonssen, Knud, 1947–   II. Title.
B1545.Z7.C36 2005
192–dc22   2005011910

ISBN-13 978-0-521-77059-0 hardback
ISBN-10 0-521-77059-9 hardback

ISBN-13 978-0-521-77924-1 paperback
ISBN-10 0-521-77924-3 paperback

Transferred to digital printing 2007

CONTENTS

List of Contributors   *page* ix

Method of Citation   xiii

Introduction: The Coherence of Smith's Thought   I
KNUD HAAKONSSEN

1. Imagination: Morals, Science, and Arts   22
    CHARLES L. GRISWOLD, JR.

2. Adam Smith, Belletrist   57
    MARK SALBER PHILLIPS

3. Adam Smith's Theory of Language   79
    MARCELO DASCAL

4. Smith and Science   112
    CHRISTOPHER J. BERRY

5. Smith on Ingenuity, Pleasure, and the
    Imitative Arts   136
    NEIL DE MARCHI

6. Sympathy and the Impartial Spectator   158
    ALEXANDER BROADIE

7. Virtues, Utility, and Rules   189
    ROBERT SHAVER

8. Adam Smith on Justice, Rights, and Law   214
    DAVID LIEBERMAN

9. Self-Interest and Other Interests   246
    PRATAP BHANU MEHTA

10. Adam Smith and History   270
    J. G. A. POCOCK

11. Adam Smith's Politics   288
    DOUGLAS LONG

12. Adam Smith's Economics   319
    EMMA ROTHSCHILD AND AMARTYA SEN

13. The Legacy of Adam Smith   366
    KNUD HAAKONSSEN AND DONALD WINCH

    Bibliography   395
    Index   401

LIST OF CONTRIBUTORS

CHRISTOPHER J. BERRY is Professor of Political Theory at the University of Glasgow. In extension of his work on the Scottish Enlightenment, he is concerned with the philosophical anthropology of politics from a Humean perspective. His books include *Hume, Hegel, and Human Nature* (1982), *Human Nature* (1986), *The Idea of Luxury: A Conceptual and Historical Analysis* (1994), and *The Social Theory of the Scottish Enlightenment* (1997).

ALEXANDER BROADIE, Professor of Logic and Rhetoric at Glasgow University, has published a dozen books on Scottish philosophy. They include *The Scottish Enlightenment: An Anthology* (1997), *The Cambridge Companion to the Scottish Enlightenment* (2003), *The Scottish Enlightenment: The Historical Age of the Historical Nation* (2003), and *Thomas Reid on Logic, Rhetoric and the Fine Arts* (2005) in the *Edinburgh Edition of Thomas Reid*.

MARCELO DASCAL is Professor of Philosophy at Tel Aviv University. He works on Leibniz, the philosophy of language, cognitive science, and pragmatics. His books include *La Sémiologie de Leibniz* (1978), *Leibniz: Language, Signs and Thought* (1987), (coed.) *Leibniz and Adam* (1991), *Pragmatics and the Philosophy of Mind* (1983), *Negotiation and Power in Dialogic Interaction* (2001), and *Interpretation and Understanding* (2003).

NEIL DE MARCHI is Professor of Economics at Duke University. He writes on the history of economic ideas and on the history and functioning of markets, in particular, markets for art. His publications include (coed.) *Economic Engagements with Art* (1999), (coed.) *Higgling: Transactors and Their Markets in the History of*

Economics (1994), and recent articles on the early modern art market and on Mandeville and Smith.

CHARLES L. GRISWOLD, JR., is Professor of Philosophy at Boston University. His publications include *Self-Knowledge in Plato's Phaedrus* (1986; reprinted in 1996); *Adam Smith and the Virtues of Enlightenment* (1999); and articles on a wide spectrum of ancient philosophy and the philosophy of the Enlightenment. He edited *Platonic Writings/Platonic Readings* (1988; reprinted in 2002). He is engaged in a major project on "Philosophy and Discontents: On Reconciliation with Imperfection."

KNUD HAAKONSSEN, Professor of Intellectual History at the University of Sussex, formerly Professor of Philosophy at Boston University, works on early modern natural law theory and on the Enlightenment in Northern Europe. He is general editor of *Natural Law and Enlightenment Classics* and of the *Edinburgh Edition of Thomas Reid* and editor of *The Cambridge History of Eighteenth-Century Philosophy* (2005). His other books include *The Science of a Legislator* (1981) and *Natural Law and Moral Philosophy* (1996).

DAVID LIEBERMAN is Jefferson E. Peyser Professor of Law and History at the University of California at Berkeley. He works on Bentham and eighteenth-century legal thought, and he has published extensively in this field, including *The Province of Legislation Determined: Legal Theory in Eighteenth-Century Britain* (1989). He is currently preparing an edition of Jean De Lolme's *The Constitution of England*.

DOUGLAS LONG teaches political science at the University of Western Ontario. He works on Hume, Smith, Bentham, and modern political thought. His publications include *Bentham on Liberty* (1977).

PRATAP BHANU MEHTA is President, Center for Policy Research, Delhi. He previously taught at Harvard and Jawaharlal Nehru University. He has published widely in areas of political philosophy, constitutional law, ethics, and intellectual history. His most recent book is *The Burden of Democracy* (2003). A book on modern constitutionalism will appear in 2005.

MARK SALBER PHILLIPS is the author of *Society and Sentiment: Genres of Historical Writing in Britain, 1740–1820* (2000) and coeditor (with Gordon Schochet) of *Questions of Tradition* (2004), as well as earlier studies of historical and political thought in the Italian Renaissance. He is Professor of History at Carleton University in Ottawa.

J. G. A. POCOCK is Harry C. Black Professor Emeritus of History at the Johns Hopkins University. His works include *The Ancient Constitution and the Feudal Law* (1957; 2nd ed., 1987); *Politics, Language, and Time* (1971); *The Machiavellian Moment* (1975); and *Virtue, Commerce, and History* (1985). He is currently working on *Barbarism and Religion*, of which three volumes have appeared so far: *The Enlightenment of Edward Gibbon, 1737–1764* (1999), *Narratives of Civil Government* (1999), and *The First Decline and Fall* (2003).

EMMA ROTHSCHILD, Director of the Centre for History and Economics at King's College, Cambridge, and Visiting Professor of History at Harvard University, is an economic historian and historian of economic thought. She is the author of *Economic Sentiments: Adam Smith, Condorcet and the Enlightenment* (2001), and she is working on a book about the American Revolution and the East India Company.

AMARTYA SEN, Lamont University Professor and Professor of Economics and Philosophy at Harvard University, was awarded the Nobel Prize in Economics in 1998 for his work on welfare economics and social choice theory. He has drawn on the writings of Adam Smith in a number of essays, including "Adam Smith's Prudence" (1986), and books, including *Poverty and Famines* (1981), *On Ethics and Economics* (1987), and *Rationality and Freedom* (2002).

ROBERT SHAVER is Professor of Philosophy at the University of Manitoba. He works on ethics. Recent publications include *Rational Egoism* (1999); "Welfare and Outcome," *Canadian Journal of Philosophy* 32 (2002); and "*Principia* Then and Now," *Utilitas* 15 (2003).

DONALD WINCH is Research Professor in the School of Humanities at the University of Sussex. His books include *Economics and Policy* (1969), *Adam Smith's Politics* (1978), (coauthor) *That Noble Science of Politics* (1983), *Malthus* (1987), and *Riches and Poverty: An Intellectual History of Political Economy in Britain, 1750–1834* (1996). He is currently working on essays that will form a sequel to *Riches and Poverty*.

METHOD OF CITATION

All references to Adam Smith are to *The Glasgow Edition of the Works and Correspondence of Adam Smith* (Oxford: Clarendon Press and Indianapolis, IN: The Liberty Fund). The references use the now standard abbreviations, listed below, and the textual divisions employed in these editions. In quotations from manuscript material, the editorial emendations have generally been adopted silently.

Corr.   *Correspondence of Adam Smith*, 2nd ed., eds. E. C. Mosner and I. S. Ross (1987).

EPS   *Essays on Philosophical Subjects*, eds. W. P. D. Wightman, J. C. Bryce, and I. S. Ross (1980), containing:

Ancient Logics	"The History of the Ancient Logics and Metaphysics"
Ancient Physics	"The History of Ancient Physics"
Astronomy	"The History of Astronomy"
English and Italian Verses	"Of the Affinity between certain English and Italian Verses"
External Senses	"Of the External Senses"
Imitative Arts	"Of the Nature of that Imitation which takes place in what are called the Imitative Arts"

Languages   "Considerations Concerning the First Formation of Languages," in LRBL

LJ   *Lectures on Jurisprudence*, eds. R. L. Meek, D. D. Raphael, and P. G. Stein (1978), containing:

LJ(A)   Report of 1762–3

LJ(B)   Report dated 1766
Early Draft   Early Draft of Part of *The Wealth of Nations*

LRBL   *Lectures on Rhetoric and Belles Lettres*, ed. J. C. Bryce
        (1983)
TMS   *The Theory of Moral Sentiments*, eds. D. D. Raphael
        and A. L. Macfie (1976)
WN   *An Inquiry into the Nature and Causes of The Wealth
        of Nations*, eds. R. H. Campbell, A. S. Skinner, and
        W. B. Todd (1976)

Introduction
The Coherence of Smith's Thought[1]

I. SMITH'S LIFE

While Adam Smith is a household name as an economist, his political economy was only part of a comprehensive philosophical system centering on the nature of human action in general. The subsequent essays analyze the main parts of Smith's system; in this introduction, I attempt a synoptic view of the coherence of that system. As we will see, Smith's systematic achievement can be understood as a bold undermining of an ancient dispute between Stoics and Epicureans, which had been revived in early modern philosophy. This is not surprising when we look at the matter from the point of view of Smith's life.[2] After schooling in his native Kirkcaldy, Smith went to the University of Glasgow (1737–40), where the main influence on him was Francis Hutcheson, who was one of the main representatives in the English-speaking world of Christianized Stoicism. However, in his twenties when he was a freelance public lecturer in Edinburgh (1748–50), Smith formed the most important friendship of his life with David Hume, the most sophisticated heir to a mixed Epicurean and sceptical tradition.[3]

---

[1] Much of this chapter derives from my Introduction, in Adam Smith, *The Theory of Moral Sentiments*, ed. K. Haakonssen (Cambridge, 2002).

[2] For comprehensive biographies, see John Rae, *Life of Adam Smith* (1895), with Introduction by Jacob Viner (New York, NY, 1965); Ian S. Ross, *The Life of Adam Smith* (Oxford, 1995); and Donald Winch, "Adam Smith," in *The Oxford Dictionary of National Biography* (Oxford, 2004).

[3] Concerning Stoicism, see Leonidas Montes, *Adam Smith in Context. A Critical Reassessment of Some Central Components in His Thought* (Houndmills, Basingstoke, Hampshire, 2004), chapter 3; James Moore, "Unity and Humanity: The Quest for the *Honestum* in Cicero, Hutcheson, and Hume," *Utilitas* 14 (2002):

What is more, while he was a student at Balliol College, Oxford, from 1740 to 1746, Smith seems to have immersed himself in this intellectual confrontation by extensive studies in recent French literature and criticism, where such disputes were prominent. In view of such a mixed background, which presumably has found expression in his Edinburgh lectures, it is hardly surprising that Hutcheson's former students received Smith less than enthusiastically when the latter took up his former teacher's professorship at Glasgow. Smith taught at Glasgow from 1751 to 1764, and was succeeded by the Common Sense philosopher Thomas Reid who was an important critic of both Smith and Hume.[4] The most distinguished student of Smith's, from an intellectual point of view, was John Millar who, as professor of law in the same university, developed Smith's analysis of social authority and law.[5]

Smith resigned his professorship to accept a lucrative position as travelling tutor for a nobleman's son, a common career move by intellectuals at the time. This entailed a few years of travel, mainly in France, where he made valuable connections with many of the leading philosophers and social thinkers, including Voltaire and physiocrats such as Quesnay and Turgot. The latter acquaintances obviously stimulated Smith in the major work in which he was already engaged. This was a development of the lectures on political economy that had formed part of this teaching in Glasgow into a comprehensive study of the modern economic system seen in the light of a new history of civil society. The tutorship carried with it a life pension, and after his return to Britain, in 1766, Smith could work undisturbed as a private scholar first at his home in Kirkcaldy and then in London while finishing his huge project. *The Wealth of*

365–86; Gloria Vivenza, *Adam Smith and the Classics. The Classical Heritage in Adam Smith's Thought* (Oxford, 2001).

[4] See Reid's manuscripts printed in J. C. Stewart-Robertson and David F. Norton, "Thomas Reid on Adam Smith's Theory of Morals," *Journal of the History of Ideas* 41 (1980): 381–98, and 45 (1984): 309–21.

[5] See especially John Millar, *The Origin of the Distinction of Ranks; Or, An Inquiry into the Circumstances Which Give Rise to Influence and Authority in the Different Members of Society* (4th ed., 1806), ed. Aaron Garrett (Indianapolis, IN, 2006); K. Haakonssen, *Natural Law and Moral Philosophy: From Grotius to the Scottish Enlightenment* (Cambridge, 1996), chapter 5; John Cairns, "'Famous as a School for Law ... as Edinburgh for Medicine': The Glasgow Law School, 1761–1801," in *The Glasgow Enlightenment*, eds. A. Hook and R. Sher (East Linton, 1995), 133–59.

Nations appeared in 1776, and it soon overshadowed Smith's name as a moral philosopher; from then on, he was the great political economist. He advised governments on such matters as trade and taxation; wrote a memorandum for the Solicitor-General on the conflict with America, recommending separation for the colonies (1778; in Corr.); and advised the government in favour of a union with Ireland (1779). He also took public office, namely as commissioner for customs in Edinburgh (1778), a well-paid position that he diligently filled for the rest of his life. At the same time, Smith had become a famous man of letters. He was a leading figure in the flourishing intellectual culture that we now call the Scottish Enlightenment, for example, as a founding fellow of the Royal Society of Edinburgh (1787); he was well connected in literary circles in London; and, although he never went abroad again, he retained good contacts in Paris.

The basis for this fame was *The Theory of Moral Sentiments* and *The Wealth of Nations*, for apart from a few smaller pieces, Smith published nothing else in his lifetime.[6] He did, however, write a good deal. First, he revised his books for new editions. The moral philosophy had six editions during Smith's life. Of these, the second (1761) was significant, containing, among other things, replies to criticism from David Hume, and the last edition was a major recasting of the work. The interpretation of Smith's revisions is a complex and open question. Here we may mention just one point, namely that the tone of Smith's treatment of the role of religion in morality becomes distinctly cooler and more sceptical in the late edition. He was widely taken to be of dubious religiosity, partly because of his association with Hume, but especially because of the warm endorsement of Hume's moral character, which Smith published soon after his great friend's death.

Smith devoted similar care to his *Wealth of Nations*, revising it repeatedly for the five lifetime editions, of which the third (1785) was particularly significant. However, he also undertook new projects. One was a "sort of theory and history of law and government," which he kept announcing in the preface to all editions

---

[6] Two articles in the first *Edinburgh Review* (1755), on Samuel Johnson's *Dictionary*, on the French *Encyclopédie*, and on Rousseau's *Second Discourse* (in EPS); and "Considerations concerning the First Formation of Languages" (1761).

of *The Theory of Moral Sentiments*. Another was "a sort of Philosophical History of all the different branches of Literature, of Philosophy, Poetry and Eloquence" (Corr., p. 287). It was presumably
drafts of these works that took up most of the sixteen manuscript
volumes which Smith got his close friends, the chemist Joseph
Black and the geologist James Hutton, to burn a few days before
his death. The former project was undoubtedly a development of
the lectures on jurisprudence, part of which Smith had realized in
The Wealth of Nations; the latter was obviously related to the early
Essays on Philosophical Subjects, published posthumously in 1795
by Black and Hutton, and to the Glasgow lectures on rhetoric and
belles lettres. Both these and the jurisprudence lectures are known
to us from students' reports on them (LRBL and LJ), but in the
absence of Smith's own words, the overall coherence of his work
remains a controversial matter of reconstruction.

Such reconstruction of a fuller image of Smith has been a task for
scholarship, especially in the last generation, whereas the popular
view of Smith has been that of the father of political economy. *The
Theory of Moral Sentiments* did, however, have an independent
legacy, although one that is ill charted. These matters are addressed
in the concluding chapter of the present volume.

2. THE NATURE OF SMITH'S MORAL THEORY

For Smith, the most basic task of moral philosophy is one of
explanation; it is to provide an understanding of those forms of
behaviour that are traditionally called moral. Like his close friend
and mentor, David Hume, Smith saw moral philosophy as central
to a new science of human nature. To this purpose, Smith analyzed
those features of the human mind and those modes of interaction
between several minds which gave rise to moral practices in the
human species. Furthermore, he traced the different patterns which
these practices assumed in response to different social, economic,
and political circumstances. He believed this procedure enabled
him to say something about which features of morality appeared
to be universal to humanity and which appeared more or less historically variable. The universality in question was entirely a matter of empirically observable generality; Smith was suggesting that
without certain elementary and quite general features we would

not be able to recognize an existence as a *human* life. Smith was, in other words, not interested in any metaphysics of morals.

Generally, Smith analyzed our moral practices in terms of the qualities of human agency, or character, but, as we will see, he also found ways of accounting for our tendency to follow rules and our inclination to give moral weight to the consequences of actions. This comprehensiveness has made Smith's theory an appealing reference point for quite different schools in modern ethics, despite the fact that he did not raise the questions of a validating foundation for morality which have been dominant since Immanuel Kant and John Stuart Mill.

Morality was, in Smith's eyes, to be approached as a matter of fact about the human species' history, but this does not mean that there is *no* normative significance to his theory. It is just a very indirect normativity. For one thing, as a natural historian of humanity, Smith sees it as his task to detail how facts guide our actions by setting limits to what we can do, and among the facts about humanity which it would be futile to ignore are such things as the constant presence of both egoistic and altruistic attitudes or the claim to some degree of individual integrity. For another thing, as a humanist, Smith obviously believed his students and readers would gain insight into their moral potential through his portraits of the complexity, even contradictions, of moral lives and moral judgments. Somewhat like a novelist, he presents a wide variety of moral characters who often judge each other but who are rarely judged directly by the author, except in his capacity as a representative of "common opinion." For the rest, judgment is up to the reader.

Smith came to the conclusion that there was a great dividing line running through human morality in nearly all the forms of it that were recorded in history. This division was between the "negative" virtue of justice, which concerned abstinence from injury, and the "positive" virtues such as benevolence or prudence, which concerned the promotion of good for others or for oneself. The indirect normativity of Smith's theory is very different for these two categories of moral virtue. No recognizably human life can be without either type of virtue, but what we can say about each in general terms and, hence, what kind of guidance such accounts can yield differs significantly between the two. Because of the individuality and, not least, the uncertainty of human life, it is impossible to formulate a universal idea of the highest good or the good life. As a consequence, the virtues that promote the goods of life can be characterized only in general terms and, across cultural and historical divides, this may amount to little more than family resemblance.

In contrast, injury is considered an evil in any type of life, and this lends a certain universality to the virtue of abstaining from injurious behaviour (i.e., the virtue of justice) because we have the ability to recognize what is harmful to another, even when we know little or nothing about that person. In other words, the action-guiding power of the positive virtues – outside our intimate life – is much more uncertain than that of the negative virtue of justice, and only the latter is so rulebound that it can be the subject of systematic treatment, namely the "science of jurisprudence." Attempts to extend such system to the positive virtues are harshly rejected by Smith as "mere casuistry," a broad category that undoubtedly was meant to include a great deal of traditional moralizing literature and not just theological casuistry.

The precision of justice that enables it to be the basis for law does, however, come at a cost. The feature of justice that makes it so important in human life is its ability to regulate behaviour between entire strangers who do not know anything about each other except that they are capable, as we all are, of injury and of being injured. However, what *counts* as injury is not a universal matter, it varies dramatically from one type of society to another. True, Smith acknowledges that every known society recognizes violence to the body, denials of personhood, and prevention of access to the surrounding world as injuries, and he is ready to recognize claims against such behaviour as "natural rights." However, his many tales of different cultures indicate that not even bodily integrity or standing as a moral agent were universal concepts and, most important, the nexus between the individual and the environment was subject to variations. There were moral facts, such as private property in land, which guided people in their social intercourse in one type of society but which were simply unknown and hence irrelevant to behaviour in other societies. Smith's "natural jurisprudence" was, therefore, very much a historical jurisprudence; you would have to know what society you were talking about if your specification of rights and duties were to be of any use. This was a cornerstone in his history of civil society, as we will see.

While jurisprudence has its foundations in ethics, it is, in other words, a separate discipline (see Chapter 8).[7] Smith planned to deal with this in a sequel to *The Theory of Moral Sentiments*, as he explained in the Preface to that work, but he never published what he wrote; as mentioned earlier, he destroyed his manuscript shortly before his death. Even so, we have a reasonable idea of what he had in mind thanks to two sets of students' notes from his lectures on jurisprudence at the University of Glasgow in the 1760s. Smith's basic course consisted of four parts: natural theology, moral philosophy, natural jurisprudence, and political theory, including political economy. Next to nothing is known about the first part, which was a traditional element in the curriculum and seems to have been very brief in Smith's hands. The moral philosophy was published as the *The Theory of Moral Sentiments* in 1759, whereas the lectures on political economy were the basis for Smith's magnum opus, *The Wealth of Nations* (1776).

Just as the virtue of justice is the foundation for natural jurisprudence, so the virtue of prudence is the basis for political economy. But while the former discipline is concerned with those characteristics or qualities that individuals acquire as rights in different societies, the latter study singles out just one quality, self-interest, without specifying its content, and then works out how people based on this one quality deal with each other. Political economy is, in other words, an attempt to work out the *relations* between "abstract" individuals, individuals about whom nothing more is assumed than that they are self-interested, or "prudent." Prices, profits, interest rates, divisions of labour, and so on are, in the famous phrase, the unintended outcome of individual actions, that is, of actions whose specific intentions are irrelevant to the explanation of these phenomena (see Chapter 12). In this connection, it should be pointed out that Smith did not mistake self-interest for selfishness (see Chapter 9); the content or object of self-interest did not seem to be of much interest for explanatory purposes.

Just as Smith never pretended that there was nothing more to human life than the assertion of rights, so he never suggested that the serving of self-interest was exhaustive of human endeavour (see Chapter 11). In both cases, he was explaining facets of the

---

[7] Cf. K. Haakonssen, *The Science of a Legislator: The Natural Jurisprudence of David Hume and Adam Smith* (Cambridge, 1981).

natural history of the human species which he thought instructive about the range of our possibilities. In both cases, he was using the theory of moral personality which he had formulated in *The Theory of Moral Sentiments*. At the end of this chapter, we look at the same phenomena as part of Smith's history of civil society.

In tracing law, politics, and economy to their basis in the operations of the human mind, Smith was in effect suggesting that these moral institutions are natural to humanity. The question is, in which sense natural? One of the most fundamental disputes in ancient philosophy had been between the Stoics and the Epicureans over this issue. The former taught that morality is natural to humankind in the sense that people have the capacity to govern their lives in accordance with the orderliness, or logos, that underlies the whole of the world. The Epicureans, in contrast, saw people as naturally self-interested and suggested that morality is a device invented to regulate self-interest so it does not become self-defeating, especially through conflict with others or through opposition between immediate and long-term interests.

The conflict between these two schools of thought was revived with great vigour in early modern philosophy. A wide variety of thinkers worked on the idea of morality as "natural" to humanity, not only on Stoic but also on Platonic (or combined Platonic-Stoic) or Aristotelian grounds, but always Christianized so that the basic idea was that natural morality was a divine gift. In Smith's immediate background, one can mention the Cambridge Platonists (Benjamin Whichcote, John Smith, Ralph Cudworth), Lord Shaftesbury and Francis Hutcheson, with their various ideas of a special moral sense as a feature of the mind, and the so-called ethical rationalists (Samuel Clarke, William Wollaston) with their view of morality as a form of rational inference. The arguments of these thinkers and their predecessors were forcefully met by a less numerous succession of neo-Epicureans who, across their many differences, agreed on the basic point that morality was a human contrivance, or artifice, to control or regulate self-interest, and they often formulated this artifice as the outcome of agreements or contracts to set up political institutions to reinforce the rules of morality. Representative and particularly influential were Thomas Hobbes, Pierre Gassendi, Samuel Pufendorf, Bernard Mandeville, and David Hume.

In the hands of the last-mentioned philosopher, the Epicurean argument received a development that was of special importance to Smith. Hume conceded that there was a certain element of natural morality in humanity, namely what I earlier called the positive virtues, but argued that this would at best sustain small social groups, such as families, whereas the big society, civil society, required justice to regulate people's pursuit of self-interest. What is more, Hume indicated that justice, although artificial, developed spontaneously as a practice among people.[8]

Smith took hold of this idea of Hume's – which also had interesting antecedents in Mandeville with which both Hume and Smith were familiar – and with one bold move Smith set aside the ancient divide over the issue of nature versus artifice in morality. This is perhaps his most original contribution to moral philosophy. Smith suggested that artifice is "natural" to humankind, that is to say, there is no condition in which people do not generate moral, aesthetic, and other conventions. Smith, therefore, completely rejected the traditional idea of a state of nature that is antecedent, whether historically or conceptually, to a civil condition, and accordingly he had no room for a social contract as a bridge between the natural and the artificial (civil) life of humanity. At the same time, he saw morality as something conventional in the sense that it is part of humanity's adaptation to the circumstances in which it happens to find itself. While a scientist of human nature, such as Smith, may divide these circumstances into types of society and may be able to discern the basic features of the human mind and personal interaction which are involved in social adaptation, he does not have access to a universal morality nor is an underlying logos any part of his concern.

3. THE THEORY OF MIND AND ACTION

David Hume had put forward a theory of the imagination which Smith developed as the core of his own theory of the mind (see Chapter 1). Elements of it are scattered through *The Theory of Moral Sentiments* but one must also turn to some of his *Essays on Philosophical Subjects*, especially the "Principles Which Lead

---

[8] See Haakonssen, *Natural Law and Moral Philosophy*, chapter 3.

and Direct Philosophical Enquiries; Illustrated by the History of Astronomy," and to the notes taken by a student from his *Lectures on Rhetoric and Belles Lettres* at Glasgow in the 1760s. For both Hume and Smith, the imagination is a mental faculty by means of which people create a distinctively human sphere within the natural world. It is the imagination that enables us to make connections between the perceived elements of both the physical and the moral world, ranging from binary relations between particular events and things to complex systems such as the national or international economy or the idea of the cosmos or of humanity as a whole. The activity of the imagination is a spontaneous search for order, coherence, and agreement in the world; satisfaction of it carries its own pleasure, whereas frustration brings "wonder and surprise" and, if prolonged, anxiety and unease.

Smith talks of this imaginative striving both in moral terms as a desire for agreement and in aesthetic terms as a concern with beauty and harmony. This reflects a distinction between two fundamentally different kinds of imagination: one is concerned with persons – both oneself and others – as agents, whereas the other has as its object things and events. We may call them – although Smith does not – practical and theoretical imagination, respectively. It is through the practical imagination that we ascribe actions to persons and see persons, including ourselves, as coherent or identical over time. In other words, the practical imagination creates the moral world. This form of imagination Smith calls "sympathy," using the word in a somewhat special sense that has led to much confusion both in his own time and subsequently (see Chapter 6).

The theoretical imagination is, in Smith's view, the foundation for all the arts and sciences (see Chapter 5). It accounts for our ability to bring order and system into things and events around us so we can orient ourselves in life. Smith is particularly good at explaining aesthetic elements of daily life, such as the craving for order and the passion for arranging things for no other purpose than that the order and the arrangement please by bringing a quietness of mind, and he uses the same principle to explain why people have a desire for machinery, gadgets, and other organised systems. Works of art, as well as of technology, are, and are appraised as, works of imaginative order. Not least, philosophy and science are products of the imagination's attempt to create order in the flux of experience (see Chapter 4). In fact, experience can only function as evidence, or be "understood," if it fits into an orderly system of beliefs. Smith underscores this view of knowledge by his frequent and self-conscious invocation of machine analogies as useful representations of the natural world and of society. Furthermore, he suggests that the human mind has a tendency to extend and secure the perceived orderliness of the world by assuming there is a supreme ordering agent with a purpose. In short, Smith sees art, technology, science, and deistic religion, including natural providence, as parts of the explanatory web that the imagination creates to satisfy its desire for order.

Smith extends these considerations to the formation of language (see Chapter 3). However, it is far from clear how we can integrate his views of language in the narrower sense with his wider and highly sophisticated theory of the communicability of our sentiments, which meshes with the rest of his theory of the mind and its social intercourse (see Chapter 2). It is particularly striking that he never employs his concept of sympathy in connection with the origins of language.[9]

Such desire for order is in many ways more urgent in our dealings with people, in contrast to the rest of nature, and the imagination with which the desire for order is pursued in this case has a special quality. When we observe the behaviour of people, we do not simply experience events, we ascribe actions to agents; we pin some change in the environment on a person as an action, and we do so because we think we see the person's point in making the change. We spontaneously see people as purposeful, and this is the central act of the practical imagination. Smith calls this sympathy and, as mentioned previously, this was a troublesome terminology. Smith does not mean that we, when we think that we see another person's point in doing something, accept or approve of that point. We cannot get to the stage of either approving or disapproving of a standpoint until we see that it *is* a standpoint. Sympathy in the most important Smithan usage is this latter process which is preparatory to any assessment of people; it is not the assessment itself. Smith

---

[9] See Hans Aarsleff, "The Philosophy of Language in the Eighteenth Century," in *The Cambridge History of Eighteenth-Century Philosophy*, ed. Knud Haakonssen (Cambridge, 2005), chapter 10.

expresses this by saying that while there is a pleasure in the mere act of understanding another's point of view, as there is in any understanding, this pleasure is distinct from whatever sentiments we may have about the object of our sympathetic understanding, sentiments which may be either pleasing or displeasing. It seems that Smith himself only came to complete clarity about this matter in the light of David Hume's criticism of his handling of it in the first edition of *The Theory of Moral Sentiments*, as we see from Smith's response (in a note to TMS, I.iii.1.9). What is more, Smith himself is far from consistent in his terminology; often he uses "sympathy" in both the traditional sense of "approval" and in the more original sense explained here.

Sympathy is characterised as an act of the imagination because we do not have access to another person's mind. What we have access to is the other person's observable circumstances, including his or her behaviour. The act of sympathetic understanding is a creation of order in the observer's perceptions by means of an imagined rationale for the observed behaviour. As agents or moral beings, other people are, therefore, the creation of our imagination. However, the most remarkable feature of Smith's theory of sympathy is that the same can be said of ourselves; as moral agents, we are acts of creative imagination. The central point is that we only become aware of ourselves – gain self-consciousness – through our relationship to others. When we observe others, we notice that they observe us, and one of the most urgently felt needs for sympathetic understanding is to appreciate how they see us. This need is heightened by the inevitability that we and our fellows have different views of our relations to each other, to third persons, and to the environment. Our imagination craves order in these actual or potential conflicts and that means a workable level of agreement about personal relations and things, as in questions of who is to lead and who to own or have the use of what. Our understanding of how others see us in these circumstances determines our view of who we are and how we stand in such relationships in life.

Through sympathy, we try to anticipate the assessment by others of ourselves, thus enabling us to adjust our behaviour before conflict arises. We internalise the external spectator and respond to this figure of the sympathetic imagination. The internal spectator has the force to prompt such adjustment of behaviour as would otherwise be demanded by external spectators to satisfy the inclination to or the need for agreement or conformity. In other words, one only learns to see oneself as a person and as a member of a moral universe of agents through sympathy with others' view of one's identity and situation in the world. Society is, as Smith says, the mirror in which one catches sight of oneself, morally speaking.

Although it is natural for people to use their sympathetic imagination as spectators of others, to form ideas of the identity of other people and themselves, and to adjust their behaviour in the light of such insight, there is obviously no guarantee that they will always succeed. The process of mutual adjustment through sympathetic search for a common standpoint often fails, and this leads to moral and social disorder. When this happens, we are commonly led to seek order in a different way, namely in our own mind. We tend to imagine how a spectator would judge us and our behaviour if he or she was not limited by prejudice, partiality, ignorance, poor imagination, or lack of ordinary good will in the way in which the actual spectators of us, including we ourselves, are limited. We imagine an ideal judgment and an ideal judge. However, this imagination is itself an act of mutual sympathy; we try to "enter into" the way in which an ideal impartial spectator would sympathize with us and thus be able to appraise us. With this imagined ideal of an impartial spectator, Smith gives a social explanation for the traditional core of each person's moral and religious being, namely his or her conscience. What is more, he suggests that our imagination commonly tends to transpose the authority of conscience to a higher plane by supposing that it is the voice of God in us. The divinity itself is a function of our imagination, the pinnacle of the dialectic of mutual sympathy that starts when we first become aware that our neighbour watches us as we watch him or her.

As Smith explained in the last part of *The Theory of Moral Sentiments*, these explanations of our moral personality in terms of empirical features of the mind were meant to set aside theories, such as those of his teacher, Francis Hutcheson, which say that we are issued with a special moral sense. In this he agreed with David Hume, just as he did in rejecting the suggestion of Samuel Clarke, William Wollaston, and others, that moral judgment and moral motivation are forms of rational inference. Finally, whatever his personal religious sentiments may have been – of which we have no real evidence – he dramatically ignored all traditional religious ideas of conscience as either an inspiration by God or a response to our fear of the might of the deity.

4. MORALS AND POLITICS

By means of this account of the human mind, its extension into its environment and, especially, its interaction with other minds, Smith provides an analysis of the structure of the moral life. The central concept is that of propriety (see Chapter 7). People judge each other and themselves by considering whether a motive is suitable or proportionate to the situation that occasions it. However, such judgments are nearly always complicated by considerations of the good or bad effects which the motive aims at. As Smith sees it, when we scrutinize our moral judgments, we consider the motivation for behaviour to be the ultimate object of our assessment. But as a matter of fact, we commonly find it difficult to reach such purity of judgment; the actual actions with their perceived merit and demerit, what Smith calls "fortune," always intervene. Indeed, it is only through actions that we have any empirical material by means of which the imagination can create ideas of motivation. The fabric of moral life is thus by no means seamless, according to Smith, because it has to be stitched together continuously from, on the one hand, the empirical evidence of a world of fortune (i.e., a world of change in which all application of standards must be uncertain), and, on the other hand, a world of minds which can only be a *common* world when the creative imagination sets up common standards for how to assess motives for action (i.e., for what counts as a proper motive for action). The ultimate act of imaginative creativity – or the highest step in our moral development – is the ideally impartial spectator of humanity, including ourselves.

Smith does not mean to say that he can specify a figure known as the ideal impartial spectator, who has the last word on what is truly proper to be done in a given situation. He is, as already mentioned, not putting forward that type of directly normative theory. Rather, his concern is to explain how people make moral assessments of the merit of their own and other people's motives and behaviour, and he suggests that this happens by an implicit invocation of their notion of ideal propriety. If he had meant this to be a criterion of right action, as opposed to an analysis of the structure of people's judgment of right action, then it would clearly have been circular and quite vacuous. The theory would in that case have said that the right action is the proper one, and the proper one is the one judged to be so by the ideal impartial spectator – who, however, is identified as the character who judges in the aforesaid manner. This type of criticism is often directed at modern virtue ethics, and because Smith is sometimes invoked as a virtue theorist, he is being tarred with the same brush. However, Smith was not a virtue theorist of the sort who could have such a problem.

Although situational propriety is the basis for people's moral judgment, it is far from enough to account for the full variety of such judgment. In the very dynamics of judging in terms of propriety lies the source of a complicating factor. When we search for an ideally impartial view of propriety, we inevitably begin to see the particular situation that we are trying to assess as one of a type: we tend to categorise, generalise, and, ultimately, universalize. This is the source of rules in our moral life; they are the unintended outcome of our actual behaviour. At the same time, moral rules tend to carry a sense of obligation because they are, so to speak, a summary of our moral experience in trying to get to the standpoint of the fully impartial spectator, with whom we sympathize in so far as we are moral beings at all (see Chapter 7). Our sense of duty is, therefore, a fear of the displeasure of the ideal impartial spectator for breach of the rules of morality, except when there are overriding rules or moral reasons. This theory of the sense of duty was crucial for Smith's idea of contract in his jurisprudence.

Smith's interesting analysis of the psychology and sociology of rule-following shows how such behaviour is found to be valuable because of its capacity for creating order and predictability in the formation of motivation and choice of action. While action in accordance with a rule is commonly found morally praiseworthy, Smith is, again, not suggesting that this is a criterion of moral rightness; it is a feature of how people judge moral rightness. What is more, the feeling of obligation to rules is only one factor among several; apart from the basic sense of situational propriety, both custom and the consequences of actions play a role. These factors will often be in tension when we try to achieve clarity about our moral standpoint. Sympathetic propriety ties us to the particularity of the situation, whereas the impartial spectator calls for the generality of rules. This becomes even more complicated when we recognize our tendency to take into account what the actual consequences, or "utility," of actions may be.

Smith's central point is that while utility certainly is a factor, it is not so much utility in the sense of the end or outcome of action as in the sense of the *means* to some end, often an end that is unspecific or entirely outside one's consideration – in other words, utility in the sense of functionality. In this connection, Smith draws ingenious comparisons between aesthetic and moral judgment in terms of utility. We appreciate the utility of a gadget such as a minutely precise watch, not because we need it to be so precise, but because such precision functions in an orderly system. In the same way, we appreciate acts of benevolence or justice, not so much because they promote the greatest happiness, but because they are of "local" utility in their specific context. However, Smith's main use of this analysis of the role of utility in our practical judgments is political. He suggests that while people commonly judge in terms of situational propriety, in the manner indicated previously, and let such judgments be influenced by their liking for how things – policies, institutions, individual politicians – function, or "fit," in a given situation, there are two types of people in particular who either misunderstand or try to go beyond this feature of ordinary moral judgment. One is the speculative philosopher who thinks that his or her own ingenuity in analysing and categorising actions in terms of their utility is also the justifying ground for agents to bring about these actions. This is the central point in Smith's criticism of David Hume's moral theory. Much less benign, let alone subtle, are the political entrepreneurs who fancy that they can think in terms of some overall goal for society, some idea of public utility or happiness. Because the latter requires a sort of knowledge that rarely, if ever, is available, it often has unfortunate political consequences, many of which receive acute analysis in Smith's *Wealth of Nations*.

Smith himself practices a subtle balancing act between philosophical theory and common-life practice in morality. He often adopts the elevated standpoint of the philosophical sage who assesses the moral and social ideas that make the world go round. In this role, Smith bases himself on an ideal of tranquility as the

end of moral life which he found equally in the Stoic and the
Epicurean traditions. At the same time, his account of moral psychology showed that everything distinctive about the life of the
human species was due to people's inability to live in tranquility.
The exercise of our productive powers, which is portrayed in *The
Wealth of Nations* and the social striving through emulative vanity
that we find in *The Theory of Moral Sentiments* were only the most
dramatic illustrations of an inescapable restlessness pervading our
lives. A dialectic tension between tranquility and activity is thus
bound to be a permanent feature of human life, and the implication is clear that it would be entirely futile for the philosopher to
defend the one over the other. Accordingly, Smith's authorial voice
assumes a tone of role-playing in these contexts; on one hand, there
is the world-weary, nearly cynical, philosophical spectator to the
world's folly, on the other hand, there is the practical man of action
with his disdain for the futility of theoretical speculation.

In addition to the analysis of moral judgment, Smith structures morality through a complex account of moral virtue. This
became especially clear in the final edition of the work, where he
added a whole new part, Part IV, devoted to the topic of virtue. He
revised the traditional schema of the cardinal virtues, which in his
hands become prudence, benevolence, justice, and self-command.
Of these, benevolence is, as we have already seen, too individual
or idiosyncratic – too "personal," as it were – in its exercise to be
constitutive of any regular social forms (which, of course, does not
detract from its moral or social value). Self-command is a sort of
meta-virtue that is presupposed in all the other virtues. Prudence
and justice are different in that both are the basis for social structures which can be accounted for in empirical terms, as we have
stressed. Prudence is concerned with the pursuit of our interests,
and this is the subject of political economy. Justice is concerned
with the avoidance of injury to our interests, and this is the subject
of jurisprudence. In both cases, history plays a crucial role because
interest is a historically determined concept; the hunter-gatherer
cannot have any interest in the stock market and, consequently,
can neither pursue nor be injured in that interest. This analysis
of the four basic virtues tallies with the division between positive and negative virtues, which we discussed earlier. In this way,
Smith provided a conceptual niche both for prudence, which he

took seriously as a virtue and whose main social effects he worked out in *The Wealth of Nations*, and for the strong theory of justice and the spectator theory of rights that provided the basis for his natural jurisprudence, as we have seen.

5. THE HISTORY OF CIVIL SOCIETY AND POLITICAL ECONOMY

Because moral personality derives from the mutual judgments of people and because such judgments depend on the social experience and imagination, the idea of personhood, including the attendant rights of persons, must vary with time and place. Smith tries to order these variations by distinguishing between four broad stages of society, defined by how wide a concept of personhood and rights they recognize.[10] In hunter-gatherer societies, little more is ascribed to persons than those things immediately necessary for their existence and recognition as persons (the latter Smith calls "reputation" in a typical fusion of concepts from Roman law and from the new history of civil society). However, with nomadic "shepherds," accumulation far beyond personal needs is accepted, and this is the basis for dependency relationships and sharp social stratification. Another qualitatively different extension of personality is the recognition of ownership in land, the agricultural stage. The latest and most abstract accretion on human personality is the formation of contractual entitlements and the associated symbolic forms of property, such as paper money and credit, which we find in commercial society.

Each extension of the concept of what can be considered a person entails a change in the interests people can have and, hence, what sort of injuries they are subject to and what rights they meaningfully can claim recognition for. The extension of rights required protection by law, and Smith's stadial history is centrally concerned with the emergence of increasingly stronger government. This is not, however, to be understood as a linear history of the past (see Chapter 10). The four stages and their inherent forces for

---

[10] See Ronald L. Meek, *Social Science and the Ignoble Savage* (Cambridge, 1976), chapter 4; and his "Smith, Turgot, and the 'Four Stages' Theory," *History of Political Economy* 3 (1971): 9–27.

the change of one stage into the next are ideal types which can be used to order the actual events of the past, although the latter have often been influenced by particular actions and events, especially the use of force and violence. In fact, the most dramatic deviation from the four-stage pattern is at the core of Smith's explanation of modern European society. He saw this society as characterized by commerce and finance, which were intimately connected with protective governments. As he explains in Book III of *The Wealth of Nations*, this alliance had its roots in feudal times, when monarchs and princes sought the assistance of the burghers of cities to curb the growing power of the major landlords, thus bringing commerce forward before agriculture had been fully developed.

Smith believed the connection between government and business was unfortunate, but not because he was concerned for business; on the contrary, he was deeply suspicious of it (see Chapter 12). His worry was for the freedom of individuals, especially those who had little more than their individuality to rely on in life. The potential in a properly functioning commercial or market society was that even the labouring poor could be free of dependence on others. The key idea was that in a market, people could sell their services without selling themselves as persons because the relationships between producer and product and between worker and employer were reduced to the circulating medium of money. However, this freedom from reliance on personal ties to employers in the traditional household "oeconomy" depended on government's ability to protect the labourers' freedom to sell their labour, a freedom that vested, corporate interests always tried to curtail by law and regulation. This was a struggle between, on the one hand, self-interest that was distorted into avarice when protected by government, and, on the other hand, self-interest that tended to be "prudent" when it was left unprotected and thus open to society's judgment of its propriety. This choice had not been open to the pre-commercial societies resting on nomadic and agricultural economies. Here, the rich could only apply their accumulated goods by consuming it, and largely this had to be done vicariously, thus creating circles of dependents in the form of extended families and tribes. In commercial society, the rich can spend their wealth on themselves by buying the goods of the marketplace, but such goods are only available if there is a division of labour that makes production on a marketable scale possible. This again requires the freedom of labourers to sell their services where there is a demand for them. The result is an unintended social order, as we have already seen, including a distribution of the wealth of the society that, although never equal, is as equitable as humanity can hope for:

[The rich] are led by an invisible hand to make nearly the same distribution of the necessaries of life, which would have been made, had the earth been divided into equal portions among all its inhabitants, and thus without intending it, without knowing it, advance the interest of the society, and afford means to the multiplication of the species. (TMS, IV.1.10)

Just as government in the interests of the common good can counteract the avariciousness of the rich, so it can remedy the corruption of the poor. The division of labour tends to enervate workers, depriving them of public spirit both as citizens and as soldiers. Smith suggests that this can be helped by education, funded in part by society, and by the multiplicity of confessional groups that tend to arise from freedom of religion. Both will tend to replace the moral community of spectators that is lost when people move away from the dependency relationships of traditional society to the "anonymity" of the wage economy in commercial society.

While, in Smith's view, law rested on the virtue of justice and the economy on the virtue of prudent self-interest, politics depended on public spirit which consisted of a great many social virtues, such as liberality, probity, generosity, courage, leadership, and distributive justice (see Chapters 9 and 11). Political activity was concerned with "police, revenue and arms," which included public works that supported commerce but that were not provided by the market; furthermore, educational and cultural measures in the wide sense indicated earlier; and, finally, defence.[11] However, politics was a much wider concept for Smith because it encompassed the great number of public offices which were certainly of a civic nature but which were not offices of the state. A wide variety of leadership roles in local communities was crucial for British society as he knew it; indeed, one could say that much Parliamentary business

---

[11] See Donald Winch, *Adam Smith's Politics. An Essay in Historiographic Revision* (Cambridge, 1978).

was an extension of such local leadership. It was politics in this sense that rested on public spirit.

As we have seen, the underlying motivation for philosophy, or science, was, in Smith's eyes, the tranquility of mind that comes with the perception of order, and order is the work of the imagination. The greater our imagination, the wider our scope for acting, for placing ourselves within a perceived order. Smith's historically based analysis of commercial society was an attempt to widen his contemporaries' imagination about what that society could be; it was no more a normative political theory than his analysis of morality was a normative ethics.

1 Imagination
Morals, Science, and Arts

Adam Smith's thought is known to us primarily through his *Theory of Moral Sentiments* and *Wealth of Nations*. We also possess a number of posthumously published essays on the history of science and the arts, as well as several sets of student notes of his lectures on jurisprudence and on belles lettres and rhetoric (none was authorized or reviewed by Smith). Smith conceived of himself as constructing a comprehensive system; what we have are parts of that system.[1] The fragmentary character of the corpus, and the absence of a treatise on "the theory of the imagination," mean that Smith's theory of the imagination must be woven together from a number of passages, of which fortunately there are quite a few. The imagination is a continuous and important theme throughout his work and would likely have been an important theme in the work he did not live to complete. In this claim about the imagination's crucial role in human life and cognition, Smith was not (and did not pretend to be) radically innovative; his emphasis on the imagination, and indeed on its creative capacity, unquestionably represents an appropriation of Hume.[2]

---

[1] In the Introduction (section 5) of C. L. Griswold, Jr., *Adam Smith and the Virtues of Enlightenment* (Cambridge, 1999), I set out the projected system. I have drawn on various parts of this book throughout this chapter, and I thank Cambridge University Press for its kind permission to do so.

[2] For helpful discussion of this point see D. D. Raphael's "'The True Old Humean Philosophy' and its Influence on Adam Smith," in *David Hume: Bicentenary Papers*, ed. G. P. Morice (Edinburgh, 1977), pp. 23–38. See also M. J. Ferreira's "Hume and Imagination: Sympathy and 'the Other,'" *International Philosophical Quarterly* 34 (1994): 39–57.

Broadly speaking, Smith presents the imagination as lying at the heart of both "sympathy" and of intellectual endeavor. In the first of these capacities, the imagination is key to sociability, common life, and morality. In intellectual endeavor, imagination is key to our ability to create illuminating and unifying accounts of the phenomena. Sympathetic imagination (examined in Section I) makes possible a complex "change of places," and enables a spectator to grasp the situation and sentiments of an actor, and an actor to see him- or herself from the perspective of a spectator (perhaps even of an impartial spectator, which is itself brought to life by the imagination). Theoretical or nonsympathetic imagination (examined in Section III) requires no such "change of places." In both practical and theoretical spheres, however, the imagination is powerfully attracted by, and productive of, order, unity, correspondence, proportion, and harmony. The imagination is narrative, not just representational; it draws things into a coherent story whenever possible, filling in gaps and searching for moral or conceptual equilibrium. The satisfaction inherent in order and completeness, rather than some further reason of utility, provides the imagination's chief motive in its various modes of activity.

The beautiful is, then, a bridge between the two capacities of the imagination. The attraction of the beautiful is also manifested in certain aspects of religious and political zeal, as well as in the admiration of wealth and power (discussed in Section II). The imagination is key to our striving to "better our condition" economically, and therefore, to the political economy set out in The Wealth of Nations. The passions of human life, including those which Smith denominates as "selfish," themselves originate in the imagination.

The possibility of moral and political corruption is inherent in the imagination's powerful drive for harmony. Smith therefore distinguishes between those "illusions" or "deceptions" of the imagination that are beneficial and those which are not, and recommends antidotes where necessary. Among the nearly irresistible impositions of the imagination is the sense of realism that accompanies moral convictions and intellectual discoveries for which we wish to claim truth and objectivity. In the concluding section of this essay, I discuss the sense in which the imagination's inventiveness is related to the convictions of ordinary life, as well as the limits to which any "theory" of the imagination is, on this account, subject.

I. IMAGINATION, SYMPATHY, AND MORALS

Selfishness and Sympathy

The fundamental problem to which Smith's moral philosophy casts itself as a response is set in the first sentence of *The Theory of Moral Sentiments*: "How selfish soever man may be supposed, there are evidently some principles in his nature, which interest him in the fortune of others, and render their happiness necessary to him, though he derives nothing from it except the pleasure of seeing it." Smith wants to oppose the view that we empathize with others only when we think it to our advantage to do so (i.e., that we treat others as means to our self-interest narrowly understood). The term "selfish" here denotes more than an undesirable trait of character; Smith is also assuming that because one person is able to "see" the situation of another, to enter into it, and to understand it, we are not "selfish" in the sense of being confined to our own selves. That is, selfishness is both an ethical and an epistemological issue. Smith is working at both normative and analytical levels in using the term.

From the first sentence of the book forward, Smith maintains that experience teaches that the gap between individuals can be bridged. The phenomenology is carefully built up from well-chosen examples. He writes:

Though our brother is upon the rack, as long as we ourselves are at our ease, our senses will never inform us of what he suffers. They never did, and never can, carry us beyond our own person, and it is by the *imagination* only that we can form any conception of what are his sensations. Neither can that faculty help us to this in any other way, than by representing to us what would be our own, if we were in his case. It is the impressions of our own senses only, not those of his, which our *imaginations* copy. By the *imagination* we place ourselves in his situation, we conceive ourselves enduring all the same torments, we enter as it were into his body, and become in some measure the same person with him, and thence form some idea of his sensations, and even feel something which, though weaker in degree, is not altogether unlike them. (I.i.1.2; emphasis added)

"Sympathy" is founded on the imagination; let us refer to it as the "sympathetic imagination." This is the bridge across our separateness. To understand the role of the imagination in Smith's *Theory of Moral Sentiments*, it is necessary to discuss his conception of "sympathy." Like "selfish," "sympathy" has two meanings: "Pity and compassion are words appropriated to signify our fellow-feeling with the sorrow of others. Sympathy, though its meaning was, perhaps, originally the same, may now, however, without much impropriety, be made use of to denote our fellow-feeling with any passion whatever" (I.i.1.5; also I.iii.1.1). In its narrow sense, sympathy is an emotion (that of compassion); in its broader Smithean sense, it is also the means through which emotions are conveyed and understood. Smith occasionally slides back and forth between the narrow and broad meanings of the term, and so between what might in a Christian tradition be thought of as a laudable sentiment or virtue, and a notion in moral psychology with bearing on epistemic issues.

The possibility of sympathy in the narrow sense of the term (as commiseration) rests on sympathy in the wider sense (as fellow feeling) because the former assumes we are able to enter into the world of another person. Furthermore, because one can sympathize with any passion, it must be possible to sympathize with someone and *not* approve of them, not even be "sympathetic" in the narrow sense of the term. Sympathy does not preclude a spectator's fellow feeling with an actor's selfish passions. Sympathy is not to be equated with approval; that would destroy the possibility of ethical evaluation and entail that disapproval amounted to no more than the inability of a spectator to enter into the situation of an actor. Sympathy is not simply a vehicle for *moral* sentiments; Smith provides examples of people sympathizing with the joy that the wealthy seem to take in their riches (I.iii.2.1). Sympathy can be distorted and distorting; it is natural to humans but must also be cultivated and refined. "Sympathy" articulates the fundamental fact of our already being, at least to some degree, "in" each others' world.

Precisely how the imagination functions in sympathy (and I use the word in Smith's broader sense unless I indicate otherwise) is a delicate matter. As we have seen, Smith writes that our senses will never carry us beyond our own situation. The imagination does not simply join us to others, it gets us "inside" their experience. It joins us to their world, to their motivations, and to the circumstances to which they are responding. Emotions are tied to objects or situations; we naturally take them as relational or intentional. Even where, as in Smith's examples at the start of the book, an emotion is communicated immediately, the imagination rushes in to fill gaps with an account or story that contextualizes the particulars under evaluation. The imagination assembles the background assumptions and narrative within which someone's emotion, action, or expression strike the observer as noble or base, graceful or offensive. The sympathetic imagination is not solely representational or reproductive. It is primarily narrative, seeking to flow into and fill up another situation, and to draw things together into a coherent story, thus bringing the spectator out of him- or herself and onto the larger stage.

All this holds whether we are observing real persons or actors in the theater; Smith almost immediately introduces examples from the arts (I.i.1.4) to illustrate our responsiveness to the situations of others. He implies that our sympathizing with imagined characters is the same kind of process as our sympathizing with "real" people in everyday life. This is one reason why drama and literature not only provide Smith with examples that nicely illustrate the workings of the imagination, but on his account are also important to our moral education. Drama and literature are central to ethics (in particular, to moral education) because the sympathetic imagination is so important to the accurate "understanding" of others and to the formation of ethical judgment.[3]

Imagination, the means by which we change places (I.i.1.3) with another, only allows us to form a proximate idea of the other's sensations or emotions, as the passage quoted previously indicates. The idea one person forms of the sensations or emotions that another is experiencing is always less lively than those sensations or emotions are to their possessor. As Smith puts it, "Mankind, though naturally sympathetic, *never* conceive, for what

---

[3] Smith's frequent use of examples and stories, as well as allusions and references to various dramas (particularly tragedies), elicit the work of the reader's moral imagination. In his lectures on rhetoric, Smith holds that successful communication is effected through "sympathy" between speaker and auditor (LRBL, i.v.56; see also i.96).

has befallen another, that degree of passion which naturally animates the person principally concerned" (I.i.4.7; emphasis added). Our fundamental separateness, then, is not obliterated through the imagination. The point is not just that one person (following Smith, let us call him or her the "spectator") does not feel the passions of the person principally concerned (the "actor" or "agent") to the same degree that the latter does. In the literal sense, the spectator does not feel the actor's feelings at all; he or she imagines being in the actor's *situation* and responds accordingly. Smith writes: "sympathy, therefore, does not arise so much from the view of the passion, as from that of the situation which excites it" (I.i.1.10). The statement is a qualified one, and importantly so, for spectators must imagine or understand the actor's response to the situation to evaluate its appropriateness. The imagination provides the spectator with access to the actor's character, or better, the actor's story, but not just from the actor's perspective.

Smith's insistence on the priority of entering through imagination into another person's *situation*, rather than simply of entering into their emotions or sentiments, is important. To begin with, it allows a measure of objectivity. If we were unable to see the situation except from the standpoint of the person affected, or if we "identified" completely with the agent's sentiments, no independent evaluation would be possible. The sympathetic imagination is not, at least when functioning properly, confined to reproducing in the spectator the sentiments of the actor.

The sympathetic grasp of the actor's situation may demand a large measure of sophisticated understanding. Because the situations that give rise to a passion can be complex and multilayered, more than one actor may be involved (as is typically the case in situations where claims about [in]justice are being made), and the facts of the matter may be complex. This is especially the case when we have a "divided sympathy" and seek to evaluate the merit of claims about unfair treatment (I.ii.4.1). Smith presents us with a spectrum of sympathy, from a sort of "contagion" view described in the third paragraph of *The Theory of Moral Sentiments* (we instinctively shrink back when we see a blow about to land on someone else's leg) to "divided sympathy" cases in which possibly elaborate assessment is required, to cases in which we do not actually stop to represent to ourselves the other's situation (say, because we just lack the time), but nonetheless express ourselves as we would had we really stopped to sympathize (I.i.3.4; this is called "artificial sympathy" at I.iii.1.12). The spectator's moral perceptions cannot simply be understood on a model of intuition or immediate apprehension. The spectator's imagination blends deliberation, understanding, and insight.

In some cases, we "feel with" the other and identify with the other's emotions; this may be termed "empathy" in the proper sense, and amounts to re-creating in oneself a sort of "analogous feeling" to that experienced by the actor.[4] In other cases, the spectator's emotions have the emotions and experiences of others as their objects; we may feel resentment at, or compassion for, the anger or grief of another. In still other cases, we "feel with" the other in that we acknowledge the actor's feelings as understandable, even though we actually feel nothing ourselves when sympathizing with the actor.

Smith's notion of sympathetic imagination is thus a supple one. In no case of "sympathy," though, do we *simply* identify with the other. If I am grieving on "your account," as Smith puts it (VII.iii.i.4), my grief will no doubt be less wrenching to me than would be my grief over my own loss of the same sort. Sympathetic imagination does not dissolve the sense of separateness of either party, as Smith tells us explicitly.[5] He thinks this appropriate, not only because it reflects our fundamental separateness as subjects, but because it also permits the spectator "emotional space" in which to comfort and assist the actor. Given the actor's desire for the fellow feeling of the spectator, the actor tries to adjust his or her responses to a level with which the spectator can sympathize. This, in turn, is both practice in self-control and helpful in alleviating the grief in question (I.iii.1.13).

Tying sympathy to situation allows Smith to explain cases in which the spectator sympathizes with the actor, even though the actor actually feels nothing of what the spectator imagines is called for. For example, we may sympathize with the insane, with infants,

---

[4] Smith himself uses the verb "identify" when speaking of the actor's attempt to see himself through the eyes of, and to adopt the sentiments of, the impartial spectator (III.3.25, 28).

[5] TMS, I.i.4.7. Similarly, see J. Deigh's "Empathy and Universalizability," *Ethics* 105 (1995): 759.

and with the dead. Imagine being in the last of these conditions, in a cold grave, "a prey to corruption and the reptiles of the earth," soon to be forgotten. The idea that death is a terrible misfortune arises "from putting ourselves in their situation [that of the dead], and from our lodging, if I may be allowed to say so, our own living souls in their inanimated bodies, and thence conceiving what would be our emotions in this case" (I.i.1.13). "Sympathizing with the dead" is obviously a widespread yet complex act. The "life" of the dead, as we picture it, is a figment of our imagination. Thus, we here seem to be sympathizing with a fictional entity of our own imagining. The immobility of the dead person is not a figment of our imagination, but our picture both of the fate of the lifeless body, and of the "dreary and endless melancholy" that seems the lot of the dead, is fanciful. Identification with the dead is an illusion in that the dead feel nothing of the misery we attribute to them.

Sympathy seems capable of entering into a situation and of grasping an actor's response to that situation even when the description of the situation and of the actor is largely made up by the sympathetic imagination. It is for this reason that in the extreme case of sympathizing with the dead, sympathy seems "selfish" in the sense that we are grieving in light of what we imagine we would feel were we in that situation. Smith refers to our "sympathy" with the dead as "illusive" (II.i.2.5, II.i.5.11). This is not to be understood as "selfish" in the sense that we care only for our welfare; in fact, Smith speaks of "illusive sympathy" in the crucial context of our resentment at the mortal harm done to another. Our sentiment that the given deed is wrong and unjust hinges on this exercise of the imagination. However, because the object of the imagination has no reality in this case, sympathy is in a sense deceptive, and the experience of "changing places" with the dead is illusory. The imagination here functions projectively.

This "illusion of the imagination" (I.i.1.13), thanks to which we sympathize with the deceased, leads us to fear our own deaths. The fear of death thus springs from what one might call the projective imagination. Here, the mechanism of sympathy produces a selfish outlook in the sense that one becomes preoccupied with one's own fate. This "selfishness" is in a crucial sense a good thing because the dread of death is "the great restraint upon the injustice of mankind" and "guards and protects the society." An illusion of the imagination is key both with respect to our desire to punish injustice and to refrain from doing it. This unintended result is a typically Smithean example of the invisible hand at work. The result is both good and bad for, as Smith himself says, the fear of death is also destructive to the happiness of the individual (I.i.I.13).

Sympathizing with the living (including with the living who are grieving on account of the death of a third person) would seem to come to more than imagining *oneself* in their situation, or else sympathy would collapse into self-centered imaginative projection. Obviously, there are disanalogies between the "illusion" of the imagination generated by sympathy with the dead, and the sense in which we sympathetically imagine the situation of living selves. Among other things, sympathy with the living can be a two-way process.

Yet, Smith's own preliminary formulations of the issue, as well as the example of sympathy with the dead, prompt the following question – is every sympathetic identification of spectator with actor an illusion in that the spectator simply projects his or her own feelings into the situation and then attributes them to the actor? The illusion would seem unavoidable when the situation is one that the spectator could not possibly experience. Let us listen to another of Smith's preliminary formulations: "As we have no immediate experience of what other men feel, we can form no idea of the manner in which they are affected, *but by conceiving what we ourselves should feel in the like situation....* Neither can that faculty [of imagination] help us to this any other way, than by representing to us what would be our own [sensations], if we were in his case. It is the impressions of our own senses only, not those of his, which our imaginations copy" (I.i.1.2; emphasis added). Formulations such as these are meant to show that we are not by nature "selfish" in the sense of incapable of entering into the situations of others or of caring about them. Yet, the process does seem, so to speak, "self-centered." This introduces a perplexing ambiguity in the whole idea of sympathetic imagination.

One could drive the point home by arguing that, in yet another respect, sympathy is fundamentally "illusive," namely in regard to the impartial spectator. Smith discusses the impartial spectator in Part III, "of Duty," and it is essential to his whole theory of duty and of autonomy that actors be able to judge themselves in light of how an impartial spectator would see them no matter how actual spectators judge. Smith refers to this imagined spectator as the "higher tribunal" or the "man within the breast, the great judge and arbiter" of our conduct (III.2.32). In such a case we evidently imagine, through illusive sympathy, a nonexistent spectator; we then imagine what we would look like from the standpoint of this imagined person, thereby sympathizing with ourselves from an external standpoint, so to speak. Our sympathizing with ourselves is not itself an act of illusive sympathy, but it is exercised from a standpoint created by illusive sympathy. The impartial spectator is meant to counter "selfishness" in the ordinary moral sense of the term (Smith speaks a great deal in Part III of conscience overawing our vanity); yet it seems, at a deep level, "self-centered." How then can this self-reflecting process provide critical perspective and detachment from oneself?

Or so one might query Smith. He certainly wants to deny that sympathy need be "selfish" in a perspective-destroying sense. Sympathy is not a matter simply of imagining what *we* would feel were we in the other's situation. Hence, he ultimately denies that sympathy is "selfish," even in this mild sense of "self-centered."[6] Consider his example, in the concluding pages of the book, of a man sympathizing with a woman's pain in childbirth:

Sympathy, however, cannot, in any sense, be regarded as a selfish principle. When I sympathize with your sorrow or your indignation, it may be pretended, indeed, that my emotion is founded in self-love, because it arises from bringing your case home to myself, from putting myself in your situation, and thence conceiving what I should feel in the like circumstances. But though sympathy is very properly said to arise from an *imaginary* change of situations with the person principally concerned, yet this *imaginary* change is not supposed to happen to me in my own person and character, but in that of the person with whom I sympathize. When I condole with you for

---

[6] Hume seeks to counter the self-love view by taking exactly the opposite of Smith's tack: "No force of imagination can convert us into another person, and make us fancy, that we, being that person, reap benefit from those valuable qualities, which belong to him. Or if it did, no celerity of imagination could immediately transport us back, into ourselves, and make us love and esteem the person, as different from us.... All suspicion, therefore, of selfish regards, is here totally excluded." *Enquiry Concerning the Principles of Morals*, in *Enquiries Concerning Human Understanding and Concerning the Principles of Morals*, ed. L. A. Selby-Bigge, 3rd rev. ed. P. H. Nidditch (Oxford, 1989), p. 234.

the loss of your only son, in order to enter into your grief I do not consider what I, a person of such a character and profession, should suffer, if I had a son, and if that son was unfortunately to die: but I consider what I should suffer if I was really you, and I not only change circumstances with you, but I change persons and characters. My grief, therefore, is entirely upon your account, and not in the least upon my own. It is not, therefore, in the least selfish.... A man may sympathize with a woman in child-bed; though it is impossible that he should conceive himself as suffering her pains in his own proper person and character. (VII.iii.i.4; emphasis added)

We seem pulled in different directions on the issue of whether the sympathetic imagination can escape the charge of being selfish. Smith began the book with the problem ("selfish" being the second word of the book proper). There it was a question of whether we naturally take an interest in the fortunes of others, regardless of the immediate benefit to us of doing so. Let us call that opening notion of selfishness "sense {1}" of the term; this is the vice selfishness. The second paragraph of the book explains how it is possible for us to identify with others, and Smith mentions the "imagination" for the first time. In the third paragraph, the process is referred to as one of "changing places"; in the fourth paragraph, the distinction between "spectator" and "the person principally concerned" arises, and we hear of an "analogous emotion" arising in them; and in the fifth paragraph, Smith introduces "sympathy" as the key explanatory term. The narrative evolves until at the end of the book (in the passage just quoted at length) we reach the more nuanced sense of selfishness. Let us call that "sense {2}" of the term. In sense {2}, "selfishness" would prevent us from entering into another's situation and person, and would deny us transcendence of ourselves. Smith rejects the reduction of sympathy to selfishness in sense {2}, arguing that we rightly take ourselves to be capable of genuinely stepping outside the circle of our own selves and our own experiences.

Is there not something paradoxical about Smith's insistence at the end of the book on the opposition between sympathy and sense {2} selfishness? Presumably, one could refrain from treating others "selfishly" in sense {1} of the term even if sympathy were selfish or "egoistic" in sense {2}. That is, I could care about others, be interested in their fortunes, and have their happiness matter to me, even if my sympathy with them could in principle come only to my imagining how *I* would feel in their situation rather than how *they* actually feel. Further, because he himself insists at the start of the book that "we have no immediate experience of what other men feel," how could I sympathize with you, *except* by imagining how I would feel were I in your situation? If Smith is right in insisting that sympathy be entirely nonselfish, he would seem to have raised the bar impossibly high, thus dooming us to what he would characterize as selfishness.

Smith must therefore deny both that sympathizing with another requires that the spectator have had an experience *analogous* to that of the actor, and that the spectator's experience form the *basis* of his understanding of the actor's experience. Otherwise, understanding another – on the relatively few occasions when the experiences of actor and spectator match each other – would come down to remembering how *I* acted or reacted in the situation. Smith plainly thinks that to sympathize with others we need not be bound by the "actual experience" condition. Part of his evidence is, I think, an appeal to ordinary experience. We do affirm that a properly attuned and informed imagination can permit a "change of situations."

It would seem to follow that, where imagination bridges the experiences of two persons, the spectator's sympathy is not "selfish" as long as it takes cognizance of the differences between the spectator and actor. For where their experiences are not identical, or even of the same sort, the spectator cannot honestly reconstruct the actor's situation in analogy with his or her own, at least not solely by analogy. Indeed, to "substitute" (to use a term from drama) one's experiences for another's, in the way that an actor on the stage does for a character when trying to get inside that character's emotional life, has as its goal the accurate representation of *that character*. It thus assumes a difference between arbitrary reconstruction and true interpretation. One has to know what experiences to substitute, how, and when.

Yet, given both that the spectator cannot feel the actor's feelings or sensations (and never does so in the same degree), and that the spectator cannot in the end escape from the fact that he or she would still be the one imagining the feeling of the actor, does it make sense to insist on the distinction between my imagining how I would feel in your situation and my imagining how you feel in your situation? I think the answer is affirmative, if it is properly qualified.

I cannot grieve on "your account" until I know what *your* situation is. Even where the two biographies overlap such that my reaction to the imagined prospect of an event taking place in my life is similar to your reaction to the event having taken place in yours, there is a difference between my sharing in the reaction because I imagine it taking place in *my* life, and sharing in it because I enter into *your* life. It is unavoidable that in imaginatively grasping how you have reacted, *I* must do the imaginative grasping. However, crucially, this does not preclude the "change of place" that Smith depicts, and consequently, does not in itself jeopardize Smith's argument that sympathy need not collapse into selfishness.

The sympathetic imagination cannot simply identify itself with "your situation" or else it would lose all critical distance; nor can it ignore the distinction in question by replacing the actor with the spectator. With this in mind, the various types of sympathetic imagination may be arranged in the following spectrum:

1. Sympathizing in cases where the object of our sympathy is not in fact "there." Smith provides us with four examples, the most striking of which is that of our "sympathizing" with the dead. The situation of the dead is not reproducible in imagination, and we have no idea, or no accurate idea, of their emotions or situation. Smith refers to this as "illusive sympathy." Sympathy here must mean imagining what we would feel if we were in the situation we have ourselves re-created on the basis of physical cues (e.g., the corpse of the deceased) and our own passions. In this instance, sympathy would be "selfish" in our second sense of the term.

2. Sympathy with someone's physical condition and sensations that cannot literally be shared with us. Smith's example is that of a spectator sympathizing with the pain felt by the man on the rack (I.i.1.2). We form some conception of what the agent feels by placing "ourselves in his situation" and conceiving "ourselves enduring all the same torments." This appears to remain "selfish" in our sense {2}; nonetheless, the spectator's imagination is not simply producing that which is sympathized with because the

living agent is in some sense there before his or her eyes. This does not appear to be selfish in sense {1}.

3. Sympathizing in cases where the actor is not primarily experiencing physical pain or pleasure, but rather of an emotion "derived from the imagination" (e.g., grief or joy, anxiety or fear). The example here is of the spectator sympathizing with a person who has lost a son (VII.iii.i.4). The spectator does not consider what he or she would feel if in the same situation as the actor; rather, he or she considers what he or she would feel if he or she *were* the actor. He or she and the actor "change persons and characters." This does not seem selfish in either sense {1} or {2}.

4. At the other end of the spectrum, we have a situation into which the spectator's imagination cannot enter. In some respects it resembles case 1, except that this time there is supposed to be real sympathy between two live persons, so to speak. However, neither is a spectator of the other; that is, neither is "outside" the other in the relevant sense. Smith's example is that of (romantic) love between two persons. Their worlds are thoroughly intertwined, but spectators cannot sympathize with the actors' mutual sympathy: "Our imagination not having run in the same channel with that of the lover, we cannot enter into the eagerness of his emotions" (I.ii.2.1). Spectators do not really understand the lovers' mutual affections; they cannot imagine or sympathize with them.

Smith often writes as though sympathy between persons is an ongoing process of adjustment, a continuous search for equilibrium. The consensus (or "mutual sympathy") reached at any point between two or more persons could be characterized from a Smithean standpoint as a fiction or story with this or that history of accommodations and claims to understanding, claims that come to be trustworthy only after standing up to repeated challenge in various contexts. It is a process with analogies in the economic sphere, not only with respect to the search for equilibrium in supply and demand (as expressed by price), but also more generally with respect to the important rhetorical dimension of selling and buying (TMS, VII.iv.25; WN, I.ii.2).

The Social Character of Sympathetic Imagination

It may seem that the theory of "sympathy" is meant to explain how an actor gets "out" of his or her own self and "into" another self, as though selves were separately constituted as isolated monads to begin with, as though the theory were intended to solve a Cartesian problem of other minds. That is quite the opposite of Smith's view. His view is, rather, that we always see ourselves through the eyes of others and are mirrors to each other.[7] We are not transparent to our own consciousness; indeed, without the mediation of the other, we have no determinate moral selves "there" waiting to be made transparent. Smith performs a thought experiment: suppose "a human creature could grow up to manhood in some solitary place, without any communication with his own species." What sort of creature would result?

To a man who from his birth was a stranger to society, the objects of his passions, the external bodies which either pleased or hurt him, would occupy his whole attention. The passions themselves, the desires or aversions, the joys or sorrows, which those objects excited, though of all things the most immediately present to him, could scarce ever be the objects of his thoughts. The idea of them could never interest him so much as to call upon his attentive consideration. (III.1.4)

Because no passion becomes the object of reflection, no passion arouses a new passion. We acquire what have been called second-order desires as a result of forming positive or negative judgments about our first-order desires.[8] We may then act to change our character and habits. For Smith, moral judgments change our desires, or in his vocabulary, our passions. This would be impossible outside society because we do not have a moral self outside the human community. Presumably, this is why he uses the striking and almost oxymoronic phrase "human creature" in the passage just quoted, a "creature" being less than fully human.

---

[7] The metaphor of the mirror is Smith's; III.1.3. For classical uses of it, see Aristotle's *Nicomachean Ethics*, 1166a30–3, *Eudemian Ethics*, 1245a28ff, *Magna Moralia*, 1213a10–27; Plato's *Phaedrus*, 255d5–6, and *Alcibiades*, I 132d–133c. Cf. Hume's *A Treatise of Human Nature*, ed. L. A. Selby-Bigge, 2nd rev. ed. P. H. Nidditch (Oxford, 1978), p. 365.

[8] I borrow these terms from H. Frankfurt's "Freedom of the Will and the Concept of a Person," *Journal of Philosophy* 68 (1971): 5–20.

Characterizations or evaluations of sensations and passions arise only in communities of specific individuals. However naturally they may arise, such characterizations of ourselves are social artifacts. By means of them, we humanize ourselves. For to "be in society" means, Smith says, to imagine ourselves as seen through the eyes of others. We cannot "be ourselves" as moral agents without imagining how we are seen by others. The asocial "creature" not only lacks a sense of "personal beauty and deformity," but it also lacks any sense of moral beauty and moral deformity. Not even the beauty or deformity of one's "own face" (III.1.3–5), let alone that of one's soul, is visible to an individual in a Rousseauan state of nature. Our natural state is in society. Spectatorship is the condition for agency – this helps explain why spectatorship is normatively prior – and imagination is a condition for seeing oneself. Smith writes: "We suppose ourselves the spectators of our own behaviour, and endeavour to imagine what effect it would, in this light, produce upon us. This is the only looking glass by which we can, in some measure, with the eyes of other people, scrutinize the propriety of our own conduct" (TMS, III.1.5). Sympathy is key to our self-conception; on Smith's account, the logic of self-knowledge is an extension of the logic of our understanding of others.[9] The privileged position of the spectator is ultimately grounded in his depiction of the natural sociability of humans, and so of our natural dependence on others for our self-conception.

In sum, we are aware of ourselves through being aware that others are aware of us; the dependence on the spectator is built in (or "natural"). We evaluate ourselves as we imagine that others evaluate us. The story does not end there – we also learn to correct mistaken views that actual spectators hold of us – but it would seem to start there. The standpoint of the spectator is privileged in its connection to evaluation, and this privileging of the spectator is internalized in the actor: we cannot see and judge ourselves except by looking at ourselves from the outside, as it were; that is just what it means to take an evaluative perspective on ourselves or others (TMS, III.1.2). Moral self-consciousness requires that I

---

[9] Cf. L. W. Beck's useful formulation of this point in *The Actor and the Spectator* (New Haven, CT, 1977), pp. 64–5.

"divide myself, as it were, in two persons" (III.1.6). The idealized judge is still a spectator – the stand-in for "the public." The theatrical relation is thus internalized; we become our own public.

Consequently, the actor has no exclusive epistemic access to his or her own emotions, none that dispenses with the spectator – with the public, with the community, and with "mankind." The claim to that privileged access cannot even be stated, except through the mediating presence of the spectator or other (language itself being a public phenomenon). Our understanding and moral assessment not just of others, but of ourselves as well, depend on an exercise of the imagination.

Imagination and the Impartial Spectator

The standard relative to which the rightness and wrongness of character and action is judged is, on Smith's account, the *impartial* spectator. Here again the imagination is crucial. The "abstract and ideal spectator" (III.3.38) is a logical development, entertained at times solely in our imagination, of traits of actual spectators. Just as we learn in childhood not only to view and judge others, but also to view and judge ourselves through the eyes of others, so too do we want to be praised for that which we find praiseworthy in them and to avoid being blameworthy for that which we find blameworthy in them.

In one passage, Smith also compares the process by which we learn to exercise balanced moral judgment to that by which we learn to make correct visual judgments. He has Berkeley's *New Theory of Vision* in mind, a book of which he thought very highly. The basic idea is that just as I cannot gauge the correct proportions of objects of different sizes and at varying distances, except by "transporting myself, at least in fancy, to a different station, from whence I can survey both at nearly equal distances," so too I cannot accurately evaluate the magnitude of my passions in comparison with another's except by viewing them "neither from our own place nor yet from his, neither with our own eyes nor yet with his, but from the place and with the eyes of a third person, who has no particular connexion with either, and who judges with impartiality between us" (III.3.3). The "natural misrepresentations of self-love can be corrected only by the eye of this impartial spectator"

(III.3.4; cf. III.5.5). Smith claims that, as in cases of sensory perception, so too in moral judgment we learn to acquire perspective by "habit and experience," not by philosophy. He once refers to the standpoint of the impartial spectator as of the "reasonable man" (II.i.2.3), but reasonableness or impartiality should not be confused with philosophical rationality. The "reasonable man" is the person of reflective and informed imagination and appropriately engaged emotions, suitably detached from the actor (or him- or herself qua actor) so as to allow perspective. The impartial spectator, and thus the moral imagination, give us at least part of what Kantian moral reason is meant to provide – and for Smith, all we really need for moral life – without any of the problematic claims about the transcendental status of reason, the reduction of emotions to "incentives" or "inclinations," the meshing of "maxims" with the a priori machinery of the categorical imperative, or claims about the mysteriously noumenal status of freedom.

The impartial spectator has normative force in part because it *defines* the moral point of view already latent in ordinary life. The verb "define" must be given its full weight here. The "precise and distinct measure" of virtue is to be found in the "sympathetic feelings of the impartial and well-informed spectator." "The very words, right, wrong, fit, improper, graceful, unbecoming, mean only what pleases or displeases those [moral] faculties," and by definition the impartial spectator exercises the moral faculties in the proper manner. Whatever this impartial spectator takes to be morally good or not, is such (III.5.5). The impartial spectator is not a heuristic procedure, one way among others of checking the accuracy of our view of things. We judge well by *becoming* impartial spectators. The impartial spectator does not look off to principles of impartiality as though to a Platonic Form. The standards for impartial spectatorship are not ultimately independent of the impartial spectator, and the impartial spectator is not an "image" of some moral "original."

Differently put, the impartial spectator is constitutive of the moral outlook.[10] Character, passions, and actions are "rendered"

---

[10] This distinction between heuristic and constitutive versions of the impartial spectator is drawn by M. Nussbaum in *Love's Knowledge: Essays on Philosophy and Literature* (Oxford, 1990), pp. 344–5.

(VII.iii.2.7) worthy of approbation or the contrary by the impartial spectator's reflective sentiments. The impartial spectator is the "natural and original measure" of virtue (VII.ii.3.21). Thus, in looking to the impartial spectator as the measure, in attempting to "identify" with and become the impartial spectator, we adopt as moral agents a standpoint that is definitive of the moral determination in question, not one from which a further search for spectator-independent standards is conducted. To characterize the impartial spectator as "constitutive" is meant to make a metaphysical point rather than describe the process of ethical evaluation. The idea is to underline the notion that the impartial spectator's evaluations are ultimately defining, in contrast with the view that such evaluations ultimately mirror an independent order of moral facts. That is, the central role played by the imagination in Smith's philosophy is the obverse of his skepticism about the "Platonic" view that there exists a knowable independent order of moral facts.

All this leads to an important issue to be pursued further in Sections III and IV, namely the constructed or projected nature of value. The nonnatural nature of moral standards is inseparable from the fact that all of morality, and indeed all the human "world," is a complex whole we communally impose on ourselves. Yet, it is also part of Smith's view that this "artificial" character of the "world" is not generally visible to actors or spectators. Correspondingly, morals are ordinarily taken as possessing a reality and authority that is external to us. Indeed, Smith himself describes how the "reality" and authority of moral norms may become understood in religious terms. Before "the age of artificial reasoning and philosophy" explicated moral rules to us, religion made them holy through the natural workings of sympathy and the passions. Smith sketches a sort of psychological anthropology of religion (III.5.4) intended to explain why moral rules are so often backed, in our imaginations, by the authority of the divine. Fortunately, "religion enforces the natural sense of duty" (III.5.13). Smith has in mind not religion as theological doctrine, but a "natural religion" composed of beliefs about God, soul, and afterlife. Unfortunately, as we will see, the imagination's deification of moral norms can also create grave risks.

Imagination and the Passions

Smith's theory of moral sentiments distinguishes between passions or sentiments whose origin is in the body, and those whose origin lies in "a particular turn or habit of the imagination" (I.ii.2.1). Phenomenologically, the key to the distinction between the two kinds of passions seems to be, on this account, that bodily passions are expressions or consequences of bodily affections or states (such as an empty stomach, an open wound), whereas this is not the case, at least at the level of ordinary experience, with states of mind such as fear and hope that depend on the work of the imagination. Furthermore, the passions of the imagination are more easily sympathized with by others than are passions of the body. Given the tremendous influence of the passions that originate in the imagination, not to mention the role that imagination plays in sympathy, we might also say – borrowing a phrase from Shaftesbury – that the imagination is the "mint and foundery" in which we are given shape.[11]

The relationship of imagination to the passions is key to whatever self-directedness humans can attain.[12] Although the passions introduce an unavoidable element of passivity into the self, passions can also be formed and directed by the imagination, and the imagination can itself be educated and directed. Smith does not explicitly connect morality with "autonomy" – not a word he uses – or with the notion of a freely legislating "will" – a word he rarely uses. His theory nonetheless insists on a place for moral agency or self-determination. By means of the imagination's capacity to reflect on self from the standpoint of the spectator, and to identify with that standpoint, one can direct one's actions and shape one's

---

[11] "Thus, I contend with Fancy and Opinion and search the mint and foundery of imagination. For here the appetites and desires are fabricated. Hence they derive their privilege and currency." From Shaftesbury's "Soliloquy, or Advice to an Author," Pt. III, sect. II, in *Characteristics of Men, Manners, Opinions, Times*, ed. L. E. Klein (Cambridge, 1999), p. 143.

[12] Joseph Cropsey argues, in contrast, that for Smith all action originates in passion. Cropsey infers that Smith cannot account for moral judgment and motivation and is, therefore, "involved in an inconsistency" of the most serious kind. Joseph Cropsey, *Polity and Economy. An Interpretation of the Principles of Adam Smith* (The Hague, 1957; reprint Westport, CT, 1977), p. 17.

character. That one type of passion is guided by an "idea" of the imagination already indicates that for Smith the emotions are in some way cognitive; beliefs are part and parcel of emotions, and beliefs may be true or false, adequate or inadequate. Smith could therefore speak of erroneous or inadequate emotions; indeed, the whole notion of rational criticism of an actor's emotions from the standpoint of a spectator is supported by this interpretation of the emotions, and he certainly speaks of our amending such emotions to better meet the standards of virtuous character and action. The proper degree of its passions is not determined by appeal to nature as much as by the judgments of the impartial spectator.

Smith divides the passions of the imagination into three: the unsocial, the social, and the selfish. His discussion implies that this tripartite division is exhaustive. The unsocial passions are above all, those of hatred, anger, and resentment. These are "unsocial" because they "drive men from one another" or assume they have thus been driven (I.ii.3.5). Judgments of justice and injustice are founded on the unsocial passions; consequently, these passions are "necessary parts of the character of human nature," and are useful both to the individual and society (I.ii.3.4).

While the unsocial passions require from the spectator a divided sympathy, the social passions elicit a "redoubled sympathy" that renders these passions particularly agreeable and becoming. These passions or affections include generosity, humanity, kindness, compassion, mutual friendship, and esteem. The selfish passions, finally, hold a "middle place" between the other two, never so odious as the one or graceful as the other. These passions include grief and joy "conceived upon account of our own private good or bad fortune" (I.ii.5.1). These passions seem not to be reducible to pleasure or pain in a physical, private sense; the selfish passions, even though there is overlap, are not passions of the body. Perhaps in this context, the term "selfish" would better be understood as "centered on self." We should note that even with respect to these passions, spectators are prepared to sympathize in some cases, particularly with great (and justified) sorrow and small (and justified) joy. Presumably, the selfish passions are at the core of the "desire to better one's own condition," whose importance Smith underlines in both *The Theory of Moral Sentiments* and *The Wealth of Nations*.

II. IMAGINATION AND CORRUPTION

Until this point, we have been examining the pivotal and constructive role played by the imagination in sociality, in one person's
understanding of another, and in self-understanding and assessment. The imagination is not, however, simply the fount of these
good things. In the area of religion, the passion for moral rectitude
easily degenerates into "erroneous conscience" or "fanaticism"
(TMS, III.6.12). The very mechanism that affords us a normative
and objective standpoint – religion – also supplies an incentive for
the corruption of norms. Vanity leads to a false exaltation of strict
duty and to the enunciation of a precise system of duties suppos-
edly derived from God (which in turn leads to casuistry), a system
that is imagined to be obligatory on all: "False notions of religion
are almost the only causes which can occasion any very gross perversion of our natural sentiments in this way" (III.6.12; "almost"
because political ideals can also have a similar influence).

Religious fanaticism is only one way in which the imagination
can loosen the bonds of custom and common sense with deleterious
results. The "delusions of self-love" press in on us: "so partial are
the views of mankind with regard to the propriety of their own
conduct, both at the time of action and after it," that this "self-
deceit, this fatal weakness of mankind, is the source of half the
disorders of human life" (III.4.5–7). Vanity is "the foundation of the
most ridiculous and contemptible vices" (III.2.4) and arises from
an "illusion of the imagination" (III.2.4; Smith also refers to this as
"self-delusion" at III.4.4). Moral blindness is thus a major theme in
Smith's vivid depiction of moral experience.

A similar pattern holds with respect to wealth-getting – a theme
present in both of Smith's books. The "desire of bettering our
condition...comes with us from the womb, and never leaves us
till we go into the grave." Between birth and death one is never
"so perfectly and completely satisfied with his condition, as to be
without any wish of alteration or improvement," and "augmentation of fortune is the means by which the great part of men propose
and wish to better their condition" (WN, II.iii.28). In *The Theory of
Moral Sentiments*, Smith argues that not "passions of the body,"
not "physical" needs, but the drive to be the object of approbation, underlies this never-ending effort to better ourselves. For in

that approbation, we think, lies happiness. The acquisitive urge is traced to a mistake brought about by the imagination:

If we consider the real satisfaction which all these things are capable of affording, by itself and separated from the beauty of that arrangement which is fitted to promote it, it will always appear in the highest degree contemptible and trifling. But we rarely view it in this abstract and philosophical light. We naturally confound it in our imagination with the order, the regular and harmonious movement of the system, the machine or oeconomy by means of which it is produced. The pleasures of wealth and greatness, when considered in this complex view, strike the imagination as something grand and beautiful and noble, of which the attainment is well worth all the toil and anxiety which we are so apt to bestow upon it. (IV.i.9)

This remarkable phenomenon is aesthetic at two levels. First, we yearn for the harmony or beauty of a correspondence of sentiments with spectators that we (rightly) imagine is the good fortune of the wealthy and powerful. Second, the spectators' approval of the wealthy and powerful is "disinterested" (TMS, I.iii.3.2), a function of their appreciation of the beauty of countless "trinkets of frivolous utility" possessed by the rich and powerful. It is not any sense of the purposes to which these goods (from watches to clothes to carriages to houses) may be put, but rather their intrinsic fineness that draws us; and this attraction of the beautiful "is often the secret motive of the most serious and more important pursuits of both private and public life" (IV.1.7, 6). Both levels of aesthetic appreciation are the work of the imagination; yet, the association of happiness with that seemingly beautiful life is fallacious. Smith refers to that association as a "deception" produced by our imagination and as imposed (his verb) on us by nature (IV.1.10).

The immediate result of this deception is that, except in those rare moments when we view beauty in an "abstract and philosophical light" (IV.1.9), we are plunged into the world of unceasing work, of "bettering our condition," and therefore of unhappiness. Bettering our condition leaves us "constantly dissatisfied" (VI.iii.51). Human life is naturally restless, driven not so much by fear (as Hobbes suggested), but by longing for a species of beauty. The comic irony of this general picture of human life is unmistakable. It is crucial to see that *The Wealth of Nations,* and so the world of wealth-getting it promotes, is painted *within* this frame. Such is a good portion of human life in modern liberal commercial society, as conceived by Smith.

In a twist so typical of his thinking, Smith argues that it actually contributes to the "happiness of mankind, as well as of all rational beings," that most individuals are *not* perfectly happy. The deception of the imagination underlying the drive to better our condition, vulgarly understood, creates "progress" or "civilization" (i.e., productive labor), which under conditions of liberty and justice may increase the wealth of nations: "it is this deception which rouses and keeps in continual motion the industry of mankind" (IV.I.10). This may in turn lead to all the social, political, and scientific improvements we prize. It is in this context of our deception by our own imaginations that Smith makes the one reference, in *The Theory of Moral Sentiments* to the famous "invisible hand," thanks to which the striving of individuals to better their condition leads to the unintended distribution of their wealth to others, thus advancing the interest of society (IV.i.10). It is good that things are arranged thus, or so Smith argues. But what will restrain the illusions of the imagination from wreaking mischief?

To begin with, moral education – the habit of deliberating with appropriate appeal to general rules, and so with an understanding that they are *general* – ought be ingrained in the character of a virtuous person. Conversation with self and others on the great stage of human life is part and parcel of this education. Much of moral education consists in training the imagination rightly. Judgment about the right choice of action in a given situation will require imagination because we must represent to ourselves possible courses of action, consider the intended effects of our choice on others and thus view the situation from their standpoint, and indeed review our own motivations from the (imagined) standpoint of an impartial spectator.[13] Other factors will be important, including proper social institutions that encourage the evolution of conscience but not religious fanaticism. In Book V of *The Wealth of Nations*, he argues that the separation of church and state, along with other liberal political and social arrangements, support this end.

---

[13] On the moral imagination, cf. C. E. Larmore's *Patterns of Moral Complexity* (Cambridge, 1987).

Smith's striking account of wealth-getting is followed by still other observations of the influence of "the same principle, the same love of system, the same regard to the beauty of order, of art and contrivance." He singles out the effect of this love of beauty on public spiritedness, and argues that public benefactors (including legislatures) are often inspired not so much by sympathy with those in need of help, as the pleasing "contemplation" of so "beautiful and grand a system" of law or a constitution or economic measures. Public spiritedness may be improved by the "study of politics," i.e., "works of speculation" that exhibit the beauty of ordered complexity (TMS, IV.1.11). Heroic self-sacrifice may also be inspired by the "unexpected, and on that account the great, the noble, and exalted propriety of such actions" (IV.2.11). Thus, the love of beauty has not only crucial moral and economic consequences, it also has decisive political consequences.

Here again, the imagination can exert its grip in a deleterious fashion. Some of Smith's most compelling passages describe the "man of system" who, "intoxicated with the imaginary beauty of this [his] ideal system," will suffer no deviation from it. "He seems to imagine that he can arrange the different members of a great society with as much ease as the hand arranges the different pieces on a chess-board" (VI.ii.2.15, 17). This is a formula for disaster, and Smith's famous prescriptions for the "system of natural liberty" is intended in part as the antidote to this particular degeneracy of the "intoxicated" imagination.

III. IMAGINATION, THEORY, AND UNITY

The love of beauty, concord, and harmony is manifested in sympathy and morals, politics, economics, and religion. It also shows itself in the "abstruser sciences" such as mathematics, which earn our admiration on account not of their utility but of their exactitude and orderliness (TMS, IV.2.7). In his essays on the history of astronomy and physics, Smith develops, at some length, the notion that good "philosophy" (in a sense broad enough to include what today we call "science") grips us because of the elegance, conceptual fineness, systematic arrangement, and capacity to explain much on the basis of few principles. Theoretical intelligence is also attracted by the beauty of the "machine," regardless of its external purpose; nature is one such machine or system, human nature another. The passages from Smith's posthumously published essay, "Of the Nature of That Imitation Which Takes Place in What Are Called the Imitative Arts," may be brought to bear here. Smith describes a "well-composed concerto of instrumental Music," noting that "in the contemplation of that immense variety of agreeable and melodious sounds, arranged and digested, both in their coincidence and in their succession, into so complete and regular a system, the mind in reality enjoys not only a very great sensual, but a very high intellectual, pleasure, not unlike that which it derives from the contemplation of a great system in any other science" (II.30, EPS, 204–5). In contemplating the vast system of nature as though it were a well-composed concerto, the theorist imagines not the utility of the system for some further purpose, but instead enjoys its intricate internal order. Both the concerto and the "system of nature" are the products, on Smith's account, of the imagination's unifying and constructive labor.

Theorizing, whether about moral philosophy or a system of religious duties or astronomy, heavily depends on the imagination. In contrast with empathetic imagining, however, theoretical imagining does not require us to put ourselves in the situation of another person. No "imaginary change of situations" is required for two persons to agree in their judgment of "the beauty of a plain" or of an intellectual matter (TMS, I.i.4.2). Morality is not primarily a philosophical, theological, or scientific matter; and these intellectual pursuits are not primarily ethical (IV.2.12). Intellectual endeavor characteristic of the natural sciences relies on the nonsympathetic imagination. Sympathy and theoretical reason are distinct for Smith, then, but both depend on the imagination's harmony-seeking, unifying, constructive character. The demand of the imagination for order, harmony, and tranquility drives our desire for both "correspondence of sentiments" and intellectual coherence.

The much debated issue of teleology in Smith's philosophy should be seen in the light of his account of both our drive for a picture of the whole as harmonious and of the beautiful as that which inspires human endeavor at all levels. Teleology, understood as the notion of an ordered nature or world, is parasitic on aesthetics, not on some independent religious faith of Smith's or on an argument from design whose fallacies Smith had already learned from Hume. Teleology is not a description of how the world is, but a postulation of the harmony we yearn for it to have. It is therefore a regulative ideal, and in terms of the theorist's demand for system, it performs work.

Thus, when Smith refers to the "invisible hand of Jupiter" in his "History of Astronomy," he uses the metaphor to characterize a mythological view held by the "vulgar superstition" of polytheism (III.2, EPS, 49). Smith has his own uses for the "invisible hand," but they are – and on his own account must be – sophisticated refinements of the same sort of exercise of the intellectual imagination. Just as the "invisible hand of Jupiter" was part of the vocabulary of ancient "superstition," the "invisible hand" is part of Smith's philosophical and protreptic rhetoric whose purpose is likewise to establish order persuasively. The many "teleological" or even, on occasion, "religious" statements in *The Theory of Moral Sentiments* must be understood in connection with this aestheticized, speculative outlook. All are ways of rendering experience whole, organized, harmonious, or presenting a picture of unity and beauty. While Smith is adamant that we not confuse teleological characterizations of the philosophical sort with appeals to efficient causality, we must still attempt such characterizations to satisfy the imagination's yearning for beauty.

Smith tells us that "nature ... seems to abound with events which appear solitary and incoherent with all that go before them, which therefore disturb the easy movement of the imagination" and that this disorganization is answered by philosophy that "endeavours to introduce order into this chaos of jarring and discordant appearances, to allay this tumult of the imagination, and to restore it, when it surveys the great revolutions of the universe, to that tone of tranquillity and composure, which is most agreeable in itself, and most suitable to its nature" ("Astronomy," II.12, EPS, 45–6). Ordinary life is also given to "this chaos of jarring and discordant appearances," as is shown by the long history of religious war, for example. The imagination's pleasure would be all the greater when the order contemplated is as seemingly unsystematic and surprising as that of a "system of natural liberty." This "system" embodies a clear understanding of both human imperfection and the great role of chance in human life.

In his accounts of philosophical inquiry, Smith seeks to show that "the repose and tranquillity of the imagination is the ultimate end of philosophy," whereas wonder and perplexity provoke philosophy ("Astronomy," IV.13, EPS, 61). Philosophical views of "the whole" are not so much discoveries of pre-existing harmonies as they are creative efforts to render appearances harmonious. The "History of Astronomy" essay sets out to explain how each system "was fitted to sooth the imagination, and to render the theatre of nature a more coherent, and therefore a more magnificent spectacle, than otherwise it would have appeared to be" (II.12, EPS, 46). The imagination converses with itself in the context of its observation of events on the great stage of nature. Whether theories "really" link up with a "cosmos" is a question about which Smith has suspended judgment because the mind shapes "nature" (understood as a mind-independent system, an intelligible whole) and what appears to us. Even when theorizing, we are in fact contemplating the phenomena as taken up in the "inventions of the imagination," and thus are in a certain sense contemplating ourselves. Similarly, at the moral level, the actor continually views him- or herself in the mirror of (i.e., from the standpoint of) the spectator or, as the occasion demands, in the mirror of the (imagined) impartial spectator.

Smith makes it abundantly clear that the beauty conceived by the imagination at the various levels is not, so far as we know, a passive assimilation of pre-existing form. The imagination is fundamentally creative, and we should see "all philosophical systems as mere inventions of the imagination."[14] The very notion of nature as a "machine" is an imaginative metaphor which commonly leads to the postulation of a designer of the machine, as if nature imitates art.[15] That Smith should use, not some organic whole, but a

---

[14] "History of Astronomy," IV.76, in EPS, 105. At IV.33, Smith remarks: "For, though it is the end of Philosophy, to allay that wonder, which either the unusual or seemingly disjointed appearances of nature excite, yet she never triumphs so much, as when, in order to connect together a few, in themselves, perhaps, inconsiderable objects, she has, if I may say so, created another constitution of things, more natural indeed, and such as the imagination can more easily attend to, but more new, more contrary to common opinion and expectation, than any of those appearances themselves" (EPS, 75).

[15] "History of Ancient Physics," 9, in EPS, 113–14; also "History of Astronomy," IV.19, in EPS, 66. See also TMS, VII.iii.3.16; also TMS, IV.2.1.

humanly created artifact (the machine) as the paradigm for unity, natural or otherwise, is itself indicative of the drift of his account.[16] A machine is designed to accomplish a certain end, whether the production of pins (WN, I.i.3) or the explanation of the movements of the celestial bodies. It is productive and expresses the fundamentally creative nature of the imagination. It is also an artificial thing invented by us for the satisfaction of our desires and, often, for the manipulation of external nature. In seeing varying sorts of organization as "machines," Smith points to the fundamentally creative nature of the human animal, even as he observes that we naturally deploy this machinery not for prudential reasons but because we find order and harmony immensely attractive.

Qua unified "system," the natural and social world is constituted by our own imaginations. Thus, *The Theory of Moral Sentiments*'s idea of nature (of "the whole" or "the universe") is itself an "invention of the imagination." In fact, both *The Theory of Moral Sentiments* and *The Wealth of Nations* are themselves, qua systems or unifying accounts, "inventions of the imagination."[17] Smith's practice of theory and theory of practice are held together by this view of imagination as a seminal, creative force in life. The implications of the theory of moral sentiments are clear: considered from a metaphysical standpoint, value is something we communally determine for ourselves, and is not founded on philosophically mysterious entities lodged outside of this-worldly phenomena of human life. Recall the thesis that the impartial spectator "defines" good and bad, and consider Smith's equally important point that:

There is no appeal from the eye with regard to the beauty of colours, nor from the ear with regard to the harmony of sounds, nor from the taste with regard to the agreeableness of flavours.... The very essence of each of those qualities consists in its being fitted to please the sense to which it is addressed. It belongs to our moral faculties, in the same manner to determine when the ear ought to be soothed, when the eye ought to be indulged, when the taste ought to be gratified, when and how far every other principle of our nature ought either to be indulged or restrained. What is agreeable to our

---

[16] The metaphor of the machine is common in Smith (see, e.g., TMS, VII.iii.1.2, I.i.4.2), but in one place he uses an organic metaphor (WN, IV.ix.28).

[17] A point also made by D. D. Raphael, *Adam Smith* (Oxford, 1985), p. 112.

moral faculties, is fit, and right, and proper to be done; the contrary wrong, unfit, and improper. The sentiments which they approve of, are graceful and becoming: the contrary, ungraceful and unbecoming. The very words, right, wrong, fit, improper, graceful, unbecoming, mean only what pleases or displeases those faculties. (TMS, III.5.5)

Hence, for Smith as for Hume, morality must ultimately be understood as arising "from us," not as established by nature or the divine.[18] For given the limits of reason, those nonhuman or suprahuman sources are in fact – although we may imagine the contrary – inscrutable to us. We are therefore left with the one remaining source, namely ourselves. Intellectual systems are to be analogously understood, as his writings on the history of philosophy and science show. As he puts it in a passage mentioned previously, he takes himself as having analyzed "all philosophical systems as mere inventions of the imagination." Our confinement to the appearances, their being "rendered" (VII.iii.2.7) or shaped by the intellectual imagination, represent the other face of the restricted role of philosophical reason.

This is, however, the philosopher's perspective on practical and theoretical activity. Things look different from the standpoint of the agent in ordinary life, or of the thinker or artist engaged in their respective day-to-day metier. In his discussion of the relationship between theory and practice early in the book, Smith declares that "we approve of another man's judgment [about "the subjects of science and taste"] not as something useful, but as right, as accurate, as agreeable to truth and reality: and it is evident we attribute those qualities to it for no other reason but because we find that it agrees with our own." That is, although *in fact* another person's judgment appeals to us because it fits with our own disposition, and persuasively addresses our "intellectual sentiments" of

---

[18] Cf. Hume's "The Sceptic," in *Essays Moral, Political, and Literary*, ed. E. F. Miller (Indianapolis, IN, 1987), p. 162: "If we can depend upon any principle, which we learn from philosophy, this, I think, may be considered as certain and undoubted, that there is nothing, in itself, valuable or despicable, desirable or hateful, beautiful or deformed; but that these attributes arise from the particular constitution and fabric of human sentiment and affection" (also p. 166). See also *Treatise*, 468–9; and Hume's point in the first appendix to the *Enquiry Concerning the Principles of Morals* that aesthetic and moral taste "has a productive faculty, and gilding or staining all natural objects with the colours, borrowed from internal sentiment, raises in a manner a new creation" (p. 294).

surprise, wonder, and admiration, we normally assume the appeal persuades because it rests on the correspondence between a judgment and reality (I.i.4.4).[19] On Smith's account, the basis of our agreement with convictions and opinions of another, and that of our agreement about moral matters, are in this respect analogous (I.i.3.2). Similarly, he does not expect that by and large we will suspend belief even in the course of our theoretical endeavors; rather, we will ordinarily see our beliefs as rationally grounded in mind-independent "reality."

A remarkable passage in his discussion of philosophy and science makes just this point. The passage occurs on the culminating page of the essay on the history of astronomy. Referring to Newton, Smith suggests that the more satisfying a proposed system is to the intellectual imagination, the more likely we are to take the system as describing how things are objectively, independent of the human mind: "And even we, while we have been endeavouring to represent all philosophical systems as mere inventions of the imagination, to connect together the otherwise disjointed and discordant phaenomena of nature, have insensibly been drawn in, to make use of language expressing the connecting principles of this one [Newton's system], as if they were the real chains which Nature makes use of to bind together her several operations." Indeed, "the most sceptical cannot avoid feeling this," he remarks.[20] Because *The Theory of Moral Sentiments* is an example of Smithean theorizing, presumably he expects it to be treated on the whole as an attempt to represent how things really are, although when spectating on his creation with detachment, he will see it as one of many "inventions of the imagination." If he had completed his "Philosophical History of all the different branches of Literature, of Philosophy,

---

[19] Smith's theory has affinities with S. Blackburn's Humean "quasi-realism" view, a summary of which may be found in Blackburn's "Errors in the Phenomenology of Value," reprinted in *Morality and the Good Life*, eds. T. Carson and P. Moser (Oxford, 1997), pp. 324–37. However, talk of "projection" would, for Smith, have to be carefully modulated so as not to suppress the roles of receptivity and responsiveness, as my discussion of "sympathy" suggests.

[20] "The History of Astronomy," IV.76, EPS, 105 (emphasis added). Knud Haakonssen refers to this passage as a "very Humean piece of teasing, double-edged scepticism." *The Science of a Legislator: The Natural Jurisprudence of David Hume and Adam Smith* (Cambridge, 1981), p. 81. See also J. R. Lindgren's "Adam Smith's Theory of Inquiry," *Journal of Political Economy* 77 (1969): 900–1.

Poetry and Eloquence," the same description applied here to astronomy would presumably have been extended to philosophy altogether.[21]

The metaphysical thrust of Smith's doctrine of the imagination easily leads to misunderstanding. It is no part of his argument that the imagination creates the world *ex nihilo*, that objects of perception are fantasies in the mind, or that science is an arbitrarily spun "story." Building on Hume's remarks about the imagination, Smith is arguing that the world as unified or coherent, as intelligible and as part of a connected narrative or account within which it has meaning or value, is formed by the imagination – but not formed out of thin air.[22] The imagination works on givens, including complex "systems" previously shaped by the imagination. It systematizes, organizes, harmonizes, gives shape, establishes correspondences and coherence, and binds together through narrative. It thereby helps render its objects intelligible and confers value. For Hume, of course, one crucial way in which the imagination unifies the world is by attributing relations of cause and effect to events in it. Our ordinary assumption that objects continue to exist through time and are independent of the mind, our memory of particulars of events as really having occurred, even systems of philosophy – all are based on the imagination. Hume remarks that "the memory, senses, and understanding are, therefore, all of them founded on the imagination, or the vivacity of our ideas" (*Treatise*, 265), and

[21] This "Philosophical History" would have included the three essays (all in EPS) entitled "The Principles Which Lead and Direct Philosophical Enquiries; Illustrated by the History of Astronomy," the "History of Ancient Physics," and the "History of the Ancient Logics and Metaphysics." Clearly, Smith viewed these three essays as parts of a single unified treatise, itself a part of a larger inquiry. Given that the imagination pervades his theory of sympathy, norm construction, and judgment, it is not altogether surprising that he attached to TMS (starting with the third edition) an early essay entitled "A Dissertation on the Origin of Languages" (first published in 1761). Smith's discussion of the evolution of language makes clear that linguistic forms are "invented" (a favorite verb in the essay). The essay is a sort of conjectural or natural history of the formation of speech and thought, thanks to which the creation of "metaphysics" can be both understood and seen as a compelling illusion. A similar point is made in his essay on "The History of Ancient Logics and Metaphysics," 6 (EPS, 125).

[22] Smith's views about the imagination's centrality to human life and in inquiry owe so great a debt to Hume that they may be seen as an extension of Hume's views. For some discussion of that connection, see A. S. Skinner's *A System of Social Science: Papers Relating to Adam Smith* (Oxford, 1979), pp. 14–41.

comments on the "illusion of the imagination," thanks to which such things as causality appear in ordinary life to be independent of the mind (267).[23]

Let us avoid another possible misunderstanding by noting that according to Smith the world is not somehow "unreal" or "subjective" because it is rendered whole by the imagination. To be sure, morals, norms, customs, science, and philosophy do not on this account "correspond" to some completely mind-independent reality; no "reality" in that "Platonic" sense in fact appears to us. Norms are nonetheless "real" in the sense that they organize the world; that we rely on them in making decisions, from the most inconsequential to the gravest; and that we both appeal to them and develop them in praising and blaming our fellows, which praise and blame, in turn, guide much of human life. These norms may be critically evaluated. Moral and intellectual mistakes may certainly be specified and corrected, on this view. This is not all that some philosophers may want from a notion of the "real," and it is not all that non-philosophers assume about the reality of what presents itself as natural. Smith's reply to the philosophers would be that it is all we in fact have, and to ordinary agents, that their exaggerated assumption is an "illusion of the imagination" (to repeat Hume's phrase), albeit a beneficial one.

IV. UNDERSTANDING IMAGINATION

The standpoint of the spectator is always emphasized by Smith whenever questions of judgment or intelligibility or perspective or knowledge are at stake. Nature does not illuminate; our viewing of it does. Smith can give no definite account of what nature is unilluminated; nature does not come pre-sorted and organized into a coherent whole, such that it can in its eidetic integrity and harmony be absorbed by the mind. The account he does provide necessarily makes the self the source of light, as it were, and in thus privileging the self, Smith is joined by many modern philosophers,

[23] For discussion, see R. Fogelin's *Hume's Skepticism in the Treatise of Human Nature* (London, 1985), chapter 5 ("Skepticism and the Triumph of the Imagination"). On pp. 89–90, Fogelin discusses Hume's view that "the imagination is the ultimate judge of all systems of philosophy."

especially when issues of value are at stake. Nature is insufficient for our moral and theoretical purposes.[24]

For Smith, the world is made livable and intelligible thanks to the imagination's shaping of it. In and of itself, abstracting from our efforts, the world is obscurity and shadows to us. Light is provided by the imagination, and this light seeks the form of harmony. At the moral level, sympathetic imagination seeks the mutual composition of harmony between actor and spectator, allowing the one to transport him- or herself into the situation of the other, to become the other in some measure. It allows selves to mirror each other, and a self to perceive itself through the eyes of an imagined spectator. The imagination in effect fashions most of the emotions that govern human life, not out of whole cloth but by reweaving them against the complex tapestry of conventions, norms, goals, and both economic and social institutions. Norms are the products of the communal imagination over time, and are regulated by the impartial spectator, itself a stance of the reflective imagination. "Natural jurisprudence" is guided not by mind-independent nature but by the impartial spectator; viewed abstractly, "rights" represent the self-assertion of the imagination in appropriate contexts.[25] The imagination provides for the "appearance" of selves on the stage. Philosopher and moral actor both seek to understand these appearances by taking the stance of the "critic" (TMS, I.i.5.10). Their imagination shapes standards for judgment of varying degrees of demandingness. At the theoretical level, the imagination stages "systems," sometimes ideal and tenseless ones, and thus presents nature or human nature to us as though it were a "machine" to be contemplated.

Just as we do not know "the real chains which Nature makes use of to bind together her several operations," we also do not

---

[24] Toward the end of their review of the last five or so decades of moral philosophy, Darwall et al. comment that "moral realists, constructivists, and quasi-realists alike look to the responses and reasons of persons, rather than some self-subsistent realm, to ground moral practice." S. Darwall, A. Gibbard, and P. Railton, "Toward *Fin de siècle* Ethics: Some Trends," in *Moral Discourse and Practice*, eds. S. Darwall, A. Gibbard, and P. Railton (New York, NY, 1997), p. 34.

[25] For further discussion, see K. Haakonssen's "Adam Smith," in *Routledge Encyclopedia of Philosophy*, ed. E. Craig (London, 1998), vol. 8, pp. 815–22.

know what the imagination is in and of itself.[26] We seem stretched between two poles – world on the one side and imagination on the other. The inner constitution of each is obscure to us. Because we lack a philosophical account of mind qua mind, we seem largely left with an account of mind in terms of how it conceives (and has come to conceive) things in this or that particular way, and this is just the sort of account Smith aims to provide in his essays on philosophical inquiry. We are limited to the appearances, including those of the imagination (the "of" being both the objective and subjective genitive). The nature of the imagination is revealed through its products; we know it by what it does.[27] From Smith's perspective, this suffices for the conduct of philosophy and – given wise provision against corruption and fanaticism – for the conduct of common life as well.[28]

---

[26] Cf. Kant's statement that the schematism of the imagination "is an art concealed in the depths of the human soul, whose real modes of activity nature is hardly likely ever to allow us to discover and to have open to our gaze" (*Critique of Pure Reason* A142/B180–1); and Hume's references to the imagination as "a kind of magical faculty in the soul, which, tho' it be always most perfect in the greatest geniuses, and is properly what we call a genius, is however inexplicable by the utmost efforts of human understanding" (*Treatise*, 24).

[27] This is similar to Hume's view, if we accept G. Deleuze's interpretation of Hume. *Empiricism and Subjectivity*, trans. C. V. Boundas (New York, NY, 1991), p. 133. Deleuze there comments: "In short, as we believe and invent, we turn the given itself into a nature.... Philosophy must constitute itself as the theory of what we are doing, not as a theory of what there is."

[28] I want to thank Knud Haakonssen for his comments on earlier drafts of this essay and the Earhart Foundation for a fellowship that supported my work on the essay.

2   Adam Smith, Belletrist

The *Lectures on Rhetoric and Belles Lettres* as we have it does not derive from Smith's own text, which on his instructions was destroyed along with other unpublished literary materials shortly before his death. Rather, we owe the recovery of the contents of the lectures to the fortunate survival of a single set of student notes. Undoubtedly, these circumstances account for the fact that the work has not attracted as extensive or as detailed a body of commentary as might be expected in relation to a significant early work of such a central writer. Nonetheless, there are at least three contexts in which the *Lectures on Rhetoric and Belles Lettres* (henceforth, LRBL) has an interest. First, Smith was a pioneer in the university teaching of rhetoric at a time when, on this as on other subjects, Scotland was emerging as one of the most fertile centers of European thought. Although Smith's lectures remained unpublished, and therefore lacked the influence of either Hugh Blair's or George Campbell's works, they nonetheless have an important place in the history of eighteenth-century rhetoric and belles lettres. Secondly, the LRBL is an extended treatment of the subject that first engaged Smith's academic interests. Although the lecture notes date from near the end of Smith's teaching of this material, the document tells us as much as we are ever likely to know about this early chapter in Smith's intellectual career. Smith subsequently moved away from criticism as such, but there are clear lines of continuity between the rhetoric lectures and later writings, especially his great work on moral psychology, *The Theory of Moral Sentiments*. Thirdly, independent of the contexts already mentioned, the LRBL offers some specific analyses that have great intrinsic interest. On historical writing, in particular, Smith seems

to me the most original voice of his times, and his extended discussion of the techniques and possibilities of historical narrative
deserves to be far better known.[1]

The student report of Smith's rhetoric lectures was first recov-
ered and published by John Lothian and subsequently re-edited by
J. C. Bryce as part of the definitive Glasgow edition of Smith's
works. Bryce's excellent edition examines what is known of the textual history of the work, and readers should consult his "Introduction" for further details.[2] Bryce is convinced that the manuscript
was not the product of direct transcription of Smith's words as they
were spoken. Rather, the manuscript appears to be the product of
a strenuous collaboration by two students anxious to recollect and
reconstitute Smith's words as accurately as possible. The report
dates from 1762 to 1763, but Smith had been teaching the subject
since 1748, first as public lectures in Edinburgh and subsequently
as part of his professorial duties at Glasgow University. It is impossible to know what modifications Smith made over time, but given
the unity of Smith's conception, it is likely that there was considerable continuity in the fundamentals of the course over much of this
period. Certainly, there are few references to works that appeared
after 1748, and these could have been inserted without disturbing
the broad outline of his text.[3]

In his biography of Lord Kames, Alexander Fraser Tytler recalled
the beginnings of Smith's teaching:

It was by his [Kames's] persuasion and encouragement, that Mr Adam Smith,
soon after his return from Oxford, and when he had abandoned all views
towards the church, for which he had been originally destined, was induced

---

[1] The striking interest of the LRBL for historiography has largely escaped the attention of scholars of eighteenth-century historical thought. For an earlier analysis,
see the discussion in M. S. Phillips, "Adam Smith and the History of Private Life:
Social and Sentimental Narratives in 18th-Century Historiography," in *The Historical Imagination in Early Modern Britain*, eds. D. Kelley and D. Sachs (Cambridge,
1997), pp. 318–42, as well as in M. S. Phillips, *Society and Sentiment: Genres of Historical Writing in Britain, 1740–1820* (Princeton, NJ, 2000), chapter 3. See also John
Pocock, *Barbarism and Religion*, vol. 2 (Cambridge, 1999), pp. 325–6, and Pocock's
contribution to the present volume.

[2] J. C. Bryce, "Introduction," in LRBL.

[3] See Bryce, "Introduction," 12, as well as Ian S. Ross, *The Life of Adam Smith* (Oxford,
1995), pp. 87–94. Ross's biography provides essential background to Smith's teaching, as well as useful commentary on his rhetorical and other academic interests.

to turn his early studies to the benefit of the public, by reading a course of Lectures on Rhetoric and the *Belles Lettres*. He delivered those lectures at Edinburgh in 1748, and the two following years, to a respectable auditory, chiefly composed of students in law and theology; till called to Glasgow.[4]

Tytler's description only hints at the national and linguistic considerations that made Kames promote the idea of public lectures and that provided Smith with a receptive audience. In the aftermath of the rebellion of 1745, Scotland's lowland elites renewed the movement toward a greater degree of economic and social union with England. The choice made by so many Scots to see themselves as North Britons meant that they labored under a degree of linguistic self-consciousness that had no counterpart among the English. As one of Smith's contemporaries put it in arguing just a few years later for the creation of a chair in rhetoric at Edinburgh, "eloquence in the art of speaking is more necessary for a Scotchman than for anybody else as he lies under some disadvantages which Art must remove."[5] This self-consciousness surely helps explain why public lectures on rhetoric were thought to be "of benefit to the public" and why the choice of lecturers fell on a young Scot with extensive English education; it will not, however, explain (as I argue here) the richness of Smith's conception of his subject or its fertility for his later thought.

I

To a large extent, scholarly interest in eighteenth-century rhetoric has been shaped by considerations of disciplinary history. Although I do not have space for a detailed survey of this scholarship, a brief look at some of the principal lines of discussion may be useful as an orientation to the different ways in which Smith's work in this area has been viewed in the past generation. Most students of the LRBL have come to it from the discipline of rhetoric. In the older literature especially, eighteenth-century rhetorics have generally been read against a background of concern for the vicissitudes of

---

[4] A. F. Tytler, *Memoirs of the Life and Writings of the Honourable Henry Home of Kames*, vol. 1 (Edinburgh, 1807) p. 190.

[5] John Home to [Lord] Milton, August, 1756; quoted from R. Sher, *Church and University in the Scottish Enlightenment: The Moderate Literati of Edinburgh* (Princeton, NJ, 1985), p. 108.

an ancient art as it survives into modern times. In a period when rhetoric often appears to dwindle into trivial lessons for schoolboys or parish clergy, scholarly attention has been drawn to writers such as Smith, whose depth and seriousness seemed capable of renewing the idea of rhetoric as the broad-based program of thought it was for Aristotle or Cicero. Inevitably, much of this scholarship is undertaken "in defence of rhetoric" and therefore has an implicitly apologetic purpose.[6]

In Wilbur Howell's *Eighteenth-Century British Logic and Rhetoric*, for example, which remains the most comprehensive and authoritative survey of the period, Smith stands as the leading figure of a small group of writers in the second half of the century who, while jettisoning most of the specific features of the Ciceronian tradition, renewed rhetoric as a serious and comprehensive discipline. Howell traces the rise of this "new rhetoric" as a response to the critique of traditional rhetoric mounted by writers associated with the scientific spirit of the Royal Society, especially Boyle, Sprat, and Locke. A second important influence was the seventeenth-century French discussion of belles lettres; instructed by the work of Charles Rollin, Jean-Baptiste Dubos, and others, eighteenth-century British rhetoric expanded its traditional concern with the arts of persuasion to include a wider body of letters and the crucial subject of taste. Calling Smith "the earliest and most independent of the new British rhetoricians of the eighteenth century," Howell proclaims the destruction of his manuscripts a "calamity" that prevented the recognition of Smith's importance as a rhetorician and seriously damaged the subsequent development of the discipline.[7]

More recently, a different approach to Scottish rhetoric has come to the fore, but one that has also been shaped by the concerns of a disciplinary history. For some time now, interest in the history of the disciplines, as well as a perceived crisis in contemporary literary theory, has given impetus to a growing literature on the history of English studies. Scholars coming to eighteenth-century rhetoric

[6] See Brian Vickers' fine book, *In Defence of Rhetoric* (Oxford, 1988).
[7] Wilbur S. Howell, *Eighteenth-Century British Logic and Rhetoric* (Princeton, NJ, 1971), pp. 536–76.

from this direction have been concerned with the institutional contexts and ideological implications of what is construed as the beginnings of the teaching of English literature. Accordingly, they have not been concerned to trace the continuities of an ancient art, but rather to capture the moment of origin of a powerful modern discourse.[8] English studies, it is argued (with varying degrees of explicitness), performed from the start the function of disciplining a variety of marginal groups through the imposition of the linguistic and cultural standards of metropolitan elites. This ideological purpose is disclosed by the circumstances under which English studies came to be institutionalized in the university curriculum. Since the first university chairs of rhetoric belong to eighteenth-century Scotland, Robert Crawford and his colleagues argue for the "Scottish invention of English literature." What is more, following on from the Scottish case, the same process of institutionalization is evident in Ireland, North America, British India, and other cultural provinces.[9] Thus, Smith and his successors have been seen as beginning a process that still has implications for understanding "just how the university teaching of English spread across the globe, and how it conditioned the emergence of the modern English departments in England."[10]

Clearly, this second disciplinary history reverses many of the assumptions discussed previously. The invention paradigm, if I can call it that by way of shorthand, emphasizes the ruptures of modernity, not the continuities of the classical. Its thrust is demystificatory, rather than apologetic, although mixed at times

---

[8] For the broader literature on the rise of "English," see Chris Baldick, *The Social Mission in English Criticism, 1848–1932* (Oxford, 1983), and Gerald Graff and M. Warner, eds., *The Origins of Literary Studies in America* (New York, NY, 1989). Those who have emphasized the place of Scottish developments in the eighteenth century include Franklin Court, *Institutionalizing English Literature: The Culture and Politics of Literary Study, 1750–1900* (Palo Alto, CA, 1992); Robert Crawford, *Devolving English Literature* (Oxford, 1992); Robert Crawford, ed., *The Scottish Invention of English Literature* (Cambridge, 1998). See also Richard Terry, "The Eighteenth-Century Invention of English Literature: A Truism Revisited," *British Journal for Eighteenth-Century Studies* 19 (1996): 47–62.

[9] See Gauri Viswanathan, *Masks of Conquest: Literary Study and British Rule in India* (New York, NY, 1989); Thomas Miller, *The Formation of College English: Rhetoric and Belles Lettres in the British Cultural Provinces* (Pittsburgh, PA, 1997).

[10] Crawford, ed., *Invention*, 17.

with a considerable degree of national celebration. Where the historians of rhetoric have offered detailed expositions of eighteenth-century rhetorical ideas against a grid provided by the traditional divisions of classical rhetorics, the proponents of the "Scottish invention" have generally been less interested in analyzing particular doctrines than in the institutional setting and social implications of rhetoric teaching.

At the center of this disagreement is a debate over what we should call the subject matter that Smith and his successors taught. Howell insists that "Smith intended them [i.e., the LRBL], not as discourses on ancient and modern literature, but as discourses to expound a system of rhetoric."[11] On the other side – overlooking how much of Smith's lectures is indeed devoted to ancient and modern literatures (continental as well as English) – scholars interested in the "culture and politics of literary study" have wanted to define the subject quite simply as English literature or English studies.[12] Hence, Crawford can claim that "English Literature as a university subject is a Scottish invention."[13]

Students of the eighteenth century will not find it novel that scholarly debate takes the form of a division between those who want to see the period as essentially continuing seventeenth-century concerns and those who see it as foreshadowing the preoccupations of the nineteenth century. In the present case, however, the concept of belles lettres – a term formulated by the French writers of the seventeenth century and naturalized into English in the first half of the eighteenth century[14] – marks out a distinctive middle ground. There are two principal reasons for giving weight to this designation. The first has to do with what it implies about

---

[11] Howell, *British Logic*, 545. The title "Lectures on Rhetoric," it should be noted, is given by the student copyist, not Smith himself.

[12] The quoted phrase is the subtitle of the study by Franklin Court, cited in footnote 8. Ian Duncan speaks of Smith's "foundational place in the early history of English" and writes that the LRBL "constitute the first significant university programme devoted to the analysis of English literary discourse." See his "Adam Smith, Samuel Johnson and the Institutions of English," in Crawford, ed., *Scottish Invention*, 37.

[13] Crawford, ed., *Scottish Invention*, 1. Similarly, Court writes: "The first serious efforts to introduce English literary study into the university curriculum in Britain were made in eighteenth-century Scotland." *Institutionalizing*, 17.

[14] See Howell, *British Logic*, 503–35, and Barbara Warnick, *The Sixth Canon: Belletristic Rhetorical Theory and Its French Antecedents* (Columbia, SC, 1993).

the scope of literary study; the second concerns its social and psychological focus.

The term "letters" highlights significant differences between the eighteenth- and nineteenth-century conceptions of the literary field. It is a notable feature of Smith's and Blair's lectures that they addressed themselves to a number of genres (including, most notably, historiography) that would later come to be regarded as standing outside the normal scope of literary study. This inclusiveness continued the pattern set by Dubos and Rollin, but it stands in contrast to the elevation of imaginative literatures that came with the Romantics. The effect of Romantic assumptions about the primacy of imagination was to privilege one part of the domain of letters, and hence, to establish a fundamental division between "literary" and "nonliterary" genres. This distinction became deeply ingrained in literary studies and – for all the efforts that scholars have made to broaden the scope of teaching and research – it still remains a constitutive feature of the discipline of "English."[15] In consequence, it is often difficult for literary scholars to reenter an eighteenth-century literary domain not yet divided in this fashion. For those who have grown up in a literary system that habitually sorts books into classes called "fiction" and "nonfiction" (the latter, of course, being simply a residual category), it is not intuitively easy to grasp the concerns of a text such as the LRBL, whose most extended formal analysis concerns historical narrative, not the novel.[16]

In short, the term "belles lettres" points us to a concept of the literary field that is differently unified and otherwise centered than the more familiar Romantic conception that succeeded it. At the

[15] For the Romantic redefinition of the idea of literature, see Timothy Reiss, *The Meaning of Literature* (Ithaca, NY, 1992); David Perkins, *Is Literary History Possible?* (Baltimore, MD, 1992).

[16] Two of the contributors to *Scottish Invention* work hard to bring the modern preoccupation with the novel into a reading of Smith and other eighteenth-century rhetorics. See Ian Duncan, "Adam Smith, Samuel Johnson and the Institutions of English," 37–54, and Paul Bator, "The Entrance of the Novel into the Scottish Universities," 89–102. In my view, however, the case is difficult to make because Smith says almost nothing about the novel. It should also be noted that Smith's library, which was rich in history, philosophy, politics, and classical and continental literatures, contained almost no prose fiction. See James Bonar, *A Catalogue of the Library of Adam Smith*, 2nd ed. (London, 1932).

same time, the idea of belles lettres also stands for a shift in the orientation of rhetorical theory that has a particular importance for understanding the place of rhetorical study in Smith's subsequent career. Classical rhetoric and its Renaissance continuation had focused on the orator's skill in producing persuasive argument. The Scottish rhetoricians, however, writing under the influence of French belletrism, refocused attention on the ways in which works in a variety of genres are read or received. Thus, rhetorical analysis shifted its concern from the *production* of persuasive *speech* to the *reception* of written *texts*. Because these texts might move readers in a variety of ways, rhetoric came to concern itself more broadly with the aesthetic and emotional power of writing and became a body of psychologically oriented criticism.

Criticism in this form has both a moral/aesthetic and a social concern. In one view, the sensitive reader who responds appropriately to the passions displayed in a tragedy or a history can be taken as a kind of receptive instrument that gauges the aesthetic and moral qualities of the work. Reciprocally, belletrist criticism also strives to elevate the taste of readers to respond only to works that are worthy of proper regard. The stress on moral and aesthetic refinement that resulted from this reciprocity gave rise to the accusations of excessive sensibility that troubled literary discussion in this period. The same preoccupation also forms the basis of a scholarly critique of eighteenth-century rhetoric that sees its central purpose as bound up with a social investment in what Nancy Struever has called "receptive competence."[17] This sort of aesthetic training would have particular interest to provincial elites such as those of Edinburgh or Dublin, whose standards of good taste and proper speech were under intense scrutiny. More broadly, eighteenth-century belletrism can also be characterized as signifying a loss of ancient ideals of eloquence associated with "civic humanism" and their replacement by new standards of politeness more appropriate to modern conditions. In commercial society, it is argued, it is not excellence in public speech, but conversational skill and elegant taste that became the path to social distinction. Accordingly,

---

[17] Nancy Struever, "The Conversable World: Eighteenth-Century Transformations of the Relation of Rhetoric and Truth," in *Rhetoric and the Pursuit of Truth: Language Change in the Seventeenth and Eighteenth Centuries*, eds. Brian Vickers and Nancy Struever (Los Angeles, CA, 1985), p. 80.

belletrism changed the focus of rhetoric by orienting criticism to the domestic settings and habits of private reading belonging to the expanded print culture of eighteenth-century Britain.[18] "Rhetorical discipline is reassembled as a new skill which is the duty, property, and talent of a new social elite; the faculties to be developed in education and social intercourse enhance, give meaning to, status and connection: taste, for example, is a mode of social commmunication, the hegemonous social competence."[19]

It is evident that the idea of receptive competence does some valuable work in identifying what is at stake from a social point of view in the eighteenth-century's revision of classical rhetoric. In much the same way, although rather more polemically, the "invention paradigm" draws attention to the considerations of national identity and social conformity that lie behind the linguistic self-consciousness of the Scots. Yet, while both frameworks provide needed contextualization, neither can really capture the richness or particularity of a thinker such as Smith. After all, if our main concern is to understand elite social competence or linguistic embarrassment, we might be better off to bypass the LRBL altogether to examine the popularity of Thomas Sheridan's writings on elocution or the circulation of contemporary periodicals such as the *Mirror*. On the other hand, to go more deeply into Smith's own understanding of letters, we may need to pay less attention to the immediate social and political uses of rhetoric and more attention to the issues of moral psychology that for him were a lifelong preoccupation.

II

Until the recovery of the lecture notes that constitute the text of the LRBL, our clearest image of Smith's concerns as a teacher of logic and rhetoric came from Smith's student and friend, John Millar, who was a leading figure in the next generation of the Scottish Enlightenment. Millar provided Dugald Stewart with an account of Smith's teaching for the memoir of Smith's life that Stewart read

[18] See especially, Adam Potkay, *The Fate of Eloquence in the Age of Hume* (Ithaca, NY, 1994).
[19] Struever, "Conversable World," 80.

to the Royal Society of Edinburgh in 1793. According to Millar, Smith replaced conventional approaches to logic and rhetoric with one built on the study of the human mind:

The best method of explaining and illustrating the various powers of the human mind, the most useful part of metaphysics, arises from an examination of the several ways of communicating our thoughts by speech, and from an attention to the principles of those literary compositions which contribute to persuasion or entertainment. By these arts, every thing that we perceive or feel, every operation of our minds, is expressed and delineated in such a manner, that it may be clearly distinguished and remembered. There is, at the same time, no branch of literature more suited to youth at their first entrance upon philosophy than this, which lays hold of their taste and feelings.[20]

For Millar, evidently, Smith's philosophical psychology was the key to his interest in rhetoric and (implicitly at least) the connecting thread between his early teaching and his later concerns. Everything in this carefully constructed account hinges on the contrast between the naturalism of Smith's system, with its focus on language and the mind, and the arbitrary and artificial teaching it replaced. Because language responds to and records everything we think or feel, both informal speech and written composition are prime laboratories for an empirical study of mind. Intriguingly, Millar also suggests that Smith saw the material that provided him with his own first opportunity for systematic study as doing the same for his students. The reference to the emotional appeal of the subject (one that "lays hold of their taste and feelings") leaves some doubt, however, whether the emphasis is on the inherent appeal of literary materials or on the attractions of the introspective methods of philosophical criticism.

Millar's description is, of course, a retrospect, not a summary of the impact of Smith's lectures as his students first heard them. In practise, as the lecture report of 1762-3 indicates, Smith's teaching was certainly more diverse in its concerns than any brief summary could indicate. We can get a useful sample of these concerns by focusing on a pair of lectures – numbers seven and eight – that center on his assessment of Swift and on the nature of humor. The point of departure here is Smith's persistent attack on the

---

[20] Dugald Stewart, *Account of the Life and Writings of Adam Smith*, in EPS, 274.

artificiality of conventional systems of rhetoric, which he dismissed as "generally a very silly set of Books and not at all instructive" (i.v.59). Despite what the "ancient Rhetoricians imagined," Smith asserts, beauty of style does not consist of the use of tropes and figures. Rather, "when the words neatly and properly expressed the thing to be described, and conveyed the sentiment the author entertained of it and desired to communicate...by sympathy to his hearers; then the expression had all the beauty language was capable of bestowing on it" (i.96). Smith's emphasis is on perspicuity and naturalness. The reader's sympathies will be most fully engaged when the object is properly described and the accompanying feelings of the author are clearly expressed. Thus, figurative language has no particular value in itself: "it is when the expression is agreable to the sense of the speaker and his affection that we admire it" (i.76).

Smith's emphasis on aptness carries with it the corollary that good style necessarily responds to differences of situation and audience. Smith has in mind two sorts of variables, both of which combine psychological typologies with formal concerns. The first has to do with the requirements of genre, the second with the author's self-presentation or persona.

Smith begins with genre and its implications for what we would now call point of view. Sentiments may be naturally expressed, he says, in a variety of different manners, according to the "circumstances" of the writer. "The same story may be considered either as plain matter of fact without design to excite our compassion, or...in a moving way, or lastly in a jocose manner, according to the point in which it is connected with the author" (i.77). Making his argument more concrete, he connects variability in style to the different purposes served by the several types of discourse the writer might employ. In doing so, he initiates what will later become a major theme in the work, namely a set of formal comparisons between history, oratory, and didactic writing. The orator and the historian, he explains, are in very different circumstances. "The business of the one [i.e., the historian] is barely to narrate the facts which are often very distant from his time and in which he is, or ought to be and endeavours to appear, noways interested." In contrast, the orator treats subjects he or his friends "are nearly concerned in." As a result, he must try to appear "deeply concerned in the matter, and [he] uses all his art to prove what he is engaged in" (i.81–2).

Smith offers no term for the sorts of choices he describes, but as a shorthand we might think of it as a question of assumed distance.[21] That is, Smith's view seems to be that by virtue of the different requirements of their genres, historians and orators will necessarily position themselves very differently in relation to the events they describe and to the audiences they address. The orator speaks about matters of immediate interest, that is, things which his audience "are nearly concerned in." Accordingly, he adopts a stance of immediacy or proximity; he "insists on every particular," and he will "exclaim on the strength of the argument, the justice of the cause." The historian, in contrast, takes up a posture of detachment: he "acts as if he were an impartial narrator of the facts; so he uses none of these means to affect his readers, he never dwells on any circumstance, nor has he any use for insisting on arguments" (i.81–3).[22]

Smith's interest in the issue of distance casts some light on his earlier remarks on style, as well as on the psychological orientation of his criticism. The ideal of perspicuity in Smith and others has generally been associated with the Royal Society's promotion of unadorned language.[23] Undoubtedly more than one explanation exists for the popularity of the plain style, but Smith's repeated emphasis on the role of sympathy suggests that for him, perspicuity has less to do with the descriptive austerity demanded by Baconian science than with a conception of reading that is attuned to sentimentalist immediacy. Of course, Smith's opening position is complicated by his subsequent thoughts on distance. Even so, his

---

[21] I have explored the subject of distance in relation to historiographical writing of this period in *Society and Sentiment*, and in "Relocating Inwardness: Historical Distance and the Transition from Enlightenment to Romantic Historiography," *Proc. of the Modern Language Association* 118 (2003): 436–49.

[22] Later, as we will see, Smith seems in part to soften this contrast by investigating the possibilities of pathetic narrative in historical writing. Here, particularity in historical description, is seen as a technique for engaging the sentiments of the reader.

[23] For an important reconsideration of the supposed hostility of science to rhetoric, see Brian Vickers, "The Royal Society and English Prose Style: A Reassessment," in *Rhetoric*, eds. Vickers and Struever, 3–76. Carey McIntosh presents Smith as an advocate of a more writerly, polite style in *The Evolution of English Prose, 1700–1800: Style, Politeness, and Print Culture* (Cambridge, 1998).

discovery that in practice various kinds of writing require different degrees of detachment or proximity only calls attention to the
fact that the general description of reading from which he departs
takes as its ideal a situation in which the flow of sympathy between
reader and author will be as unmediated as possible.

Smith then introduces a second variable into his discussion of
good style, which is the author's choice of persona. By way of illustration, he offers two modes of self-presentation that he sees as
closely related, but distinct, namely the style of the plain man and
that of the simple one. As a typology, this is both simpler and more
familiar than the issue of distance, but as an instrument of criticism
it leads to some interesting results:

When the characters of a plain and a simple man are so different we may
naturally expect that the stile they express themselves in will be far from
being the same. Swift may serve as an instance of a plain stile and Sir Wm
Temple of a simple one. Swift never gives any reason for his opinions but
affirms them boldly without the least hesitation; and when one expects a
reason he meets with nothing but such expressions as, I have always been of
opinion that, etc. because etc. It seems to me.... He is so far from studying
the ornaments of language that he affects to leave them out even when
naturall; and in this way he often throws out pronouns etc. that are necessary
to make the sentence full but would at the same time lead him into the
uniformity of cadence which he industriously avoids. This however makes
his stile very close. (i.91–2)

In his serious works, Smith continues, Swift avoids figurative language, just as he avoids smoothness of cadence. "He never expresses
any passion but affirms with a dictatorial gravity" (i.93).

A parallel description of Temple's authorial personality and style
follows, but it is evident that Swift remains the central figure. Thus,
lecture eight finds Smith commenting at length on the popularity of Swift as a humorist and the reasons why his most serious
works are little read or understood. This, it is worth noting, represents a venture into literary history, a genre which has a greater
presence in this period than has generally been recognized. Smith's
literary history, however, bears little resemblance to later romantic
narratives, with their interest in poetry and the national spirit.
Rather, in keeping with his belletrist framework, Smith's focus is
on questions of taste, and his central figures are not so much poets

as men of letters – principally, Swift and Temple, but also Lucian, Shaftesbury, and Addison.

Smith's inquiry into "the causes of this general taste" reviews several broad cultural factors that shaped Swift's reception, including the nature of his religious views and his aversion to abstract speculation. In the end, however, Smith suggests that it may be Swift's plain-spoken manner itself that is most responsible for the "generall disregard" for his more serious works, whereas in contrast Shaftesbury and Thomson are admired for their artificial diction. In a passage that addresses the linguistic self-consciousness of his countrymen as plainly as any recent critique, Smith suggests that the Scots have special difficulties in recognizing the virtues of the plain style. "We in this country are most of us very sensible that the perfection of language is very different from what we commonly speak in. The idea we form of a good stile is almost conterary to that which we generally hear. Hence it is that we conceive the farther ones stile is removed from the common manner ... it is so much the nearer to the purity and the perfection we have in view" (i.103).

We can finish this brief survey of lectures seven and eight of the LRBL with yet another topic related to Swift, namely an investigation of humor or ridicule. Smith's anatomy of humor, which owes a good deal to Hutcheson, is more extended than I have space to reproduce here, but its manner is well represented in an opening passage that outlines the starting point of a characteristically Smithian psychological thought experiment. "Whatever we see that is great or noble excites our admiration and amazement, and whatever is little or mean on the other hand excites our contempt. A greatt object never excites our laughter, neither does a mean one, simply as being such. It is the blending and joining of these two ideas which alone causes that Emotion" (i.107).

The various combinations of meanness and grandeur occupy Smith for the remainder of the lecture, which he ends by making a further distinction between two kinds of objects of ridicule and hence two classes of humorist. This distinction, resumed and completed in the ninth lecture, amounts to a contrast between the type of humor that exposes the pettiness of some object by describing it as if it were actually great, and (contrastively) humor that takes some object that appears to be great and brings it into ridicule

by exposing its elements of pettiness. Swift, the plain-spoken mis-
anthrope who castigates the "prevailing gay follies of his Time" is
the exemplar of the first type, whereas the more jovial personality
and pompous targets of Lucian stand for the second. For Smith, this
evidently amounted to a satisfying symmetry, and he concludes
that the two humorists together "form a System of morality from
whence more sound and just rules of life for all the various characters of men may be drawn than from most set systems of Morality"
(i.119, 125).

   In another author, this conclusion might be taken as little more
than a flourish – the complacencies of a literary man levelled
against the pretensions of philosophy. In Smith, however, this kind
of opposition can hardly be allowed because literary structure and
moral choice characteristically converge. This does not mean that
Smith's criticism ignores the formal qualities of texts, but rather
that he regards literary structures as capturing habits that reflect
wider regularities of moral psychology. Thus, in a later summary
that recapitulates the ground we have gone over and brings this
section to a close, Smith answers the objections of an imaginary
critic by agreeing that his observations are little more than common sense: indeed, "all the Rules of Criticism and morality when
traced to their foundation, turn out to be some Principles of Common Sence which every one assents to" (i.133). The issue, he continues, is simply to show the application of these rules to particular
subjects. "Tis for this purpose we have made these observations on
the authors above mentioned. We have shewn how fare they have
acted agreably to that Rule, which is equally applicable to conversation and behaviour as writing" (i.135).

III

Throughout the LRBL, Smith frequently uses illustration from historians, who evidently made up some of his favorite reading. In
lectures twelve through twenty, however, Smith turns his attention to narrative and description, and here historiography becomes
the central literature under consideration.[24] This attention to

---

[24] History is not his explicit and exclusive subject until lectures seventeen through
   twenty; nonetheless, narration and history seem more or less interchangeable

historical writing reflects, in part, Smith's affinity to the bel-letrist tradition with its wide definition of letters. The differences, however, are instructive. In contrast to Rollin, for instance, whose extensive discussion of history never questions the standard humanist cliches about learning by example, Smith clearly aims to create an analysis of narrative that is not beholden to any existing body of prescription. In fact, Smith had a real love for the ancient historians, and much preferred them to their modern successors. Nonetheless, his naturalism committed him to regard the ancients not as a source of authoritative rules of composition, but as superior posts of observation for investigating the powers of narrative. In this spirit – and keeping both reader and writer in mind – he sets out to classify the various objects and functions that properly belong to narrative. The result is a genuine independence from the routine justifications of the classical tradition in a writer who, nonetheless, was deeply attracted to its literary achievements.

Smith's starting point is to distinguish between two fundamental aims of discourse. "Every discourse," he states, "proposes either barely to relate some fact, or to prove some proposition" (i.149). The first intention gives us narrative; the second – depending on the balance between persuasion and instruction – gives us either didactic or rhetorical discourses. Thus, narrative emerges as one of three primary literary modes, whereas persuasion, once the focus of rhetorical analysis, is reduced to one of several possible ends.

In historiographical terms, this is an important revision because the classical idea of exemplarity had done its best to bring history under the general rules and purposes of rhetoric as "philosophy teaching by example."[25] From the standpoint that Smith was to explore in the LRBL, the weakness of the doctrine of exemplarity is that it thinks of narrative as little more than an inert medium, whereas all the active interest lies in the examples. Smith, in contrast, assimilates historiography not to rhetoric but to narrative, which (as we have seen) he simultaneously raises to a central position among literary modes. This move – coupled with his psychological method – requires him to make a serious attempt to produce

---

terms for Smith, so there are good grounds to consider the entire section on narrative and description as constituting a single unit.
[25] The formulation, of course, belongs to Bolingbroke, an eighteenth-century author, but it nicely summarizes an ancient idea.

a theory of history in which narrative effects rather than moral examples would be key.

In fact, Smith carried the identity between history and narrative so far that he wanted to exclude rhetorical, and especially didactic elements, from historical composition altogether (ii.37–43). When first formulated, this strictly narrativist position must have seemed a straightfoward expression of support for the traditions of classical historiography over the political and religious disputatiousness endemic in British historiography. By 1762, however, when these lectures were recorded, Smith purism put him in opposition to the most innovative historians of his day, whose works increasingly incorporated essayistic enquiries on matters that lay beyond the ken of Thucydidean narrative. There is a real irony in all this because Smith's stance on narrative stands in obvious tension with his own efforts to pioneer new forms of social enquiry. No one, in fact, did more than Smith to extend the reach of social analysis. Nonetheless, as a critic of historiography, he championed a classical view of narrative that excluded both the domain of commerce analyzed in *The Wealth of Nations* and the world of private life and inward experience explored in *The Theory of Moral Sentiments* – and all of this, of course, was occurring at just the time when enlightened historians such as his friend David Hume were seizing on the didactic elements Smith disliked as a way to acknowledge the enormous importance of commerce, manners, and opinion to their understanding of history. It is no wonder, then, that Smith left behind the lasting impression that on questions of historical narrative he was a severe classicist and a deep conservative, as indeed in some ways he was. Yet, if Smith limited history to what could be narrated, he also discovered new possibilities that extended the range of narrative in significant ways. In particular, he pointed to the technique he called "indirect narrative," by which history acquired a potential to explore dimensions of experience beyond the purview of conventional description.[26]

Smith begins his analysis of narrative – which he also calls "the historicall stile" (LRBL, ii.12) – by examining the different classes

---

[26] For Smith's reputation as a conservative on matters of narrative, see my discussion in "Adam Smith and the History of Private Life," as well as *Society and Sentiment*, chapter 3.

of objects that narrative can be called on to describe. His principal point is to distinguish between "facts" that are externally observable and those that are not, and then to develop a parallel distinction between direct and indirect techniques of narration. "There are two different Sorts of facts, one externall, consisting of transactions that pass without us, and the other internall, towit the thoughts sentiments or designs of men, which pass in their minds" (i.150). He also makes a parallel distinction between simple and compound objects, thus yielding a matrix of objects that runs from simple and visible objects to those that are compound and visible ("as of an Action"), those that are compound and invisible ("a character"), and finally, mixing the two, "the Historicall Style or descriptions of Actions and Characters" (i.151). However, this is, perhaps, to leave too tidy an impression because the lectures loop back a number of times to the original distinctions, each time underlining the difficulty narrative faces as it attempts to describe internal or invisible objects. "But whatever difficulty there is in expressing the externall objects that are the objects of our senses; there must be far greater in describing the internal ones, which pass within the mind itself and are the object of none of our senses." If the easiest way of describing an object is by its parts, "how then describe those which have no parts?" (i.162).

Smith's desire to confront the difficulties that arise when so much that needs to be accounted for is not available for immediate inspection demonstrates both the strength and fertility of his narrativist and empiricist commitment. His solution is to widen the range of narrative effects by examining two different, but complementary approaches to problems of description.

That way of expressing any quality of an object which does it by describing the severall parts that constitute the quality we want to express, may be called the direct method. When, again, we do it by describing the effects this quality produces on those who behold it, may be called the indirect method. This latter in most cases is by far the best. (i.160)

For history, self-evidently, the importance of indirect description has a good deal to do with the fact that invisible objects like the "passions and affections" can only be described indirectly (i.181–2). Even in the case of simple physical objects, however, Smith was convinced that indirect description is often more moving or more satisfying. In Addison's description of St. Peter's, for instance, we gain a better idea of the size and proportions of the church from its effect on the beholder than would be possible from an exact enumeration of dimensions. However, the situations that occupy Smith most are the more complex realms of character and action that enter into historical description. Here, too, although both approaches are often possible, Smith generally prefers the indirect. In the description of character, for instance, direct description takes an almost impossible degree of penetration to be successful on its own. Accordingly, Smith favors the indirect method, "when we do not enumerate its severall component parts, but relate the effects it produces on the outward behaviour and Conduct of the person" (i.192).

Smith's fascination with indirect description in the LRBL bears some analogy to the central conceptual device of *The Theory of Moral Sentiments*, the impartial spectator. The spectatorialism of the LRBL, however, stops well short of impartiality; on the contrary, one of the chief attractions of the indirect method is its power to heighten readerly sympathy, especially in relation to scenes of distress.

Thucydides might have given us in a very few words the whole acount of the sieze of Syracuse by the Athenians, which has filled the best part of the 7th Book of his history, but no such account could have had [a] chance of equalling the animated and affecting description he has given of that memorable event.

Equally, he argues, many passages in Livy and elsewhere would serve to illustrate the point that "when we mean to affect the reader deeply we must have recourse to the indirect method of description, relating the effects the transaction produced both on the actors and Spectators" (ii.6–7).

Smith's views on the two writers he considered the greatest historians of Greece and Rome would not be out of place in a prologue to a novel, a form of reading he affected to despise (ii.30). In fact, we could sum up much of what is most striking in these lectures as a result of thinking about historiography from the standpoint of the sentimental reader.

On the other hand, it remains unclear how Smith meant to reconcile his sentimentalist aesthetic with the traditional idea (referred to more than once) that history provides materials that will "assist us in our future conduct" (ii.18). Is history's ability to rouse the "Sympatheticall affections" (ii.16) central to its functions, or simply an enhancement of its traditional didactic role? Was history, which for so many generations had aimed to instruct humanist readers, now ready to educate sentimental ones in a substantially different way?[27]

Smith's judgments on the history of historiography (the subject of lectures nineteen and twenty) certainly suggest that he regarded the power to mobilize sympathy as a key aspect of historical reading. We have already seen that his sentimentalist aesthetic is central to his appreciation of Thucydides and Livy, his favorites among the classical historians. The same views also enter into his general preference for the ancients and his dislike of anything that takes history away from a strictly narrative mode. Proofs and demonstrations, he argues, are not only inconsistent with the historical style, they also interrupt the thread of the narration, and "withdraw our attention" from it. The dissertations which are such a prominent feature of modern histories, Smith concludes, "contribute...not a little to render them less interesting than those wrote by the Antients" (ii.41, ii.v.39).

The most remarkable application of Smith's sentimentalist aesthetic, however, is certainly his revaluation of Tacitus. According to Smith, Tacitus understood the advantages of indirect narrative and therefore set out to "write a history consisting entirely of such events as were capable of interesting the minds of the Readers by accounts of the effects they produced" (ii.62–3). Furthermore, Tacitus realized that in peaceful times the incidents of private life, although less important than public ones, "would affect us more deeply and interest us more than those of a Publick nature" (ii.66). For this reason, Tacitus largely disregarded the importance of events, paying heed instead to their affective power. As a result, although the events of his history may often be considered secondary, "the method [by which] he describes these is so interesting, he leads us far into the sentiments and mind of the actors that they are some of the most striking and interesting passages to be met

---

[27] I have discussed evidence for sentimental reading in "'If Mrs. Mure Be Not Sorry for Poor King Charles': History, the Novel, and the Sentimental Reader," *History Workshop Journal* 43 (1997): 111–31, as well as *Society and Sentiment*, chapter 4.

with in any history." The consequence is that his account may not instruct us in the causes of events; "yet it will be more interesting and lead us into a science no less usefull, to wit, the knowledge of the motives by which men act; a science too that could not be learned from [lacuna in text]" (ii.67).

For Smith, Tacitus's approach to history was more than a personal choice. It was also the product of peaceable times and an atmosphere of luxury and refinement, a condition which the Roman Empire in the age of Trajan shared with contemporary France.

Sentiment must bee what will chiefly interest such a people.... Such a people, I say, having nothing to engage them in the hurry of life would naturally turn their attention to the motions of the human mind, and those events that were accounted for by the different internall affections that influenced the persons concerned, would be what most suited their taste.

It is for this reason, Smith concludes, that Tacitus so much resembles Marivaux and Crebillon – "as much as we can well imagine in works of so conterary a nature" (ii.63–4).

As Smith well knew, this is an extraordinary comparison to make; after all, Tacitus's name had long been a byword for a ruthless, unsentimental acceptance of political reality, whereas in Britain more recently Tacitus had figured as the scourge of tyrants and the champion of republican virtue. Smith obviously felt the novelty of what he was doing, and he closes the lecture with an uncharacteristic flourish: "Such is the true Character of Tacitus," he proclaims, "which has been misrepresented by all his commentators from Boccalini down to Gordon" (ii.69).

IV

The rhetoric lectures are far too striking and inventive to be reduced to a preamble to Smith's later accomplishments; nonetheless, we should not leave them without underscoring the importance of the LRBL's theme of persuasion and intersubjective exchange to Smith's later, more famous works. Both *The Theory of Moral Sentiments* and *The Wealth of Nations*, after all, build on a view of human nature that stresses the communicableness of the passions and the passion to communicate. Let me conclude, then, with one last quotation from Smith's teaching that points the way to these continuities of interest. "Men always endeavour to persuade others to be of their opinion," Smith writes,

even when the matter is of no consequence to them. If one advances any thing concerning China or the *more distant moon* which contradicts what you imagine to be true, you immediately try to persuade him to alter his opinion. And in this manner every one is practising oratory on others thro the whole of his life. (LJ[A] vi.56)[28]

This passage, which so enlarges the sphere of eloquence in human life, does not appear in the rhetoric lectures themselves, but rather in the *Lectures on Jurisprudence*. The subject he is addressing, later resumed in *The Wealth of Nations*, is the psychological foundation of trade, or as Smith himself puts it, "the principle in the human mind on which this disposition of trucking is founded, ... the naturall inclination every one has to persuade." Smith continues:

You are uneasy whenever one differs from you, and you endeavour to persuade <?him> to be of your mind; or if you do not it is a certain degree of self command, and to this every one is breeding thro their whole lives. In this manner they acquire a certain dexterity and adress in managing their affairs, or in other words in managing of men; and this is altogether the practise of every man in the most ordinary affairs. (LJ[A] vi.56–7)

---

[28] For a comparable statement on the ubiquity of the desire for persuasion, see Hume, *Political Essays*, ed. K. Haakonssen (Cambridge, 1994), p. 37.

3 Adam Smith's Theory of Language

Adam Smith's lasting fame certainly does not come from his work on language. He published little on this topic, and he is not usually mentioned in standard histories of linguistics or the philosophy of language. His most elaborate publication on the subject is a 1761 monograph on the origin and development of languages, "Considerations Concerning the First Formation of Languages." Smith's monograph joins a long list of speculative work on this then fashionable topic (cf. Hewes, 1975, 1996). The fact that he later included it as an appendix to his successful *Theory of Moral Sentiments* indicates that Smith "set a high value" on this monograph (Stewart, 1793: 32) – an appreciation he did not bestow on his lecture notes on rhetoric and literature, which he consigned to the flames.[1] Although Smith devoted most of his teaching to language-related topics, and certainly developed an organized body of convictions about the subject, it would be an exaggeration to say that he had a "theory of language." In contrast to *Theory of Moral Sentiments*, Smith did not call his monograph a "theory," preferring the modest "considerations."

Nevertheless, as I try to show, his reflections on language are worth examining, for several reasons. First, they reveal the assumptions about the nature and functions of language underlying the work of an extremely self-conscious writer, whose care for style and clarity of exposition was apparent in all his writings – a fact that was highly praised by his contemporaries and by present-day readers

---

[1] Stewart (1793: 74). Despite Smith's unwillingness to publish the lecture course, it occupies a central place in his reflections on language, whose broader scope it reveals, as we will see.

alike. Second, they highlight interesting connections between the better known parts of his work, which might help to reconstruct his general underlying epistemology. Third, they help to situate his work in the context of a century where the relationship between language and knowledge often functioned as an indicator of a thinker's stance on other philosophical and social issues.

In this chapter, we begin with a brief summary of the agenda of language studies legated by the seventeenth to the eighteenth century, highlighting the issue of the relationship between language and mind. We then analyze Smith's *Languages*, and explore other aspects of his philosophy of language as expressed in his rhetoric and moral philosophy. Finally, some suggestions are made about the significance and eventual influence of his reflections on language.

LANGUAGE AND MIND: FROM THE SEVENTEENTH TO THE EIGHTEENTH CENTURY

The eighteenth century inherited from the seventeenth a philosophical agenda where language loomed large. Locke had made language an "official" philosophical topic by devoting one of the four books of *An Essay Concerning Human Understanding* (1690) entirely to language. This gesture crowned a century-old burgeoning concern with language, especially its relationship with thought and knowledge. Whether to warn against the danger of falling prey to the linguistic "idols of the marketplace" (Bacon) or to raise natural language to the position of the reasoning tool par excellence (Hobbes), all major seventeenth-century philosophers addressed the question of language's epistemic vices or virtues.[2] The eighteenth century followed suit, albeit with some noteworthy differences in emphasis and method.

The central items in the linguistic-epistemic agenda at the turn of the century are, for the most part, represented in Locke's *Essay*, which was extremely influential throughout the eighteenth

[2] The seventeenth century also displayed other interests in language, not directly connected with epistemic issues. However, the latter gradually overshadowed and even influenced these other concerns. For a survey, see Dascal (1994, 1996) and the bibliography therein. For specific authors, issues, and currents, see Aarsleff (1967, 1982), Auroux (1992), Dascal (1978, 1987, 1990, 1998a), Formigari (1988, 1992), and Knowlson (1975).

century. Locke's views on the relationship language-mind were by no means unanimously accepted, but they provide an excellent vantage point for understanding the issues under discussion.

Chapter 7 of Book III of Locke's *Essay*, devoted to the "particles," epitomizes the central issue. Particles are words that function as "marks of some action or intimation of the mind" (3.7.4). Their analysis, therefore, lead directly into the study of "the several views, postures, stands, turns, limitations, and exceptions and several other thoughts of the mind" (3.7.4; see also 3.7.6). Leibniz, in the corresponding chapter of his *Nouveaux essais*, aptly summarized, generalized, and somewhat twisted the previous suggestion by Locke, while enthusiastically endorsing it: "I truly believe that the languages are the best mirror of the human mind, and that a precise analysis of the meaning of words would provide, more than anything else, knowledge of the understanding's operations" (*Nouveaux essais*, 3.7.6; Leibniz, 1879, vol. 5, 313).[3] In the formula "language (s) = mirror of the mind" he concisely formulated the most important theme in the linguistic-epistemic agenda of the seventeenth and eighteenth centuries. This formula is conveniently ambiguous as to the precise nature, causes, and consequences of the "mirroring" relation it makes use of, as well as of the languages and mental attributes and functions it refers to – an ambiguity that permits it to stand for the variety of positions on the language–mind relationship that thrive in the seventeenth and eighteenth centuries.

The main underlying question is whether language mirrors the mind only because it serves to convey to others one's language-independent mental contents or because it also somehow participates in the mental operations involved in the formation of such contents. The answer to this question entails the choice of a favored mode and direction of explanation. For those who hold the first view, the linguistic should ultimately be explained in terms of the mental because the latter is the "primary" phenomenon, whereas the former is the "derivative" one. On this view, linguistic observations can be useful in our inquiries about the mind, just as the observation of effects is useful in understanding their causes. For those who hold the second view, language plays a constitutive

---

[3] Notice the plural "language*s*" (Dascal 1990, 1998b).

causal role in mental life, and therefore is part and parcel of the explanation of at least some of its aspects. Locke held the first view, along with most of the thinkers of the period; Leibniz, along with Hobbes and Condillac, held the second, minority view.

Although Locke suggests that "knowledge...has greater connexion with words than perhaps is suspected" (*Essay*, 3.1.6), this connection – within his theoretical framework – can only have the auxiliary role of supporting his theory of ideas and of helping to avoid the mistaken inferences about the mind suggested by a careless consideration of words.[4] Whatever its supporting role, language, in so far as it mirrors the mind, does so "from the outside." This view is shared by most seventeenth-century rationalists. Descartes, to be sure, considered human linguistic behavior to be the proof that humans – unlike animals and machines – have a mind, but he and his followers rejected with horror Hobbes's suggestion that words might play any role whatsoever in what goes on within the mind itself (see Dascal, 1994, 1996, 1998b). Similarly, the Port Royal logicians and grammarians, although viewing logic and grammar as symbiotic disciplines, did not question the priority of the former. For them, all languages share a "deep grammatical structure" – an idea that is the core of their "general grammar" research program – because the logical structure of thought underlies them.[5]

An alternative – and minority – view was proposed by Hobbes and by Leibniz (cf. Dascal, 1998a, 1998b). Each in his own way defends the idea that language has, in addition to its communicative function, a *constitutive* role in thought. On this view, important cognitive functions cannot be performed without the assistance of linguistic or other signs. While Hobbes talks of all reasoning as "reckoning" or computation performed by means of words, Leibniz insists on the necessary role of signs in virtually all cognitive operations, from the formation of mildly complex

---

[4] Among the inferences he considers helpful is the remark – often relied on in the eighteenth century – that words for "notions quite removed from sense have their rise thence, and from obvious sensible ideas are...made to stand for ideas that come not under the cognizance of our senses" (3.1.5). His prime example are terms referring to mental operations such as "imagine," "apprehend," "comprehend," "conceive," as well as to the mind itself ("spirit").

[5] This program's pivot was the *proposition* (rather than individual *words*, on which Locke's semantics focused). Its founding symbiotic works were Arnauld and Lancelot (1676) and Arnauld and Nicole (1683).

concepts to the performance of any moderately long inference (see Dascal, 1998a). From this point of view, language "mirrors" the mind in a much more intimate way than an effect mirrors its cause. Because mental processes are not language independent, by examining language we are somehow looking at the mental operations themselves, and we are in a position to provide a fuller explanation of them. The "particles" found in natural languages, in this respect, acquire a special significance, because they both give "form" to discourse *and* weave the relational structure or form of thought (Dascal, 1990).

The critique of language and the search for remedies for its deficiencies was part and parcel of the philosophical concern with language. The two camps described were concerned with it because – whether only communicative or also constitutive – only a duly "sanitized" language could be a reliable epistemic tool. Accordingly, there was considerable agreement as to the sanitation measures required. For example, the exclusion of figurative language was viewed as a sine qua non for language to perform properly its cognitive functions. As a result, rhetoric or dialectic, which had been in the renaissance a major component of the *ars inveniendi* (method of discovery), was removed from the epistemic agenda and relegated to noncognitive tasks. Agreements such as these, however, did not obliterate the divergence regarding the explanations given to language's deficiencies and the steps proposed to overcome them. For the "communicativists," the problem lay not so much in language as in thought itself and linguistic reform per se would be of no avail. The "constitutivists," who viewed language not merely as a tool for the transmission of knowledge, but also for its acquisition, were willing to invest more effort in devising suitable notations, careful definitions, and even in designing new, transparent, and precise languages which – they hoped – would improve the quality of thought and knowledge.[6]

In the eighteenth century, where the Newtonian paradigm of science is extended to the "moral sciences" and an unprecedented

---

[6] In 1668, the Royal Society of London created a committee to examine the "philosophical language" it had commissioned one of its founding members, John Wilkins, to design. Despite Wilkins's (1668) effort and ingenuity, his "Real Character" was never used. On universal languages in the seventeenth and eighteenth centuries, see Pombo (1987) and Knowlson (1975).

systematization of knowledge is undertaken by the *encyclopé-distes*, the epistemic significance of language can no longer be treated as a relatively marginal topic. Academies offer prizes for the best essays on the relationship between language, mind, and the advancement of knowledge, and the best minds of the century comply. The discussion of these issues becomes so intense in the second half of the century that Kant's silence about them in his *Critique of Pure Reason* (1781) is sharply criticized by his contemporaries Herder and Hamann (cf. Dascal and Senderowicz, 1992). Some of the seventeenth century's concerns arouse less interest[7] and other themes, such as inquiries about "the origin of language," become more fashionable, but the issue that organizes the whole field remains that of the precise role of language in cognition.[8]

Although initially repudiated as dangerously antiscientific, atheistic, and materialistic, the idea that language is an indispensable constituent of cognitive processes slowly gains adherents, even among the champions of the ideationist theory of mind,[9] and by midcentury the view that language is an indispensable component of cognition is no longer in the minority. It is Condillac, who describes himself as a follower of Locke, that articulates forcefully and influentially this view (cf. Aarsleff, 1982: 146–209; Dascal, 1983; Formigari, 1993: *passim*). In the *Essai sur l'origine des connaissances humaines* (1746), Condillac examines in detail all the operations of the mind, from perception to reasoning, to show "how and in what order" the former engenders (*produit*) all the others (*Essai*, Introduction, 4). The underlying principle of this progress from the simplest to the most sophisticated mental

---

[7] For example, universal language and general grammar. The latter, after reaching its peak in midcentury, is replaced by a concern with the specificity of each language (Joly and Stéfanini, 1977).

[8] In this, as in other domains, continuity between the two centuries is the rule (Haakonssen, 1998: 1350).

[9] For instance, Berkeley's nominalist theory of generality, where a general *noun* grants to a collection of particular ideas the stability and coherence required for its use in reasoning (*Principles*, Introduction #18: *Works*, II, 36). Along this nominalistic path, Berkeley – comparing words to algebraic signs – points out that "they should not, every time they are used, excite the ideas they signify in our minds" (*Alcyphron, Works*, III, 292; *Principles*, Introduction #19: *Works*, II, 37).

operations is what he calls the *liaison des idées*.[10] Because signs play a crucial role in this *liaison* (*Essai*, Introduction, 4), Condillac pursues a parallel inquiry about the development of our semiotic systems, to show how full-fledged conventional, articulated languages, writing, poetry, and scientific notations emerge step by step from a natural, inarticulate, and primitive *langage d'action*. The "history of language," he claims, "will show the true meaning of signs, will teach us how to avoid their abuse, and will leave no doubt about the origin of our ideas" (ibid). The *Essai* is thus an account of the simultaneous and interdependent "evolution" of language and mind. It becomes the classical model for a type of inquiry with more emphasis on logical reconstruction than on chronology and where appeal to supernatural causes is replaced by the search for a "natural origin" and a "natural history" of mind and language. Smith's "Considerations Concerning the First Formation of Languages," as well as several of his other works, belong to this type of inquiry.[11]

Condillac reaches the conclusion that the higher mental operations (beginning with "reflection") could not evolve without the appearance of articulated language (*Essai*, 1.2.11.107). Unlike other empiricists, he points out that sensations, which provide the "materials" for the mind's operations, are complex conglomerates of stimuli, far from Hume's "impressions," which were taken to be the sensory counterparts of "simple ideas." To reach the building blocks out of which concepts, judgments, and reasonings are composed, we need an "analytic tool" that decomposes sensations. We acquire this tool with the emergence of language. Just as the availability of numerical signs is essential for calculating,

---

[10] Which differs from the association of ideas (Aarsleff, 1982: 29).

[11] Many important thinkers of the eighteenth century, in addition to Condillac and Smith, wrote on the origin of language in this vein (e.g., Rousseau, Maupertuis, Turgot, Herder), and it has been suggested that "detailed attention to this discussion ought to be one of the best means to gain true understanding of the Enlightenment" (F. Venturi, *La jeunesse de Diderot*, 1939, pp. 238–40; quoted in Aarsleff, 1982: 199). Smith was familiar with this discussion. In his *Letter to the Edinburgh Review* (1755), he reviewed the French *Encyclopédie*, that devoted many articles to language (*Letter to the Edinburgh Review*, EPS, 5). He possessed copies of Condillac's *Essai* and *Traité des sensations* and, while in Paris, he held many conversations (and later also corresponded) with Turgot (Stewart, 1793: 47–8).

so, too, are words essential for thinking in metaphysics and ethics (*Essai*, 1.4.1.5). Despite his praise for Locke, Condillac blames him for assuming that "the mind makes mental propositions where it connects or separates ideas without the intervention of words" (*Essai*, 1.4.2.27). Condillac, thus, seemed to reinstate – in the new "origins" terminology – the Hobbesian thesis that thinking is nothing but mental word juggling. Horne Tooke, an influential and controversial figure in English philology in the second half of the eighteenth century, put this bluntly by claiming that "what are called [the mind's] operations are merely the operations of Language" – a thesis he sought to demonstrate with the help of etymological evidence.[12]

However, not everyone was so eager to accept this reduction of thought to language, for a variety of reasons. Apart from the charge that it led to atheism, it was seen by many (e.g., Shaftesbury, Hutcheson, Harris, Reid) as a *materialist* reduction that deprived the mind of its spiritual, active powers. Furthermore, its underlying antiessentialism or nominalism, which made thought dependent on arbitrary linguistic signs, challenged the assumption of the universality of knowledge and raised the specter of relativism and skepticism. This was viewed as particularly dangerous for ethics and politics, and efforts were made to protect our "inner moral sense" from this danger by separating it from language.[13] The same danger was perceived in aesthetics, and was the subject of the extensive debate throughout the century about the "standard of taste" and the principles of criticism (e.g., Shaftesbury, Hume, Burke, and also Smith).[14] Ultimately, the possibility that language – unequivocally a result of social interaction – is deeply

---

[12] John Horne Tooke, *Diversions of Purley* (1786), II, 51b (quoted by Aarsleff (1967: 13).

[13] For example, by Hutcheson: "It is an easy matter for men to assert any thing in words; but our own hearts must decide the matter" (*An Inquiry into the Origins of our Ideas of Beauty and Virtue*, 1725); "Morality does not consist in significancy" (*An Essay on the Nature and Conduct of the Passions and Affections*, 1728). Both quoted in Formigari (1993: 16–17).

[14] The view, advanced by Condillac and developed by Rousseau in his *Essai sur l'origine des langues*, that language at its origin is "metaphorical," with its implication that primitive men were "natural poets," prompted the need to distinguish between such a natural poetry from "poetry proper," which could not (e.g., for thinkers such as Shaftesbury) be reduced to its alleged natural linguistic origins.

and essentially involved in our mental life brought to the fore the tension between the traditional view of humans as individual, autonomous subjects and the emerging awareness of the importance of humanity's social nature. In an age where the very idea of social sciences was taking shape, this issue was crucial. It was not by chance that Rousseau (1755) discussed it in one of his social treatises (see footnote 19). Nor was it by sheer accident that the Berlin Academy in 1769 offered a prize (won by Herder) for the best essay on the topic.

SMITH ON LANGUAGE

In Search of a System

In his earliest linguistic publication, a review of Samuel Johnson's *Dictionary of the English Language*, published in the *Edinburgh Review* (1755), Smith praises the pioneering character of this work, but criticizes it for not being systematic enough. Its plan, he says, is not "sufficiently grammatical"; the different significations of a word are "seldom digested into general classes, or ranged under the meaning which the word principally expresses"; and "words apparently synonymous" are not carefully distinguished (EPS, 232–3). He proposes his own alternative to two of Johnson's entries, one of which, *but*, had been analyzed by Locke. According to Smith, *but* is a particle that holds the place of various grammatical categories "according to the different modifications of the general sense of opposition" (EPS, 236). Johnson's eighteen meanings of *but* are then accommodated into seven grammatical categories and subcategories and, for the two main senses, "adversative" (= *however*) and "alternative" (= *unless, except*), Smith explains the difference between *but* and its English synonyms. These explanations employ a mixed lot of syntactic, stylistic, and semantic considerations. Although his semantic explanations refer to "mental operations," he does not seem to follow Locke in taking this to be the main criterion for explaining the particles' meanings. Unlike Locke, who expresses his dissatisfaction with grammatical terminology and seeks a systematic account in terms of the "several relations the mind gives to the several propositions" (*Essay*, 3.7.5), the systematicity Smith seeks is rather that of a conservative grammarian.

Nor is he concerned – as Leibniz (*Nouveaux essais*, 3.7.5; 1879, V: 312) – with providing a precise definition for each meaning and with subsuming them under a more specific notion than "opposition."

Eight years later, commenting on the abstract of Ward's "plan for a Rational Grammar," Smith praises it as a blueprint for "the best System of Grammar," as well as for "the best System of Logic in any Language" and "the best History of the natural progress of the Human mind in forming the most important abstractions upon which all reasoning depends."[15] He goes on to describe what his own plan for treating the same subject would look like. He would begin with the verbs; then show how subject, attribute, and object were separated from the verb; and likewise investigate "the origin and use of all the different parts of speech and of all their different modifications, considered necessary to express all the different qualifications and relations of any single event" (ibid). This brief description sums up the essence of *Languages*, published 2 years earlier.[16] *Languages*, however, *does not* begin with the verb, although at about midway attention is shifted to verbs, which "must necessarily have been coëval with the very first attempts towards the formation of language" (*Languages*, 27). This discrepancy hints at the different principles of organization underlying *Languages* and perhaps the whole of Smith's reflections on language.

LANGUAGE ORIGINS: STRUCTURE AND COGNITION. *Languages* begins with proper names, "probably . . . one of the first steps towards the formation of language" (*Languages*, 1). By inventing proper names, "two savages, who had never been taught to speak," would be able to indicate to each other those particular objects which were most familiar to them. Next, they would naturally apply these names to other objects *exactly resembling* the original ones. This diachronic antonomasia – Smith observes – is parallel to its

---

[15] Letter to George Baird, 7 February 1763 (Corr. 87–8). William Ward's *An Essay on Grammar, as it may be applied to the English language* was published in London in 1765.

[16] *Languages* was published in the first volume of the London series *Philological Miscellany* (1761) and later appended without significant revisions to the third edition (1767) of *Theory of Moral Sentiments*. It is reprinted in LRBL, but not in the Glasgow edition of *Theory of Moral Sentiments*, contrary to Smith's express instructions.

synchronic counterpart, which we still use when we call an orator a Cicero or a philosopher a Newton. This procedure generates
general names and gives occasion to the formation of classes "of
which the ingenious and eloquent M. Rousseau of Geneva finds
himself so much at a loss to account for the origin" (*Languages*, 2).

Rousseau's difficulty was a chicken-or-egg puzzle. Generalization, he said, requires words, but words in turn depend on the
ability to generalize. Smith's solution at first seems to break the
circle by espousing a nominalist position: classes arise by virtue
of using a name for a multitude of objects. On closer inspection,
however, he is claiming that it is not the name that creates the
class, but rather the resemblance between its members, which enti-
tles one to apply to them the same name.[17] Just as he assumes
"familiar objects" as the natural prelinguistic candidates for proper
names, he also assumes "natural kinds" defined in terms of a natural similarity of space as prelinguistically given bearers of general
names.[18] It is questionable whether, by side-stepping in this way
Locke's antiessentialism, Smith has indeed addressed Rousseau's
problem.[19]

The next problem for the savages is finding a way of particu-
larizing a general name to refer to an individual object for which

[17] "It is this application of the name of an individual to a great multitude of
   objects...that seems originally to have given occasion to the formation of those
   classes"; "what constitutes a species is merely a number of objects, bearing a certain degree of resemblance to one another, and on that account denominated by a
   single appellation" (*Languages*, 2).
[18] On "natural kind" and "similarity space," see Quine (1969: chapter 5).
[19] Rousseau's problem is presented in a series of aporetic circles exploring the difficulties of explaining how man could acquire cognitive abilities beyond those of the
   animals. "The more one meditates on this subject" – he says (1755: 50) – "the bigger
   is the distance from pure sensations to the simple bits of knowledge." Communication is introduced as a possible way out: "It is impossible to conceive how a man
   would be able, by his own forces, without the assistance of communication...to
   overcome such an enormous interval" (ibid.). However, language, the tool of communication that alone would be able to overcome the gap, raises a "new and worse
   difficulty," namely "if men needed speech in order to learn to think, they were
   much more in need of thoughts in order to discover the art of speech" (52). The
   reason is that "general ideas can penetrate the mind only with the help of words,
   and the understanding only grasps them through propositions" (54). Assuming –
   as Smith does – that general ideas arise independently of language so *green* can be
   "from the very first start" a general word (*Languages*, 7), or – as Condillac suggests
   (*Essai*, 1.4.25–6) – that both evolve together, is hardly a solution to the problem
   (Dascal, 1978).

no proper name is available. This can be done either through the individual's qualities or through its relations to other things. Thus come into being two other categories of words – adjectives and prepositions. The invention of the former presupposes the capacities to compare objects and distinguish those having a quality from those not having it, to distinguish the quality from the object to which it belongs, and to conceive the object as subsisting without the quality. "The invention, therefore, even of the simplest nouns adjective, must have required more metaphysics than we are apt to be aware of" (*Languages*, 7). "More metaphysics" means "more mental operations,"[20] and Smith concludes this paragraph by stressing that these operations – some of which remind of Condillac's "analysis" – "must all have been employed, *before . . .* nouns adjective, could be instituted" (ibid; italics added). From this he infers "that when languages were beginning to be formed, nouns adjective would by no means be the words of the earliest invention" (ibid).

Here, too, Smith is ambivalent regarding the language–mind relationship. His inference may be warranted either by the need of an earlier stage of language which was necessary for developing the mental operations required for inventing adjectives, or else simply by the fact that it is more likely that other words requiring "less metaphysics" were invented earlier. What is clear, at any rate, is the criterion he has been using so far to establish the chronological order of appearance of the different kinds of words: the more mental operations are involved, the later a category of words will be invented.

The next category to appear is the preposition, which requires more powers of abstraction, generalization, distinction, and comparison than the invention of adjectives (*Languages*, 12). Not all prepositions are equally "general, abstract and metaphysical." For example, *above* and *below*, which denote specific spatial relations, are less so than *of*, which denotes "relation in general." The latter's interpretation is context dependent (i.e., the particular relation

---

[20] In the eighteenth century, "metaphysics" was a term generally used to refer to the theory of mind (cf. Goldschmidt, 1974: 267–8). However, Smith also uses "metaphysical" in a more traditional sense, both in *Languages* (as when he says that "a relation is, in itself, a more metaphysical object than a quality") (*Languages*, 12) and elsewhere (e.g., in "Ancient Logics").

it denotes "is inferred by the mind"), thus requiring more mental machinery than the more specific prepositions. According to the principle "more metaphysics, later invention," this means that prepositions such as *of*, *to*, *for*, and *with* "would probably be the last to be invented" (ibid). After the preposition comes number, which, "considered in general, without relation to any particular set of objects numbered, is one of the most abstract and metaphysical ideas ... and, consequently, is not an idea, which would readily occur to rude mortals, who were just beginning to form a language" (*Languages*, 22).

The sequence of inventions described previously amounts to the conjectural development of languages Smith calls "compounded" (later to be called analytic, e.g., English). However, he also describes a parallel sequence that would have led instead to "original" (later to be called "synthetic" or "agglutinative") languages (e.g., Latin). The latter evolve when, instead of creating separate words for qualities, relations, and numbers, the inventors of language resort to the "expedient" of attaching to substantives different terminations. The qualities of having or not having a sex and, in the former case, of being male or female are expressed in this way in Latin and Greek; and the expression of relations in these languages by means of cases instead of prepositions "is a contrivance of precisely the same kind" (*Languages*, 13). Languages that follow this path are "original" because the expedients they use require "less metaphysics," so those "rude" first inventors of language would "naturally" tend to invent them instead of their analytical counterparts.[21]

Smith is thus employing consistently the same principle (i.e., the amount and degree of sophistication of the mental operations required) in establishing the chronology of appearance of the parts of speech and of the types of languages.[22] Compounded languages

---

[21] "To express relation, therefore, by a variation in the name of the co-relative object, requiring neither abstraction, nor generalization, nor comparison of any kind, would, at first, be much more natural and easy, than to express it by those general words called prepositions, of which the first invention must have demanded some degree of all those operations" (*Languages*, 17).

[22] This does not rule out the possibility that the two types of language evolve simultaneously. In fact, simultaneous evolution seems to be required by his later explanation of the rise of "mixed" modern languages.

would tend to appear earlier because of a "least effort" principle. However, Smith points out, their "synthetic" method has severe limitations: how many qualities, relations, and numbers can be represented by nominal declensions without encumbering the linguistic system so as to make it useless? Greek, for example, has five cases, three numbers, and three genders, not to speak of the "infinitely more complex" verb conjugations (*Languages*, 24–6). It seems, thus, that there is a trade-off between parsimony regarding mental operations (i.e., simplicity at the mental equipment level) and complexity of the linguistic system. However diachronically "natural," easier, and useful within the limited range of notions used by primitive men, the latter puts a heavy burden on the synchronic use of language for the communicative needs of more advanced humans. If they were to use only the limited number of declensions and conjugations available for expressing qualities, numbers, relations, persons, time, and aspect, they would in fact need to rely more rather than less on a wider range of mental operations such as memory and contextual inference.

However, even within the presumed limited scope of the original compounded languages, is it the case, as Smith claims, that the invention of morphological variations of words does not require as much analytic powers as the invention of separate words? In his discussion of the synthetic way of expressing relations, Smith argues that 1) *abstraction* was not needed because the relation is expressed here "as it appears in nature, not as something separated and detached, but as thoroughly mixed and blended with the co-relative object" (*Languages*, 14); 2) *generalization* was not needed because, although a word like *arboris* ("of the tree") contains "in its signification" the same relation expressed by the English preposition *of, arboris* (unlike *of*) is not a general word that "can be applied to express the same relation between whatever other objects it might be observed to subsist" (*Languages*, 15); and 3) *comparison* is not needed because the rule assigning the same termination to other nouns to express the same relation would arise

without any intention or foresight in those who first set the example, and who never meant to establish any general rule. The general rule would establish itself insensibly, and by slow degrees, in consequence of that love of analogy and similarity of sound, which is the foundation of by far the greater part of the rules of grammar. (*Languages*, 16)

Argument 2 emphasizes the grammatical distinction between *morphs* and *lexemes*, and assigns to it a semantic significance it hardly has: first, because both are equally syncategorematic (i.e., the interpretation of both depends on the words they are "attached" to), as Smith himself remarked when discussing the extreme generality of prepositions such as *of*, which "in modern languages hold the place of the ancient cases" (*Languages*, 19); second, because once the same morph is regularly used to express *the same relation* when attached to other nouns, it becomes just as general a symbol of that relation as the corresponding preposition. Smith, perhaps anticipating this objection, argues in argument 3 that this rule or regularity emerges "naturally" (i.e., without design or intention). However, this is immaterial to the issue at hand, for as soon as the termination *-is* is applied to another word in the genitive case, *it* (not *arboris*) has been generalized; and this implies the same power of generalization as that involved in applying the adjective *green* to two different objects, referring to the same color. Perhaps he has in mind the further step of abstraction (not *generalization*) involved in the invention of a word such as *greenness*. However, it is doubtful that not performing this step differentiates between the inventors of the synthetic *-is* and those of the analytic *of*. It takes a logician or a metaphysician, not a regular language inventor (nor a later language user) to conceive of such things as "ofness" (or "-isness") and greenness.

In argument 1, Smith appeals again to the notion of "nature." Here, the idea is that "in nature" what the first inventors of language encounter are "thoroughly mixed and blended" wholes, not yet analyzed into components of various sorts. The synthetic representation of relations fits better this presumed preanalytic stage of our perception of the world because it is analogous to it (i.e., because its *form* structurally corresponds to it). With this iconic conception of the naturalness of a language, Smith is introducing a new criterion of anteriority. He is assuming that the better a linguistic form *mirrors* sensory input, the closer it is to nature (at least as it appears to us), and consequently, the earlier it is likely to be created. This is a semiotic criterion, based on the type of relation that links signifier and signified. Its correlation with the mental operations criterion presupposes that iconic representation is mentally less onerous than other forms of representation, presumably because it relies on a pre-existing ability to detect similarities – an assumption Smith had already made use of. The similarity in question here, however, does not require an imagetic or pictorial relation between the sign and its meaning. Smith does not question the arbitrariness of the sign, nor does he appeal to the onomatopoetic speculations about word origins that animated the etymological imagination of his century. He is talking about a structural analogy that could in principle be displayed by analytic languages as well, whenever what they represent is itself segmented.

Smith's use of this semiotic criterion to support the anteriority of synthetic language thus entirely depends on the belief that sensations are "thoroughly blended and mixed" wholes, as Condillac argued, against Locke and the other empiricists.[23] Condillac's initial language – the *langage d'action* – was also synthetic. However, it was, semiotically speaking, *indexical*. Its cries, gestures and "agitations of the whole body" (*Essai*, 2.1.2.2) do not *depict* the feelings and desires they express – they form with them a single behavioral whole. This, not iconicity, is what makes the *langage d'action* natural and different from the articulated languages that segment these initial behavioral and sensorial wholes. Furthermore, the savages who used the *langage d'action* had no leisure to contemplate and describe the world; what they were concerned with was "demanding and giving help to each other" (ibid).

Condillac's savages performed directive and expressive speech acts (e.g., requesting, warning, ordering, offering, expressing fear, comforting), while Smith's language inventors were more concerned with assertive ones: "We never speak but in order to express our opinion that something either is or is not" (*Languages*, 27). However, both discover soon that they need the verb: "No affirmation can be expressed without the assistance of some verb" (ibid). Because there is no real speaking without verbs, their invention – to repeat – "must necessarily have been coëval with the very first attempts towards the formation of language" (ibid).

With the verb, *Languages* returns to the beginnings of language and follows again the path described for the noun. Generalization,

---

[23] Even the analysis of sensations that "seem capable of a certain composition and decomposition," such as taste or sound, require the skill of a cook or an experienced ear ("External Senses," 31).

abstraction, and analysis led from impersonal verbs "which express in one word a complete event" (*Languages*, 28) to the division of this event into its "metaphysical elements" (*Languages*, 30) and to the institution of new words, or the use of the already available nouns for denoting "not so much the events, as the elements of which they were composed" (ibid). Thus appear the distinctions of persons (which express "ideas extremely metaphysical and abstract," especially the first person – *Languages*, 32), subject and complement, tenses, voices, and modes. Again, "original" and "compounded" languages diverged in their ways of representing these distinctions, the former morphologically, the latter lexically.

The verb narrative differs from the noun narrative in two important respects. First, it makes use of the semiotic criterion from the outset. Second, it introduces in the discussion, for the first time, a rhetorical comparison between the two types of language. These two considerations are interrelated. Impersonal one-word verbs "preserve in the expression that perfect simplicity and unity, which there always is in the object and in the idea" (*Languages*, 28). They mirror, thus, "that perfect simplicity and unity with which the mind conceives it in nature," "a complete affirmation, the whole of an event" (ibid). Smith mentions here several times the *simplicity* of the event and of the idea corresponding to it: "in nature, the idea or conception of Alexander walking, is as perfectly and completely one simple conception, as that of Alexander not walking" (ibid). He is stressing that, unlike relational complexes, which are *mixtures* (albeit "thoroughly blended"), events are inherently simple. Whereas the semiotic adequacy of a one-word representation of the former lies in the way they appear to us, that of the latter seems to lie at the deeper level of what "really is." Therefore, to divide an event into parts is an *artificial* move. It results from the imperfection of a language that employs a multiple-word "grammatical circumlocution" when one word would suffice – a procedure whose "significancy is founded upon a certain metaphysical analysis" (ibid). This procedure is not only needless, but also misleading in the sense of Ryle's (1932) "systematically misleading expressions," for the structural analogy suggested by grammar, instead of revealing the logical form of things, hides it.

One can discern here a critical attitude vis-à-vis natural language that can be traced back to the tradition initiated by Bacon.

However, Smith does not espouse the wholesale Baconian critique of the false classifications embedded in the languages created by vulgar unscientific minds – the critique that inspired the research program of a complete reform of scientific language.[24] Nor does what he says indicate that he would endorse Reid's reliance on natural language in his critique of the empiricists' "way of ideas" (see Aarsleff, 1967: 101). Smith's attitude is more nuanced. Natural languages, as we know them today, are the result of a process of "mixture of several languages with one another, occasioned by the mixture of different nations" (*Languages*, 33). Consequently, they contain at best only *some* epistemologically and metaphysically reliable elements. These must be carefully distinguished from the unreliable ones, with the help of – among other means – the kind of conjectural history and typology undertaken by Smith.

This nuanced attitude probably results from Smith's realization that Gabriel Girard's fundamental parallelism *parole/pensée/monde* does not strictly hold. Girard, whose *Les vrais principes de la langue françoise* (1747) Smith recommended to Ward as the linguistic book from which he "received more instruction than from any other,"[25] defined speech as "the manifestation of thought through words," thought as arising from "the union of ideas," and ideas as "the simple images of things" (Girard, 1747: 5). As pointed out by Swiggers (Introduction to Girard, 1982: 32), following Foucault (1966), Girard assumes that the structured world pre-exists thought and language, and that its structure is transitively transferred to thought and language. However, despite his efforts, this presumed transitivity is precisely what Smith could not find, as we have seen. Consequently, the best system of grammar, the best system of logic, and the best history of the natural progress of the human mind are not mirror images of each other. The interest of undertaking these three enterprises together, as *Languages* presumably purports to do, lies in the instructive divergences one discovers between them.

---

[24] This program culminated, via Condillac's claim that science is nothing but *un langage bien fait*, in Lavoisier's reform of chemical nomenclature (see Crosland, 1978: part II, chapter 5).

[25] Letter to Baird, 7 February 1763 (Corr., 88).

In addition to the epistemic, metaphysical, and grammatical perspectives, *Languages* displays Smith's rhetorical concerns as relevant to the assessment of language evolution, structure, and function. When he speaks of metaphysically artificial "grammatical circumlocutions," he is also condemning prolixity as stylistically wrong. When he praises the iconicity and analogy of "original" languages, he is also suggesting the value of apposite metaphors.[26] To be sure, progress in analysis has the functional cognitive advantage of yielding a system of language that is "more coherent, more connected, more easily retained and comprehended" (*Languages*, 30). However, its price is a loss of unity and simplicity of expression, which becomes instead "more intricate and complex." The trade-off between these two desiderata is formulated by Smith as an "inverse law":

In general it may be laid down for a maxim, that the more simple any language is in its composition, the more complex it must be in its declensions and conjugations; and, on the contrary, the more simple it is in its declensions and conjugations, the more complex it must be in its composition. (*Languages*, 36)

"Composition" here is more a rhetorical than a syntactical notion, and for Smith, it has a considerable weight vis-à-vis the cognitive advantages of analytic "simplicity."

TOWARD A THEORY OF LANGUAGE USE. This "rhetoricization" of the discussion in *Languages* reaches its peak in the final paragraphs, which compare the evolution of languages to the evolution of machines – a rather expected simile in the Newtonian era. After

---

[26] Smith does not favor the use of metaphor per se, but only when it is appropriate (LRBL, i.13–15, i.v.56–8, i.76). His positive valuation of iconicity and analogy in *Languages* can be compared, on the one hand, to Rousseau's thesis that language in its origin is metaphorical and, on the other hand, to Leibniz's *lex expressionum*, according to which a relation of "expression" obtains between two things "when there is a constant and ordered relation between what can be said of both" (Letter to Arnauld, September 1687; Leibniz, 1879, II, 112) (i.e., where no similitude between them is required other than structural analogy) ("What is an idea"; VII, 263). Neither Rousseau's nor Leibniz's relevant texts could have been known to Smith. Condillac's *langage d'action*, however, was based on a *metonymic* relation of representation. Vico's ideas on the role of metaphor and poetry in the formation and evolution of language had their counterparts in Britain at the beginning of the eighteenth century (Formigari, 1993: 24ff.), and may have influenced Smith.

showing how English is able to express all the tenses with the help of a few auxiliary verbs, Smith writes:

It is in this manner that language becomes more simple in its rudiments and principles, just in proportion as it grows more complex in its composition, and the same thing has happened in it, which commonly happens with regard to mechanical engines. All machines are generally, when first invented, extremely complex in their principles, and there is often a particular principle of motion for every particular movement which it is intended they should perform. Succeeding improvers observe, that one principle may be so applied as to produce several of those movements; and thus the machine becomes gradually more and more simple, and produces its effects with fewer wheels, and fewer principles of motion. In language, in the same manner, every case of every noun, and every tense of every verb, was originally expressed by a particular distinct word, which served for this purpose and for no other. But succeeding observation discovered, that one set of words was capable of supplying the place of all that infinite number, and that four or five prepositions, and half a dozen auxiliary verbs, were capable of answering the end of all the declensions, and of all the conjugations in the ancient languages. (*Languages*, 41)

This sounds as the description of the ultimate linguistic achievement, especially for a self-proclaimed Newtonian such as Smith. However, it is surprisingly followed by the claim that, instead of perfection, it marks indeed imperfection:

But this simplification of languages, though it arises, perhaps, from similar causes, has by no means similar effects with the correspondent simplification of machines. The simplification of machines renders them more and more perfect, but this simplification of the rudiments of languages renders them more and more imperfect, and less proper for many of the purposes of language. (*Languages*, 42)

These "other purposes" are nothing but the rhetorical virtues of eloquence, beauty, rhyme, mobility of words within a sentence, and conciseness. On all these counts, the "original" synthetic languages reach "much greater perfection" than the modern languages, whose expressive power is severely limited by their inherent "prolixness, constraint, and monotony" (*Languages*, 45).

Smith lectured on "rhetoric and belles lettres" from 1748 to 1763. The third lecture of his last course, delivered on November 22, 1762, is a summary of *Languages*, which shows that he viewed that essay's thematic as belonging to a broader concern with "explaining and illustrating the powers of the human mind" through an examination of "the several ways of communicating our thoughts by speech" and of "the principles of those literary compositions which contribute to persuasion or entertainment".[27] This, and not the "taedious [sic] and unentertaining" (LRBL, i.16) details of traditional rhetorical treatises, is for him what rhetoric is all about, for "there is no art whatever that hath so close a connection with all the faculties and powers of the mind as eloquence, or the art of speaking."[28]

Smith's rhetoric extends and deepens his theory of language in three significant ways. The first is a shift from a diachronic (even though conjectural) frame to an overtly synchronic one. Granted that English has "such great defects" due to "the very manner of its formation," the question is now how English speakers and writers remedy them (LRBL, i.37). Phonetic contractions of all sorts help overcome the inherent prolixity of the auxiliary verbs system; the compositional constraints of fixed order can be overcome by anteposition of "whatever is most interesting in the sentence," as well as by contractive stress (LRBL, i.v.46): only "ideots" and "a man who felt no passion" use "the most plain" syntactical order. Those who are affected by what they say will let the idea that affects them most "thrust itself forward" and will utter it "strongest" (LRBL, i.v.45–6).

Secondly, the range of mental operations related to language is extended well beyond the limited set of basic cognitive ones discussed in *Languages*, for "stile . . . not only expresses the thought but also the spirit and mind of the author" (LRBL, i.v.47). The expression "spirit and mind" covers, in addition to the author's emotions, his character, ethical virtues, ability to argue, the knowledge he has of the theme treated, and his sensitivity to the intended audience and circumstances. The correspondence between these mental properties and their suitable expression is ruled, according to Smith, by a general principle of propriety: "expression ought to be suited to the mind of the author" (LRBL, i.79). Given the

---

[27] From a report by John Millar, who had attended Smith's lectures (Stewart, 1793: 11).

[28] George Campbell's opening sentence in *The Philosophy of Rhetoric* (1776). Quoted in the editor's Introduction to LRBL, 36.

variety of "spirits and minds," there is a corresponding variety of styles. The capital crime is to fashion to oneself a style (and a character) that does not fit one's cast of mind, and therefore, is artificial and sometimes ridiculous – as Smith claims referring to Shaftesbury (LRBL, i.137–9, 145–6). Having extended as far as this the range of mental traits relevant for assessing the propriety of one's linguistic behavior, Smith reaches an encompassing notion of "naturalness" of which the "metaphysical" and semiotic versions discussed in *Languages* are nothing but particular cases (LRBL, i.133–6).

Finally, I think we can detect in Smith's rhetoric a shift from language structure to language use as particularly relevant to the language–mind relationship. The previously mentioned notions of naturalness and of what is of primary interest for the speaker (or writer) in each sentence he utters exemplify this shift. None of them can be accounted for in terms of language structure alone because grammar is insufficient to express the "spirit and mind" of the author (LRBL, i.v.47). The propriety of such an expression can only be judged by reference to the context where language is put to use to express a particular mental state. Writing that is unrelated to context is unnatural (LRBL, i.144), and the writer must take into account his readers: the ease of understanding, care not to overburden the reader's processing capabilities, and an awareness for what one *suggests* (in addition to what one *says*).[29] This regard for the addressee is essential, along with clarity and true passion, for communication to proceed *by sympathy* (LRBL, i.v.56). Smith's account of language use thus links up, unequivocally, with its ethical underpinnings.

TOWARD AN ETHICS OF COMMUNICATION. Leaving aside the more obvious connections between LRBL and *Theory of Moral Sentiments* pointed out by the former's editor (Introduction to LRBL,

---

[29] On the two first points, see LRBL, i.9–10, i.v.52, i.133–6. A good example of the third is Smith's rule: "Your Sentence or Phrase [should] never drag a Tail" (LRBL, i.52). Hedging or qualification at the beginnings of a sentence is okay because it suggests accuracy, whereas at the end it suggests "a kind of Retractation and bears the appearance of confusion or disingenueity" (ibid.). Suggestions such as these belong to a family of nonsemantic inferences whose study has been one of the mainstays of pragmatics ever since Grice's groundbreaking articles on the "logic of conversation" (collected in Grice, 1989).

18–19), I want to mention a few other significant relations between Smith's theories of language and of morality.

First, just as Smith's ethics is a theory of the propriety of action, his rhetoric is a theory of the propriety of *linguistic* action. The fundamental notion of Smithian ethics, sympathy, is in fact a principle of correspondence based on the instinctive analogy between what the other feels and what one would feel in similar circumstances (TMS, 1.1.1.4). We have seen the role of correspondence and analogy in the relationship between signifier and signified (*Languages*), and in the proper expression of a speaker's or writer's "spirit and mind" (LRBL). In *Theory of Moral Sentiments*, the emphasis is rather on the *mutual* correspondence that must obtain between interacting human beings in order to create and sustain social life. Accordingly, Smith stresses the human ability of mentally *changing places* with a sufferer (TMS, 1.1.1.3, 1.1.1.5).[30] Natural sympathy, cultivated and perfected by deliberate effort (TMS, 1.1.5.5), yields a principle of "distribution of the effort" each of the participants in the "communication of sentiments" is required to perform:

[the effort] of the spectator to enter into the sentiments of the person principally concerned, and [the effort] of the person principally concerned, to bring down his emotions to what the spectator can go along with. (TMS, 1.1.5.1)

To be sure, the "interval" between the participants' sentiments (TMS, 1.1.1.6) cannot be entirely eliminated by this concerted effort, but its reduction is indispensable for ensuring the sharing of sentiments. Furthermore, it is essential that the effort be more or less equitably divided between the persons interacting. It would be morally improper, as well as inefficient, for any of them to lay on the other the whole burden. The "spectator" is required to make an effort to identify him- or herself with the feeling of "the person principally concerned," whereas the latter is required to make an effort to restrain the spontaneously strong expression of his or her emotion to let the spectator identify with his or her

---

[30] For Leibniz, this principle was of fundamental ethical, social, and communicative importance. His notion of tolerance and his attempts to reconcile opposing views were largely based on it (Dascal, 1993, 1995). Unlike Smith, who tended to focus on its "altruistic" reading (TMS, 1.1.5.5, 2.2.1.1), Leibniz acknowledged also a selfish "strategic" use of the principle.

feeling, for, not being directly involved in what produced it, he or she cannot be expected to identify with its strongest expression. Replace "spectator" by "hearer," "person principally concerned" by "speaker," and "identify" by "understand," and the dialectics of emotion sharing described by Smith becomes a formulation of the basic principle of communicative cooperation – the "division of communicative labor." We encountered the rudiments of this principle in the rhetoric, and it comes as no surprise that, in *Theory of Moral Sentiments*, he straightforwardly applies it to communicative acts such as excessive questioning motivated by unrestrained curiosity (TMS, 7.4.28).

The other parallel between Smith's views on language and his ethics has to do with the notions of rule and system. Smith distinguishes between two kinds of rules in morality and in language (TMS, 7.4.1), which I would call "algorithmic" and "heuristic." The former admit of no exceptions, whereas in the latter exceptions are the rule. Grammatical rules that admit of exceptions are simply bad rules that should be replaced by better ones. Smith criticizes the Greek and Roman grammarians for not having done so:

> when they came to find that many expressions could not be reduced to these rules, they were not candid enough to confess the grossness of their error and allow that these were exceptions to the generall they had laid down but stuck close to their old scheme. (LRBL, i.v.55)

Rules of justice are of this kind. In contrast, moral rules for all the other virtues, cannot, by their very nature, be without exceptions (TMS, 3.6.9). The reason for multiplication of exceptions in this kind of rules is their context dependence (TMS, 3.6.9, 7.4.3–5).[31] Heuristic rules cannot provide, therefore, a decision procedure for choosing a particular action in specific circumstances (TMS, 3.6.11). Their function is not to decide mechanically for the agent, but to provide him or her with general guidelines for deciding by him- or herself. Algorithmic rules, on the contrary, are perfect only when they give "infallible directions" that determine the correct choice. This is the ideal to be pursued by a correct grammar, as well as by jurisprudence (TMS, 3.6.10). To achieve this

---

[31] For instance, character and circumstances vary so much that virtually all the terms of the retribution rule ("equal," "superior," "value," "service," "as soon as," "you can") can receive widely different values.

ideal, such rules are to be made as "context free" as possible, by incorporating all the relevant contextual specifications (ibid), thus lending them infallibility, in grammar and in jurisprudence (TMS, 3.6.11). Because they are absolutely dependable, they should be followed with "the most sacred, ... reverential and religious regard" and often it is "a crime to violate them" (ibid).

Algorithmic rules characterize the machine-like structure of what might be called the "basic institutional systems" underlying communication and social life. Without the existence and unquestioned respect for such "structural laws," neither could exist. In this sense, they constitute an indispensable infrastructure that should be valued as such, much like we appreciate the intricacy and cleverness of machines and contrivances independently of the ends for which they were contrived (TMS, 4.1.3). However, these rules must be complemented by another set of rules, the heuristic ones, which – so to speak – lift us above this structural ground. For we need also guidance in evaluating the different communicative and social ends we can pursue, as well as the propriety of the linguistic and moral tools we use to that effect. Casuistry attempts to reduce the second type of moral rules to the first, and for this reason, it is sharply criticized by Smith (TMS, 7.4.16, 7.4.33); so, too, are the moralists, for their exclusive reliance on imprecise heuristic rules. Smith's message is crystal clear: moral philosophy requires the two different types of rule. Neither can be dispensed, nor can one of them be reduced to the other. *Mutatis mutandis*, this message should be applied to Smith's philosophy of language. In addition to its grammatically and semantically codifiable part, a proper treatment of language should cover also the whole domain of language use (exemplified but not exhausted by rhetoric), a domain where the most appropriate rules are of the heuristic type (Dascal, 1992).

SIGNIFICANCE

Smith's monograph on the formation of languages is extremely brief, if compared with the voluminous works by his contemporaries on the same subject. Although he addressed in it the main issue on the agenda of such studies – the relationship between language and mind – in a way that permits us to locate him within Condillac's "research programme," his voice in the intensive dialogue that his century sustained on this topic was a relatively minor one.[32] With characteristic moderation, he avoided taking a clear stance on the priority of language or thought, preferring simply to show how they are correlated in the various phases of language evolution. At times, as we have seen, he came close to suggesting a decisive influence of language on the development of mental operations, but on the whole he remained faithful to the traditional Cartesian and Lockean mind → language direction of explanation. He avoided the nominalist and materialist positions that authors such as Tooke sought to develop from Locke's observation that names of mental operations are derived from names for sensory and physical operations. Similarly, although he pointed out the complexity of the mental operations required for discerning qualities and relations, he avoided the ontological issue of whether they exist "out there" or are simply creations of our mental (and linguistic) efforts, and – as far as substances are concerned – he assumed, contra Locke, the former.

Smith's thesis of the originality and epistemic-semiotic primacy of the impersonal verb, which corresponds to a whole event, has been hailed by Land (1974: 87) as a significant step in both logic and linguistics because it emphasizes the proposition as the basic unit of form and meaning. Arnauld, in the *Port Royal Grammar*, had posited an invariable subject-copula-attribute syntactic "deep structure," from which all "surface structures" are derived. On this view, shorter sentences would be the result of a process of abbreviation or ellipsis. Contrary to this, just as he had rejected the cryptoanalyticity of morphologically represented relations, Smith (*Languages*, 30) rejects the suggestion of Sanchez – an influential sixteenth-century grammarian – that even in impersonal verbs there is an underlying subject (so that *pluit* results by ellipsis from *pluvia pluit*). He also rejects the Port Royal formula on the grounds that it presupposes a logical sophistication the language creators could not have, including the ability to use the copula, "the most abstract and metaphysical of all verbs" (*Languages*, 34). On epistemological grounds, Smith seems convinced that it is much more natural, both diachronically and synchronically, to take

[32] Yet, in so far as strictly linguistic matters are concerned, Smith was "more directly influential than Condillac on later philologists: Monboddo draws heavily upon the *Considerations* and Smith anticipates A. W. Schlegel's important distinction between analytic and synthetic structures" (Land, 1974: 80).

nonanalyzed propositions that express whole events, rather than an abstract analytical formula, as the primitive linguistic structure from which the others are derived. However, Smith did not develop farther this insight,[33] so it is a bit far fetched to see in it the seeds of propositional logic, not to say of the detachment of the study of linguistic form from the study of cognition (Land, 1974: 93).

However important *Languages* may have been, it seems to me that the broader significance of Smith's theory of language is to be gathered from what transpires in his other works, as I have tried to show.[34] As far as the mind–language issue is concerned, he went beyond the prevalent approach of considering mainly their cognitive and structural correspondence and interdependence. Thereby, he extended considerably the range of "mental operations" and linguistic phenomena to be considered within the tradition that put the mind–language relationship at the center of its concerns.

Unlike the dominant tendency among the rhetoricians of his time, who focused on the "ornamental" role of language, Smith viewed style as a comprehensive mirror of the mind, and redefined beauty in terms of this mirroring relation (LRBL, i.80–5). This provided the guidelines for a kind of criticism that could appreciate Swift's "plain" style and be contemptuous towards Shaftesbury's "dungeon of metaphorical obscurity" (LRBL, i.13). It also permitted him to recover the forgotten Aristotelian rhetorical tradition that emphasizes persuasion as a main discursive function ("Ancient Logics," 1) – a tradition that distinguishes between a "rhetorical" discourse that "endeavours *by all means* to persuade" (LRBL, i.149; italics added) and a "didactic" one that "endeavours to persuade us only so far as the strength of the argument is convincing" (ibid).[35] In

---

[33] Elsewhere, he even took for granted the universality of the Port Royal formula: "in every [phrase] there are generally three principall parts or terms because every Judgement of the humane mind must comprehend two Ideas between which we declare that relation subsists or does not subsist; concerning Two of these we affirm some thing or other, and the third connects them together and expresses the affirmation" (LRBL, i.43).

[34] For lack of space, I have not gone into his few remarks on language in the WN or into the many connections with language one can find in the LJ.

[35] The urge to persuade others is so strong and basic, according to Smith, that he even suggests that it may be "the instinct upon which is founded the faculty of speech" (TMS, 7.4.25). The connection of this urge with ambition, with the desire of "leading and directing other people," however, suggests that the kind of persuasion a man motivated by this desire would undertake would be of the "rhetorical," rather than of the "didactic," kind.

terms of Smith's functional approach, the "propriety" of discourse had to be assessed in terms of the speaker's "cast of mind," his current interest and communicative intentions, the hearer's capacity of understanding, and – in general – the context of use. He thus naturally moved from an exclusive interest in language structure and semantics to an awareness of the parameters relevant for language use or pragmatics.

One of his disciples, Dugald Stewart, may have picked up his own sensitivity for the pragmatic aspects of language from the incipient theory of language use he detected in Smith's writings.[36] Stewart observed that context dependence or "ambiguity," and consequently the need for a constant interpretive effort, is an ineradicable feature of language use in all the sciences, except mathematics. For this reason, whereas in mathematics "the solution of [a] problem may be reduced to something resembling the operation of a mill," in the other sciences (especially the moral sciences)

the words about which our reasonings are conversant, admit, more or less, of different shades of meaning; and it is only by considering attentively the relation in which they stand to the immediate context, that the precise idea of the author in any particular instance is to be ascertained. (Stewart, 1854–60: III, 106; in Land, 1974: 113)

This fact puts on the mind an extra burden, possibly even a new set of pragmatically required mental operations:

the mind must necessarily carry on, along with the logical deduction expressed in words, another logical process of a far nicer and more difficult nature, – that of fixing, with a rapidity which escapes our memory, the precise sense of every word which is ambiguous, by the relation in which it stands to the general scope of the argument. (ibid, 107; in Land, 1974:121)

These acute observations cannot but remind one of Smith's distinction between the algorithmic and the heuristic types of linguistic (and moral) rules. It is a pity that Smith himself did not further develop his pragmatic insight along similar lines.

[36] Stewart is customarily perceived as more of a follower of Reid than of Smith (Harris, 1994: vii; Aarsleff, 1967: 101–2), but I think some of his most original linguistic ideas can be traced back to Smith. Contrary to what Harris suggests (ibid), Stewart did not detach himself entirely from the language–mind research programme. He only condemned its abuses, as exemplified mainly by Tooke, and redirected the program's agenda to previously unexplored aspects of language and mind, as is shown.

He might also have elaborated on other aspects of language use that his moral philosophy in general and his ethics of communication in particular imply. I have in mind especially the linguistic and mental operations aspects of the activity of moral criticism, embodied in the central Smithian figure of the impartial spectator. However, I cannot develop this point here. Nor can I analyze, unfortunately, the methodological significance of his linguistic work. Let me only mention two points. First, the fact that *Languages* was hailed as a "very beautiful specimen" of "theoretical or conjectural history," which "may be traced in all his [Smith's] different works" (Stewart, 1793: 33, 36, 37). Like other theoretical systems, it is an "invention of the imagination, to connect together the otherwise disjointed and discordant phaenomena of nature" ("Astronomy," IV.76). When such a connecting job succeeds, a scientific system – just like a linguistic system – can be compared with a machine (IV.19). Nevertheless, and this is my second point, this machine-like model is not the only model available in Smith's repertoire, pace his Newtonianism. As we have seen, the language–machine analogy in *Languages* has a coda, which is absent from its counterpart in "Astronomy." Because languages are multifunctional, simplification and reduction in their case, unlike in machines, breeds imperfection, rather than perfection. Because language use is inherently context dependent, the variability of the circumstances of use, and of the characters and intentions of the users, cannot be abstracted away or accounted for in terms of a set of simple algorithmic rules. At most, only a small part of language can be treated in this machine-like way, the rest requiring systematization in terms of imprecise heuristic rules. Even for this small structural part, *Languages* did not succeed in accounting for the conjectural evolution of language structure in terms of a single criterion.

The expansion of his linguistic interests toward a more comprehensive treatment of language required Smith to account for an unexpected language-related "wealth of notions."[37] As a result, he had to depart from the esprit de système that had inspired

---

[37] The phrase "wealth of notions" is used by Stam (1976: 39ff.) to refer to Smith's "capitalist ideology" as revealed in *Languages* by the "nominalization of all actions and reification of all relations" and by the contradictions of his analysis of the first person pronoun, which makes "the self" both "one out of an infinity of particular objects" and "the most abstract and metaphysical of all ideas." It seems to me that

his original plan for *Languages*.[38] This seems to have suggested to Smith a model of system that could function as an alternative for the mechanical model, if not in the natural sciences, at least in the moral ones. Although this model does not supersede the Cartesian-Newtonian one, it seeks "something more than mere tidiness and intellectual coherence" – as pointed out by the editors of LRBL (Introduction, 35). It focuses not on the components of a whole but on the whole itself; it stresses the "variety of the parts" rather than their uniformity, as well as the harmonious whole that can result from such a variety ("Imitative Arts," II.30); and it insists not on the sequential (axiomatic-like) mode of presentation but on the non-linear, parallel, and simultaneous way of "connecting" the parts to obtain a complete effect. In such a model, different approaches may complement each other and do a better descriptive and explanatory job than the reductionist temptation to rely exclusively on one set of assumptions. After all, in so far as different theories "are founded upon natural principles, they are all of them in some measure in the right" (TMS, 7.1.1). Perhaps it is to this sort of critical-eclectic, nonreductionist alternative that Dugald Stewart is alluding when he says that

when different theoretical histories are proposed by different writers, [they] are not always to be understood as standing in opposition to each other . . . for human affairs never exhibit, in any two instances, a perfect uniformity. (Stewart, 1793: 37)

At any rate, if the two different methodological models here sketched do indeed coexist in Smith, this might help at least explain how authors who considered themselves to be followers of Smith (e.g., Malthus, Ricardo) could diverge so much not only in method, but also in their conception of what the proper "style" – i.e., the "spirit and mind" – of a social science should be (see Cremaschi and Dascal, 1996, 1998).

his Marxist *parti pris* did not allow Stam to realize how wealthy Smith's reflections on language are.

[38] Smith praises French talent for method and systematicity, but points out that this talent, most beautifully exemplified by Descartes, did not prevent Descartes's physics from being "now . . . almost universally exploded" (*Letter to the Edinburgh Review*, EPS, 5). For a comparative study of the meaning of "Cartesian" for several Scottish thinkers, including Smith, see Cremaschi, 2000.

REFERENCES

Aarsleff, Hans, 1967. *The Study of Language in England, 1780–1860*. Princeton, NJ.

Aarsleff, Hans, 1982. *From Locke to Saussure: Essays on the Study of Language and Intellectual History*. Minneapolis, MN.

Arnauld, Antoine and Lancelot, Claude, 1676. *Grammaire générale et raisonnée*, 3rd ed. Paris.

Arnauld, Antoine and Nicole, Pierre, 1683. *La logique ou l'Art de penser*, 5th ed. Paris [re-edition 1970].

Auroux, Sylvain, 1992. "La tradition rationaliste dans la philosophie du language." In *Philosophy of Language – An International Handbook of Contemporary Research*, eds. Dascal et al., vol. 1, pp. 184–97.

Berkeley, George, 1948/57. *The Works of George Berkeley*, 9 vols. eds. A. A. Luce and T. E. Jessop. Edinburgh.

Condillac, Etienne Bonnot de, 1746. "Essai sur l'origine des connoissances humaines." In *Oeuvres philosophiques de Condillac*, vol. 2, ed. G. le Roy. Paris, 1947.

Cremaschi, Sergio, 2000. "Les lumières écossaises et le roman philosophique de Descartes." In *Descartes: Reception and Disenchantment*, eds. Y. Senderowicz and Y. Wahl. Tel Aviv.

Cremaschi, Sergio and Dascal, Marcelo, 1996. "Malthus and Ricardo on economic methodology." *History of Political Economy* (3): 475–511.

Cremaschi, Sergio and Dascal, Marcelo, 1998. "Malthus and Ricardo: Two styles for economic theory." *Science in Context* (11): 229–56.

Crosland, Maurice P., 1978. *Historical Study in the Language of Chemistry*. New York, NY.

Dascal, Marcelo, 1978. "*Aporia* and *Theoria*: Rousseau on language and thought." *Revue Internationale de Philosophie* (124/125): 214–37.

Dascal, Marcelo, 1983. "Signs and cognitive processes: Notes for a chapter in the history of semiotics." In *History of Semiotics*, eds. A. Eschbach and J. Trabant. Amsterdam, pp. 169–90.

Dascal, Marcelo, 1987. *Leibniz: Language, Signs, and Thought*. Amsterdam.

Dascal, Marcelo, 1990. "Leibniz on particles: Linguistic form and comparatism." In *Leibniz, Humboldt, and the Origins of Comparativism*, eds. T. de Mauro and L. Formigari. Amsterdam, pp. 31–60.

Dascal, Marcelo, 1992. "On the pragmatic structure of conversation." In *(On) Searle on Conversation*, eds. J. Searle et al. Amsterdam, pp. 35–56.

Dascal, Marcelo, 1993. "One Adam and many cultures: The role of political pluralism in the best of possible worlds." In *Leibniz and Adam*, eds. M. Dascal and E. Yakira. Tel Aviv, pp. 387–409.

Dascal, Marcelo, 1994. "Lenguaje y conocimiento en la filosofía moderna." In *Del Renacimiento a la Ilustración I* (= *Enciclopedia Ibero Americana de Filosofía* 6), ed. E. de Olaso. Madrid, pp. 15–51.

Dascal, Marcelo, 1995. "Strategies of dispute and ethics: *Du Tort* and *La Place d'Autruy.*" In *Leibniz und Europa: VI. Internationaler Leibniz-Kongress*, pp. 108–16.

Dascal, Marcelo, 1996. "The dispute on the primacy of thinking or speaking." In *Philosophy of Language – An International Handbook of Contemporary Research*, 2 vols., eds., Dascal, Gerhardus, Lorenz, and Meggle. Berlin, 1992/1996, vol. 2, pp. 1024–41.

Dascal, Marcelo, 1998a. "Language in the mind's house." *Leibniz Society Review* (8): 1–24.

Dascal, Marcelo, 1998b. "O desafio de Hobbes." In *Descartes, Leibniz e a Modernidade*, eds. L. R. dos Santos, P. M. S. Alves, and A. Cardoso. Lisbon, pp. 369–8.

Dascal, Marcelo and Senderowicz, Yaron, 1992. "How pure is pure reason? Language, empirical concepts, and empirical laws in Kant's theory of knowledge." *Histoire, Epistemologie, Langage* (14): 129–52.

Formigari, Lia, 1988. *Language and Experience in Seventeenth-Century British Philosophy.* Amsterdam.

Formigari, Lia, 1992. "The empiricist tradition in the philosophy of language." In *Philosophy of Language – An International Handbook of Contemporary Research*, eds. Dascal et al., vol. 1, pp. 175–84.

Formigari, Lia, 1993. *Signs, Science and Politics: Philosophies of Language in Europe 1700–1830.* Amsterdam.

Foucault, Michel, 1966. *Les mots et les choses: Une archéologie des sciences humaines.* Paris.

Girard, Gabriel, 1747. *Les vrais principes de la langue françoise.* Paris [Reprint with an introduction by P. Swiggers, Geneva, 1982].

Goldschmidt, Victor, 1974. *Anthropologie et politique. Les principes du système de Rousseau.* Paris.

Grice, Paul, 1989. *Studies in the Way of Words.* Cambridge, MA.

Haakonssen, K., 1998. "Divine/natural law theories in ethics." In *The Cambridge History of Seventeenth-Century Philosophy*, eds. D. Garber and M. Ayers. Cambridge.

Harris, Roy (ed.), 1994. *Comparativist Controversies.* London.

Hewes, Gordon H., 1975. *Language Origins: A Bibliography.* The Hague.

Hewes, Gordon H., 1996. "Disputes on the origin of language." In *Philosophy of Language – An International Handbook of Contemporary Research*, eds. Dascal et al., vol. 2, pp. 929–43.

Joly, A. and Stéfanini, J. (eds.), 1977. *La grammaire générale des modistes aux idéologues.* Lille.

Knowlson, James, 1975. *Universal Language Schemes in England and France 1600–1800*. Toronto.

Land, Stephen K., 1974. *From Signs to Propositions: The Concept of Form in Eighteenth-Century Semantic Theory*. London.

Leibniz, Gottfried Wilhelm, 1879. *Die philosophischen Schriften von G. W. Leibniz*, 7 volumes, ed. C. I. Gerhardt, [Reprint Hildesheim, 1965].

Locke, John, 1690. *An Essay Concerning Human Understanding*. Ed. J. W. Yolton. New York, NY, 1967.

Pombo, Olga, 1987. *Leibniz and the Problem of a Universal Language*. Münster.

Quine, William van Orman, 1969. *Ontological Relativity and Other Essays*. New York, NY.

Rousseau, Jean-Jacques, 1755. "Discours sur cette question proposée par l'académie de Dijon: Quelle est l'origine de l'inégalité parmi les hommes et si elle est autorisée par la loi naturelle." In J.-J. Rousseau, *Du Contrat Social*. Paris, 1954.

Ryle, Gilbert, 1932, "Systematically misleading expressions." *Proceedings of the Aristotelian Society*. (31): 139–70.

Stam, James H., 1976. *Inquiries into the Origin of Language: The Fate of a Question*. New York, NY.

Stewart, Dugald, 1793. *Account of the Life and Writings of Adam Smith LL.D.* In D. Stewart (1858).

Stewart, Dugald, 1854–60. *The Collected Works of Dugald Stewart*, 11 vols. ed. W. Hamilton. Edinburgh.

Wilkins, John, 1668. *An Essay Towards a Real Character and a Philosophical Language*. London.

4   Smith and Science

There is a deliberate ambiguity about the title of this chapter. It refers at one and the same time to Smith as a commentator on and as a practitioner of "science." In the former role, he explicitly addresses issues of method and implicitly reflects a pervasive Enlightenment commitment to the progressive agenda associated with science. In the latter role, his actual investigations, if liberally interpreted, manifest both the method and the agenda.

The analysis that follows is divided into four parts. I examine first the "Enlightenment commitment" – the high value placed on science – and note what can be gleaned of Smith's own exposure to scientific thinking. Next, the focus is on Smith as a commentator, his specific account of science as the discovery of connecting principles. The third and longest part discusses "Smith the scientist" – outlining and illustrating by means of a few case studies his commitment to causal explanation and to what I call "soft determinism." In the brief final part, the point is made that Smith does not divorce scientific "findings" from moral significance.

I

The Enlightenment was a self-conscious movement of intellectuals who thought of themselves as *Aufklärer* striving to make their age *un siècle des lumières*. This implied that earlier times were comparatively benighted. This contrast is encapsulated in the contrast between science, on the one hand, and ignorance, prejudice, and superstition, on the other hand. Hence, any institutions such as slavery, torture, witchcraft, or religious persecution that still existed were to be opposed as relics of darker ages, which the light of scientific reason would clear away. This Baconian implication that science is to be put to use for the good of humanity meant a unity of theory and practice.

Nowhere is this unity better exemplified than in one of the Enlightenment's key products, the *Encyclopédie, ou Dictionnaire raisonné des sciences, des arts et des métiers* (a text that Smith was instrumental in purchasing for Glasgow University Library). In its *Discours préliminaire* (1751), D'Alembert, after commending Bacon's path-breaking role, attached particular weight to the work of Newton. This is typical; Newton is *the* hero of the Enlightenment. His perceived achievement was to have explained the full range of natural phenomena, celestial and terrestrial, by using only a few simple principles (laws of motion plus gravity). It became a challenge to emulate his work, to achieve for the moral or social sciences what he had done for natural science. Newton himself, in his *Optics*, had effectively thrown down the gauntlet when he remarked that if, through pursuit of his method, natural philosophy becomes perfected so, in like fashion, "the bounds of Moral Philosophy will be also enlarged."[1]

The Scottish universities led the way in adopting Newton's framework. In a period of about half a century from 1660, Aristotle was replaced with Descartes who was in turn superseded by Newton. Of the Scottish universities, Glasgow was perhaps the slowest to adapt, although by 1712 Newton was on the curriculum.[2] Its eventual dominance was facilitated by two factors – one particular, the other general. In particular, the adoption of Newton's system was aided by the establishment of designated subject "chairs" to replace the regenting system (1727), where one individual had to teach a cohort of students the full run of subjects throughout the 4 years of their university career. More generally, Newton's system gradually became assimilated as a buttress to natural theology and, beyond that, to the established social order. In this process, his work and name came to stand as a sort of cultural shorthand which, as such, paid little detailed attention to

---

[1] *Optics*, Question 31, in *Newton's Philosophy of Nature*, ed. H. Thayer (New York, NY, 1953), p. 179.

[2] Cf. C. Shepherd, "Newtonianism in Scottish Universities in the Seventeenth Century," in *The Origin and Nature of the Scottish Enlightenment*, eds. R. Campbell and A. Skinner (Edinburgh, 1982), p. 75.

his own priorities and tended to subsume, more or less indiscriminately, the work of other experimental scientists within his. This is symptomatic of the interweaving of "science" and "society" that the term "Newtonianism" came to represent. As we will see later, while Smith was a Newtonian, there are some grounds for questioning the extent of his subscription to Newtonianism.

When Smith entered Glasgow in 1737, "natural philosophy" was the special responsibility of Professor Robert Dick (primus), whereas mathematics was taught by Professor Robert Simson. Indirectly there is evidence that these two subjects were Smith's favourites.[3] Smith would have had lessons in mathematics in his "semi" year (his own first, but the third year in the usual progression). Simson, his teacher, was (or became) a leading authority on Euclid (Smith owned a copy of the second edition of his *Sectionum Conicorum*). Much later, Smith called him one of the two greatest mathematicians of his time (TMS, III.2.20). The other was the Edinburgh Professor Matthew Stewart (father of Dugald, Smith's first biographer) and a fellow student of Simson with Smith. In his final year, he would have attended Dick's classes in experimental philosophy, using instruments that had been bought as part of a self-conscious "modernising" drive[4] to elucidate the "doctrine of bodies" as "improved by Sir Isaac Newton."[5]

Smith himself compared his Glasgow education favourably with that on offer at Oxford where he went in 1740 as a Snell Exhibitioner. Commenting on the Oxford curriculum, his most recent biographer ventures that Smith "must have been struck at Balliol... by the lack of commitment to providing instruction in the New Philosophy and Science of Locke and Newton."[6] The justified presumption is that Smith spent his time at Oxford cultivating his linguistic skills and developing the study of human nature in all its branches.[7] However, it does not seem that Smith's interest

---

[3] Cf. D. Stewart, *Account of the Life and Times of Adam* Smith (1794), who cites the recollections of Archibald Maclaine, one of Smith's undergraduate contemporaries; EPS, I.7.

[4] Cf. R. Emerson, "Politics and the Glasgow Professors," in *The Glasgow Enlightenment*, eds. A. Hook and R. Sher (East Linton, 1995), p. 29.

[5] J. Chambelayne, quoted in I. Ross, *The Life of Adam Smith* (Oxford, 1995), p. 55.

[6] Ross, *Life*, p. 73.

[7] Stewart, *Life*, I.8.

in natural philosophy atrophied. In part, this is supported by the probable construction of the "History of Astronomy" shortly after leaving Oxford and, in part, from some of his activities when he returned to Glasgow University in 1751. Aside from his pedagogic duties, Smith also occupied a variety of administrative posts. In the latter capacity he used his discretion to support scientific expenditure. On one occasion, against the objections of the Principal, he explicitly defended the outlay for a new chemical laboratory.[8]

Undoubtedly, Smith was sustained in this conviction by his friendship with William Cullen and Joseph Black, two of the leading chemists of the eighteenth century and successively professors of chemistry at Glasgow and then Edinburgh. This friendship is symptomatic of a prominent strand in the Scottish Enlightenment – the clubbability of its members and the breadth of their interests. These features are embodied in the innumerable "societies" that existed in all the major cities. Smith was a member of several, both in Glasgow and Edinburgh. From the extant evidence of their meetings, it is clear they were centrally engaged in fostering the Baconian association between science and "improvement" (the appliance of science to agriculture in particular, but also, as with Cullen's work on bleach for the linen industry,[9] increasingly to wider aspects of the burgeoning economy). For example, the Glasgow Literary Society (which Smith helped establish), and despite what its name might suggest, included among its topics for discussion papers on chemistry, physics, and medicine, and it was at a gathering of that society that Black read a paper on latent heat.[10] It is a significant feature of the period that "science" did not exist in some separate intellectual compartment but permeated the polite and literary culture.[11]

Undue stress should not be placed on these snippets of biographical information. The principal evidence of Smith's scientific

---

[8] Cf. Ross, *Life*, p. 150.

[9] Cf. D. Guthrie, "William Cullen and His Times," in *An Eighteenth Century Lectureship in Chemistry*, ed. A. Kent (Glasgow, 1950), p. 62.

[10] Cf. R. Sher, "Commerce, Religion in the Enlightenment in Eighteenth Century Glasgow," in *Glasgow: Beginnings to 1830*, eds. T. Devine and G. Jackson (Manchester, 1995), pp. 335ff.

[11] Cf. R. Emerson, "Science and the Origins and Concerns of the Scottish Enlightenment," *History of Science* 26 (1988): 333–66.

concerns has to be his writings. Nevertheless, there is clear evidence that he had a basic grounding in the principles of the paradigmatic physical sciences of his age and that, judged by the contents of his library, he had the means to keep himself abreast of the century's developments, including the ownership of twenty-one volumes of the *Philosophical Transactions of the Royal Society*.

II

Reflecting again the seamless nature of personal and intellectual links, Smith appointed two of his close, scientific friends – Joseph Black and James Hutton – as his executors. He instructed them to destroy his manuscripts but allowed them, at their discretion, to publish a set of essays. This set appeared in 1795 with the title *Essays on Philosophical Subjects*. The most substantial component is a "History of Astronomy." This essay has occasioned much scholarship. In part this is due to the belief that *anything* a recognised "great mind" or "seminal thinker" wrote is bound to be of interest, but the "Astronomy" does have intrinsic merits, and these, not unexpectedly, bear on the theme of this chapter. The major point of interest in the scholarship, as it also is for us, is less Smith's impressive erudition than the "methodological" views he appears to express. These are captured in the full title of the essay "The Principles which Lead and Direct Philosophical Enquiries: Illustrated by the History of Astronomy." There are two other shorter essays that also illustrate these principles, namely "Ancient Physics" and "Ancient Logics and Metaphysics," but they scarcely live up to their billing, being for the most part expositions of, respectively, Empedoclean accounts of the four Elements and Greek philosophy, with Plato prominent.

There is a body of circumstantial evidence as to when the "Astronomy" was written. As noted in Part I, it is probable that its outlines were drafted after his departure from Oxford, and parts of it were, perhaps, used in a series of lectures Smith gave in Edinburgh in 1748/50.[12] Smith himself called his "a history of Astronomical Systems...down to the time of Des Cartes' a 'juvenile work'" (*Correspondence*, 137). In addition, the reference in the published text to the predicted appearance in 1758 of Halley's

[12] Cf. Ross, *Life*, p. 99.

comet ("Astronomy," IV.74) suggests that even the final Newtonian part was written before that date. Access to Smith's motives being unavailable, it is fruitless to speculate at any length on why Smith wrote the essay. Certainly, it was not to add to an existing genre. He did own John Keill's *Introductio ad Veram Astronomiam* (1718), which is a printed version of his lectures at Oxford and would have been the source of the subject when Smith was at Balliol. Keill's work, however, is analytical rather than historical, devoted to expounding the Newtonian (the "true") system.

Before addressing some of the issues that have been raised by the "Astronomy," it is necessary to outline synoptically the argument of the essay. Underlying the argument are a series of claims about the constituents and dynamics of human nature. These all betray an acceptance of an empirical, Lockean approach, especially, as we will see, in its Humean guise. Thus his opening sentence declares humans to possess certain sentiments. He mentions three – wonder, surprise, and admiration – which he maintains are distinct, although they are often confounded. Without any supporting argument he stipulates that wonder as a sentiment is excited by what is new and singular, surprise by what is unexpected, and admiration by what is great and beautiful. Just as *The Wealth of Nations* was titled an enquiry into its "nature and causes" so Smith says at the end of the preliminary section of "Astronomy" that the design of the essay is to consider the "nature and causes" of the three sentiments because their influence is greater than might be thought (Intro., 6). The next two sections deal with surprise and wonder; however, admiration rather unexpectedly does not receive a separate treatment. Instead, the third section is devoted to the question of the "origin of philosophy." The bulk of the essay's content is section four which provides the illustrative "history of astronomy."

The key point made about surprise is that the opposition of contrasted sentiments heightens their vivacity, whereas resemblance renders them more languid (I.9). This, Smith observes, accounts for the deadening effect of habit and custom (I.10). The section on wonder contains more meat. The mind is declared to take pleasure in the observation of resemblances and it endeavours to sort or classify them (II.1). This does not sit altogether happily with the earlier reference to their deadening effect, and while not inconsistent, the requisite conceptual tidying up is absent, as perhaps reflects the "unfinished" nature of the manuscript. Smith illustrates the point about classification with an example drawn from language – "animal" is a general name that classifies together all those things endowed with a power of self-motion. This example is not totally random and intimates Smith's typical Enlightenment concern with language, as represented by his "Considerations Concerning the First Formation of Languages" (see later). Because the roots of that essay have been linked to his Edinburgh lectures, it gives some mild corroboration to the notion that the "Astronomy" was composed at the same time. Smith proceeds to observe that the inclination to classify and subclassify develops along with the growth of knowledge, and he makes, in effect, a distinction between the expert and the lay person. This has bearing later. Wonder properly occurs when something "new or singular" occurs, when something defies classification, when neither memory nor imagination is able to place it (II.3). Because it is a postulated fact about human nature that the inability to classify induces "uncertainty and anxious curiosity" then, given that it is another fact about the dynamics of human nature that anxiety or unease prompts remedial action, it follows that wonder is a psychological state to "get rid of"(II.4).

Wonder is generated not only by a singular event but also equally by an irregular succession. Here Smith, in his most conspicuously Humean passage,[13] remarks that it is a break in the customary succession of two objects "constantly" presenting themselves to the senses in a particular order that generates first surprise then wonder. The languid, non-anxious, state occurs when the "association of ideas" is so well established that the "habit of imagination" passes from one to the other without any break or gap (II.7). However, if there is a gap, that is when customary connection is interrupted, then:

the supposition of a chain of intermediate, though invisible, events, which succeed each other in a train similar to that in which the imagination has been accustomed to move, and which link together those two disjointed appearances, is the only means by which the imagination can fill up this interval, is the only bridge which, if one may say so, can smooth its passage from the one object to the other. (II.8)

---

[13] Cf. D. Raphael, "'The True Old Humean Philosophy' and Its Influence on Adam Smith," in *David Hume: Bicentenary Papers*, ed. G. Morrice (Edinburgh, 1977), pp. 23–38.

Once this is achieved, wonder vanishes (II.9). The emphasis on custom here reflects not only an endorsement of Humean empiricism, but also nonreflective experience. The expert/lay distinction here re-emerges. Humans in general do not wonder how the consumption of bread is converted into flesh and bones; more particularly, artisans do not wonder about their craft, but philosophers are aware of gaps, and thus perceive a need for bridges, where others ("the bulk of mankind") experience no such break in their imagined associations (II.11). Smith builds on this last point to characterise philosophy as the "science of the connecting principles of nature" (II.12). (He echoes this characterisation in "Ancient Logics," I) Philosophy introduces order into chaos by "representing the invisible chains" that bind together disjointed objects. In doing this, it allays the "tumult of the imagination" and restores it to tranquility. Given this, then philosophy can be "regarded as one of those arts which address themselves to the imagination," a remark that has prompted several commentators to regard Smith's account of science as ultimately aesthetic.[14]

The third section changes tack by developing a sociological rather than a psychological argument.[15] His concern here is to identify the circumstances originally conducive to philosophy. There is, he conjectures, a pre-philosophical age where, because subsistence is precarious, order and security are absent. As a consequence, the "savage" has no curiosity about the seemingly disjointed appearances of nature, which are dealt with by invoking the favour or displeasure of gods; a response Smith identifies as the origin of polytheism (III.1.2).[16] However, with the gradual establishment of order and security, there comes, for those of "liberal fortune," sufficient leisure to enable them to attend to the world around them (III.3). These individuals now become "embarrassed"

[14] Cf. H. Thomson, "Adam Smith's Philosophy of Science," *Quarterly Journal of Economics* 79 (1965): 219; M. Brown, *Adam Smith's Economics* (London, 1988), p. 47; J. Christie, "The Culture of Science in Eighteenth Century Scotland," in *The History of Scottish Literature*, vol. 2, ed. A. Hook (Aberdeen, 1987), p. 301; D. Reisman, *Adam Smith's Sociological Economics* (London, 1976), p. 45.

[15] Cf. S. Moscovici, "A propos de quelques travaux d'Adam Smith sur l'histoire et la philosophie des sciences," *Revue d'Histoire des Sciences* 9 (1956): 5.

[16] Cf. C. Berry, "Rude Religion: The Psychology of Polytheism in the Scottish Enlightenment," in *The Scottish Enlightenment: Essays in Reinterpretation*, ed. P. Wood (Rochester, NY, 2000).

by incoherences and are placed in the uneasy state of wonder. This they seek to allay not through the "pusillanimous superstition" of the savage (III.2; "Ancient Physics," 9), but by the philosophical pursuit of the "concealed connections that unite the various appearances of nature" (III.3). This pursuit, Smith declares, is a disinterested affair; as befits the social status of its first practitioners, philosophy/science does not originate in any material need to extract advantage from its discoveries.

The first societies developed enough to practise philosophy were Greece and its colonies. The final section of the essay – the illustrative history of astronomy – now traces this practice. Smith's initial formulation, however, is unexpected. With no preparation, he reinvokes "greatness and beauty" because these are the characteristics of the "celestial appearances," but instead of linking them with admiration (as the opening section did) he says it made them the "object of curiosity." The link with admiration is duly made in the "Ancient Physics" (9), but a much more consistent explanation is given in The Wealth of Nations. There Smith comments that (inter alia) the "revolutions of the heavenly bodies . . . necessarily excite wonder so they naturally call forth the curiosity of mankind to enquire into their causes" (WN, V.i.f.24). In the "Astronomy" itself Smith charts its history from the system of concentric circles through Ptolemy to Copernicus, Galileo, Kepler, Descartes, and finally Newton. In telling this story Smith draws particular attention to the transition from one system to another, and it is here perhaps that the chief interest and the most debated aspects lie.[17]

Much of the commentary on "Astronomy" has an overblown air to it in as much as it seeks to elicit Smith's "philosophy of science" or, a shade less grandiosely, his "history of the philosophy of science." Smith, however, does not articulate anything so substantial.

A common ploy is to explicate the various principles or criteria of scientific explanation that lie within the text. Along these lines we find, for example, Cremaschi identifying simplicity, familiarity, coherence, and comprehensiveness, whereas both Lindgren and Reisman have the same first three but substitute beauty for the last. Christie comes up with unity, simplicity, and harmony;

---

[17] Smith characterises a "system" as "an imaginary machine invented to connect together in the fancy those different movements and effects which are already in reality performed" (IV.19).

Brown with familiarity, uniformity, coherence, and generality; and Campbell with coherence, simplicity, and familiarity.[18] Although all these identifications have textual support, the shades of difference between them indicate that nowhere is Smith himself explicit.

The imposition on Smith of a philosophy of science has itself generated a debate about quite what that philosophy is. A prominent line of interpretation has been that Smith adopts a conventionalist or an "anti-realist" posture.[19] There are seemingly two strands to this interpretation. The first, weaker, one is developed around the issue of the criteria, whereby one system of astronomy is replaced by another. Skinner, for example, fastens on the development of the first system of concentric spheres, Brown on the acceptance of Copernicus's heliocentric theory, and Cremaschi on the relation between Descartes and Newton.[20] Because the stronger of the two strands in the anti-realist interpretation focuses on Smith's wording in his discussion of Newton, it will be most apt to deal with the final case.

Smith argued that after Galileo removed the problem over the velocity of motion that had been associated with Copernicus' theory, and after Cassini's observations had established the accuracy of Kepler's laws, the only embarrassment suffered by the Copernican system was the gap between the ponderousness of the Earth and its rapid revolution (IV.60). In accordance with his psychological theory, this "gap" had to be bridged by some "connecting chain." Descartes attempted to identify this invisible chain with his theory of vortexes. This was successful in as much as it conceived of the planets as "floating in an immense ocean of ether" (IV.65), which was an idea or analogy familiar to the imagination so "mankind could no longer refuse themselves the pleasure of going along with

[18] S. Cremaschi, "Adam Smith: Skeptical Newtonianism, Disenchanted Republicanism and the Birth of Social Science," in *Knowledge and Politics*, eds. M. Dascal and O. Gruengard (Boulder, CO, 1989), p. 86; J. Lindgren, "Adam Smith's Theory of Inquiry," *Journal of Political Economy* 77 (1969): 905; Reisman, *Sociological Economics*, p. 39; Christie, "Culture of Science," p. 301; Brown, *Smith's Economics*, p. 31; T. Campbell, *Adam Smith's Science of Morals* (London, 1971), p. 39.

[19] This is not a first-order debate. Like all other participants whose concern is with Smith, I also refrain from direct involvement in the disputes between realists and their opponents, who in fact articulate a variety of arguments.

[20] A. Skinner, *A System of Social Science* (Oxford, 1996), p. 35; Brown, *Smith's Economics*, p. 37; Cremaschi, "Skeptical Newtonianism," p. 86.

so harmonious an account of things."[21] Yet despite this, while Copernicus remains universally accepted, Smith observes that the Cartesian system is now almost universally rejected in favour of Newton's.

The advantages of the Newtonian system were that it explained all planetary irregularities (something Descartes failed to do), its predictions had proved accurate, and it had linked into one system all celestial and terrestrial phenomena and had done so by using the principle of gravity which is "so familiar a principle of connection" that it "completely removed all the difficulties of the imagination" (IV.67). In consequence, Smith declares, here echoing the standard Enlightenment judgment, that it was "the greatest and most admirable improvement that was ever made in philosophy" (ibid) and Newton's principles "have a degree of firmness and solidity that we should in vain look for in any other system" (IV.76). Cremaschi, however, quotes Smith's remark that:

even we, while we have been endeavouring to represent all philosophical systems as mere inventions of the imagination, to connect together the otherwise disjointed and discordant phaenomena of nature, have insensibly been drawn in, to make use of language expressing the connecting principles of this one, as if they were the real chains which Nature makes use of to bind together her several operations. (IV.76)

The consequence he draws from this passage is that for Smith we cannot suppose Newton's theory is superior on the grounds that it is a "better reproduction of reality" since every theory (Newton's included) is an invention of the imagination. This same passage indeed is quoted by most of those who subscribe to the stronger strand in the anti-realist interpretation.[22]

Such an interpretation is difficult to sustain. It needs to be recalled what Smith's aim is in the essay. "The History of Astronomy"

[21] Smith had earlier noted the significance of analogy; all individuals, philosophers included, explain phenomena strange to them in terms of those familiar to them, and in intellectual systems, what in some is an analogy that occasions a "few ingenious similitudes" becomes in another the "great hinge upon which every thing turned" (II.12).

[22] Cf. Cremaschi, "Skeptical Newtonianism," p. 87; D. D. Raphael, "Adam Smith: Philosophy, Science and Social Science," in *Philosophers of the Enlightenment*, ed. S. Brown (Brighton, 1979), p. 90; H. Thomson, "Philosophy of Science," p. 222; Reisman, *Sociological Economics*, p. 41; Brown, *Smith's Economics*, p. 37.

is meant to illustrate how philosophy is an activity that addresses itself to the imagination, and Smith is explicit in this context that this is a "particular point of view." There is no implication that philosophy is nothing but an imaginative exercise. More pointedly, Smith continues that this particular perspective is distinct from any regard to the "absurdity or probability" of the various systems of nature, of "their agreement or inconsistency with truth and reality" (II.12). Lindgren and the others seem guilty of overgeneralising the particular. There is, of course, a sophistication in Smith's account that has seemed to some reminiscent of T. S. Kuhn's account of the development of science as a series of paradigm shifts,[23] but that does not establish an anti-realist posture.

The actual argument of the text also serves to cast doubt on the accuracy of that posture as portrayal of Smith's position. A case in point is the replacement of Cartesianism. Newton's triumph is inseparable (we recall) from two facts. First, Descartes' system could not account for the minute irregularities in the movement of the planets that Kepler had ascertained and which Cassini had established, whereas Newton's could (IV.66, 67). Secondly, each predicted a different shape for the earth and this was resolved by actual measurements in Newton's favour (Smith possessed a copy of the English translation of Maupertuis' expedition to Lapland that undertook the measurements). What these two "facts" indicate is that Smith (no more than Kuhn[24]) does not dissociate the history of astronomy from the accumulation of data. The imagination of scientists (experts) is disconcerted in the presence of wonder, but it is the independent increase in data, accessible only to the expert and itself consequent on the development of increasingly sophisticated equipment, that generates the gap in the first place. In addition, elsewhere, in a different context, Smith describes Descartes' work as "a fanciful, an ingenious and elegant, tho fallacious system" (*Letter to the Edinburgh Review*, 5). In the light of these

---

[23] Cf. T. S. Kuhn, *The Structure of Scientific Revolutions*, 2nd. ed. (Chicago, IL, 1970). He is cited by A. Skinner, "Adam Smith: Science and the Role of the Imagination," in *Hume and the Enlightenment*, ed. W. Todd (Edinburgh, 1974), p. 180; C. Longuet-Higgins, "'The History of Astronomy': A Twentieth Century View," in *Adam Smith Reviewed*, eds. P. Jones and A. S. Skinner (Edinburgh, 1992), p. 91.

[24] See T. Kuhn, *The Essential Tension* (Chicago, IL, 1977).

considerations, it seems a sounder interpretation of that oft-quoted passage from IV.76 to treat it as a self-reprimand by Smith. He is chiding himself for transgressing his own announced particular perspective and, as such, this is not a positive endorsement of the view that Newton's system is only a "more ingenious device" no better than that of his predecessors.[25]

Conceivably, there is in this disputed passage another, complementary, agenda. Almost from its inception Newton's philosophy had been assimilated and appropriated. As noted in Part I, his authority was used to underwrite the providential foundations of the Hanoverian social order and to buttress natural theology. This latter role is clear in, for example, Keill's *True Astronomy* and in Colin Maclaurin's influential *General View of Sir Isaac Newton's Method* (1748).[26] Because eighteenth-century Newtonianism was more than a narrow methodology, it meant that to discriminate within it required a certain fastidiousness. It is, at least, arguable that Smith's relative reticence, like that of Hume,[27] in citing Newton in his major works betrays some such caution. If that is granted, then it allows that fastidiousness in the self-inflicted reprimand (as I have presented it) to be read as pertaining less to some abstract "philosophy of science" than to a need

---

[25] Cremaschi, "Skeptical Newtonianism," p. 103. Similarly, *pace* Christie ("Culture of Science," p. 301), Smith does not explicitly disavow claims that the new chain of ideas that constitute scientific theories have a warrantable correspondence with the real world of external nature. Defenders (on a variety of grounds) of a realist reading include R. Olson, *Scottish Philosophy and British Physics 1750–1880* (Princeton, NJ, 1975), p. 123; D. Oswald, "Metaphysical Beliefs and the Foundations of Smithian Political Economy," *History of Political Economy* 27 (1995): 454f; J. Becker, "Adam Smith's Theory of Social Science," *Southern Economic Journal* 28 (1961): 16; N. Hetherington, "Isaac Newton's Influence on Adam Smith's Natural Laws in Economics," *Journal of the History of Ideas* 44 (1983): 502.

[26] In his opening pages Maclaurin comments, "But natural philosophy is subservient to the purposes of a higher nature, and is chiefly to be valued as it lays a sure foundation for natural religion and moral philosophy; by leading us, in a satisfactory manner, to the knowledge of the Author and Governor of the Universe." *General View* extracted in *The Scottish Enlightenment: An Anthology*, ed. A. Broadie (Edinburgh, 1997), p. 782. Keill's book opens with similar sentiments.

[27] Cf. D. Forbes, who emphasises this point, *Hume's Philosophical Politics* (Cambridge, 1975), chapter 2. See also M. Barfoot, who makes the point that "Newtonian" became something of a "catch-all" such that, for example, the views of Boyle were conflated with those of Newton, "Hume and the Culture of Science in the Early Eighteenth Century," in *Studies in the Philosophy of the Scottish Enlightenment*, ed. M. A. Stewart (Oxford, 1990), pp. 151–90, at 162.

to disentangle (say) Maclaurin's mastery of Newtonian mathematics (cf. IV.58) from his Newtonian theology.[28]

What is indisputable is the high regard in which Smith held Newton. In his Rhetoric lectures he explicitly identified, within what he termed the didactical mode, a style of writing as the "Newtonian method." This method lays down "certain principles known or proved in the beginning, from whence we account for the severall Phenomena, connecting altogether by the same chain" (LRBL, II.134). Such a procedure is the "most philosophical," especially in contrast to its chief alternative – the Aristotelian method – where a different principle is given to every phenomenon. Because it is the most philosophical, then, in "every science whether of Moralls or Naturall philosophy" there is presumptive reason to pursue it.

Some commentators have sought out Smith's Newtonianism. Hetherington, for example, thinks there are 'obvious similarities' between Smith's effort to discover general laws of economics and Newton's success in discovering natural laws of motion and Raphael judges that "Smith clearly regards sympathy as the gravitational force of social cohesion and social balance."[29] Others have been less confident that Smith himself carried out this project, although this is largely because of their more historically informed appreciation of what Newton's system in fact represented.[30] As Raphael acknowledges, and as we have already noted, Smith himself is not very helpful – there are, despite his emblematic status, minimal references to Newton in his two major works. Certainly contemporaries drew parallels. For example, John Millar (pupil then Glasgow colleague of Smith) declared him to be the "Newton of political economy" because he had discovered the principles of commerce.[31] While of Smith's more acute early critics, Governor

---

[28] Cf C. Griswold, Jr., who identifies a deliberate scepticism in Smith with respect to certain metaphysical views about reality or God in this passage, *Adam Smith and the Virtues of Enlightenment* (Cambridge, 1999), p. 169.

[29] Hetherington, "Newton's Influence," p. 497, cf. pp. 504–5; Raphael, "Philosophy, Science and Social Science," p. 88.

[30] Cf. inter alia D. Redman, "Adam Smith and Isaac Newton," *Scottish Journal of Political Economy* 40 (1995): 210–30; S. Hollander, "Adam Smith and the Self-Interest Axiom," *The Journal of Law and Economics* 20 (1977): 133–52; Campbell, *Science of Morals* (although he differentiates between the TMS and the WN in this regard, p. 31); Griswold, *Virtues of Enlightenment*, pp. 72f.

[31] J. Millar, *Historical View of the English Government*, vol. II (Edinburgh, 1803), pp. 429–30n.

Pownall opened his assessment of *The Wealth of Nations* by noting that Smith's treatise had fixed "some first principles," becoming a *"principia* to the knowledge of politick operations" (see Smith's *Correspondence*, 337). The very prestige of Newton not only meant that to liken someone's work to his was to pay it the highest possible compliment, but also that this was not very discriminatory, as when, for example, both Hume and George Turnbull claimed a Newtonian inspiration for their very different philosophies.[32] The prudent conclusion is that while there is no reason to doubt the presence of that inspiration in Smith, it is better understood as a general orientation rather than a specific agenda. With that counsel in mind we can now turn to Smith's own "scientific" practice.

III

According to Newton, "Nature is pleased with simplicity and affects not the pomp of superfluous causes" so the first rule of reasoning in natural philosophy is: admit only such causes as are "true and sufficient to explain appearances."[33] Here two familiar points are being made – the aim should be economy so a lot is explained by a little, and the explanation is achieved through the identification of causes. It is scarcely saying anything of moment to state that Smith adopts these two commonplaces. More informative is how this adoption is manifest.

While the issue of causal explanation does not figure prominently in the "Astronomy," the role that Smith does allot to it conforms to the psychological account that he there outlines. The connecting principles that bridge the gap in the imagination are most satisfactorily grasped in the form of causes. In his Rhetoric lectures (in the context of historical composition), he again remarks that "the very notion of a gap makes us uneasy" (LRBL, II.37), and it is the connection of cause and effect that best satisfies us (LRBL, II.32). This is not unexpected. The underlying argument, derived from Hume, was itself articulated in an account of causation, and the imagery of invisible chains made in the "Astronomy"

---

[32] Hume subtitled his *Treatise of Human Nature* (1739/40) "an attempt to introduce experimental reasoning into moral subjects"; Turnbull quoted Newton's statement in *Optics*, Qn. 31 (see supra) on the title page of his *Principles of Moral Philosophy* (1740).

[33] I. Newton, "Rules of Reasoning," in *Newton's Philosophy of Nature*, p. 3.

harmonises with the standard image of explanation as the identification of a chain of causes and effects.

The fact that these last points have been drawn from Smith's discussion of history is more than coincidental. Along with his fellow Scots, Smith held that humans are naturally social and that this sociality expresses itself in institutions that differ over time. These are facts that are just as much a part of experience as apples falling to the ground. Although the latter fact might be classified as "physical" or "natural" and the former as "moral," they cohabit the one experienced world. The natural aspect of that world has, since the Renaissance, been systematically investigated and causal explanations provided with great success. As we have already noted, the expectation throughout the Enlightenment was that a similar success, both theoretical and practical, beckoned for the moral aspect. Given that the moral and the physical are of the same species (a point to which we return) then the way forward was to explain human institutions causally. Since to study society scientifically means tracing the chain of causes and effects, then it builds into the study a temporal or historical aspect – causes precede effects.

Sociality is true of all humans, but it is evident to experience that its institutional expression is not uniform. Nevertheless by seeking a causal explanation for these expressions they can be revealed as non-random. Because the hallmark of successful natural science is the reduction of multiplicity to simplicity, then the hallmark of successful social science is the reduction of the diversity of institutions to some intelligible pattern. Smith's work bears this out. Perhaps its most celebrated manifestation is the "four-stages theory" (see below), but that itself is only an expression of a more general approach that was labelled definitively by Dugald Stewart in his *Life of Smith* as natural, theoretical, or conjectural history.

The lynchpin of this history is the relation between the principles of human nature and external circumstances. The "principles" are fixed and constant. The "circumstances" in any particular situation are, given the uniformity of nature, inferable from what is known generally to be the case. Between them they can, in the absence of direct evidence, license a "theoretical" reconstruction with explanatory power. As, Stewart puts it, "in examining the history of mankind" when "we cannot trace the process by which an event *has been* produced, it is often of importance to be able to show how it *may have been* produced by natural causes." As examples of this approach he cites, among others, the "works of Mr Millar," as well as the pretext for this entire digression, Smith's "Dissertation" on the origin of language.[34]

Smith's account of language is worth briefly pursuing. The question of the origin and development of language was a hotly debated Enlightenment topic, notable in particular for its endeavour to treat the subject naturalistically. The argument of Smith's essay is that the various elements in language (e.g., verbs, nouns, adjectives, prepositions) develop *pari passu* with the maturing of human faculties. This developmentalism he believes will resolve Rousseau's puzzlement as to how linguistic categories such as genera and species arose (*Languages*, in LRBL, 2). For Smith, words that were originally the proper names of individuals "insensibly become the common name of a multitude" (*Languages*, 1). Echoing the account in "Astronomy," the "mechanism" at work here is resemblance. Smith gives two telling instances of this process – first, a child when just learning to speak calls everyone who comes to the house its 'papa' or 'mama' (ibid) and, secondly, a savage 'naturally bestows' on each new object the 'same name' that had previously been given to a similar object when it was first encountered (ibid). This conjunction between the savage and the child is also echoed in "Astronomy" when Smith notes how a child "beats the stone that hurts it," and the savage punishes the axe that had accidentally caused a death (III.2).

This conjunction reveals once more the presence of an effectively Lockean model of human nature. Locke himself remarked that "children, idiots, savages and illiterate people" function without any capacity to refer to general maxims and universal principles.[35] Savages thus represent, in a favourite phrase in the Enlightenment (and in Scotland especially), "the infancy of mankind." *Both* children and savages, it follows from this model of cognitive development, are confined to the world of immediate sensation, which means that they are unacquainted with all universal or abstract ideas.

---

[34] Stewart, *Life*, pp. 293, 294–5 (Stewart's emphases).
[35] *Essay Concerning Human Understanding* (1689) Book 1, chapter 2, sect. 27; cf. 1.2.12.

If we now return to *Languages*, we find these themes repeated. For example, he says of "number" that it is "one of the most abstract and metaphysical ideas ... and consequently is not an idea which would readily occur to rude mortals who were just beginning to form a language" (*Languages*, 22). Similarly, substantive nouns predate adjectives, so the word "tree" is developed before the word "green," which itself precedes the word "greenness." By the same token, impersonal verbs predate personal, whereas prepositions and pronouns "expressing so very abstract and metaphysical an idea, would not easily or readily occur to the first formers of language" (*Languages*, 32).

Smith's adoption of this genetic or Lockean model of cognitive development pervades his thought and, in so doing, it establishes out of the diversity of social experience a coherent pattern or structure. This structure is that of a natural, that is predictable, development from infancy to maturity, from the simple to the complex, from the concrete to the abstract. The four-stages theory is best understood against this backcloth. Although it may have been essayed in his Edinburgh lectures, Smith articulated this theory in his Glasgow lectures on jurisprudence, in particular those on property rights. The move from the first stage of the hunter-gatherer through to the fourth commercial age is thus marked by increasing abstraction. A telling case is his remark that "among savages property begins and ends with possession and they seem scarce to have any idea of anything as their own which is not about their own bodies" (LJ[B], 150). In contrast to this "concreteness," by the time of the age of commerce property is not only conceptually distinguished from physical possession but itself assumes an increasingly "abstract" form in, for example, the guise of credit and "paper money" as promissory notes (WN, II.ii.28).

The same story can be told using the growth in complexity as the index. The division of labour has developed from its rudimentary form in the first stage to one where the "very trifling manufacture" of pins is divided into the labour of ten individuals. A society where tasks such as pin-making are minutely divided must necessarily be complex and its members deeply interdependent. The fact of interdependence means that each individual "stands at all times in need of the co-operation and assistance of great multitudes" (WN, I.ii.2); a state of affairs that is illustrated by the fact that "many thousands" are involved in the production of a coarse woollen coat (WN, I.i.11).

Although, along these lines, Smith's reduction of the variety of historical experience to a simple structural model can be labelled "scientific," this is too generalised to be of telling significance. In particular, the causal model remains unspecific. Before proceeding to a more precise treatment, an implication of the social scientific approach that Smith is apparently pursuing needs to be picked up. To say that the miserable poverty of savages (WN, Intro. 4) and the opulence experienced universally in a commercial society (WN, I.ii.10) are effects caused by the differential extent of the division of labour is to deny that the relations are accidental, just as eclipses are not random but caused by the orbits of the earth and the moon. This is a fraught issue. Some Smith scholars see his thought as implying a sharp division between natural and social sciences,[36] others hold that he places them on a similar footing.[37] While the latter are more nearly correct, a more precise account of Smith's position is needed.

Smith adopts what can be called a "soft determinist" position.[38] In eighteenth-century terminology, as spelt out by Hume, he is an advocate of moral not physical causes. Whereas physical causes "work insensibly on the temper," moral causes are "all circumstances which are fitted to work on the mind as motives or reasons and which render a peculiar set of manners habitual to us."[39] Moral causes are a species of soft determinism because they operate through habituation or socialisation. These are still *causes* and are still deterministic but, unlike the hard determinism of physical causation, they can accommodate change or variation. The difference between the philosopher and the porter is not physical but moral, since it arises from "habit, custom and education" (WN,

---

[36] Cf. Lindgren, "Theory of Inquiry," pp. 912–13; Skinner, *System*, p. 41; Redman, "Smith and Newton," p. 220.

[37] Cf. Brown, *Smith's Economics*, p. 37; Thomson, "Philosophy of Science," p. 232; Campbell, *Science of Morals*, p. 41; J. Young, *Economics as a Moral Science: The Political Economy of Adam Smith* (Cheltenham, 1997), p. 10; H. Bitterman, "Adam Smith's Empiricism and the Law of Nature" (1940), reprinted in *Adam Smith. Critical Assessments*, 7 vols., ed. J. Wood (London, 1983–94), vol. 1, p. 196.

[38] Cf. C. Berry, *Social Theory of the Scottish Enlightenment* (Edinburgh, 1997), chapter 4.

[39] D. Hume, "Of National Characters" (1748) in *Essays: Moral, Political and Literary* ed. E. Miller (Indianapolis, IN, 1987), p. 198.

I.ii.4), yet neither is it random; there are real *causes* at work here, it is a predictable effect that different social experiences produce different characters.[40] This does not mean that human nature is a mere blank sheet; moral causation presupposes certain universal structures and dynamics in human nature, including necessarily a capacity to learn and to form habits.

To bring out the bearing of this on Smith's social scientific practice and to attempt to move beyond the hitherto generalised discussion, I consider two more particular cases – each chosen for its wider resonance:

1. In nomadic society, the second of the four stages, the leaders are those with the greatest herds and similarly in the third, agricultural stage, power lies with the landlords or, as Smith calls them, the "great proprietors." These individuals use their surplus in the same way as a Tartar chief (cf. WN, V.i.b.7) had done, namely to maintain a multitude of retainers and dependents who in return for their keep can offer only obedience (III.iv.5). Since the king was only another proprietor, the administration of justice lay in the (local) hands of those with the means to execute it (III.iv.7). At this point Smith observes that it is a mistake to see the origin of these "territorial jurisdictions" in feudal law (III.iv.8). The source of this mistake is faulty social science, a misunderstanding of social causation. The cause of feudal power lies not in the deliberative and purposive decrees of law but in "the state of property and manners" from which it "necessarily flowed" (ibid). For the properly informed expert (social scientist), this necessity is not a singular event causing wonder and surprise because it is duplicated in the histories of the French and English monarchies and is exemplified by the case "not thirty years ago" of Mr. Cameron of Lochiel "a gentleman of Lochaber in Scotland" (ibid). It is therefore a regularity amenable to scientific explanation; as Smith says explicitly, "such effects must always flow from such causes" (ibid).

Similarly, to explain the collapse of feudal power – both secular and ecclesiastical (WN, V.i.g.25) – an appropriate social or moral

---

[40] Cf. WN, III.iv.3, where the "different habits" of the merchant and the country gentleman "affects the temper and disposition in every sort of business." Hume distinguished the soldier and the priest similarly, *National Characters*, pp. 198–9.

cause has to be found. Once again, "the feeble efforts of human reason" (V.i.g.24) lack sufficient explanatory power. Exemplifying Dugald Stewart's two lynchpins of theoretical history, Smith finds the requisite causal power in the conjunction of the principles of human nature and external circumstances. The former is represented by the selfish desire of those in power, the latter by "the silent and insensible operation of foreign commerce." Thanks to this commerce, the great proprietors in exchange for a "pair of diamond buckles," or similarly frivolous but privately consumable trinket, gradually bartered their whole power and authority (III.iv.10). As the effects of a cause, there is an implicit regularity here. Smith provides a counterfactual when he observes that the sway of the Tartar chief stems from his using his surplus to maintain a thousand men *because* "the rude state of his society does not afford him any manufactured produce, any trinkets and baubles of any kind for which he can exchange that part of his rude produce which is over and above his own consumption" (V.i.b.7). However, the presence of foreign commerce in the feudal era, by making available these baubles, resulted ultimately in the members of a commercial society being free of the thrall of personal dependency because the proprietors "were no longer capable of interrupting the regular execution of justice" (III.iv.15).

This process of social change is, for Smith, a general truth about social life. The truth it bespeaks is that social life is pervaded by unintended consequences or the operation of the "invisible hand." As Smith himself acknowledged in the one reference to the invisible hand in *The Wealth of Nations* the phenomenon applies in "many other cases" (IV.ii.9). In this instance, the collapse of feudalism, which Smith calls a "revolution of the greatest importance to the publick happiness," cannot be put down to any purposive individualistic explanation. Neither the proprietors nor the merchants had the "least intention to serve the publick" and neither had "knowledge or foresight of that great revolution" (WN, III.v.17). The public happiness, the general good, was not brought about by deliberate human policy. Smithian social science does not turn individuals into socially constructed ciphers; they do indeed have intentions (e.g., to obtain diamonds), but these of themselves do not provide an adequate causal explanation of either social statics (institutions) or dynamics (change). To provide that, and presupposing a given model of human nature, moral causes have to be identified.

2. A pervasive theme in *The Theory of Moral Sentiments* is that morality is a learnt phenomenon. Hence society would "crumble into nothing" if "by discipline, education and example" individuals were not impressed with a "reverence" for rules of conduct (TMS, 5.1.2), or it would "crumble into atoms" (II.ii.3.4) without the observance of justice, but the rules of justice may be taught to all (III.6.11). In these and other ways, moral behaviour is an effect of socialisation and thus exhibits the traits of soft determinism. Individuals internalise moral standards so in practice the authority possessed by conscience is the effect of "habit and experience" (III.3.2). The fact that it is habitual, so "we are scarce sensible" that we do appeal to it, means that, building on the given natural dynamics of human nature, it is a learnt resource.

The most graphic presentation of this theme is where Smith likens society to a mirror (TMS, III.1.3). Supposing "a human creature could grow up to manhood in some solitary place, without any communication with his own species," then such a person "could no more think of his own character, of the propriety or demerit of his own sentiment and conduct, of the beauty and deformity of his own mind, than of the beauty or deformity of his own face." Society, however, acts as a mirror wherein it will be seen "that mankind approve of some of them [passions] and are disgusted by others." According to Smith's reading of human nature, in the former case, "he will be elevated" but "cast down in the other." The given universal dynamics of human nature are such that humans seek pleasure and shun pain (cf. TMS, VII.iii.2.8) so socially approved passions will be reproduced and disapproved ones shunned.

This emphasis on morality as learnt seems to entail a conflation of social conformity and ethical standards. Smith however denies that his account of morality precludes criticism or is, in effect, an endorsement of cultural and ethical relativism. He openly admits that virtues differ between "rude and barbarous nations" and "civilized nations" (TMS, V.2.8). Nonetheless, he believes "the sentiments of moral approbation and disapprobation are founded on the strongest and most vigorous passions of human nature; and though they may be somewhat warpt, cannot be entirely perverted" (V.2.1).

As an example he cites the practice of infanticide. He accounts for this by the fact that "in the earliest period of society" infanticide was commonplace and the "uniform continuance of the custom had hindered them [the practitioners] from perceiving its enormity" (TMS, V.2.15). Echoing the language of "Astronomy," Smith refers to "we" not being in a state of wonder or surprise about this. The social scientist armed with the notion of moral causation is able to explain it. However, Smith does not subscribe to the maxim *tout comprendre, tout pardonner*. He does allow the practice to be "more pardonable" in the rudest and lowest state of society, where "extreme indigence" obtains so, human nature being what it is, the infant is abandoned that the adult might live. However, the practice was inexcusable "among the polite and civilized Athenians." Smith is adamant that just because something is commonly done does not mean it is condonable when the practice itself is "unjust and unreasonable" (ibid). According to Smith, the Athenian practice in exposing their infants was the effect of the moral cause since such a policy was their "uninterrupted custom." So powerful is this, Smith implies, that even the most acute minds of the time, such as Plato and Aristotle, accepted it as normal.

IV

The normative tenor that Smith's treatment of infanticide exhibits runs throughout his writings. This does not, however, compromise his scientific credentials; on the contrary, in his eyes, it underwrites them.

We noted previously that Smith added a sociological thesis to his psychological account of philosophy, or science. Those living in the concrete, simple, immature era of polytheism are prone to superstition, but with the growth of leisure, philosophy becomes possible. In due course, this produces the growth of genuine knowledge so those in the fourth stage *know* more. One consequence of that greater (scientific) knowledge is not only their greater opulence and improved material living standards, but also, concurrently, their greater command of their environment. The "natural progress of improvement" (WN, V.i.a.43) brings about not only the superiority associated with gunpowder, but also all that "ennobles human life" as "the whole face of the globe is changed" by turning "the rude forests of nature into agreeable and fertile plains," making the "trackless and barren ocean a new fund of subsistence and the great high road of communication to the different nations of the earth" (TMS, IV.1.10).

Smith is here a fully paid-up member of the Enlightenment "family." One of the clearest expressions of his membership occurs in *The Wealth of Nations*. In the context of the public good of education, he remarks unequivocally that "science is the great antidote to superstition" (WN, V.i.g.14). He advocates making the "middle ranks" study philosophy and science because, if they are immunised, then the spread of the poison to the "inferior ranks" is liable to be countered. This policy prescription, as with all the others which *The Wealth of Nations* contains, is not breaking some supposed fact/value dichotomy but is, rather, what science is truly about. Although Smith may well have laid the foundations for the subsequent development of positivist, scientific economics, this, as more historically nuanced commentators have long held, cannot be regarded as an accurate reflection of his own position.

Social life in *all* its manifestations – economic, political, aesthetic, religious, and moral – consists of data to be analysed, of causal relations to be uncovered. Moral philosophy or social science is that analytical causal enterprise as it pertains to the moral or social world. Smith essentially shares Hume's conviction that a "science of man," or as he himself puts it, a "science of human nature" (TMS, VII.iii.2.5), is possible. This science demonstrates as a universal fact about the constitution of human nature that (for example) material well-being is better than miserable poverty, whereas the "science of a legislator," operating from "general principles" (WN, IV.ii.39), will determine that this can be achieved by allowing the "natural effort of every individual to better his condition...to exert itself with freedom and security" and by removing the "impertinent obstructions with which the folly of human laws too often incumbers its operations" (WN, IV.v.b.43). In sum, for Smith, science identifies folly and points out the road to enlightenment.[41]

[41] I am grateful to Roger Emerson for running his (nonpersuaded) eye over a draft of this article and to Knud Haakonssen for editorial support.

5 Smith on Ingenuity, Pleasure, and the Imitative Arts

SMITH'S PREOCCUPATION WITH THE IMITATIVE ARTS

After Smith returned to Kirkaldy from London in June 1777, one of "Several Works" that occupied him was an essay on the imitative arts (Corr., no. 208). Progress was interrupted, as he feared it would be, by his duties, from January 1778, as a Commissioner of His Majesty's Customs for Scotland. Nonetheless, he returned to this particular essay as time allowed, maintaining his interest in the subject right up to his last days.

Twice in the 1780s that we know of, Smith laid out his ideas before competent audiences on what it is about imitation in the arts that gives pleasure. In the summer of 1782, at a meeting in London of the Johnson literary club, he conversed on this theme. The painter Sir Joshua Reynolds was present, told Smith afterward that he perfectly agreed with his notions, and subsequently wrote to his friend Bennet Langton that the subject was clearly one Smith had "considered with attention."[1] Then, in December 1788, when Smith was in Glasgow for his investiture as Rector of the University, he addressed the Literary Society there, reading a paper

---

[1] The letter is reprinted in Frederick W. Hilles, *Portraits by Sir Joshua Reynolds. Character Sketches of Oliver Goldsmith, Samuel Johnson, and David Garrick, Together with Other Manuscripts of Reynolds Discovered Among the Boswell Papers* (New York, NY, 1952), pp. 173–5, and in Charles N. Fifer, ed., *The Correspondence of James Boswell with Certain Members of the Club*, vol. 3 (New York, NY, 1976), pp. 125–6. Reynolds states that he told Smith after the meeting that he completely shared his notions and asked if he would read an ordered version of various notes he had on the topic. Smith declined on the ground that he hoped to publish an essay on the subject that winter. Some of Reynolds's notes are printed in Hilles, op. cit., pp. 175–6.

of two hours length, on the same subject.[2] The essay remained incomplete at that late date, and it is doubtful whether Smith was able to add much to it before he died. Nonetheless, that he considered his ideas worth preserving may be inferred from the fact that he spared this essay, along with the "History of Astronomy," and several others, from the destruction he ordered of his lecture notes and other manuscript materials a week or so before his death.[3]

The full title of the essay was "On the Nature of that Imitation which takes place in what are called the Imitative Arts." Smith's literary executors, James Hutton and Joseph Black, chose to publish it in 1795, along with the other surviving essays, in a volume entitled *Essays on Philosophical Subjects*. The modern edition of this essay, edited and introduced by W. P. D. Wightman, appears in volume III of the Glasgow edition of Smith's *Works*, both volume and essay bearing the same titles as in 1795.

Smith was interested in the imitative arts – for him, sculpture, painting, music, poetry, theater, opera, and dance – as illustrative material for certain principles, a pattern followed in virtually all the preserved essays. Chief among those principles, as Smith's disquisitions in the 1780s would lead us to expect, was the notion that imitation conveys pleasure.

Smith's view of imitation was quite distinct from that common among his contemporaries, which was that it is copying, mere replication, and therefore inferior.[4] His desire to explain pleasure

---

[2] Ian Ross, Smith's modern biographer, reprints a brief summary of the paper by William Richardson, Professor of Humanity at Glasgow, Smith's former student and his choice to be Vice–Rector. It reads, in part: "The subject was the Imitative Arts: and the design was to illustrate the general principle by which they please. He treated of statuary, Painting, and Music – and is still to treat of Poetry and Dancing. Yes, Dancing, for he conceives it to be an Imitative art; and I believe means to prove, that the Greek tragedy was no other than a musical Ballet" (Ian Simpson Ross, *The Life of Adam Smith* [Oxford 1995], pp. 379–80).

[3] Joseph Black and James Hutton, in an advertisement to their edition of the *Essays*, state that Smith "left them in the hands of his friends to be disposed of as they thought proper, having immediately before his death destroyed many other manuscripts which he thought unfit for being made public" (EPS, 32). The destruction of those other materials is discussed in Ross, op. cit., pp. 404–5.

[4] The entries on "imitate" and "imitation" in Johnson's *Dictionary of the English Language* (1755) convey the prevailing sense of imitation as replication. The common view was well expressed by Edward Young. An imitator, even the most excellent, "yet still ... but nobly builds on another's foundation; his debt is, at least, equal to his glory; which therefore, on the balance, cannot be very great" (*Conjectures on*

required that he fashion his own definition. Negatively, because "Uniformity tires the mind," whereas variety pleases, replication was ruled out as an unsuitable characterization of imitation (LJ [B], 208). Positively, Smith connected imitation with his well-known general interest in the forging of links between apparently unconnected phenomena. A connectedness that is natural and readily appropriable – "proper variety, easy connection, and simple order" (ibid) – soothes the imagination and brings us closer to that state of tranquility that is true happiness, a proposition he applied to moral sentiments (TMS, III.3.30), to systems of planetary motion ("History of Astronomy," ii.12, iv.67, iv.76) and to music ("Imitative Arts," ii.20–3). Imitation in the arts, as we will now see, also partook of an additional property: resemblance that transcends, yet at the same time respects, differences in kind.

THE NATURE, AND QUALITY, OF IMITATION

An example from the essay will clarify this cryptic definition. The illustration Smith himself used both in an early, brief mention of imitation, and in the essay, once difference had been introduced, involves painting. "In Painting, a plain surface of one kind is made to resemble, not only a plain surface of another, but all the three dimensions of a solid substance" ("Imitative Arts," i.6; cf. LJ [A], iv. 14–15; LJ [B], 208–9). A stretched canvas, in other words, is a substitute for any surface, whether a carpet or a landscape. Remarkably, however, pile and its softness, grass, trees, and hills, can also be represented on the flat canvas, and from the hand of a good artist will look just like their real counterparts, although there is no physical depth to the canvas. What is transferred is the appearance of solidity

Original Composition [London, 1759; facsimile edition, Leeds, 1966], p. 11]. James Malek notes that by the late eighteenth century other questions had begun to displace interest in imitation ("Thomas Twining's Analysis of Poetry and Music as Imitative Arts," *Modern Philology* 68 (1971): 260–8, at 260). Smith should probably be viewed as one of those who led the shift, the interest he displayed in invention (as distinct from traditional imitation) in the arts (see following text and footnote 5) being matched by his interest in invention in machinery, and in his treatment of arrangement and style in rhetoric and poetics. On the latter, see Michael Carter, "The Role of Invention in Belletristic Rhetoric: A Study of the Lectures of Adam Smith," *Rhetoric Society Quarterly* 18 (1988): 3–13.

only (cf. "External Senses," 50). Therein lies the artifice. The artist creates a plausible resemblance between natures that are distinct and remain so after the connection has been made.

Having approached imitation in this way, Smith at once addressed two likely misunderstandings. First, imitation does not require exact resemblance: merit does not attach to deception (i.15). Second, although in general we are pleased by beauty, imitative merit is independent of the beauty of the subject (i.7–8). What does please us then in an imitation, if it is neither deception nor beauty as such? Our pleasure stems from ingenuity, from the very design and contrivance shown in overcoming a disparity of kinds by linking them in appearance.[5]

Not all artifice, however, is equal. To be truly admirable, artifice must be understandable, not a matter of mystery or an object of wonder only. This is an idea that appears and reappears across Smith's work, and we can piece together his reasoning from sources as diverse as the "History of Astronomy," the lectures on rhetoric and belles lettres, and the essay on the arts. Wonder is a sentiment produced by effects, but effects that we do not understand. Anything that appears to us to be "new and singular," resisting classification according to all known orders and "assortments," can excite wonder ("Astronomy," Intro 1 and ii.3). The pleasure of wonder, however, being essentially that of "uncertain and undetermined thought," manifests itself strictly through the senses, its effects ranging from a rolling of the eyes, breathlessness, and swelling of the heart, to rapture, and even ecstasy (ibid, ii.3; "Imitative Arts," i.17). After a while, however, wonder ceases, because familiarity with the effect causes us to stop thinking that any explanation is required. Pleasure also then disappears, as in the case of most mirror images. If we can see the original we quickly lose interest in its "shadow" (i.17). The relative inadequacy and fleeting nature of the pleasure of wonder was Smith's reason for holding, for example, that the true pleasure in painting or statuary is not just independent of deception but "altogether incompatible with it" (i.16).

---

[5] As Smith put it in the lectures on rhetoric and belles lettres, speaking of the greater interest we find in histories that deal with men and with the great changes that affect them, than in histories of insects, "Design and Contrivance is what chiefly interests us" (LRBL, ii.15).

Unlike wonder, understanding gives pleasure to the mind, and that pleasure is both deeper and longer lasting. What pleases the mind is "observing the resemblances that are discoverable betwixt different objects," hence some "principle of connection" is essential to intellectual satisfaction ("Astronomy," ii.1; iv.67). Smith also noted that, where disparity is greater the art that can overcome it also appears "evidently...to be founded upon a much deeper science, or upon principles much more abstruse and profound" ("Imitative Arts," i.18). Finally, this issues in a rule of thumb: "the pleasure arising from the imitation seems to be greater in proportion as this disparity is greater" (i.6).

Dugald Stewart read in this last observation a principle, that pleasure increases with difficulty surmounted (*Account*, iii.14 in EPS), but that was not Smith's emphasis. Certainly, the greater the disparity, the greater the ingenuity involved in producing a connection; however, it is the ingenuity that pleases, and ingenuity may have little or nothing to do with difficulty. Against what standard should we judge whether Newton's or Descartes's theory of motion involves the greater "difficulty"? Smith did not even pose such questions. He did insist, however, that Newton's achievement in connecting so many natural phenomena together under the single principle of gravity was "vastly more ingenious" than Aristotle's, which required that a separate principle be assigned to each effect. Being more ingenious it was, "*for that reason* more engaging" (LRBL, ii.133, emphasis added; cf. TMS, V.i.9; LJ [A], vi.12–13).

A second requirement of superior imitation is that the means it employs to bridge disparity should be reasonably transparent. Not that full or very deep understanding can be had in an instant, or without training, but "the nobler works" of statuary and painting – once again serving as leading examples – do seem to "carry, as it were, their own explication along with them." They "demonstrate, even to the eye, the way and manner in which they are produced." For instance, "a certain modification of figure" allows the sculptor to express "with so much truth and vivacity, the actions, passions, and behaviour of men." The same results can be reached in painting, from the combined use of shading and tonality. Such artifices are apparent even to "an unskilful spectator" ("Imitative Arts," i.16).

At least one modern critic has questioned whether an uninformed viewer can discern *how* representation is achieved in, say, a sculpture or a painting.[6] Smith, however, does not impute insight beyond what education could possibly allow. That would be unlikely coming from an advisor to the Foulis School for the Art of Design, who must have understood very well the importance of training in drawing to students preparing to become artists.[7] Smith's statement is not general – there is no mention of poetry or music – nor is he asserting anything very profound. He refers here explicitly only to expression, or to the way mood and passion are conveyed through gesture, body positioning, and facial "motion." It is not asking much of a viewer to discern how posture can help convey passion, or coloration and the shading of a face various feelings. What is presupposed here is simply an ability to connect depictions with common experiences of people and their situations, which is no more than is required for the device of the impartial spectator to work. Being able to project oneself into another's situation,

---

[6] See Peter Jones, "The Aesthetics of Adam Smith," in *Adam Smith Reviewed*, eds. Peter Jones and Andrew S. Skinner (Edinburgh, 1992), pp. 56–78, at p. 70, where, however, Smith's position is distorted by a quotation being used to suggest that the fine arts require "little labour" of a spectator (LRBL, i.140). In fact, in the passage quoted, Smith seems to be referring to physical labor only. He points out that those whose bodies are feeble and who are dogged by ill health, of which the Third Earl of Shaftesbury is the prime example, tend to cultivate pursuits suited to their limited physical capabilities. Slightly earlier, it is true, Smith had spoken of feebleness of body *and* mind, yet the passage as a whole offers no support for the view that the arts yield their secrets without training.

[7] This school was established in 1753 by Robert Foulis, University Printer for class texts and volumes of the classics, and self-styled disciple of Hutcheson, "to teach designing in the University with the approbation and protections of the masters i.e. professors" (Richard B. Sher, "Commerce, Religion and the Enlightenment in Eighteenth-Century Glasgow," in *Glasgow. Volume I: Beginnings to 1830*, eds. T. M. Devine and Gordon Jackson (Manchester, 1995), pp. 312–59, esp. pp. 327, 333–4. Jones notes that Smith advised Foulis on paintings and sculptures that the students might copy or that might be available in print form (Jones, op. cit., p. 57). Smith's involvement also extended to helping resolve space problems for the school (Ross, op. cit., pp. 146–7), and possibly to drafting "a memorandum to enlist government support" (Jules Lubbock, *The Tyranny of Taste. The Politics of Architecture and Design in Britain, 1550–1960* [New Haven, CT, and London, 1995], p. 220). In 1761, the school organized an open air display of paintings in the courtyard of the university, recorded by the artist David Allan, a pupil in the school. An engraving after Allan's original is in the Mitchell Library, Glasgow. It is attractive to think that Smith might have been active in setting up this exhibition, but I know of no supporting evidence.

and perceiving how a representation connects distinct spheres, are similar in that each supposes that a person is able to intuit the nature of the disparity to be overcome.

The ease of access to the means of imitation in the arts – in some of them anyway – was contrasted by Smith with the remoteness through abstraction of much explanation in natural philosophy. Wonder is removed when understanding is reached; for "Who wonders at the machinery of the opera-house who has once been admitted behind the scenes?" Yet, "In the Wonders of nature . . . it rarely happens that we can discover so clearly this connecting chain" ("Astronomy," ii.9). Again, it seems that Smith is not so much insisting that understanding is available to all in the arts, as that an intuitive grasp carries one farther in the arts than in natural philosophy, where it is just the starting point of a plausible account.

IMITATIVE POTENTIAL IN THE SEVERAL ARTS

Smith's essay appears in part to be an exercise in ranking, to see which of the arts involves more and which less of imitation, properly understood. Imitation, it turns out, is just one of the sources of our pleasure in the arts, although it might have seemed to Smith an appropriate initial focus, given that the arts had been regarded from antiquity as essentially imitative.[8]

However, perhaps that is the wrong way to understand Smith's attitude to ancient preconceptions. It is possible that he undertook the ranking exercise based on imitation knowing full well its inadequacy, and meaning thereby to undermine, as he tries to do in more direct ways, ancient preconceptions that the arts are inferior precisely because they imitate nature. His point may be

[8] If Artistotle's *Poetics* may be regarded as a brief for the defence of poetry against Plato's charges in Book 10 of *The Republic*, then Smith's excursions into the nature of imitation constitute additional evidence, in which ingenuity, as a peculiarly intellectual, yet at base technical, source of pleasure, is pitted against the idea that the arts are removed from reality and cater principally to the emotions. A pithy characterization of the Platonic and Aristotelian positions is to be found in Gerald F. Else's introduction to his edition and translation of the *Poetics* (Ann Arbor, MI, 1967). A useful overview of better and lesser-known eighteenth-century critics on imitation is contained in John L. Mahoney, "The Anglo-Scottish Critics: Toward a Romantic Theory of Imitation," in *Johnson and His Age*, ed. James Engell (Cambridge, MA, 1984), pp. 255–83. Jones, op. cit., offers both a more complete and balanced survey, as well as references useful for understanding the context in which Smith wrote.

that the richness of the arts as a source of pleasure cannot possibly be exhausted when we have identified merely the ways and degree to which they imitate.

Smith's subversive intent, if that is what it was, emerges in a variety of contexts, all, however, having to do with the role of nature in informing our critical judgments. For example, he showed that, although it might seem, and had often been said to be, unnatural to sing when we want to persuade, the use of song to convey a meaning is an excellent example of imitation (in his sense). For using vocal music in place of speech is exactly the sort of making "a thing of one kind resemble another thing of a very different kind" in which the merit of imitation consists ("Imitative Arts," ii.11). An even more direct challenge to ancient doctrine occurs in *The Theory of Moral Sentiments*, at a point where Smith argues that there is no "certain measure of verse . . . by nature appropriated to each particular species of writing" (TMS, V.i.6). Here Smith's distancing of himself from nature was part of a defence of the role of custom in influencing the arts. Plausible though the idea of a natural measure for each kind of verse might be, a new manner of writing or of music can introduce "a considerable change in the established modes" (V.i.7). Thus, after noting the objections made by the nature-bound among the ancients to various writers whom he considered admirable – Seneca, Sallust, Tacitus – Smith concluded that the objections were self-defeating. They merely served to show that, "After the praise of refining the taste of a nation, the highest eulogy, perhaps, which can be bestowed upon any author, is to say, that he corrupted it" (ibid).

Bearing in mind, then, that Smith's ranking of the arts by their imitative capacities may have been intended to reveal the shortcomings of the traditional imitative preconception itself, I will summarize his exploration of the imitative capabilities inherent in each of the arts.[9] First, however, a note on order.

[9] This is just one way of approaching Smith's essay. Peter Jones offers a rich account of the essay as an exercise in aesthetics, setting Smith's views against those he expresses in the lectures on rhetoric and belles lettres and in *The Theory of Moral Sentiments*, and identifying influences and the ways in which Smith differed from contemporaries. See Jones, op. cit. Partly because this excellent account exists, I have felt free to choose a somewhat different focus.

Smith's order in the essay was to treat in Part I sculpture and painting, with short sections each on tapestry and topiary. Then followed a discussion of music and dancing, with remarks on poetry, and some asides on opera. A very short, and clearly unfinished, final section floats the idea that Greek theatre was more or less a form of pantomime and dance. On this point, William Richardson, Smith's Vice-Rector, took away from Smith's 1788 reading in Glasgow that it was meant to demonstrate "that the Greek tragedy was no other than a musical ballet" (Ross, *Life*, 380).

The progression in Smith's essay appears to have been dictated by the principles he wanted to display, rather than because it matched the rank order of imitative potential. Thus sculpture and painting served to show what he meant by imitation; tapestry, his idea that we must make allowance in evaluating imitative success for the "awkwardness of the instruments" available ("Imitative Arts," i.12); and topiary, the notion that fashion greatly influences our ideas about beauty. Music, dance, and poetry had often been treated together, as sister arts; however, a separate note printed immediately following the essay probes the adequacy of the traditional basis for the affinity of the three, *Rhythmus*, or measure. Smith had already discussed elsewhere, in his lectures on rhetoric and belles lettres, measure as number in architecture (LRBL, ii.126–30), although even earlier he had urged that it is custom, not nature, which decides the propriety of certain traditional proportions in buildings (TMS, V.i.5). His remarks on the French opera in Part II of the essay (music, dance, and poetry) were introduced to illustrate the notion that effects may please, even though they are excessive, cheap, and contrary to the very nature of an art. These various ideas and principles get in the way of a simple analysis of imitation; nevertheless, it is imitation that supplies the binding thread of the essay.

Dance and instrumental music offer convenient points of entry to Smith's rankings, although neither stands very high on the scale of imitative potential. Dance, he suggests, is like instrumental music in that "it can produce very agreeable effects, without imitating any thing." Indeed, neither is it "essentially imitative" ("Imitative Arts," iii.1; cf. ii.22). However, dance accompanied and directed by music becomes imitative, as does instrumental music itself, when it is married to poetry (iii.2; ii.9). In both these combinations "art conquers the disparity which Nature has placed between the imitating and the imitated object" (iii.2).

Dance, however, is an easy form of imitation, because mimicry itself is so natural, and the very idea of using gestures and motion to express common experiences is obvious (ii.6). The natural disparity overcome is therefore typically greater in sculpture or painting. Yet, dance encompasses all the subjects of those two arts, while also being able to represent action as a sequence of causes and effects. Sculpture and painting, in contrast, are confined to capturing a moment (iii.2).

Strictly in terms of imitative power, however, vocal music exceeds dance and indeed all the other arts, including instrumental music. "Poetry...is capable of expressing many things fully and distinctly, which Dancing either cannot represent at all, or can represent but obscurely and imperfectly," including ideas, fancies, and the passions (ii.7). Vocal music has the same power as dance or poetry to convey "a distinct sense or meaning," no matter how unnatural it may be to sing an argument or express a serious intent (ii.9). The words of vocal music, however, also "commonly...express the situation of some particular person:" a joyous companion, a lover, a warrior, a generous spirit, or a person in prosperity (ii.10). Through sympathy, we participate in these situations, and our pleasure is thereby increased (ii.22). "The more complete Music of an air" enjoys yet another advantage. Persons in the grip of a passion tend to be absorbed by it and return constantly to whatever is agitating them. Unlike instrumental music, poetry, or prose, vocal music "can venture to imitate those almost endless repetitions" characteristic of such absorption, and with positive effect, which is normally impossible with repetition (ii.12).

Finally, to the power of resembling discourse and expressing the sentiments and situations of particular persons, vocal music adds a third imitative capability, the expressive acting of the singer (ii.15).

Contrast all this with instrumental music: although it can engage our minds with "a train of objects," producing real pleasure and delight, it does this by affecting our emotions, not through any imitative power (ii.21–2, 31–2). It is true that music can be bent so as to resemble the tone or movement of feelings or conversation; moreover, it represents best the amiable and social passions, those that bind us together, a merit it shares with sculpture and painting (ii.12–13). Music, in addition, adds beauty to its subjects, which neither painting nor sculpture can do, "clothes them with melody and harmony," and in the process heightening color, adding lustre, and enhancing grace (ii.14). Nevertheless, and to repeat, these are statements of our emotional responses to music, not demonstrations that it has any strictly imitative power. "Whatever we feel from instrumental Music is an original, and not a sympathetic feeling: it is our own gaiety, sedateness, or melancholy; not the reflected disposition of another person" (ii.22).

AFFECT

The arts then are pleasurably affecting as well as imitative. Is the one inferior to the other? Pleasing effects, Smith pointed out, can be produced abusively, as in French operas, where "easy tricks" are regularly employed: a hail of peas or a snow of paper. Such imitative excesses merit no esteem or admiration, being "unfit to be represented upon the stage." At the same time, it is undeniable that they are not only used often but received with "the most complete approbation and applause" by audiences in France, "that ingenious nation." Similarly, in Italian opera, although it had become less extravagant than formerly, frequent changes of scene were now quite acceptable, even though they violated the "sacred law" of the unity of place in common drama (ii.26–7).

Given Smith's lack of reverence for the established rules of artistic performance and his fascination with ingenuity, it is hard to believe that he felt deeply troubled by these developments. Recall that one of his cherished insights in *The Theory of Moral Sentiments* was the notion that the ingenuity embodied in an object can be a source of pleasure, quite apart from any fitness it may have for use (TMS, IV.i.3). In fact, his response was to attribute pleasure in effects to the external senses, distinguishing these from pleasures of the mind, yet without any hint that the former are inferior. That he wrote, and preserved, another essay, "Of the External Senses," seems to confirm that sensory registrations of, and pleasure in, effects, was for him a subject of investigation on a par with the "inventions of the imagination" known as philosophical systems ("Astronomy," iv.76). It is true, as has been shown, that the effects of surprise and wonder are more immediate than those linked to our understanding of causes. They also decline quickly and are gone. However, although admiration increases only slowly (as understanding dawns), it also has a maximum; it "comes to its greatest height and again decreases" (LRBL, i.165). We may assume pleasure here follows the course of the effect. It is not, therefore, that science and understanding represent absolutely superior sources of pleasure, but that the pleasure they give lies deeper and is more sustained – although it too decays. The point about opera is that it is an entertainment, designed wholly with a view to producing pleasing effects. If those effects can be produced as well by "other powers" than "the most exact imitation of nature, which the most perfect observation of probability, could produce," then so be it ("Imitative Arts," ii.28). As Smith noted of the different effects produced by studying the plans of a building versus seeing it realized, the two experiences are not only "vastly different," but "the amusement derived from the first, never approaches to the wonder and admiration which are sometimes excited by the second" (TMS, II.iii.2.3).

Smith's discussion of imitation in the arts leads to the conclusion that, while pleasure is the goal, imitation, or rational ingenuity in overcoming disparity, is just one way of generating pleasure. Knowing *how* effects are produced heightens pleasure in all cases; nonetheless, performance in the arts can produce greater pleasure than, say, studying a play or a piece of music "in the closet." The effect of performance is passing, but no less real for that while it lasts, and as in this case, may be more powerful.

A CONJECTURE: THE ESSAY ON THE ARTS AS PENDANT TO *THE WEALTH OF NATIONS*

This conclusion alerts us to a possible position for the essay on the arts in Smith's overall work that I outline now and explore more fully in a moment. Consider "unproductive" labor, which is defined in *The Wealth of Nations* as labor issuing in no concrete or lasting product (II.iii.1–2). Performing artists are mentioned as prime examples of unproductive laborers. "[P]layers, buffoons, musicians, opera-singers, opera-dancers, &c." all produce "nothing which could afterwards purchase or procure an equal quantity of labour...the work of all of them perishes in the very instant of its production." Productive labor, in contrast, has the advantage from the point of view of assisting growth that its products are concrete and durable. Such products fix living labor for a time but can be sold again for money with which to employ new productive labor. Thus a second or third value can be added, by creating new durable products. Productive labor, in other words, has transformative potential. Nothing of the sort is possible in the performing arts, whose product is fleeting, insubstantial. These arts may please, but the pleasure they generate is due to labor that perishes in the act. Smith, however, was convinced that pleasure is the main purpose of activity once we have satisfied our survival needs,[10] and he wanted to make value added in the form of (mere) pleasure just as acceptable as that brought about by productive labor (LJ [B], 206–7; LJ [A], vi.161–2; WN, II.i.26; "Imitative Arts," ii.20–1, 29–30).

Smith set about this task in two stages. First, he argued that the pleasure we derive from objects describes a similar path whether the pleasure itself is caused by something as insubstantial as, say, color, form, or ingenuity (the idea), or follows from an objective property (uniqueness, or novelty in an actual object). The path in all cases shows rising pleasure at first, but with a maximum, followed by decline. This reality provided Smith with a basis for treating unproductive labor as analogous to productive labor. A second step was required to allow him to deal with the problem that there is no common, objective measure of pleasure; to get around this difficulty, he applied the same general principles to the pricing of physical goods and to artistic services, including services in the unproductive performing arts. These are certainly moves that Smith made; I read them as advancing steps toward a case for viewing the essay on the arts and *The Wealth of Nations* as complements. I must now recover that joint project in Smith's work.

THE PATTERN OF PLEASURE

We first encounter pleasure and imitation together in the section on "police" (policy) in Smith's moral philosophy course at Glasgow, of which we have student notes from the sessions of 1762–3 and (probably) 1763–4. In his lectures, Smith laid out a logical sequence

---

[10] I am consciously enlarging on Smith's declaration in that an understanding of the causes of growth is only a necessary counterpart to the real end, which is consumption, "the sole . . . purpose of all production" (WN, IV.viii.49).

running from needs of nature through artificial wants to those qualities that lead us to prefer some objects over others.

The chain begins with the question how "plenty and abundance" can be introduced into a nation. First, Smith observed, we must understand these terms, and for that we must "consider what are the naturall wants and demands of mankind" (LJ [A], vi.8). Natural wants comprise our strictly physical needs: food, shelter, and clothing. However, we humans are never satisfied to accept nature's provisions for these needs, unimproved. We have been given "reason and ingenuity, art, contrivan[c]e, and capacity of improvement far superior to that . . . bestowed on any of the other animalls," and we exercise those capabilities most energetically (ibid). Our insistence on modifying everything supplied by nature is the source of artificial wants, or "demands." "Man alone of all animalls . . . is the only one who regards the differences of things which no way affect their real substance or give them no superior advantage" in supplying our natural needs (vi.12–13).

In the civilized world, Smith noted, basic needs are readily met; however, since we demand "more elegant nicities and refinement," artifice quickly comes to comprise the greater part of our activities. To supply our artificial demands "allmost the whole of the arts and sciences have been invented and improved" (vi.12, 16). This has everything to do with plenty for, on the one hand, "Cheapness is in fact the same thing with plenty" (LJ [B], 205; cf. LJ [A], vi.31–2), whereas on the other hand, cheapness comes about through specialization and division of labor (e.g., LJ [A], vi.28–9).

Reading this argument backward, division of labor, which is the mainspring of growth, is facilitated by specialization. However, the pattern of specialization will be a reflection of the goods people prefer. "[T]he ground of preference" in turn is the pleasure-giving properties of objects (LJ [B], 209; cf. LJ [A], vi.13). Reading forward, once again, pleasure and choice stand at the head of a chain that ends with division of labor. Pleasure is thus established as logically prior to and as undergirding the line of argument that dominates *The Wealth of Nations.*

Smith identified four general properties of objects that are directly associated with pleasure and which help turn some into objects of desire. These are imitation; color; form or figure, where pleasure is linked to variety; and rarity, which may also be combined with variety. What is the form of the curve tracing the pleasure that arises from each of these four properties considered separately?

1. To start with Smith's common illustration, painting, imitation in that art is essentially a technical problem, one of bridging two distinct worlds, that of solidity and touch, and that of objects of sight ("External Senses," 50). Through the use of combinations of color and shading, plus perspective, the bridging can be effected, the solid can be convincingly represented on a plane. However, there is implicit in this achievement the idea of an optimal degree of accuracy, to be determined in reality by our needs as viewers and in art by the purposes of the painter (51). In a strict sense, therefore, understanding cannot be ignored. That constraint, which will be reflected in *de facto optima*, tells us that in practice the trace of pleasure with respect to imitation will increase until some maximum is reached, after which it will decline.

2. As to color, although it is "the most flimsy and superficiall of all distinctions, [it too] becomes an object of...regard" (LJ [A], vi.13). Indeed color, although it belongs to the category of the insubstantial, is said to be no less important than figure "in directing...choice" (ibid). It is the reason, for example, why diamonds and other precious stones "have at all times been distinguished from the more ordinary peb[b]les of less splendid hues" (ibid). Smith speaks of the copper and zinc alloy known as Pinchbeck as being virtually the equal of gold in color. He also mentions "preparations of paste and glass" that fall not far short of the brilliance of real gems. He notes that the English imitation called "French plate" captures much of the "splendor" of silver (vi.16). We should understand from these remarks that brilliance, splendor, or richness of hue are the chief qualities that give color its appeal, although brilliance is not so much color-related as it is a term referring to the intensity of light caused by the manipulation of refraction and reflection. Brightness, nonetheless, and high value of color seem to yield pleasure. At the same time, "Man is the only animal who is possessed of such a nicety that the very colour of an object hurts him" (LJ [B], 208). Thus pleasure in color also has a maximum; it will rise with intensity, brilliance, and hue to a certain point but then diminish.

3. Notions of figure too are insubstantial, although Smith slips back and forth between notions of form and their substantiation in

objects. Whether in a line, then, or a wall, too much uniformity, as we have seen, "tires the mind," and is to be shunned. A circle, in contrast, has a constantly changing local shape and is therefore preferable. Sharp angles, however, introducing as they do discontinuities, give no pleasure. An artist or architect therefore who uses many-sided figures risks overwhelming us with their complexity: we are unable to grasp at a glance the nature of the form involved, and experience displeasure (LJ [A], vi.14). Figure, in short, is a complex variable whose quality changes from simplicity to complexity, the associated pleasure curve rising to a maximum and then falling with the change, as complexity begins to overwhelm us.

4. Rarity is not discussed in terms of increasing and then declining pleasure; rather, Smith stresses that our pleasure in unique objects is very great, partly because we like to know that we alone can afford such possessions (WN, I.xi.c). Strictly speaking, pleasure in rarity/uniqueness cannot be diluted by the existence of cheap copies. Nonetheless, we do take less pleasure in the familiar, so if uniqueness is not available, then variety at least is to be preferred above replication. The pleasure curve for uniqueness may then be thought of as a composite, involving variety as compensation for loss of strict uniqueness. Pleasure in other words can be sustained for those who must make do with copies, through adding variety, as in a collection; however, even variety, as we have seen, may become overwhelming, after which pleasure will decline (LJ [B], 208; LJ [A], vi.13–14).

Broadly speaking, Smith's four causes all produce a curve of rising, then declining pleasure, although true rarity (in isolation from variety) does not quite fit this treatment. Notwithstanding, there is sufficient uniformity here for us to be able to speak of an approximately standard *form* of response to the four basic causes of pleasure. The form of response being roughly similar whether the cause of pleasure is insubstantial or objective and physical, Smith had a basis for comparing values added whether of the lasting or ephemeral sort. He had still to address the assessment of pleasure. Normally this would have involved him in a discussion of taste. However, for the most part, Smith trod carefully around taste, preferring, it seems, to stick with analysis closer to the modern concept of willingness to pay.

TASTE AS ANALYSIS, AND WILLINGNESS TO PAY

Eighteenth-century taste involved the proper application of critical judgment. Just or proper criticism of course presupposed an agreed set of criteria, and these arose from the prior supposition of a certain nature being possessed by each art. Natures were broken down into component aspects or properties, or what might be called modal characteristics – modal in the sense that they were what made a particular art what it was and not something else. Thus Smith, following long tradition, spoke of the art of painting as comprising drawing, coloring, and expression. Music, more originally, he viewed as comprising melody and harmony (expression being merely the effect of these two characteristics) ("Imitative Arts," ii.32).

Each art being analysed into characteristics, the performance of an individual artist, or the execution of a particular work, could be assessed by paying attention to the corresponding categories of skill or "art." In judging painting, Smith was able to draw on the French theorist and adviser to the duc de Richelieu, Roger de Piles (1635–1709). In 1708, de Piles, although with no very serious intent, drew up a table of renowned painters and assessed their performance along the dimensions of drawing, coloring, composition, and expression, each on a scale from zero to twenty.[11] Such judgments did not amount to objective measures of taste; the exercise was valuable rather because it could be conducted across many works and many artists, issuing in relative rankings according to a consistent method. Moreover, by combining the assessments of individual critics, perhaps informed consensus could be reached. That the method held some appeal for Smith may be inferred from the fact that he conducted his own exercise in ranking, applying it as we have seen to the imitative potential of the several imitative arts. Not only that, but he cited de Piles in substantiation of his conviction that an artist may excel in one or more characteristics of an art without excelling in all. Smith applied this in a more radical way to music, saying that imitation is not essential to the art of music itself, hence not essential either to the merit of a piece of music ("Imitative Arts," ii.32).

---

[11] The table appeared at the end of *The Principles of Painting* (English translation of 1743, from the original French of 1708).

After such exercises in analysis are completed, it still remains to assess the overall impact of a work of art or a performance. Smith, we have seen, attempted this, but in terms of pleasure, for which he lacked an objective standard. At that point he might have withdrawn into the language of aesthetics; instead he subsumed the valuation of pleasure from the arts under the general principles of pricing, here applied explicitly to the services of performing artists. Thus we read that although players, buffoons, and so on produce nothing substantial, yet "[t]he labour of the meanest of these has a certain value, regulated by the very same principles which regulate that of every other sort of labour" (WN, II.iii.2). Those principles Smith set out in Book I, chapter X of *The Wealth of Nations*. We do not need to go into them here; I note merely that for Smith the principles determined the relative rewards of different kinds of labor and involved such elements as cost of training, steadiness of employment, and so on. What is important is that, because the arts in Smith's Britain were to a large extent privately provided and charged for, prevailing rates of pay for artists' services were market rates.[12] Of course, any rate of pay was an average for some whole category of workers, yet it was at times determined directly, and in every other case as part of the mix of costs, fixed and variable, in an overall accounting.[13] Costs, and a sense of demand, determined the prices charged for admission and seating or standing positions, better and worse. Willingness to pay those charges measured the value patrons set on particular performers and a performance. For a patron pleasure was the motive and willingness to pay the measure of satisfaction anticipated.

My conjecture, then, is that Smith deliberately undertook to put the performing arts (and by implication, since they were the

---

[12] The case for this characterization of the arts in eighteenth-century Britain is made in Neil De Marchi and Jonathan A. Greene, "Adam Smith and Private Provision of the Arts." *History of Political Economy* 37/3 (2005). Much relevant material on the point is available in convenient form in John Brewer, *The Pleasures of the Imagination. English Culture in the Eighteenth Century* (London, 1997).

[13] Many sorts of performing artists in eighteenth-century London were paid an annual salary (a fixed cost), plus a percentage of the box office for "benefits" after "charges" were covered; however, the salary was usually broken down into a per performance fee: no performance, no fee (so, in effect, a variable cost). See contract documents in Allardyce Nicoll, *A History of Early Eighteenth Century Drama, 1700–1750* (Cambridge, 1925), pp. 286ff.

least obviously productive, the arts in general) on the same footing as durable, physical products. He did this by showing first that the pleasure we derive from objects follows a common pattern whether due to insubstantial or substantial characteristics of goods. This removed the bias consciously espoused in *The Wealth of Nations* that only durable, physical products are part of productive capital. Second, Smith made a connection between the general principles of pricing and the pricing of artistic services, particularly mentioning in this context the services of performing artists. Pleasure is pleasure, in other words, whatever the character of its cause(s); moreover, pleasure need not be rejected as a measure because it is subjective. Individuals express their anticipated pleasure in their willingness to pay for artistic services, and in well-functioning markets the going rates for such services are a sufficient if approximate indicator of the pleasure they generate.

CONCLUSION: PLACING SMITH'S ESSAY

Smith's essay on the arts has attracted little modern commentary, and that small amount mostly from scholars who view the essay as a contribution to aesthetics.[14] A prominent recent assessment is that the essay is uneven and derivative, with heavy borrowings from Hume in particular, and thus indirectly from the Abbé Dubos.[15] It certainly holds for painting that Smith's remarks are fairly commonplace, except for his notion of imitation. Only his insights on music escape negative judgment.[16] Jones claims that Smith's views had "little if any influence" on subsequent writings.[17]

However, the essay was important to Smith, and this fact creates a dilemma. Either he was mistaken about the significance of this particular enterprise, or his modern critics have missed something.

---

[14] Jones, op. cit.; James S. Malek, "Adam Smith's Contribution to Eighteenth-Century British Aesthetics," *The Journal of Aesthetics and Art Criticism* 31 (1972–3): 49–54.

[15] Jones, "Aesthetics," 58–9, 64, 68–9. See also Jones, "Hume's Literary and Aesthetic Theory," in *The Cambridge Companion to Hume*, ed. David Fate Norton (Cambridge, 1993), pp. 255–80, esp. p. 277.

[16] Malek, p. 49; Jones, "Aesthetics," p. 71.

[17] Jones, "Aesthetics," p. 77.

The view I have taken here is that the essay does not receive its due considered as a contribution to aesthetics. On this point, I have argued that we get a better sense of what Smith was about if we accept that his interest in the imitative arts was to some extent instrumental, that the essay was important to him as part of a larger set of concerns. These last, I urge, had to do with seeing that preference and choice are grounded in (anticipated) pleasure, and with exploring the consequences of that insight.

The nature of the pleasures yielded by the imitative arts certainly dominates in the essay itself, and that is the topic on which Smith spoke when he outlined his ideas to audiences in the 1780s, even if pleasure is not mentioned in the title of the essay. Smith used the essay to put forward a new view of imitation, and with it built a connection back to his analysis of preference in his earlier lectures on jurisprudence, where the causes and pattern of pleasure, imitation among them, were of paramount concern. He showed there that the intensity of our pleasure is independent of whether its cause is insubstantial or substantial.

This connection between the lectures and the essay would be of minor interest if that is all there is. In taking up the essay as he completed the revisions for the second edition of *The Wealth of Nations*, however, it seems likely that Smith was planning to revert to his earlier discussion of the ground of preference for some additional reason. A rationale is available if we think of the essay as offering him a chance to pick up and tie a loose thread left dangling in his treatise on wealth. The thread, I suggest, was the hint, undeveloped in *The Wealth of Nations* itself, that even unproductive labor "has a certain value" (II.iii.2).

That statement might seem to ring hollow set alongside its companion assertion, that even "the noblest and most useful [unproductive labor], produces nothing which could afterwards purchase or procure an equal quantity of labour" (ibid). Moreover, focusing on the arts in a separate essay might have accentuated the distance commonly assumed to exist, then and now, between the arts and commerce – here, the analysis of *The Wealth of Nations* – in a way paralleled by Smith's opposing of beauty to utility in *The Theory of Moral Sentiments*. Recall that there he insisted that fitness "bestows a certain propriety and beauty" that may have little or nothing to do with use ("convenience") (TMS, IV.i.1.).

I have attempted to argue that, certain such appearances notwithstanding, Smith was in fact looking for a way to place the arts – even the performing arts – and productive labor (and its products) on an equal footing. This basis he found in pleasure, the value of which is approximated by the market prices of artistic services in the case of the arts, privately supplied and charged for, as in large part they were in his day. In this way, without undermining the importance of productive labor for growth, Smith made a secure place for the arts.

The case can even be pressed further. Division of labor, vigorously applied, Smith protested, produces individuals of distorted character and mental decrepitude, unable to take an interest in others or in social affairs, unfit to take any decisions and unfit to function in society (WN, V.i.f.50, 61). Exposure to the arts is an important way to counteract these tendencies (V.i.g.15). However, leaving this aside and sticking with pleasure, the conceptual link between the arts, on the one hand, and goods and their accumulation, on the other hand, was solid enough.

Value added captured as pleasure experienced is a common element binding the outputs of productive and unproductive labor. It encompasses pleasures rooted in the objective, physical characteristics of goods and those originating in insubstantial causes, which may result only in a personal and transitory affect. With these realignments of thinking, Smith made the essay on the arts into a counterweight and pendant to *The Wealth of Nations*.

The argument that Smith's essay is a pendant to *The Wealth of Nations* hits a snag in his own incomplete blending of the causes of pleasure and the analysis of the nature of each art. His causes of pleasure do not relate at all well to the non-visual arts. We can connect variety and form with instrumental music, and even color in a metaphorical sense, yet he acknowledges that imitation scarcely applies to them. Again, as Jones has noted, whereas we might expect texture to play a role in the explanation of how statuary pleases, as it might also in painting, this too is missing from Smith's discussion.

That said, some such argument as I have proposed is required if we are to take seriously Smith's regard for his own essay, and the unfinished business of the value of unproductive labor in *The Wealth of Nations*, which jars with his sustained commitment to finding connections between apparently unrelated phenomena. The result of stressing the particular connections adumbrated previously between the arts and productive wealth is that we end up with an enlarged conception of "wealth" as that which has a capacity to please. Consumer choice and, ultimately, division of labor itself are shown to be founded on pleasure. The arts provided Smith with an opportunity to assert these things as general propositions, an opportunity he sensed and gripped firmly.

6 Sympathy and the Impartial Spectator

THE BROAD CONTEXT

For Smith, sympathy cannot be detached from spectatorship, for it is spectators who sympathise. According to the doctrine of sympathy as developed in *The Theory of Moral Sentiments*, sympathy is consequent on a spectator's cognition of a person's feelings or emotions. I therefore begin with the concept of the spectator, and then turn to sympathy and to the relation between the two concepts.

The concept of the spectator, central to Smith's moral philosophy, had already been put to work, within the context of moral philosophical investigations, by both Hutcheson and Hume, and it is plausible to see Smith's writings on the spectator as a development of the work of his older colleagues. That the concept should have held their attention is easily explained. Wanting to pass judgment on whether I have acted well or badly, I have to consult others, for in so far as my judgment is not shaped by the views of others, it may be shaped instead, and therefore distorted, by my self-love or self-interest. At least I cannot be sure that my judgment is not distorted by these motives. Because I want to know what a disinterested judge would say, and because there are evident obstacles to my being a disinterested judge of my own acts, it is necessary for me to turn to others.

In thinking along these lines, Hutcheson and Hume were motivated by philosophical considerations relating to the development of a theory concerning the content of concepts. Arguably, Hutcheson maintains that the concept of a spectator – and here he clearly has in mind the disinterested or impartial spectator – is part of the content of the concept of the "amiability or loveliness of a virtue." He writes:

Virtue is then called Amiable or Lovely, from its raising Good-will or Love in Spectators toward the Agent; and not from the Agent's perceiving the virtuous Temper to be advantageous to him, or desiring to obtain it under that View. A virtuous Temper is called Good or Beatifick ... from this, that every Spectator is persuaded that the reflex Acts of the virtuous Agent upon his own Temper will give him the highest Pleasures.[1]

Hutcheson is not content here to refer only to the agent. The spectator's role is crucial, and indeed there is plainly a sense in which, for Hutcheson, the spectator's judgment has priority over the agent's, for it is in virtue of a fact about the spectator that the agent's temper is called good or beatific.

The spectator resurfaces in Hutcheson's writings in the discussion of merit or worthiness of reward, for he suggests that "Rewardable" denotes "That Quality of Actions which would make a Spectator approve a superior Nature, when he conferred Happiness on the Agent, and disapprove that Superior, who inflicted Misery on the Agent, or punished him."[2] Again there is a sense in which Hutcheson prioritises the spectator's judgment as against that of the agent observed. The intention behind the prioritisation is plain; it is to identify a perspective that has a claim to disinterestedness or impartiality. More than a decade before Hume's *Treatise* was published, therefore, and about three decades before the first edition of *Theory of Moral Sentiments*, seeds of the concept of the impartial spectator had already been sown by Smith's teacher.

Hume's position was also close to Hutcheson's, at least in broad outline, as is plain from many considerations. For example, he distinguishes between, on the one hand, terms such as "enemy" and

[1] *An Inquiry into the Original of Our Ideas of Beauty and Virtue in Two Treatises*, ed. Wolfgang Leidhold (Indianapolis, IN, 2004), p. 218 (*Treatise II*, sect. 1, para. 8), a passage added in the 3rd ed. of 1729. The reflex acts here invoked are the agent's acts of *reflecting* on his temper, for Hutcheson is concerned to make the anti-Hobbesian claim that although there is indeed a close relation between virtue and pleasure, the pleasure is being considered not as a cause of the virtuous temper, but as an effect, in the agent, of his awareness of the virtuousness of his temper. Nevertheless, Hutcheson is not content to refer only to the agent.

[2] *An Essay on the Nature and Conduct of the Passions and Affections, with Illustrations on the Moral Sense*, ed. Aaron Garrett (Indianapolis, IN, 2003), p. 182 (*Illustrations*, sect. v).

"antagonist," with which a person "is understood...to express sentiments, peculiar to himself," and, on the other hand, terms such as "vicious" and "depraved," with which he "expresses sentiments, in which he expects all his audience are to concur with him. He must here, therefore, depart from his private and particular situation, and must choose a point of view, common to him with others."[3] Here, therefore, the distinctive feature of moral terms is that their use implies a perspective shared with others, one that is not self-interested but impartial. Again the spectator's perspective as against the agent's is prioritised. This feature of Hume's moral theory is underlined when he gives as a definition of "virtue": "*whatever mental action or quality gives to a spectator the pleasing sentiment of approbation.*"[4]

By the time Smith began to lecture at Glasgow University, the concept of sympathy, no less than that of the spectator, was firmly on the moral philosophical agenda in the Scottish Enlightenment, chiefly because of the role accorded sympathy by Hutcheson and Hume. For Hutcheson the fact of sympathy was a crucial part of his anti-Hobbesian doctrine that benevolence is natural to humans. By sympathy or compassion,

we are dispos'd to study the Interest of others, without any Views of private Advantage...Every Mortal is made uneasy by any grievous Misery he sees another involv'd in, unless the Person be imagin'd evil, in a moral Sense: Nay, it is almost impossible for us to be unmov'd, even in that Case.[5]

However, while Smith, and indeed Hume, would accept the position just articulated, they must have seen that Hutcheson's teachings on sympathy left a great deal of work to be done, and in particular that he does not tell us in detail what he takes sympathy to be. If the concept is to be allotted a leading role within the context of a system of moral philosophy, it is necessary to have a firm grasp of the concept. Hume and Smith provide details. I give consideration to Hume's position, with a view to providing a basis for a fruitful comparison with Smith's own doctrine.

---

[3] *Enquiry Concerning the Principles of Morals*, IX, Pt.1, in *Enquiries Concerning Human Understanding and Concerning the Principles of Morals*, eds. L. A. Selby-Bigge and P. H. Nidditch (Oxford, 1975), p. 272.

[4] *Enquiry Concerning the Principles of Morals*, App. I, p. 289.

[5] *Inquiry*, p. 159 (II. 5. 8).

First, however, it is necessary to note, although briefly, that the concept of sympathy has a home in several disciplines, and the familiar phrase "sympathetic nervous system" reminds us that it belonged in Graeco-Roman physiology and medicine and in particular figured significantly in Stoic thought. In the Scottish Enlightenment the term was used by physicians both in respect of physiology and physical sickness and also in respect of the psychology of physician/patient relations. For example, James Crawford (d. 1732), for twenty years a teacher of medicine at Edinburgh University, presents a tripartite classification of causes of disease in parts of the body:

That a Part is affected by *Protopathia*, when it is essentially in itself lesed [= diseased], and owes not its Origin to any Communication from another Part. Or by *Idiopathia*, when tho' it be essentially lesed, yet the hurt was at first propagated to it from some other Part. Or lastly, by *Sympathy* or Consent, when the Part in itself is yet whole and sound, and is only affected by the fault of some other Part...Diseases by Consent are propagated from a Distance, (in which case only I shall consider them) either by long Muscles or Nerves.[6]

It has been argued that Hume, while a student at Edinburgh and a member of the Physiology Library[7] (of which Crawford also was a member), might well have been familiar with the medical concept of sympathy,[8] a concept deployed by physiologists to explain how damage and therefore pain in one part of the body can have an effect at a distance in the form of damage and therefore pain in another part of the body. This concept is plainly very similar in form to philosophical concepts of sympathy, under which fall cases in which a feeling of pleasure or pain, or an emotion undergone by one person can have an effect in the form of a like feeling or emotion

---

[6] See James Crawford, "Practical Remarks on the Sympathy of the Parts of the Body by the Late Dr. James Crawford Professor of Medicine in the University of Edinburgh," article XV, in *Medical Essays and Observations, Revised and Published by a Society in Edinburgh*, vol. 5, pt. 2, (1744); quoted in Laurence B. McCullough, *John Gregory and the Invention of Professional Medical Ethics and the Profession of Medicine* (Dordrecht, 1998), p. 50.

[7] For details of the library, see Michael Barfoot, "Hume and the Culture of Science in the Early Eighteenth Century," in *Studies in the Philosophy of the Scottish Enlightenment*, ed. M. A. Stewart (Oxford, 1990), pp. 151–90, esp. pp. 150–60.

[8] McCullough, *Gregory*, 52.

in someone at a distance. I do not spell out further parallels here, but proceed instead to a discussion of Hume's philosophical analysis of sympathy.[9]

Although Hume occasionally uses "sympathy" to refer to a feeling, the whole weight of his exposition is to see sympathy as a principle of communication, not only of feelings, but also of opinions; however, it is with the communication of feelings that I am concerned. Because as a result of the communication the spectator might share the agent's feeling of dismay, anger, joy, or delight, it is wrong to understand Hume's "sympathy" as compassion or pity. The term is a technical one for Hume, not least because it is deeply imbedded in his philosophy of impressions and ideas, and it has to be understood on that basis. It should perhaps be added that its technical nature does not imply that the term is further adrift of the common meaning than is Smithian sympathy. Indeed, as we will see, Smith employs the Humean terminology of impressions and ideas in the exposition of his own concept of sympathy.

The spectator observes in the countenance and conversation of the agent qualities that he takes to signify a given passion or feeling, and in doing so he forms an idea of that feeling. "This idea is presently converted into an impression, and acquires such a degree of force and vivacity, as to become the very passion itself, and produce an equal emotion, as any original affection."[10] The spectator's idea of the agent's passion does not of course always become so vivid as to attain the status of a real passion. Hume, emphasising the role of the relations of resemblance, contiguity, and causation, which relate spectator and agent, explains why the process of vivification of the idea of a passion sometimes occurs and sometimes does not. He explains, that is, why it is that sometimes the spectator sympathises with the agent and sometimes does not.

However, what has to be attended to here is the fact that the spectator's sympathetically acquired passion is acquired by means of the observation of those features or acts of the agent that the spectator interprets as signifying the passion. If the spectator does not believe the agent to have a given passion, then he does not

---

[9] For detailed discussion of Enlightenment concepts of sympathy, medical and philosophical, see especially Lisbeth Haakonssen, *Medicine and Morals in the Enlightenment: John Gregory, Thomas Percival and Benjamin Rush* (Amsterdam, 1997).

[10] *A Treatise of Human Nature*, eds. David Fate Norton and Mary J. Norton (Oxford, 2000), Book II, Part 1, Section 11.

sympathise with the agent because Humean sympathy is essentially a principle of communication by which the spectator comes to have a passion that he believes the agent to have and he comes to have it because of this belief. Precisely this doctrine of Hume's is rejected by Smith, who holds on the contrary that it is possible for a spectator sympathetically to have a passion that he does not believe the agent to have, or even that he knows the agent cannot have. There are, then, significant differences between Hume's concept of sympathy and Smith's, which is not of course to deny that there are also significant similarities. I turn now to Smith's concept.

SMITH'S CONCEPT OF SYMPATHY

It is our imagination that does most of the work. We, as spectators, on seeing the agent suffer, form in our imagination a copy of such "impressions of our own senses" as we have experienced when we have been in a situation of the kind the agent is in. We "form some idea of his sensations" and even feel something "which, though weaker in degree, is not altogether unlike them," and we do this by means of the imaginative experiment of placing ourselves in the agent's circumstance: "we enter as it were into his body, and become in some measure the same person with him" (TMS, I.i.1.2). This last point, that we "become in some measure the same person with the agent," is a crucial part of the case that can be made in defence of Smith against Thomas Reid's criticism that Smith's is essentially a "selfish" system, "selfish" given that the baseline in the formation of a moral judgment about a person's attitude or behaviour is how *I* would feel if *I* were in that person's shoes.[11] For Smith stresses that in sympathising, the spectator imagines not being himself in the agent's situation but being the *agent* in that situation: "But though sympathy is very properly said to arise from an imaginary change of situations with the person principally concerned, yet this imaginary change is not supposed to happen to me in my own person and character, but in that of the person with whom I sympathize." If I sympathetically grieve with you in your bereavement my "grief ... is entirely upon your account, and not in the least upon my own. It is not, therefore, in the least selfish"

---

[11] See J. C. Stewart-Robertson and David F. Norton, "Thomas Reid on Adam Smith's Theory of Morals," *Journal of the History of Ideas* 41 (1980): 381–98, and 45 (1984): 309–21.

(TMS, VII.iii.1.4).[12] I do not mean to imply that this can be taken as an effective rebuttal of Reid's criticism, but only to point out that Smith was well aware of the likelihood of an attack from that direction.

The feeling that the spectator comes to have by these means is not necessarily one of pity or compassion; it may instead be of delight or happiness or, indeed, any passion whatever. Thus, in the *Lectures on Rhetoric and Belles Lettres*, Smith deals explicitly with the power that a historian has to produce a wide range of sympathetic responses in the reader: "We enter into their [*sc.* human beings'] misfortunes, grieve when they grieve, rejoice when they rejoice, and in a word feel for them in some respect as if we ourselves were in the same condition" (LRBL, 90). Smith reserves the term "sympathy" for "our fellow-feeling for any passion whatever," and emphasises the fact that he is extending the scope of the term. "Sympathy" is therefore to be understood as a technical term in Smith's system, and misunderstandings can, and do, arise when his particular account of it is ignored.

Sympathy, ordinarily understood, is one feeling or emotion among many and resembles pity or compassion. However, as Smith uses "sympathy," the spectator's anger would count as sympathy *qua* fellow-feeling with the agent's anger, and his joy, qua fellow-feeling with the agent's joy, would likewise count as sympathy, and so on for all the spectator's emotions. It is perhaps more appropriate, therefore, to think of sympathy as an adverbial modification of a given feeling, in the sense that the term indicates the way that the spectator has the feeling – he has it *sympathetically*. It is the way he is angry, or is joyful, and so on. In that sense, Smithian sympathy has a kind of universality that has to be contrasted with the singularity of each feeling (including the feeling of sympathy in the non-Smithian sense).

The foregoing points are sufficient to resolve the so-called "Adam Smith Problem," which takes as its starting point the claim that Smith bases his moral philosophy on the motive of sympathy and his economic theory on the motive of self-interest. Indeed, if the claim is correct, an account is certainly required of how *The Theory of Moral Sentiments* and *The Wealth of Nations* can

---

[12] Cf. Charles L. Griswold, *Adam Smith and the Virtues of Enlightenment* (Cambridge, 1999), pp. 90–6.

be squared with each other. Might the two books simply contradict each other? Yet, in 1762, a year after the second edition of *The Theory of Moral Sentiments* and five years before the third, Smith was lecturing on the material that grew into *The Wealth of Nations*.[13] The economic theory was developed therefore within the context of a moral theory that goes wide and deep, a context that carries the message that an economic theory has to be developed within a moral philosophical framework. It is incredible that Smith should forget his moral theory while expounding his economic ideas in the course of an exposition of the moral theory, and incredible also that he should not forget the moral theory but instead simply fail to notice the contradiction. H. T. Buckle's solution is that our nature has two aspects, one sympathetic and the other selfish, these being exhaustive, and in *The Theory of Moral Sentiments*, Smith investigates one, in *The Wealth of Nations*, the other.[14] However, this interpretation rests on a mistake. For Smith, sympathy is not the motive for moral action nor indeed is it a motive at all. The contrast between sympathy and self-interest, considered as two sorts of motive, is therefore ill founded.[15]

The claim that sympathy has a universality not possessed by any of the particular feelings can also be made of sympathy in the Humean sense, to this extent, that if the spectator has a given feeling as a result of the operation of the mechanism of sympathy, then the feeling he has is the one he believes the agent to have, no matter what that feeling is. So in sympathising with the agent's anger or joy, he himself also has anger or joy. In that respect, knowledge of the spectator's sympathy does not imply knowledge of the spectator's feeling but, rather, knowledge of the way he came by the feeling. This is not to say that it is wrong to think of Humean sympathy as a feeling. The point is that it is a feeling to which the mechanism of sympathetic communication has made an essential contribution. That feeling is sympathy, or is a sympathetic feeling, which

---

[13] TMS, editors' Introduction, 38–9. Cf. Ian S. Ross, *The Life of Adam Smith* (Oxford, 1995), pp. 122–3.

[14] H. T. Buckle, *History of Civilization in England* (London, 1861), vol. 2, chapter 6.

[15] There is a large body of literature on this topic. See TMS, editors' Introduction, 20–4; Laurence Dickey, "Historicizing the 'Adam Smith Problem': Conceptual, Historiographical, and Textual Issues," *Journal of Modern History* 58 (1986): 579–609, reprinted in *Adam Smith*, ed. Knud Haakonssen (Dartmouth, NH, 1998), pp. 457–87.

has been produced by the operation of the mechanism. Hume uses the term "sympathy" to refer both to the sympathetic feeling and also to the mechanism by which the feeling is generated. The same is true of Smith.

At first sight, Smith's account of sympathy seems very Humean, even his vocabulary, which invokes a contrast between the *impressions* of the spectator's senses and the *idea* that the spectator forms of the agent's feelings. However, a feature of sympathy to which Smith frequently refers, and which is demonstrably crucial to his account, seems not to form part of Hume's account: "By the imagination we place ourselves in his [*sc.* the agent's] situation," and sympathy "does not arise so much from the view of the passion, as from that of the situation which excites it" (TMS, I.i.1.2, 10).[16] It is plausible to suppose that Smith has Hume in his sights. On Hume's account, sympathy arises precisely from the spectator's view of the agent's passion and he does not discuss the agent's situation. Instead, all that we learn is that the spectator's perception of signs of the agent's passion results in the same passion in the spectator; the impression causes an idea of the agent's passion, and the spectator's idea of the agent's passion becomes so enlivened as to be a passion in the spectator. In contrast, emphasis on the situation of the agent leads Smith to downplay the significance of the spectator's perception of the agent's passion in the formation of the spectator's sympathetic feeling. Indeed, emphasis on the situation leads Smith to say that the spectator may sympathise with the agent even though he, the spectator, does not have the same feeling as the agent. This is clearly a radical departure from Hume's position.

Some of Smith's examples of sympathy fit the Humean prescription quite well. He writes:

Upon some occasions sympathy may seem to arise merely from the view of a certain emotion in another person.... Grief and joy, for example, strongly expressed in the look and gestures of any one, at once affect the spectator with some degree of a like painful or agreeable emotion. (TMS, I.6)

Here, evidently, the progression is from the spectator's impression to an idea of the agent's passion, and thence to that same passion in

---

[16] See Knud Haakonssen, *The Science of a Legislator* (Cambridge, 1981), pp. 46–9, for discussion of the significance of these statements.

the spectator. Admittedly, Smith does not here mention the intermediate idea, but he had previously told us (TMS, I.i.1.2) that it is via an idea of the agent's passion that the spectator comes to have that very passion. However, he adds immediately that what holds for grief and joy does not hold universally, and in effect Smith thereby criticises Hume for treating passions such as grief and joy as typical of all passions when in fact they are exceptions. Mere expression of anger is not sufficient to arouse sympathy. It is necessary to know first the situation of the angry person, in particular the causal factors of his anger. If however, we know the situation of those with whom he is angry, the situation being the violence to which they may be exposed by the enraged person, we are if anything inclined to sympathise with them instead. Indeed, for Smith knowledge of the situation plays a role even in the case of grief and joy because the expressions of those passions suggest to us the general idea of some good or bad fortune that has befallen the agent, and without this concept of the situation of the agent, the spectator would not sympathise with him. However, sympathy with a grieving person would not, even if accompanied with this general idea, lead to much sympathy. The agent's lamentations "create rather a curiosity to inquire into his situation . . . than any actual sympathy that is very sensible" (TMS, I.i.1.9).

The fact that knowledge of the situation is factored into the account of sympathy is therefore demonstrable. It has to be noted however that while knowledge of the situation plays a leading role in the spectator's sympathetic reaction, the agent's own feelings often play a correspondingly insignificant role, and in some cases can play no role at all in view of the fact that the agent does not have the feeling that the spectator has sympathetically for the agent. Smith presents two spectacular examples of a sympathetic feeling which does not correspond to the agent's own. The first concerns the agent who has lost his reason. The spectator's sympathetic feeling of sorrow for the agent is not matched by the agent's own feeling because he is, on the contrary, happy, being blissfully unaware of the tragedy that has befallen him. In this case the spectator considers how he himself would feel if he were reduced to the same unhappy situation. In this imaginative experiment, in which the spectator is operating on the brink of a contradiction, the main point, for the moment, is that the idea of the agent's situation plays a large role, whereas the idea of the agent's feelings has a role only in the sense that the happiness of the agent is itself evidence of his tragedy. Smith's second example is the spectator's sympathy for the dead. Here the spectator, again operating on the brink of contradiction, has sympathetic feelings which are plainly not matched by the agent's own feelings. Again Smith invokes explicitly the agent's situation, emphasising the fact that the spectator comes to sympathise by imagining himself in the agent's situation, and imagining how he himself would feel if so situated.

It is in light of the conceptual structure of these examples that we should interpret Smith's statement that "sympathy" may "without much impropriety" be made use of to denote "our fellow-feeling for any passion whatever." The term "fellow-feeling" evidently has to be treated as a technical term in *Theory of Moral Sentiments* just like "sympathy." The existence of fellow-feeling does not imply that two people have feelings of the same kind, even though in many cases, perhaps in cases which are in some sense standard, the spectator and the agent do have feelings of the same kind, that is, the spectator shares the agent's feeling. Of course, in ordinary usage my fellow-feeling for you is my commiserating with your sorrow and my rejoicing at your joy, and in this respect Smithian sympathy is even less like sympathy ordinarily understood than is Humean sympathy, for in the case of Humean sympathy a sympathetic feeling is a fellow-feeling at least in the sense that it is shared – spectator and agent both have it.

Yet it is difficult to say that Smithian sympathy is not really sympathy, citing the fact that Smithian sympathy does not necessarily involve shared feelings for, as already emphasised, it is a technical term, and Smith is free to stipulate its meaning. According to that stipulated meaning, sympathy is of such a nature that it is possible to sympathise with a person who has lost his mind but is happy, and it is also possible to sympathise with the dead. We might think it very odd to speak of sympathising with such persons (if a dead person is still a person), and Smith acknowledges this. However, that oddity lies in the seemingly contradictory mental posture in which the living and rational spectator imagines himself in the agent's situation and therefore imagines himself to be not rational or not even alive.

Smith uses several expressions to indicate what it is that the spectator does that results in his sympathetic feeling. "We enter as it were into his [sc. the agent's] body"; we "become in some measure the same person with him"; "it is by changing places in fancy with the sufferer"; the spectator, by "bringing the case home to himself," imagines what should be the sentiments of the sufferer; "we put ourselves in his case." All these phrases point to the strangeness of Smith's concept of sympathy with the dead. I stress the point because for Smith a great deal depends on the "illusion of the imagination" involved in this particular sort of act of sympathy. "From thence arises," he affirms, "one of the most important principles in human nature, the dread of death, the great poison to the happiness, but the great restraint upon the injustice of mankind, which, while it afflicts and mortifies the individual, guards and protects the society" (TMS, I.i.1.13).

In the phrase just quoted, "we enter as it were into his body," the "as it were" has to be given due weight, as has "in some measure" in "we become in some measure the same person." Even in the case where there is fellow-feeling in the sense that the spectator shares the agent's feeling, the spectator's feeling is significantly different in that it is a product of an imaginative act that not only brought the feeling into existence but that also sustains it. The spectator's sympathetic suffering, for example, is due not to his actually being in the situation he sees the agent in, but to his being sympathetic. He has not actually suffered the bereavement, the injury, or the insult as the agent has done. He is only imagining how he would feel if he had done so, and in consequence the imaginative act "excites some degree of the same emotion, in proportion to the vivacity or dulness of the conception" (TMS, I.i.1.2).

The difference between the two sides of fellow-feeling is acknowledged by Smith as a matter of great practical importance: "What they [the spectators] feel, will, indeed, always be, in some respects, different from what he [the agent] feels, and compassion can never be exactly the same with original sorrow; because the secret consciousness that the change of situations, from which the sympathetic sentiment arises, is but imaginary, not only lowers it in degree, but, in some measure, varies it in kind, and gives it a quite different modification" (TMS, I.i.4.8).[17] The correspondence,

---

[17] Cf. TMS, I.i.4.7: "The thought of their [sc. the spectators'] own safety, the thought that they themselves are not really the sufferers, continually intrudes itself upon them; and ... hinders them from conceiving any thing that approaches to the same degree of violence."

although imperfect, is however "sufficient for the harmony of society" and "this is all that is wanted or required." Smith, here, as always, has the larger picture in mind.

SYMPATHY AND PLEASURE

So far I focus on sympathy as something explicable in terms of natural causation. However, Smith believes that even though some cases of sympathising are explicable in such terms, many are not. The starting point is the fact (as Smith believes) that sympathy always gives pleasure. Smith believes that "nothing pleases us more than to observe in other men a fellow-feeling with all the emotions of our own breast" (TMS, I.i.2.1). If an agent suffers, the awareness of a spectator's sympathy brings him relief by admixing with the original suffering the pleasure afforded by the sympathy, and if the agent is happy, then a spectator's sympathetic joy enhances or heightens that happiness by adding to the original happiness the pleasure afforded by the sympathetic joy. It appears to be pleasure that links sympathy with approval or approbation. We learn that for the spectator to approve of the agent's feeling is for him to observe that he sympathises with the agent, and for him to disapprove is to observe that he does not sympathise (I.i.3.1), in which case approbation should perhaps be classed as a judgment, *pace* Hume for whom it is a feeling. It should be added that Smith's position appears to be revised shortly thereafter when he speaks of approbation not as an observation but as a feeling: "This last emotion, in which the sentiment of approbation properly consists, is alway agreeable and delightful" (I.iii.1.9, note). The settled doctrine, however, so far as discernible, is that it is not a sentiment but an observation or judgment.

Where we observe disagreement, we are motivated to see whether the disagreement can be smoothed out. It is as if by our nature we find it disagreeable to disagree. The efforts a spectator makes to modify his sentiments so they agree with the agent's may be hard work; he must "endeavour, as much as he can, to put himself in the situation of the other," he must "strive to render as perfect as possible, that imaginary change of situation upon which his sympathy is founded" (TMS, I.i.4.6); a person's "natural feeling of his own distress, his own natural view of his own situation, presses hard upon him, and he cannot, without a very

great effort, fix his attention upon that of the impartial spectator"
(TMS, III.3.28). It has been maintained that it was Smith's awareness of the effort we may have to make to secure agreement, or at
least to determine whether agreement is possible, that led him to
stress the pleasure associated with sympathy.[18] Simply stated, if
we know that the effort will bring reward in the form of pleasure,
or enhanced pleasure, we are more strongly motivated to make the
effort. However, although this is part of the explanation of our willingness to make the effort, another part that is possibly much more
significant for Smith concerns moral considerations of fairness to
the agent, in light of the possibility that his feelings may be more
appropriate than we had first supposed. Whatever love of our neighbour may be it is at least a willingness to make the effort to see
things from our neighbour's point of view and Smith sees this as
a Christian stance. Nevertheless, even if the duty to exercise this
Christian virtue is a major part of the motivation for the exercise of
our sympathetic imagination, it is undeniable that Smith insists on
the close relation between pleasure and sympathy, and I therefore
have to consider the relation in detail.

It will be helpful to compare Smith's position to that of Hume,
who is also interested in the relation between sympathy and pleasure. One reason is his idea that the spectator's moral approval
of the agent arises from his sympathy with the pleasure of the
person acted on. Here Smith diverges significantly from Hume
who accounts for sympathy, as already indicated, in terms of natural causation and the principles of association of impressions
and ideas. Smith, in contrast, stresses the role of will as against
nature. Perhaps the spectator does not naturally sympathise with
the agent, and it is by will rather than by nature that he seeks a
way to iron out the disagreement. Of course, Hume, no less than
Smith, writes of the process by which we modify sympathetic feelings,[19] and, indeed, such processes of modification are essential to
Hume's account of the genesis of moral judgment. Smith factors
these modifications into the process of sympathy itself; for Hume
they occur after the mechanism of sympathy has already done
its work.

---

[18] See Eugene Heath, "The Commerce of Sympathy: Adam Smith on the Emergence
of Morals," *Journal of the History of Philosophy* 33 (1995): 447–66.
[19] *Enquiry Concerning the Principles of Morals*, 227–8.

Smith's claim that sympathetic feeling is agreeable for the spectator who has it, and no less agreeable for the agent who discovers that someone sympathises with him, is plausible as a generalisation. Whether the claim is universally true is less certain. There are occasions when the spectator will derive pleasure from the observation of the agreement of his feelings with those of the agent, where the pleasure is the pleasure of relief. The agreement is seen by the spectator as, so to say, validating his own position and reinforcing his judgment. However, observation of agreement between spectator and agent does not always cause pleasure. The spectator may be mortified to find himself in agreement with the agent, for the sympathetic feeling that has come upon the spectator by purely natural means, and therefore without the aid of will, might make him wonder whether he has, say, a racist or some other deplorable attitude. In such a case, which seems a perfectly credible one, sympathy is associated with pain on the side of the spectator and prompts a reexamination of his values.

Smith might reply by distinguishing between the pleasure of sympathy and the pain of an unpleasant self-realisation. The sympathy is related, although in different ways, to both the pleasure and the pain. The pleasure is internally related to the sympathetic feeling in the sense that, given "the original constitution of his frame" (TMS, III.3.9), it is not possible for him to have the sympathy unaccompanied by pleasure. However, discovery of the sympathetic nature of the feeling leads the spectator to see something disagreeable in his character, something the sight of which pains him, and perhaps pains him so much that the pain overwhelms the pleasure, leaving the latter barely detectable.

Smith draws a distinction rather close to the one just deployed to deal with a criticism famously made by Hume in a letter to Smith:

I wish you had more particularly and fully prov'd, that all kinds of Sympathy are necessarily Agreeable. This is the Hinge of your System, & yet you only mention the matter cursorily in p. 20.[20] Now it woud appear that there is a disagreeable Sympathy, as well as an agreeable: And indeed, as the Sympathetic Passion is a reflex Image of the Principal, it must partake of its

[20] Hume here indicates TMS, I.i.2.6: "As the person who is principally interested in any event is pleased with our sympathy, and hurt by the want of it, so we, too, seem to be pleased when we are able to sympathise with him, and to be hurt when we are unable to do so. We run not only to congratulate the successful, but to condole with the afflicted."

Qualities, & be painful where that is so. Indeed, *when we converse with a man with whom we can entirely sympathize*, that is, where there is a warm & intimate Friendship, the cordial openness of such a Commerce overpowers the Pain of a disagreeable Sympathy, and renders the whole Movement agreeable. But in ordinary Cases, this cannot have place. An ill-humord Fellow; a man tir'd & disgusted with every thing, always *ennuié*; sickly, complaining, embarass'd; such a one throws an evident Damp on Company, which I suppose wou'd be accounted for by Sympathy; and yet is disagreeable. It is always thought a difficult Problem to account for the Pleasure, receivd from the Tears & Grief & Sympathy of Tragedy; which would not be the Case, if all Sympathy was agreeable. An Hospital woud be a more entertaining Place than a Ball.[21]

In the second edition of *Theory of Moral Sentiments*, published in 1761, two years after receipt of Hume's letter, Smith replies to Hume by making a distinction:

I answer, that in the sentiment of approbation there are two things to be taken notice of; first, the sympathetic passion of the spectator; and, secondly, the emotion which arises from his observing the perfect coincidence between this sympathetic passion in himself, and the original passion in the person principally concerned. This last emotion, in which the sentiment of approbation properly consists, is always agreeable and delightful. The other may either be agreeable or disagreeable, according to the nature of the original passion, whose feature it must always, in some measure, retain. (TMS, I.iii.1.9, note)

The distinction that Smith here makes is clear and evidently fully justified. Surely there is a real distinction between, on the one hand, the feeling that the spectator has that is the "reflex Image" of the agent's and, on the other hand, the spectator's feeling that arises from his observation of the perfect coincidence of his feeling with that of the agent. However, would Smith's reply have cut any ice with Hume? I believe Smith's claim to have "entirely discomfitted" him is almost certainly false.[22] For Smith's rebuttal

---

[21] J. Y. T. Greig, ed., *The Letters of David Hume*, 2 vols. (Oxford, 1932), vol. 1, pp. 311–14, at p. 313. The letter is dated 28 July 1759, some three months after the publication of the first edition of the TMS.

[22] In a letter to Gilbert Elliot, dated 10 October 1759 (Corr., 49). For valuable discussion on these matters see David R. Raynor, "Hume's Abstract of Adam Smith's *Theory of Moral Sentiments*," *Journal of the History of Philosophy* 22 (1984): 51–79. Simon Blackburn also sides with Hume against Smith on this matter. See his *Ruling Passions: A Theory of Practical Reasoning* (Oxford 1998), pp. 202–4, esp. fn. 6.

begs the question, namely whether observation of agreement gives rise to an agreeable feeling. Smith's reply simply states that it does. Yet Hume has already said that "in ordinary Cases, this cannot have Place," and gives as an example an ill-humoured person, always *ennuié*, who throws an evident damp on company, which is to be accounted for by sympathy, and yet the spectators in the company do not derive any pleasure whatever from observing the agreement in feelings. By implication, Hume is accusing Smith of treating an exceptional case as if it is typical of all cases. The exceptional case in question is that in which a person sympathises with a friend. In such cases it might well be, as a matter of empirical fact, that the spectator's observation of agreement of feeling with his friend, the agent, gives rise to pleasure. However, in the case of friendship, a good deal of baggage comes along within the relationship which might easily explain why sympathy is associated in a special way with pleasure. Yet, what of cases where the spectator is not on friendly terms with the agent, and perhaps even dislikes him? Smith, in Hume's view, is silently assuming the agent is indeed a friend of the spectator.

If Hume is right in regard to this particular example, then Smith cannot be right in saying that the emotion which arises from observation of the agreement in feelings is *always* agreeable. Hume plainly believes the issue can be settled by empirical means, and it is difficult to believe Smith would disagree. He is not simply stipulating usage for the term "sympathy"; he is telling us how things are and must say what is wrong with Hume's counterexample. Nor is Smith's case defended effectively by pointing out that his concept of sympathy is significantly different from the one Hume develops in the *Treatise*. First, it is highly unlikely that Hume, having read *Theory of Moral Sentiments*, would then make the methodologically flawed move of attacking Smith's account of sympathy on the basis of a concept of sympathy that is not Smith's. Secondly, it is in any case difficult to see how Smith, even on his own terms, can deal plausibly with Hume's counterexample.

SYMPATHY AND MORAL CATEGORIES

One important matter at stake is our motivation to strive for coincidence of feeling. I turn to this striving and therefore to

Smith's discussions of propriety, impropriety, merit, and demerit, and his account of the impartial spectator. The systematic relations between propriety and impropriety on the one side, and merit and demerit on the other, are expounded in detail in *Theory of Moral Sentiments*.

A natural desire both to approve and to be approved of has the consequence that sympathy must be of such a nature as to be able to operate within an essentially dynamic social context. Where a spectator's immediate reaction to an agent's behaviour is not one of approval, he does not necessarily let the matter rest there. It may be that Hume's interest in the distinction between an agent who is a friend and one who is not may be pertinent here because the spectator's natural tendency may well be to leave his disapproval in place if the agent is an enemy or at least not a friend. For, setting aside obvious qualifications, it is easier to think ill of one's enemies than to think well of them, and on the contrary, if a friend's behaviour prompts an immediate reaction of disapproval, the spectator's natural tendency is to determine whether the agent's behaviour was as improper or inappropriate as it seemed at first. If, in the latter case, the spectator will naturally move to see whether the disagreement can be ironed out, then in the former case, he will move (if at all) in light of the moral injunction to be fair. In both cases, however, his tactic is the same – by an exercise of informed imagination, to fit himself as well as he can into the situation of the agent, and see whether there are features of that situation that he overlooked initially. The spectator's question, "What is he seeing that I am failing to see?" can therefore lead to a change not only in his perspective but also in his feelings.

This imaginative process is a critique, in the sense of "critical analysis," where the analysis is made by the spectator with a view to determining whether his initial reaction was appropriate and with a view also to improving that reaction if the spectator judges it to have been inappropriate. Two basic concepts of the Enlightenment, therefore, critique and improvement, underlie Smith's account of the spectator. The element of critique in the spectator's acts of judgment becomes even more significant in the impartial spectator's acts, so much so that it is possible to portray Smith's impartial spectator as a hero of the Enlightenment. We turn to that shortly.

Smith provides telling examples of a spectator asking himself: "What is he seeing that I am not?" He considers the case in which we no longer derive amusement from a book or poem, but take pleasure in reading the work to another person: "we consider all the ideas which it presents rather in the light in which they appear to him, than in that in which they appear to ourselves, and we are amused by sympathy with his amusement which enlivens our own" (TMS, 14). A variation on this idea is to be found in his *Lectures on Rhetoric and Belles Lettres* (LRBL, 90), where he considers the interesting fact that it is possible to read a tragedy repeatedly, yet without the play palling, and this despite the fact that the suspense is essential to the play. Smith's explanation is that although the play is not new to us who have read it many times, the dramatic events, as they unfold, are new to the *dramatis personae*, and we readers place ourselves in their shoes and see the unfolding sequence through their eyes. They do not know what the gods have in store for them, and so, in imagination, neither do we. Likewise, in reacting to the agent's display of feeling, where those are not the feelings that the spectator approves of or thinks appropriate in those circumstances, the spectator asks himself questions that probe the agent's intentions and motives and his beliefs about his circumstances. By such means the agent might, for example, decide that he himself would have acted in the same way, and his disapproval of the agent's act might then be replaced by approval, or his initial weak approval might be greatly strengthened so that it approaches the agent's own feelings about the act.

There is here a parallel with the sequence of surprise, wonder, and admiration that Smith discusses at length in his "History of Astronomy" (sections i–ii). First, we are surprised at a natural event or object, we then wonder about it, wonder why the event happened or what class of thing the object is, and at last, having answered the scientific question, the new insight into not only the rich diversity, but also the tightly knit unity of things, makes us admire God's creation the more. In many cases that come under the heading of sympathetic imagination, the spectator is first surprised at the agent's behaviour, then wonders at it, works toward a resolution of the problem by carrying out the psychological experiment of imagining himself into the agent's shoes, and having done so comes to understand the agent's behaviour, and so comes to admire the agent's behaviour instead of disapproving of it as previously. There are of course significant differences between the two sorts of case, most especially the fact that our admiration of the agent's behaviour comes after the exercise of our sympathetic imagination, and in contrast the scientist exercises an imagination which cannot be sympathetic in so far as the object under scientific study does not have mental states into which the scientific spectator can enter sympathetically. However, despite this, there is an evident parallel.

In *The Theory of Moral Sentiments* Smith invokes surprise, wonder, and admiration, and it is past belief that he was not aware of the parallel with the sequence he deploys in his exposition of the psychology of scientific discovery.[23] In both cases the spectator is not a merely passive onlooker, staring out stupidly on the world. Unlike the term "sympathy," "spectator" is not introduced in *The Theory of Moral Sentiments* as a technical term, nor is it defined. However, it is plain that the spectator who matters to Smith is a thoughtful, critical observer, directed by virtuous considerations, whether of the intellectual sort or some other, and seeking to understand. Both processes can end in admiration, but there is an added dimension in the case of the moral agent, for the spectator qua moral agent can effect a change in the person whom he observes by revealing to the person his reaction to him. In having the resources to make a constructive response to the spectator's response to him, the agent is of course utterly unlike the sun, moon, and stars. The astronomer does not effect change in the celestial phenomena.

A main reason for the spectator's ability to effect a change is the other's desire to be approved of. For while the spectator seeks to approve, the agent seeks his approval, and if he sees that he will be judged to have feelings which are excessive (or deficient) in relation to his situation, he will engage in an exercise that corresponds rather precisely to the spectator's in relation to him. For he will

---

[23] TMS, I.i.4.3; I.i.1.12. It is probable that the material in the "History of Astronomy" on surprise, wonder and admiration, was composed before Smith began work on the TMS, perhaps long before during Smith's days as a student at Oxford. He may have completed the work in Kirkcaldy immediately after Oxford. See especially EPS, editor's Introduction, pp. 5–9; also Ian S. Ross, *The Life of Adam Smith*, 99.

seek to see his own situation through the eyes of the spectator, and he might then for the first time grasp the real significance of previously noted features of his situation. In light of these new perceptions, gained by an exercise of his creative imagination, his feelings will naturally change, probably toward conformity with the feelings of the spectator. Disagreement in feeling will be transformed into agreement, and in effect each will come to sympathise with the other. Sympathy will be mutual.

This account of the contrivance of mutual sympathy is suggestive of Smith's famous sequence of "truck, barter and exchange" in *The Wealth of Nations*. Two people meet and disagree about the worth of their goods; they haggle, with each edging the other closer to his own valuation; finally, they reach an agreement and the exchange is effected. Likewise spectator and agent approach each other, with the spectator disagreeing with the agent about the propriety of the agent's feelings on some matter. Each then modifies his own judgment and consequent feeling in the direction of the other, until the judgments and consequent feelings are in line with each other. Consensus is achieved, the product of mutual accommodation.

The spectator's judgment of the propriety of the agent's sentiment is either to be identified with the spectator's approval of the agent's sentiment or is an intellectual act in conformity with that approval; however, in either case it is a product of interaction between spectator and agent. Smith devotes no less attention to a trilateral relation, between a spectator, an agent who acts on someone, and the person who is acted on, to whom I refer as the "recipient" (in preference to "patient" – although the latter, in its old-fashioned sense as correlative with "agent," is more accurate even if loaded with unhelpful connotations). The recipient's response to the agent's act may be of several kinds. Smith focuses on two, a grateful and a resentful.

If the spectator judges that the recipient's gratitude is proper or appropriate, then he approves of the agent's act as meritorious or worthy of reward. If he judges the recipient's resentment proper or appropriate, then he disapproves of the agent's act as demeritorious or worthy of punishment. Judgments of merit or demerit concerning a person's act are therefore made on the basis of an antecedent judgment concerning the propriety or impropriety of another person's reaction to that act. Sympathy underlies all these judgments because, in the cases just mentioned, the spectator sympathises with the recipient's gratitude and with his resentment. He has direct sympathy with the affections and motives of the agent and indirect sympathy with the recipient's gratitude, or judging the agent's behaviour improper, the spectator has indirect sympathy with the agent's resentment (TMS, II.i.5.1–2).

In each of the cases just considered we have supposed that the recipient really does have the feeling in question, whether of gratitude or of resentment. However, the spectator's belief about what the recipient actually feels about the agent is not important for the spectator's judgment concerning the merit and demerit of the agent. The recipient may, for whatever reason, resent an act that was kindly intentioned and in all other ways admirable, and the spectator, knowing the situation better than the recipient, puts himself imaginatively in the shoes of the recipient while taking with him into this spectatorial role information about the agent's behaviour that the recipient lacks. The spectator judges that in the recipient's situation he would be grateful for the agent's act; on that basis, and independently of the recipient's actual reaction, he approves of the agent's act and judges it meritorious. Here the spectator regards himself as a better (because better informed) spectator of the agent's act than the recipient is.

In regard to judgments of merit and demerit, therefore, although Smith sets up a model of three people, the three differ in respect to the weight that has to be given to their work. In an important sense the recipient does almost nothing. He is acted on by the agent, but apart from that he is, so to say, no more than a placeholder for the spectator who will imaginatively occupy that place and make a judgment concerning merit or demerit on the basis solely of his conception of how he would respond to the agent if he were in the place of the recipient, and he does not judge on the basis of the actual reaction of the recipient, who might approve of the agent's act or disapprove or have no feelings about it one way or the other.

THE IMPARTIAL SPECTATOR

As with judgments of propriety so with judgments of merit, there is a real person into whose shoes the spectator imaginatively places himself. However, in the case to which I now turn, there seems not to be. In situations with two or three persons, one person judges another, but how is he to know what to think of his own acts? In judging of the other, the spectator has the advantage of disinterest but may lack requisite information, and the creative imagination has to rectify the lack. In judging himself he has, or may be presumed to have, the information but has to overcome self-love or self-interest. He does this by imagining a spectator, an *other* who observes him at a distance. Distance creates the possibility of disinterest, but how is it actually achieved if the spectator is the creature of the agent's imagination?

Who or what is imagined into existence? Is it the voice of society, the representative of established social attitudes? At times in the first edition of *The Theory of Moral Sentiments* Smith comes close to saying this; and in a letter to Smith, Sir Gilbert Elliot interpreted him in that way. As a consequence, the second edition is rather clearer that this is not the role of the impartial spectator for the latter can, and occasionally does, speak against established social attitudes; or, as Smith puts the matter in his reply to Elliot: "real magnanimity and conscious virtue can support itselfe under the disapprobation of all mankind."[24] The impartial spectator cannot simply be a repository of social opinion, nor is it possible to reduce the judgment of the impartial spectator to the judgment of society, even where those two judgments coincide. In light of that consideration, it is necessary to carry lightly the judgment of T. D. Campbell: "to talk of *the* impartial spectator is simply a shorthand way of referring to the normal reaction of a member of a particular social group, or of a whole society, when he is in the position of observing the conduct of his fellows."[25] Nevertheless, the impartial spectator owes its existence to the real spectators. Were it not for our discovery that while we observe and judge other people, they

---

[24] For discussion of this change in emphasis between publication of the first and second editions see D. D. Raphael, "The Impartial Spectator," in *Essays on Adam Smith*, eds. A. S. Skinner and T. Wilson (Oxford 1975), esp. pp. 90–1; also D. D. Raphael and A. L. Macfie, Introduction, in TMS, 15–17. Smith's reply to Elliot is the letter (Corr., letter 40) referred to earlier, in which he claimed to have "entirely discomfitted" Hume.

[25] T. D. Campbell, *Adam Smith's Science of Morals* (London, 1971), p. 145.

observe and judge us, we would not form the idea of an impartial spectator of us.

There is no doubt that the impartial spectator is the product of an act of imagination and therefore has intentional being – what medieval philosophers termed *esse intentionale* as against *esse naturale*. Hence, in one sense it is not a real spectator who has the merit of being impartial, but an ideal spectator, one that exists as an idea. This terminology has the sanction of Smith.[26] In another sense the impartial spectator is indeed real, for it is no other than the agent who is imagining it into existence.

In so far as the agent is imagining how he would be judged by an impartial spectator, the judgments he is imagining are his own. In so far as the impartial spectator exists as a product of imagination, there is additional ground to be wary of Campbell's judgment just cited for this stresses the exteriorisation of the impartial spectator, whose interiority is repeatedly emphasised by Smith.

The impartial spectator is "the man within the breast" and the key to Smith's account of the faculty of conscience:

The all-wise Author of Nature has, in this manner, taught man to respect the sentiments and judgments of his brethren.... But though man has, in this manner, been rendered the immediate judge of mankind, he has been rendered so only in the first instance; and an appeal lies from his sentence to a much higher tribunal, to the tribunal of their own consciences, to that of the supposed impartial and well-informed spectator, to that of the man within the breast, the great judge and arbiter of their conduct. The jurisdictions of those two tribunals are founded upon principles which, though in some respects resembling and akin, are, however, in reality different and distinct. The jurisdiction of the man without, is founded altogether in the desire of actual praise, and in the aversion to actual blame. The jurisdiction of the man within, is founded altogether in the desire of praise-worthiness, and in the aversion to blame-worthiness. (TMS, III.2.31–2)

This is not of course to deny that Smith acknowledged that there are real spectators who judge their fellow human beings impartially. Nor is it to deny that on a highly plausible interpretation

---

[26] Cf. TMS, III.3.26: "not only the judgment of the ideal man within the breast, but that of the real spectators who might happen to be present, would be entirely overlooked and disregarded." We will see that the impartial spectator is not ideal in the sense of being perfect in respect of his judgments.

Smith's impartial spectator, considered as an inner man, is constructed by a process of internalisation of such outer people, using them as mirrors to reflect ourselves as we seek images of the proper action to take. The point here is that, by whatever means the impartial spectator, considered as our conscience, comes into being, it is not a member of society.

The account I have given of the metaphysical relation between the agent and the impartial spectator has an implication for the question of how many impartial spectators there are. Following Smith, commentators speak about *the* impartial spectator. I have followed this practice. However, sometimes Smith uses the indefinite article, and sometimes he refers to *every* impartial spectator: "[Gratitude and resentment] seem proper and are approved of, when the heart of every impartial spectator entirely sympathizes with them, when every indifferent by-stander enters into, and goes along with them" (TMS, II.i.2.2.). This interesting passage indicates that we have to be on our guard. It is probable that the reference to "every indifferent bystander" is not to the impartial spectator, understood as a creature with merely intentional being, but to real live witnesses, and neither can it be ruled out that in this case the reference to an "impartial spectator" is also to a real live bystander. However, even if we think of the impartial spectator as having merely intentional being, it might still be said that there are many impartial spectators because each person creates his own.

The impartial spectator as a creature of a person's imagination has no more (nor less) information about what is to be judged than the agent, for the creature cannot be better informed than its creator. In so far as the agent has information about his own situation that is not possessed by the external spectators, "the great demigod within the breast" is better placed than are external spectators to make a judgment about the propriety of his behaviour. So the agent asks himself what the judgment of the external spectators would be if they knew what he knows. In seeking to answer this question, the agent tries to see his own situation in a disinterested way, while benefiting from the level of information that the agent himself has.

Of course, even if the agent is better informed than the spectators, he may still not be sufficiently well informed. He may be failing, perhaps culpably, to note features in his situation that would make all the difference to his judgment about his own acts and attitudes. However, the information he has is all that is available to the impartial spectator, whose judgment therefore is not indefeasible. Hence, we can never say categorically that the impartial spectator's judgment is true, and in that sense every such judgment is no more than a holding operation. Smith distinguishes between two standards that we can apply in judging our character and conduct. One is the idea of exact propriety and perfection, and the other is the idea of such an approximation to propriety as is commonly attained in the world. The wise and virtuous man, we are told, directs his principal attention to the first of these standards: "There exists in the mind of every man an idea of this kind, gradually formed from his observations upon the character and conduct both of himself and of other people. It is the slow, gradual, and progressive work of the great demigod within the breast, the great judge and arbiter of conduct.... Every day some feature is improved; every day some blemish is corrected" (TMS, VI.iii.25). This demigod within the breast is therefore recognised by Smith not to be infallible. However, there is one particular form of fallibility to which the impartial spectator is subject, namely that arising from moral luck. I cannot enter into the moral complications of the matter; my concern is simply to clarify Smith's concept of the impartial spectator.[27]

Smith's starting point is the alleged fact that however proper and beneficent may be a person's intention, if he fails to produce the good effect intended his merit will seem imperfect. Smith continues:

Nor is this irregularity of sentiment felt only by those who are immediately affected by the consequences of any action. It is felt, in some measure, even by the impartial spectator ... if, between the friend who fails and the friend who succeeds, all other circumstances are equal, there will, even in the noblest mind, be some little difference of affection in favour of him who succeeds. (TMS, II.iii.2.2)

[27] Smith's discussion of the relation between luck and the moral sentiments is in the section, "Of the Influence of Fortune upon the Sentiments of Mankind, with regard to the Merit or Demerit of Actions," TMS, 92–108. For helpful comment on Smith on moral luck, see Charles L. Griswold, *Adam Smith and the Virtues of Enlightenment*, 240–4. The classic modern discussion on moral luck is Bernard Williams, *Moral Luck* (Cambridge, 1988).

Smith describes this "irregularity of sentiment" as "unjust," from which it follows that the impartial spectator can pass unjust judgment. This appears to be the settled doctrine of Smith. For subsequently he notes the case of a person who, without any ill intention, harms another, but apologises to the sufferer: "This task would surely never be imposed upon him, did not even the impartial spectator feel some indulgence for what may be regarded as the unjust resentment of that other" (TMS, II.iii.2.10). If the impartial spectator feels some indulgence for what may be regarded as the unjust resentment of the other, he must surely have some sympathy for that unjust resentment, and to that extent he is sympathizing unjustly. Here, then, is clear evidence that the impartial spectator, already noted to be imperfect in being no better informed than the creator-agent, also possesses at least one moral weakness. In the light of the foregoing comments we have to recognise that despite Smith's reference to "the judgment of the ideal man within the breast" (TMS, III.3.26), the doctrine of the impartial spectator is not a contribution to, even less is a version of, the "ideal observer theory" that has been on the agenda of moral philosophers at least since Roderick Firth's work. The impartial spectator is simply not ideal, but instead the best, for all its many faults, that we can manage. That best is constrained by limited information admixed with error and by an affective nature that can yield to pressure from outside forces and, in yielding, distort the agent's moral judgments. The impartial spectator is after all only a demigod, to use the term Smith repeatedly employs, not God.[28]

One further imperfection should be mentioned. Smith speaks of a case where "this demigod within the breast appears, like the demigods of the poets, though partly of immortal, yet partly too of mortal extraction." Smith has in mind the case where the demigod becomes fearful and hesitant in judgment in response to a fearsome clamour of real spectators who violently proclaim a judgment which is contrary to the one that the impartial spectator would have passed. Then our only recourse is to the all-seeing judge of the

[28] See Roderick Firth, "Ethical Absolutism and the Ideal Observer," *Philosophy and Phenomenological Research* 12 (1951–2): 317–45, with criticisms by T. D. Campbell in *Adam Smith's Science of Morals*, chapter 6, and by D. D. Raphael in "The Impartial Spectator," 94–5.

world "whose judgments can never be perverted" (TMS, III.2.33), as contrasted with the human impartial spectator. God, therefore, is the impartial spectator of the universe, better placed than the humanly created spectator who can bow to social pressures and is only imperfectly informed, unlike God who, as the all-seeing judge, is perfectly informed.

There is here an implicit acknowledgment of the importance of Sir Gilbert Elliot's concern whether the impartial spectator's judgment is anything other than a reflection of an actual attitude of society. Smith replies affirmatively, but here acknowledges that actual social attitudes can nevertheless be hard to resist. It may be added that aside from this possibly malign influence of real external spectators, they can in a sense have a benign influence by prompting the impartial spectator to spectate: "The man within the breast, the abstract and ideal spectator of our sentiments and conduct, requires often to be awakened and put in mind of his duty, by the presence of the real spectator" (TMS, III.3.38). The assumption is not that the impartial spectator characteristically will reject the judgment of the real spectator; the point is that the real spectator's judgment naturally prompts a question as to whether that judgment is appropriate. The real spectator sets the agenda for the impartial and, but for the prompting, the latter might have stayed asleep and the agent would not have reacted appropriately to his situation.

Smith's account of second- and third-person moral judgments is simpler than his account of first-person moral judgments. In the former cases, the spectator need do no more than imagine himself in the shoes of the agent, and observe an agreement, or lack of agreement, between the way he himself would feel or behave in that situation and the way the agent actually does feel or behave. Where there is agreement the spectator approves, and where there is disagreement the spectator disapproves, or at least does not approve, of the agent's feelings or behaviour. A much more complex story needs to be told in the case of first-person judgments because there the agent has to imagine himself as an impartial spectator of his feelings or acts, and has to note the impartial spectator's agreement or otherwise with the agent's feelings or acts. If he agrees, then the agent morally approves of his own acts; if not, then not.

It has been argued that Smith's concept of the impartial spectator is too complex: "It seems to me that his concept of the impartial spectator is too complicated to be acceptable when one works it out fully in terms of his general theory of approval.... The process is not impossible but it seems too complicated to be a common occurrence."[29] Yet, we humans can do very complex things and spend our days doing them. The construction of an ordinary sentence, with its clauses and nested subclauses, is a very complex act – modern syntactic theory is giving us a glimpse into the extraordinary complexity involved – and yet we manage to construct syntactically well-formed sentences more or less effortlessly, indeed hardly noticing we are constructing them, so focused are we on the sense we are seeking to convey. The complex act, described by Smith, by which an agent passes moral judgment on his own acts, seems no more complex than the acts involved in speaking.

SMITH'S NATURALISM

Smith reaches the concept of conscience by a direct route that starts with the idea of the human agent as a spectator of other people's behaviour. It progresses to the idea of the spectator as not only a judge, but also as a person aware that he is being judged. His awareness of the gaze of others prompts a response. He considers first whether he is doing what will gain praise, and then finds that praise does not satisfy him if he is not worthy of it. So he comes to scrutinise his acts and attitudes to determine not whether they will be praised, but whether they are praiseworthy. In light of countless observations of the kinds of act that we have regarded as praiseworthy, we form moral rules, and in due course we revere these rules and act out of reverence for them.

I do not discuss here the question of the proper way to interpret Smith's assertion that these rules are laws of God, but want to note that we do not come by our individual moral judgments by applying the rules, but come by the rules by way of the individual moral judgments. I believe the initial materials for Smith's analysis are thoroughly naturalistic. While most commentators have held that

[29] D. D. Raphael in "The Impartial Spectator," 99.

Smith's account of the process by which the impartial spectator or conscience comes into being does not require the theological framework that Smith lightly sketches,[30] others have disagreed.[31] God is certainly invoked at several points in the exposition of the role of the impartial spectator, most spectacularly, as we saw, when the impartial spectator yields to the violent clamour of the mob and becomes fearful and hesitant in judgment (TMS, III.2.32). However, the fact that humbled and afflicted man can find consolation in an appeal to God does not contribute to an enrichment of the concept of the impartial spectator. True it makes the point that the impartial spectator has the limitations of a human being, but that point had previously been made in some detail without God being invoked. An atheist or agnostic would not on that account have a concept of the impartial spectator different from that of a person who finds consolation in an appeal to a yet higher tribunal. I do not believe that the theodicy is a mere rhetorical device within *The Theory of Moral Sentiments*, for it is plain that Smith sees belief in a just God to be a *natural* phenomenon, and he is interested in the question of how such a belief stands in relation to the moral categories with which we operate. He does, however, hold that a person can operate with a set of moral categories, such as propriety, impropriety, merit, demerit, duty, and moral rules, without having those categories in a synthetic unity with categories of a religious or theological sort. It is therefore possible to see Smith as seeking to demonstrate that a theory of moral sentiments, one sufficient to accommodate the moral framework within which most of us operate, can be developed without recourse to theological materials. The interpretative problem is, however, a live one.

If the interpretation I have just suggested is correct, then it is possible to see *The Theory of Moral Sentiments* as "an attempt to introduce the experimental method of reasoning into moral subjects."[32]

[30] See especially A. L. Macfie, *The Individual in Society, Papers on Adam Smith* (London, 1967), chapter 6; Haakonssen, *Science of a Legislator*, 74–9.

[31] A. Kleer, "Final Causes in Adam Smith's *Theory of Moral Sentiments*," *Journal of the History of Philosophy* 33 (1995): 275–300, reprinted in *Adam Smith*, ed. Knud Haakonssen (Aldershot, Hantshire, Brookfield, VT, 1998), 139–64.

[32] Subtitle of Hume's *Treatise*.

As we have noted, Hume had serious doubts about the principle that was, in his view, the "hinge" of the system developed in *The Theory of Moral Sentiments*, but the scientific spirit that moved Smith to write the work is the same as that underlying the *Treatise of Human Nature*.

7   Virtues, Utility, and Rules

The Theory of Moral Sentiments was a great success upon publication[1]; now it is obscure. An analysis of Smith's arguments against utility and his position on rules, duty, and virtue may explain why. I begin with a sketch of Smith's basic theory.

THE BASIC THEORY

Alexander the Great "put Calisthenes to death in torture, for having refused to adore him in the Persian manner" (VI.iii.32). According to Smith, I judge Alexander in two ways. First, I imagine what I would feel if I were in Alexander's place and was presented with Calisthenes's refusal. This act of imagination does not produce in me the affront Alexander feels, and when I do not react to the refusal as Alexander does, I judge Alexander to lack "propriety." Secondly, I imagine what I would feel were I in Calisthenes's place. I would feel resentment, and do so now, irrespective of what Calisthenes actually feels (II.i.2.4, II.i.3.1, II.i.5.11). If I have found that Alexander lacks propriety, I now judge him guilty of "demerit" and deserving punishment.

In other words, a passion has propriety or impropriety according to whether, after imagining myself in the relevant situation, I feel the passion in the same degree as it was felt originally. A passion has merit or demerit provided 1) it has propriety or impropriety and 2) I feel gratitude or resentment when imagining that I was affected by the resultant action. Since reward is the "natural consequence" of gratitude, and punishment is the natural consequence of

---

[1] For details, see the editors' introduction to TMS, 25–31.

resentment, judgments of merit or demerit justify reward and punishment (II.ii.2.3).² Three things thus need clarification:

1. It is easy to read Smith as claiming that propriety arises from correspondence between the passion of the agent and the passion I believe I would feel were I in the agent's place.³ Expressions such as "we must...be affected in the same manner as he is" (II.i.5.11) suggest this reading, but it is wrong. Smith makes clear that it is the *actual resultant feeling in me of this act of imagination* that is compared with Alexander's feeling. This fits Smith's initial illustrations of sympathy, which involve the production of actual passion in the spectator (I.i.1), and it fits Smith's judgments of propriety. Consider his explanations of why "to eat voraciously is universally regarded as a piece of ill manners" or why "to cry out with bodily pain, how intolerable soever, appears always unmanly and unbecoming," or why "[a]ll serious and strong expressions" of romantic love "appear ridiculous to a third person" (I.ii.1.1, I.ii.1.5, I.ii.2.1). I do not become violently hungry by imagining your hunger; I can acquire only a small bodily pain by imagining your bodily pain; I do not acquire your romantic love by imagining your loved one. In each case, I do not "enter into," "go along with," or "keep time to" your passions – even if I believe that, were I in your position, I would eat as voraciously, cry out as loudly, or love as much as you do. When we are with grieving friends, we may "be sensible...that their passion is...no greater than what we ourselves might feel upon the like occasion"; yet, our "insensibility" ensures our grief is "the slightest and most transitory imaginable" and our friends must "silence those violent

² For discussion of the "natural consequence" claim for punishment, see Paul Russell, *Freedom and Moral Sentiment* (New York, NY, 1995), pp. 145–9.

³ D. D. Raphael writes that propriety arises when I believe that "I would have responded in the same way if I had been in her shoes... [The spectator] observes a correspondence between the feeling... which he would have and that which [the agent] evidently has. Likewise the spectator's 'sympathy' with the... gratitude [of the person benefited] is a perception that, if he were in [that person's] situation and were helped, he would have the same feeling of gratitude.... The sympathy that causes approval or disapproval is not necessarily awareness of an actual feeling which reproduces here and now the motives of those who act or the reactions of those whom the action affects. It is the thought of a feeling which you would have if you were in their shoes, an awareness that comes from imagining yourself in the situations of those who are actually involved." *Adam Smith* (Oxford, 1985), pp. 30–1.

emotions" to bring about a correspondence of sentiment and hence propriety (I.iii.12–13). Similarly, in the case of one "sunk in sorrow and dejection . . . [w]e cannot bring ourselves to feel for him what he feels for himself, and what, perhaps, we should feel for ourselves if in his situation: we, therefore, despise him" (I.iii.1.15).

The same holds for my act of imagining gratitude or resentment. When I put myself in the place of Calisthenes, what is directly relevant is not my belief that I would feel resentment, but rather the resentment I actually feel from the exercise of imagination. It is this real resentment, rather than a belief about hypothetical resentment, that motivates punishment, and so allows Smith to defend resentment as necessary for keeping society together (II.i.5.8–10). A victim's resentment is appropriate when our act of imagining ourselves in his or her place has the result that "we ourselves would upon this account even desire to be the instruments of inflicting" punishment (II.i.5.8). This level of resentment can differ from the level of resentment I believe I would feel were I in the victim's place. Typically, resentment must be "brought down to the level of the sympathetic indignation of the spectator" (II.i.5.8, II.i.3.1, II.i.5.4–11).

One might ask *why* I do not reproduce some passion. Sometimes, as in the case of hunger, a passion may require a cause largely outside what the imagination can produce. When the imagination can produce the passion, often it produces only a pale version because the

imaginary change of situation . . . is but momentary. [Mankind's] thought of their own safety, the thought that they themselves are not really the sufferers, continually intrudes itself upon them; and though it does not hinder them from conceiving a passion somewhat analogous to what is felt by the sufferer, hinders them from conceiving any thing that approaches to the same degree of violence. (I.i.4.7)

The case of Alexander is more difficult. One might think that I do not reproduce his passion because I believe that, were I in his situation, I would not feel that passion; I might respect rather than hate Calisthenes. However, Smith stresses that I must, as far as possible, take on the character of Alexander. The

imaginary change is not supposed to happen to me in my own person and character, but in that of the person with whom I sympathize. When I condole with you for the loss of your only son, in order to enter into your grief I do not consider what I, a person of such a character and profession, should suffer, if I had a son, and if that son was unfortunately to die: but I consider what I should suffer if I was really you, and I not only change circumstances with you, but I change persons and characters. (VII.iii.1.4)

If this change were entirely successful, I would always agree with Alexander. Presumably Smith's point is either that my character prevents me from successfully imagining myself as Alexander – "I cannot imagine reacting as Alexander did" – or that my character prevents the reproduction of Alexander's passion in me, even when the imagining is perfect.

2. Smith does not distinguish sharply between a passion and its expression. A judgment of propriety seems better understood as a judgment of the expression of a passion rather than as a judgment of the passion itself. That I cannot reproduce your hunger or pain does not show that your hunger or pain lacks propriety; Smith's objection is to voracious eating as ill mannered, not to voracious hunger, and to "crying out," not the agony. In the case of romantic love, it is "serious and strong expressions" that appear ridiculous (I.ii.2.1; also I.ii.1.3). Grieving friends must "silence" their grief by not expressing it rather than by not feeling it. The point is clearest for the virtue of "self-command." What lacks propriety is "clamorous grief,...sighs and tears and importunate lamentations" (I.i.5.3; also I.ii.1.12, VI.iii.17). Cato is admirable for not "supplicating with the lamentable voice of wretchedness, those miserable sympathetic tears which we are always so unwilling to give" (I.iii.1.13). Indeed, there is no self-command unless one "feels the full distress of the calamity which has befallen him" (VI.iii.18). Of the "savage" whom he so respects, Smith writes "[h]is passions, how furious and violent soever, are never permitted to disturb the serenity of his countenance or the composure of his conduct and behaviour" (V.2.9; also V.2.11). When sentenced to death, he hears the sentence "without expressing any emotion" (V.2.9). It is the "behaviour of the sufferer," the "conduct," that counts: Smith admires one in danger who "suffers no word, no gesture to escape him which does not perfectly accord with the feelings of the most indifferent spectator," or "that reserved, that silent and majestic sorrow, which discovers itself only in the swelling of the eyes, in

the quivering of the lips and cheeks, and in the distant, but affecting, coldness of the whole behaviour" (I.i.5.8, VI.iii.18, VI.iii.5, I.i.5.3).

The basic theory requires more careful statement: the expression of a passion has propriety or impropriety according to whether I feel that passion to a degree that would produce that expression, after imagining myself in the relevant situation.

3. I have not mentioned the famous impartial spectator. The impartiality of the spectator is not stressed by Smith until he applies his basic theory to judgments of oneself (discussed later). However, even before that application, Smith sometimes writes that the spectator relevant for judging propriety and merit is impartial (e.g., I.i.5.4, I.i.5.8, I.ii.4.1, II.i.2.2, II.ii.1.3, II.iii.2.1–3). He has good reason to do so for my judgments of the propriety and merit of others can be as corrupt as my judgments of myself. In "war and negotiation...[t]he ambassador who dupes the minister of a foreign nation, is admired and applauded. The just man...in those public transactions is regarded as a fool and an idiot" (III.3.42). No doubt I acquire a passion to dupe after putting myself in the place of my ambassador; but the relevant question is whether a neutral party would also acquire this passion.

One might ask whether impartial spectators can disagree. Smith usually writes "the spectator," "every spectator," or "mankind,"[4] but he admits disagreements. For example, the spectator constructed by a Russian would find in French manners "effeminate adulation"; the spectator constructed by the French would find in Russian manners "rudeness and barbarism." Civilised nations construct spectators who stress humanity more than self-command; "rude and barbarous" nations reverse this (V.2.7–8). Smith may hold that the spectator constructed by a given society sets propriety for that society; "the style of manners which takes place in any nation, may commonly upon the whole be said to be that which is most suitable to its situation" (V.2.13). If so, Russian and French spectators can disagree about a Russian's manners, but the Russian spectator is decisive. Yet, this cannot be Smith's whole view. He condemns infanticide in later Greece while noting its universal

---

[4] For references and other variants, see T. D. Campbell, *Adam Smith's Science of Morals* (London, 1971), pp. 134–5.

support at the time (V.2.15), yet Smith disqualifies the Greek spectator by arguing that "custom" wholly explains this verdict. The decisive spectator is created by the group to which the evaluated person belongs, with verdicts due entirely to custom discounted.[5]

AGAINST UTILITY

Smith takes moral theories to answer two questions. The first question asks for a description of the virtuous person. A virtuous person might be perfectly prudent (Epicurus), perfectly benevolent (Hutcheson), or possess a range of passions governed by propriety (Plato, Aristotle, the Stoics, Clarke, Wollaston, Shaftesbury, Hume, Smith). Hume differs from Smith by taking utility, rather than the approvals of the impartial spectator, to specify the passions of the virtuous person (VII.ii.3.21). The second question concerns the source of our approval of the virtuous person. I might approve out of self-love (Hobbes), reason (Cudworth), or sentiment. Approval from sentiment might come from a moral sense (Hutcheson) or sympathy (Hume, Smith). However, Hume explains approval by the spectator's reproduction of the pleasure of those affected by a virtuous trait; Smith explains it by the spectator's reproduction of the passions of the agent and of the gratitude of those affected (VII.iii.3.17). Smith offers two main arguments against Hume:

1. The most common argument claims that Smith's theory fares better than utility as an explanation of our particular approvals (of the intellectual virtues [I.i.4.4, IV.2.7], of self-command [IV.2.12, IV.iii.4, VI.concl.6], of the rich [I.iii.2.3]) or disapprovals (of criminals, of resentment [I.ii.3.1–4]). Take the punishment of criminals. The utilitarian explanation of my approval of punishment cites the good effects of punishing (II.ii.3.6). Smith's explanation cites the resentment I feel after imagining myself in the place of the victim. To decide between these explanations, Smith offers two criminals; first, a sentinel who falls asleep during his watch and is executed, although no one is hurt by his lapse. Smith has no objection to the punishment. It is justified – even "just" – on utilitarian grounds, yet it "always appears to be excessively severe.

---

[5] I put aside related problems – for example, differences in the ability to reproduce passions will also lead to different spectators. Smith cannot escape by requiring perfect ability because again the result would be no impropriety.

The natural atrocity of the crime seems to be so little, and the punishment so great, that it is with great difficulty that our heart can reconcile itself to it.... [T]he thought of this crime does not naturally excite any such resentment, as would prompt us to take such dreadful revenge" (II.ii.3.11; also II.iii.2.8). The second criminal is "an ungrateful murderer or parricide" (II.ii.3.11). The same utilitarian grounds justify punishment. However, here we feel no reluctance. Our retributive sentiments are explained by resentment rather than considerations of utility because they vary with the presence or absence of victims to whom we ascribe resentment rather than with utility. (Smith adds another example in the *Lectures on Jurisprudence*: when exporting wool was a capital crime, juries refused to convict, even when they believed that exporting wool really was harmful. The absence of resentment, rather than utility, guided the jurors [LJ (A), ii.91, (B), 181–2]).

As the example makes clear, Smith's main concern is the explanation of our approvals rather than justification.

[T]he present inquiry is not concerning a matter of right... but concerning a matter of fact. We are not at present examining upon what principles a perfect being would approve of the punishment of bad actions; but upon what principles so weak and imperfect a creature as man actually and in fact approves of it. (TMS, II.1.5.10)

The issue is what "first animates us" in favour of punishment, what "originally interests us in the punishment of crimes," what is "the first or principal source of our approbation," what is the "natural and original measure" (II.ii.3.9–10, IV.2.3, VI.ii.3.21; also I.i.4.4, VII.iii.1–4, VII.iii.3.17). Even people who have not reflected on the utility of punishment demand it (II.i.2.5, II.ii.3.9, VII.iii.1.2). One might conclude that Smith has no objection to normative utilitarianism because he offers an explanatory rather than normative theory.

This conclusion is premature because Smith does not hesitate to offer normative judgments. For example, punishing a lack of gratitude would be "improper" (II.ii.1.3). Exceptional benevolence "deserve[s] the highest reward" (II.ii.1.9). "The violator of the laws of justice ought to be made to feel himself that evil which he has done to another" (II.ii.1.10). Mere justice "is entitled to very little gratitude" (II.ii.1.9). Smith answers the question "[i]n what cases the Sense of Duty ought to be the sole principle of our conduct; and in what cases it ought to concur with other motives" (III.6, heading). To hurt another for reasons other than proper resentment for injustice is "a violation of the laws of justice, which force ought to be employed either to restrain or to punish" (VI.ii.intro.2). "[E]ach nation ought, not only to endeavour itself to excel, but...to promote...the excellence of its neighbours" in happiness and prosperity (VI.ii.2.3). Smith opposes infanticide (V.2.15), suicide (VII.ii.1.34), and monks (III.2.35), and criticises the Stoics for recommending an apathy rejected by the impartial spectator (III.iii.14, VII.ii.1.46). He often pictures the "man of the most perfect virtue" – as one expects from a theory offered as on a par with that of Plato, Aristotle, Epicurus, the Stoics, and Hutcheson (III.iii.35, VI.i.15, VI.iii.11, VI.iii.18). In general, theories of propriety specify "the proper degree of all the affections" (VII.ii.4.1). "To direct the judgments" of the spectator, to "correct...our natural sentiments," is "the great purpose of all systems of morality" (VII.ii.1.47, VII.iv.6). (Similarly, the other useful part of moral philosophy, jurisprudence, is "a theory of the general principles which ought to run through and be the foundation of the laws of all nations" [VII.iv.34, VII.iv.37].)

Moreover, what one "ought to perform" throughout is "what every impartial spectator would approve of him for performing" (II.ii.1.3). The justifications Smith offers in *The Theory of Moral Sentiments* almost always consist of the spectator's approvals rather than appeals to utility. Utility enters largely to "confirm" or "defend" judgments of propriety and merit. For example, utility reinforces initial judgments of demerit that waver when we come to carry out the punishment (II.ii.3.7). Against those (such as the young) who do not accept our condemnation of certain principles, we "cast about for other arguments" and so appeal to utility – even though the fact that "we ourselves hate and detest" the principles is "conclusive"[6] (II.ii.3.8; also IV.ii.7).

This suggests a puzzle: Smith's arguments against utility concern the explanation of our sentiments, but he also has a nonutilitarian normative theory. One solution is to argue that Smith

---

[6] Similarly, appeals to self-interest are "most apt to occur to those who are endeavouring to persuade others to regularity of conduct...[w]hen men...show that the natural beauty of virtue is not like to have much effect upon them." However, this appeal is merely "additional" to the "proper character" or "natural beauty" of conduct (VII.ii.2.13).

gives normative weight to the actual workings of our sentiments by invoking God's design of these workings.

Though man...be naturally endowed with a desire of the welfare...of society, yet the Author of nature has not entrusted it to his reason to find out that a certain application of punishments is the proper means of attaining this end; but has endowed him with an immediate and instinctive approbation of that very application which is most proper to attain it. (II.i.5.10)

Although God must maintain "the greatest possible quantity of happiness" in the world, and benevolence is His "sole principle of action," our business is not to aim at maximising happiness, nor to purge ourselves of all motives other than benevolence (VI.ii.3.2, VII.ii.3.18; also II.iii.3.2, III.5.7, VII.ii.1.45–6). We are neither smart enough to make reliable utilitarian calculations nor motivated by appeals to utility.[7] Our business is to follow propriety (e.g., III.5.5–6, 11; VI.ii.3.6; VII.ii.1.21). God's design ensures that doing so will maximise happiness. Nature has "so happily adjusted our sentiments of approbation and disapprobation...that after the strictest examination it will be found" that it "is universally the case" that our approvals of traits coincide with what utility recommends (IV.2.3).[8] On this view, appeal to propriety rather than utility can and should be *our* final justification.[9]

On this interpretation, however, Smith becomes an ineffective critic of normative utilitarianism. The utilitarian can simply agree that, given Smith's happy theological assumptions, there is no need to appeal to utility. Utility remains, however, the ultimate justification. Smith denies the view of serious anti-utilitarians such

---

[7] Smith may be following Butler: see Sermon XII, paragraph 31n, and especially "A Dissertation Upon the Nature of Virtue," paragraphs 8 and 10, in Joseph Butler, *Five Sermons*, ed. Stephen L. Darwall (Indianapolis, IN, 1983). Neither of the suggested explanations, however, is obvious in Smith. For the explanations and some textual evidence, see T. D. Campbell and I. S. Ross, "The Utilitarianism of Adam Smith's Policy Advice," *Journal of the History of Ideas* 42 (1981): 76–7, and Campbell, "Adam Smith and Natural Liberty," *Political Studies* 25 (1977): 532.

[8] For a nontheological explanation of this coincidence, see Knud Haakonssen, *The Science of a Legislator* (Cambridge, 1981), pp. 73–4. Smith sometimes offers explicit explanations. For our retributive sentiments, see LJ(A), ii.92–3 and 169–71.

[9] This interpretation has the advantage of defending Smith against Russell's charge that, as a pure retributivist, Smith cannot show any point or value in punishment. Smith is not a pure retributivist, as the sentinel example shows. More important, Smith can defend our retributive sentiments by appeal to God's utilitarian design. See Russell, pp. 142–6.

as Cudworth, Butler, Price, and Reid, who attribute benevolence-limiting aims to God.[10] In politics he holds that "[a]ll constitutions of government...are valued only in proportion as they tend to promote the happiness of those who live under them" (IV.1.11).[11] As T. D. Campbell and I. S. Ross note, Smith's own advice, on issues such as trade policy and smuggling, is typically backed by appeals to utility rather than rights or the impartial spectator.[12] Smith's verdict in the sentinel case shows that the spectator relevant to justification judges by utility rather than resentment (II.ii.3.11).[13]

Smith also uses utility to explain oddities found in both everyday and impartial spectator approvals. He gives a catalogue of examples of the effect luck has on judgments of merit: we feel more gratitude toward those who succeed in helping us than toward those who try but fail, even when we realise that their intentions were identical; brilliant plans that would have succeeded, but through no fault of the planner are not put into practice, reflect less well on the planner than equally brilliant plans realised; attempted crimes are punished much less severely than successful ones (if punished at all), even when the difference is entirely lucky, and it sometimes "gives great ease to [the failed criminal's] conscience...to consider that the crime was not executed, though he knows that the failure arose

---

[10] See J. B. Schneewind, *The Invention of Autonomy* (Cambridge, 1998), pp. 209–10, 352–3, 383–4, 402.

[11] See Campbell, *Science*, chapter 10, and "Adam Smith and Natural Liberty."

[12] See Campbell and Ross, "Utilitarianism." Elsewhere, Campbell finds an argument for utilitarianism in Smith. Smith writes that "we cannot form the idea of any innocent and sensible being, whose happiness we should not desire" (235). Sentiments such as this, unavoidable on reflection, are justified simply because they are unavoidable on reflection (Campbell, "Scientific Explanation and Ethical Justification in the *Moral Sentiments*," in *Essays on Adam Smith*, eds. Andrew S. Skinner and Thomas Wilson [Oxford, 1975], p. 77). For this argument to work, Campbell must show that for Smith this is the *only* (relevant) sentiment unavoidable on reflection.

[13] Henry Sidgwick gives a similar negligence case to show that "[c]ommon sense is forced, however reluctantly, into practical agreement with Utilitarianism." See *The Methods of Ethics* (Indianapolis, IN, 1981), p. 446; also pp. 72n, 292–3. For more on punishment, see Raphael, "Hume and Adam Smith on Justice and Utility," *Proceedings of the Aristotelian Society* 73 (1972–3): 87–103 and, especially, Haakonssen, pp. 116–23. Haakonssen sees Smith as a retributivist, but only for laws of justice based on resentment reproduction. Utility justifies laws of defence (such as the sentinel), police, and revenue, and even some laws of justice (concerning contracts). For a thorough mix of utility (as both explanation and justification) and resentment, applied to theft, fraud, forgery and perjury, see LJ(A), ii.147–61; LJ(B), 194–200.

from no virtue in him"; we are much more indignant at negligence that causes harm than at negligence that does not, even when the difference is bad luck; indeed, a "want of the most anxious timidity and circumspection" is often praised, but it is blamed if, through bad luck, harm results (II.iii.2.5, 10). Still, Smith defends rewarding luck, not by simply stating that these are the impartial spectator's judgments, but rather by appeal to utility.[14] If judgments of merit attached solely to intentions, "every court of judicature would become a real inquisition"; rewarding realised rather than "latent virtue" encourages more vigorous attempts; punishing unintended negligence, and feeling distress at even blameless harm, encourages the highest standard of care. Rewarding luck is desirable because it contributes to "the happiness and perfection of the species" or because of its "utility" (II.iii.3.2, 3; VI.iii.30).

Smith's recourse to utility, particularly when convincing others on policy, suggests that he agrees with the central argument for normative utilitarianism offered by Hutcheson and Hume, and later stressed by Bentham: appeals to utility have a privileged place in attempts to convince others or justify ourselves.[15] Smith concedes this in the discussion of convincing the young, quoted previously. He also concedes it in one of his replies to Hutcheson. Hutcheson argues, Smith writes, that "in all the disputes of casuists...the public good...was the standard to which they constantly referred; thereby universally acknowledging that whatever tended to promote the happiness of mankind was right" (VII.ii.3.8). Smith replies that

[t]hough the standard by which casuists frequently determine what is right or wrong...be its tendency to the welfare or disorder of society, it does not follow that a regard to the welfare of society should be the sole virtuous motive of action, but only that, in any competition, it ought to cast the balance against all other motives. (VII.ii.3.17)

Smith's concession that benevolence trumps other motives is surprising. However, more important, Smith does not contest, apart

---

[14] For a comparison of Smith and Hume on moral luck, see Russell, pp. 130–3, 136, notes 31, 32.

[15] The appeal to self-interest might have the same privileged place in convincing others. However, Smith notes that an appeal to one's own self-interest is unpersuasive as a justification of one's conduct. "Though it may be true...that every individual, in his own breast, naturally prefers himself to all mankind, yet he dares not look mankind in the face, and avow that he acts according to this principle" (II.ii.2.1).

from the unelaborated "frequently," the privileged place of utility in resolving debates.

Where Smith does offer normative arguments from the impartial spectator, they are sometimes unimpressive, particularly for controversial issues. It is unhelpful to note that "no regard to the approbation of the supposed impartial spectator...seems to call upon us" to commit suicide, and that "[i]t is only the consciousness of...our own incapacity to support the calamity with proper manhood and firmness" that drives us to suicide (VII.ii.1.34). It is unclear why the spectator does not approve: imagining the calamity can make a spectator want to end the sufferer's life, as in euthanasia cases. To insist that the spectator will not feel this, and so will view suicide as improper, seems unwarranted. This threat – the threat of conflicting impartial spectators within a group – is not always met by insisting on impartiality, since the difference between spectators can lie in their brute response rather than residual partiality.[16] Smith's objection to rival theories, that they fail to give "any precise or distinct measure by which...propriety of affection can be ascertained," undercuts his own theory as well (VII.ii.1.49).

There is a related worry for Smith's theory, to which utility is a solution. Recall that the decisive spectator does not decide on the basis of custom, but it is often hard to detect custom. For infanticide, Smith explains that the early Greeks had some justification: few children could be supported. The later Greek view is due to custom because it repeats the earlier view when this justification is gone (V.2.15). To identify what is merely customary, then, Smith requires an account of justification. The approvals of the impartial spectator cannot supply this account; Smith gives this role to utility. This holds not only for infanticide, but for most of Smith's examples of noncustomary spectator reactions. We approve of different traits in a parent and a general, a clergyman and an officer, an officer at war and a city guard, and a savage and a "polished" person; Smith argues that these approvals are not due to custom by noting the usefulness of the trait in each circumstance (V.2.5–14).

There is a different reply to the puzzle that rejecting explanatory utilitarianism seems irrelevant to establishing a non-utilitarian

---

[16] For this point, see Raphael, *Adam Smith*, pp. 39–40.

normative theory. Rather than trying to find a connection, as previously, one might try to justify the non-utilitarian normative theory on independent grounds. Perhaps Smith could argue that his theory best systematises our considered moral judgments. However, there is a general problem. If Smith retains his belief that normative utilitarianism and his theory agree, it will be hard to find an argument that favours his theory. If Smith claims that normative utilitarianism and his theory disagree, Smith himself seems, as in the sentinel case, to side with utilitarianism.

The case against explanatory utilitarianism remains. Here Smith is probably right that we often do not, and did not originally, arrive at our approvals by reflection on utility.[17] However, Hume *might* agree. In an explicit discussion of Smith's objection, Hume concedes that because of "education and acquired habits," we "are so accustomed to blame injustice, that we are not, in every instance, conscious of any immediate reflection on the pernicious consequences of it." He adds that "what we have very frequently performed from certain motives, we are apt likewise to continue mechanically, without recalling, on every occasion, the reflections, which first determined us."[18] The "first" makes Hume prey to Smith, but often Hume argues only that utility "determines" us in the sense that our approvals track utility.[19] If explanatory utilitarianism takes this (watered-down) form, Smith has no objection. (The wool example might seem to count against tracking. However, Smith deploys it to show that utility is not the original or motivating explanation of punishment, rather than to show that

---

[17] In the *Lectures on Jurisprudence*, Smith adds another argument against explanatory utilitarianism: the good effects of punishing attempted crimes are the same as the good effects of punishing successful crimes, but we do not punish attempts as severely as successes. Smith very plausibly explains the difference by citing the different amounts of resentment caused (LJ[A], ii.174–7; LJ[B], 201). The normative utilitarian might reply by citing Smith's own utilitarian defence of rewarding luck.

[18] David Hume, *An Enquiry Concerning the Principles of Morals*, in *Enquiries*, ed. P. H. Nidditch (Oxford, 1975), p. 203.

[19] Sidgwick offers utilitarianism "not as the mode of regulating conduct with which mankind began, but rather as that to which we can now see that human development has always been tending." See *Methods*, pp. 455–7. Marie Martin notes tracking to defend Hume against Smith but takes the tracking to establish Hume's claim that utility is the "foundation" of our approvals. If "foundation" means "origin," this is a bad inference. See Martin, "Utility and Morality: Adam Smith's Critique of Hume," *Hume Studies* 16 (1990): 111.

our approvals conflict with utility. The reason is that, unlike the jurors, Smith thinks the ban on exporting wool lacks utility. The approvals of the jurors conflict with their beliefs about utility, but not with utility.)

2. Smith objects that

it seems impossible that the approbation of virtue should be a sentiment of the same kind with that by which we approve of a convenient and well-contrived building; or that we should have no other reason for praising a man than that for which we commend a chest of drawers. (IV.2.4)

Hume again notes the worry. He replies that

[t]here are a numerous set of passions and sentiments, of which thinking rational beings are, by the original constitution of nature, the only proper objects....There is something very inexplicable in this variation of our feelings.[20]

Here Smith has the better of Hume, offering an explanation of what Hume finds inexplicable. My approvals of a building and a person differ, despite the utility of both, because the person expresses passions which I can approve; the building lacks passions (VIII.iii.3.17).[21]

Nevertheless, I think the explanatory utilitarian has a better defence because it is not obvious that there *is* a special sentiment of approval felt only toward persons. I approve of qualities in persons that are not found in buildings (and vice versa), but it does not follow that the feeling of approval itself is different. Smith himself notes that other moral sentiments do not differ with their objects. For example, we feel resentment at "the instrument which had accidentally been the cause of the death of a friend, and we should often think ourselves guilty of a sort of inhumanity, if we neglected to vent [an] absurd sort of vengeance upon it" (II.iii.1.1; also LJ[A], ii.118–20, 178; LJ[B], 188–9, 201). Similarly, for gratitude,

The sailor, who, as soon as he got ashore, should mend his fire with the plank upon which he had just escaped from a shipwreck, would seem to be guilty

---

[20] Hume, *Enquiry*, p. 213n, *A Treatise of Human Nature*, ed. P. H. Nidditch and L. A. Selby-Bigge (Oxford, 1978), p. 617; see also *Treatise*, pp. 471–3.

[21] Smith also claims that "no machine can be the object" of the sympathy "by which we go along with the gratitude of the persons who are...benefited" (VII.iii.3.17). However, if people feel grateful toward a machine, I can surely go along with their gratitude, just as I can go along with their gratitude toward a person.

of an unnatural action. We should expect that he would rather preserve it with care and affection.... A man grows fond of a snuff-box, of a pen-knife, of a staff which he has long made use of, and conceives something like a real love and affection for them. If he breaks or loses them, he is vexed out of all proportion to the value of the damage.[22] (II.iii.1.2)

If so, there may be no need for Smith's account of the special sentiment.

Suppose, however, that there is a special sentiment of approval felt only toward persons. Sidgwick offers an explanation compatible with utilitarianism: when I judge persons, I believe such a judgment can or could have motivated them; "the habitual consciousness of this will account for almost any degree of difference between moral sentiments and the pleasure and pain that we derive from the contemplation of either extra-human or non-voluntary utilities and inutilities."[23]

RULES

Smith's basic theory concerns judgments of others but he extends it to cover judgments of oneself. I take myself to act with propriety when I believe that my expressed passion corresponds to what a spectator would feel, after he has put himself in my place. I take myself to have merit when I believe that a spectator would feel gratitude, after he has put himself in the place of those affected by me. The relevant spectator has two features not found in all real spectators. First, he is well informed about my passions and place; at least, he is as well informed as I am, given that he is my creation. Secondly, the relevant spectator is impartial. He is not, for example, someone partial to me and hence predisposed, when putting himself in my place, to feel all the resentment I feel about an injury, or predisposed, when putting himself into the place of those I affect, to feel no resentment at my harsh treatment.

[22] Smith goes on to argue that inanimate things cannot be the "proper object of gratitude or resentment" because these passions "cannot vent themselves with any sort of satisfaction" on what lacks passions (or on what cannot understand which of its acts are targeted by the gratitude or resentment) (II.iii.1.3). When these conditions are not met, "there is something wanting to [the] entire gratification" of gratitude and resentment (II.iii.1.4). However, Smith has admitted that the difference in our attitudes toward animate and inanimate things is a matter of the degree of gratification of a passion – a "sentiment of the same kind" – rather than of completely different passions.

[23] Sidgwick, pp. 426–7; see also p. 220.

Here Smith foresees a problem. Since the relevant spectator is my creation, it is tempting for me to create one who will let me approve of myself. Even in retrospect, I can exaggerate the wrong done to me to conclude that an impartial spectator would approve of my furious resentment (III.4.4, III.4.12). At the moment of action, things are still worse: the "fury of our own passions" allows "but instantaneous glimpses, which vanish in a moment, and which...are not altogether just" of the approvals of a truly impartial spectator (III.4.3, 4, 12; also III.5.2).

Smith's "remedy" is to introduce "general rules" (III.4.7). These are formulated by induction on past impartial approvals (rather than by deduction from utility or by direct intuition). If I always disapprove of "sanguinary revenges" performed by historical figures or fictional characters (III.4.12), this justifies a rule against them. When tempted to revenge myself, it is preferable to recall the general rule than to create the relevant spectator because I am likely to cheat in the latter. Smith calls a regard for general rules "a sense of duty"[24] and claims that this is "the only principle by which the bulk of mankind are capable of directing their actions.... Without this sacred regard to general rules, there is no man whose conduct can be much depended upon." Without them, "society...would crumble into nothing" (III.5.1-2; also VII.iii.2.6).

One might object that general rules allow the same cheating as the creation of a spectator because induction from particular impartial judgments will rarely produce exceptionless rules. The rules are formed "by finding from experience, that all actions of a certain kind, or circumstanced in a certain manner, are approved or disapproved of" (III.4.8, VII.iv.12). For example, I am unlikely to arrive at a rule banning all promise breaking. When tempted, I must judge whether my case is exceptional, and this judgment seems as prone to self-deception as my creation of a spectator. Smith himself stresses the imprecise nature of general rules, other than those concerning justice, and even notes that in some of these cases the

---

[24] Haakonssen suggests that Smith refines this account of duty when, in the LJ, he argues that a promise obliges by creating a reasonable expectation of performance such that nonperformance causes harm resented by the spectator (*Legislator*, p. 113; LJ[A], ii.42-4 and 56-8; LJ[B], 175-6). In TMS, however, the sense of duty goes beyond cases of resented harm. It stems from any general rule (such as gratitude or benevolence).

decision "must be left altogether to . . . the man within the breast" (VI.ii.1.22; also III.6.8–11; VII.iv.12, 18, 33).

Smith might reply that, at least in the case of justice, there are precise rules easily applied to one's situation. Because Smith also holds that justice, unlike the other virtues, is "essential to the existence of society," this could explain why he finds general rules so important (II.ii.3.3). However, there is a problem. Against a rule of gratitude such as "make a return of equal, and if possible of superior value," Smith objects:

> If your benefactor attended you in your sickness, ought you to attend him in his? or can you fulfil the obligation of gratitude, by making a return of a different kind? If you ought to attend him, how long ought you to attend him? . . . If your friend lent you money in your distress, ought you to lend him money in his? How much ought you to lend him? When ought you to lend him? . . . And for how long a time? (III.6.9)

Justice is different:

> the rules of justice are accurate in the highest degree, and admit of no exceptions or modifications, but such as may be ascertained as accurately as the rules themselves. . . . If I owe a man ten pounds, justice requires that I should precisely pay him ten pounds, either at the time agreed upon, or when he demands it. (III.6.10; also VII.iv.1, 7–8)

The problem is that justice is not so different. Smith distinguishes between "jurisprudence" and "casuistry." Jurisprudence concerns "only what the person to whom the obligation is due, ought to think himself entitled to exact by force. . . . It is the end of jurisprudence to prescribe rules for the decisions of judges and arbiters." These rules are precise. Casuistry concerns "what . . . the person who owes the obligation ought to think himself bound to perform. . . . It is the end of casuistry to prescribe rules for the conduct of a good man" (VII.iv.8). Smith argues that these rules are imprecise, even concerning issues of justice such as restitution, veracity, and promises. Consider a forced promise to a highwayman. Jurisprudence is clear – no judge would or should enforce payment. Casuistry is unclear – we think a good person should have some regard for her promises; the degree of regard depends on (among other factors) the size of the promised sum, the use to which the money would be otherwise put, and on whether "the promiser had been treated with a great deal of that sort of gallantry, which is sometimes to be met with in persons of the most abandoned characters" (VII.iv.12). Even one who disregards such a promise for good reason has departed from the ideal; no one who breaks such a promise "would be fond of telling the story" (VII.iv.13). However, "[t]o fix...by any precise rule, what degree of regard ought to be paid to it, or what might be the greatest sum which could be due from it, is evidently impossible" (VII.iv.12).[25] Even if one could give a precise rule in one case, it would be useless because "what would hold good in any one case would scarce do so exactly in any other, and what constitutes...propriety...varies in every case with the smallest variety of situation" (VII.iv.33). If so, the precision of rules of justice does not avoid the worry that self-deception enters when rules are imprecise. The precise rules of justice are guides for magistrates – who are usually not concerned personally in their cases anyway – rather than for ordinary persons deciding what to do and fearing self-deception.

I think Smith has a different reply. One can reconcile his enthusiasm for general rules with his condemnation of casuistry. Casuistry offers precise rules for specific circumstances, whereas useful general rules presume to cover several circumstances by dropping many of the details. (Smith's description of the induction may suggest this: he writes of "all such actions," "acting in this manner," "actions of a certain kind," and "action[s] of the same kind" [III.5.7–8].) Also, invoking a presumption against promise breaking has an advantage over creating a spectator: a presumption requires arguments to override it, and so puts the onus on the voice of self-deception, whereas the creation of a spectator offers no similar initial bias against this voice. General rules, understood as presumptions, certainly allow self-deception, but they do seem an improvement.

To this, Smith can add that general rules are necessary for society, not because they block the effects of self-deception, but because, as he also suggests, they provide a ready method for making moral decisions – a method much quicker and easier than that

---

[25] For a similar but greatly expanded treatment of justice – perhaps influenced by Smith – see Sidgwick, Book III, chapter V.

suggested by the basic theory (I.i.3.4, III.4.12). This point has a cost, however, for it compromises Smith's case against explanatory utilitarianism. Smith's basic theory, like appeals to utility, is less evident in everyday moral deliberation when it is replaced by appeal to rules. The explanatory utilitarian might then argue that utility, rather than Smith's theory, explains these rules.

Smith resembles (and perhaps influenced) Kant in his pessimistic view of our propensity to self-deception, the unreliability of our unaided passions as guides to conduct, and in his resultant stress on duty.[26] However, unlike Kant's, Smith's explanation of how duty motivates is not mysterious: when my motivation is not simply habitual, I fear my disapproval of myself and the disapproval of others, and so follow general rules to avoid both (e.g., III.4.7, 12).

Smith differs from Kant also by treating duty as often a second-best motivation and offering a careful discussion of when one ought to so act. In the case of "naturally agreeable" passions, such as love and gratitude, acting out of duty is very much second best. For example, "a benefactor thinks himself but ill requited, if the person upon whom he has bestowed his good offices, repays them merely from a cold sense of duty, and without any affection to his person" (III.6.4; also III.5.1). Similarly, in the case of imprecise general rules, it is both difficult and pedantic to act entirely out of regard to the rule (III.6.9; also VI.ii.1.22). In contrast, if the passion is naturally disagreeable, such as resentment, it is preferable to be motivated by regard to the rule rather than by the passion. "Nothing is more graceful than the behaviour of the man . . . who, like a judge, considers only the general rule, which determines what vengeance is due" rather than acts from a "savage disposition to revenge" (III.6.5). For justice, "the actions which this virtue requires are never so properly performed, as when the chief motive for performing them is a reverential and religious regard to those general rules which require them" (III.6.10). The "selfish" passions, neither naturally agreeable nor disagreeable, are more complex: regard for general rules should motivate "in all common, little, and ordinary cases," such as the pursuit of a single shilling; however, for grander ambitions, such as a prince's defence of his kingdom, one motivated only by this

---

[26] See Samuel Fleischacker, "Philosophy in Moral Practice: Kant and Adam Smith," *Kant-Studien* 82 (1991): 249–69.

regard, rather than by a relish for the object, appears poor spirited (III.6.6).[27]

Smith's account is attractive. It avoids two familiar caricatures: the Aristotelian virtuous agent, acting and feeling rightly with never a thought of rules or experience of duty, and the Kantian virtuous agent, feeling anything whatsoever but always acting with explicit regard to rules and duty. It should appeal to those contemporary virtue ethicists who, like Smith, take character to be the source and main object of moral evaluation but do not want to jettison deontic concepts such as duty.

VIRTUE

For Smith, the "real essence of virtue" is a "keen and earnest attention to the propriety of our own conduct" (VI.iii.17). Virtue, as opposed to "mere propriety," is "excellence, something uncommonly great" (I.i.5.7). When determining "the degree of blame or applause," we use two standards: "complete propriety," and the "degree of . . . distance from this complete perfection, which the actions of the greater part of men commonly arrive at" (I.i.5.9; also VI.iii.23). When judging oneself, Smith recommends the standard of complete propriety; grading oneself on a curve encourages arrogance (VI.iii.26–8). However, either complete propriety, or conduct much closer to complete propriety than the average, is virtuous.

One might ask whether Smith requires the virtuous agent, keenly attending to propriety, to deliberate in terms of the impartial spectator. This may look unappealing; hopefully, I do not buy my wife a gift only after asking myself what an impartial spectator would feel after imagining him- or herself in my place. It is tempting to reply that, as with general rules, Smith finds explicitly moral deliberation attractive for some virtues and not others.

---

[27] Smith adds a discussion of something Kant does not: "a wrong sense of duty." When this motivates a bad action, one "will never feel . . . that indignation which he feels against other criminals, but will rather regret, and sometimes even admire their unfortunate firmness" (III.6.12). One can also act contrary to a wrong sense of duty: "A bigoted Roman Catholic, who, during the massacre of St. Bartholomew, had been so overcome by compassion, as to save some unhappy Protestants, whom he thought it his duty to destroy, would not seem to be entitled to that high applause which we should have bestowed upon him, had he exerted the same generosity with complete self-approbation" (III.6.13).

When he describes the best examples of benevolence, he notes "affection," "affectionate reverence," and "fatherly fondness" (III.6.4). The spectator is not mentioned.

However, when Smith describes self-command, one who "governs his whole ... conduct according to those ... corrected emotions which the great inmate ... within the breast prescribes" is "alone the real man of virtue." The governance must be carried out in these terms for Smith sees no virtue in a natural Stoic, one who expresses precisely what an impartial spectator would express after occupying his or her place, but as a result of insensibility (VI.iii.18). Self-command requires not merely conduct that has propriety but conduct out of regard for propriety. Smith adds that self-command "is not only a great virtue, but from it all the other virtues seem to derive their principal lustre." "To act according to the dictates of prudence, of justice, and proper beneficence, seems to have no great merit where there is no temptation to do otherwise" (VI.iii.11). If so, there is little virtue without deliberation in terms of the spectator.

This need not be a problem: perhaps this degree of explicitly moral deliberation is desirable. However, Smith's admiration of self-command is worrisome. He divides the traits that manifest our attention to propriety into benevolence, prudence, and self-command. The treatment of self-command is equal in length to that of benevolence and prudence combined. His history of "those systems which make virtue consist in propriety" devotes twenty-one pages to Zeno, whereas Plato and Aristotle share five. This is no surprise. Smith's basic theory, requiring agreement between the expressed passion of the agent and the passion actually reproduced in the spectator, makes it difficult for any violent expression to have propriety, and so makes self-command vital.[28]

---

[28] Smith may intend an argument for the importance of self-command that is independent of the basic theory. Perhaps, as the merit-requires-temptation claim suggests, self-command is vital because there is no virtue without effort. However, requiring effort for virtue is controversial; as Hume notes, it is implausible for "non-moral" cases, and Smith (like Hume) is not one to insist on a distinction between the moral and the nonmoral. (See Hume, *Treatise*, pp. 606–10, *Enquiry*, pp. 312–23.) Smith's approval of self-command may also be brute, in that it goes beyond what the basic theory supports. Of the death of Socrates, he writes that "the sympathetic grief of the spectator appears to go beyond the original passion in the person principally concerned" (I.iii.1.14). One expects Smith to condemn Socrates for too much self-command, just as he condemns those (few) who show too little resentment (II.i.5.8), but he does not.

This is not yet an objection. Smith can argue that our approvals attach to just the rather muffled expressions he admires, and so his basic theory, which generates these approvals and the importance of self-command, is correct. It certainly captures a streak in our approvals downplayed by the tearful "sensibility" literature. But Smith goes too far. His virtuous person lives a tormented life, constantly defeating temptation. This ideal seems badly suited to one of the tasks of "ethics" (as opposed to casuistry and jurisprudence), that of "animat[ing] us to the practice of virtue" (VII.iv.6; also VII.iv.28).

The problem stems from the basic theory. Reconsider the examples that make the basic theory clearest. The expression of violent hunger "is always indecent" because "we do not grow hungry" by putting ourselves in the place of a hungry person (I.ii.1.1). Smith should conclude that *no* expression of hunger has propriety.[29] "[A]ll strong expressions" of sexual desire, even in private, are "upon every occasion indecent" (I.ii.1.2). "[T]o cry out with bodily pain, how intolerable soever, appears always unmanly and unbecoming.... [I]f he makes any violent out-cry, as I cannot go along with him, I never fail to despise him" (I.ii.1.5). "[I]f he should...be led out to a public execution, and there shed one single tear upon the scaffold, he would disgrace himself for ever in the opinion of all the gallant and generous part of mankind" (I.iii.1.15). Expressions of romantic love are "always laughed at" and "appear ridiculous;" again, this should hold even in private (I.ii.2.1). These judgments do seem to follow from the basic theory[30] and make clear the need for extensive self-command, but they also suggest that the basic theory is flawed. (Smith himself notes that his theory condemns expressions of romantic love that are "just as reasonable as

---

[29] He may be trying to avoid this conclusion – which he does not want (I.i.5.7) – by writing that there is "some degree of sympathy...with hunger.... The disposition of body which is habitual to a man in health, makes his stomach easily keep time... with [non-violent hunger]" (I.ii.1.1). However, this conflicts with the claim just cited.

[30] As Martha Nussbaum notes, the impropriety of expressions of sexual desire may not follow, given pornography. It would be odd, however, to defend the expression of sexual desire by noting that spectators are stimulated by imagining it. For discussion of Smith on sexual desire and romantic love, see Nussbaum, *Love's Knowledge* (New York, NY, 1990), pp. 338–46.

any of the kind" [I.ii.2.1].) Similar problems arise even for passions that are easier to reproduce. Many see nothing wrong with expressions of grief that go beyond what an impartial spectator would express. As Allan Gibbard notes, we might even blame one who, like the narrator of Camus's *L'etranger*, expresses so little grief.[31] Many see nothing wrong with expressions of gratitude (or joy or parental love) that go beyond what an impartial spectator would express. Such expressions seem not only excusable, as Smith sometimes implies (e.g., III.3.13–14); again, we might even blame one who expresses less.[32]

A different basic theory would give a different account of the extent of self-command. Consider the theory often attributed to Smith: propriety arises from correspondence between the passion of the agent and the passion an impartial spectator believes he or she would feel if he or she were in the agent's place. This permits much greater expression because the correct amount is no longer held hostage to the abilities of impartial spectators to reproduce it. Self-command could remain a virtue, but it would ask much less of the agent than Smith asks. (Smith should be sympathetic to asking less; he criticises Hutcheson for making the "condition of human nature...peculiarly hard" by taking benevolence to be the only virtue [VII.ii.3.18].) Omitting the reproductive abilities of spectators also helps Smith's normative aspirations. The spectator's inability to reproduce a passion – unlike his or her impartiality

---

[31] Allan Gibbard, *Wise Choices, Apt Feelings* (Cambridge, MA, 1990), p. 281, note 2. Gibbard writes of appropriate passion rather than expression, but the point remains. He also objects that "[o]n Smith's theory, the proper feelings for everyone in a group are the same. On ordinary views, the ways it makes sense to feel about things can depend on one's position. It makes sense for intimates to grieve in a way it does not make sense for strangers" (281). This criticism is mistaken. The spectator feels differently after imagining the place of one who has lost an intimate and after imagining the place of one who hears of the death of a stranger. Smith notes that "[t]he man who should feel no more for the death or distress of his own father, or son, than for those of any other man's father or son, would appear neither a good son nor a good father" (III.3.13).

[32] In the case of gratitude, Smith thinks the spectator will be "naturally transported towards" the benefactor. The spectator "applaud[s]" recompense and has "a very high sense of the merit of [the] benefactor" (II.i.5.3, I.ii.2.1). However, whether this is a feeling equal to what we think the actual beneficiary should feel is dubious, particularly if Smith's insistence on our insensibility is correct.

and informedness – is not a recommendation, and so it is unclear why the verdicts of Smith's spectator should guide one. Even if Smith were right to find the inability important for explaining our approvals, in this instance, explanatory gains would bring normative losses.

Yet, the theory just noted, on which propriety arises from correspondence between the passion of the agent and the passion a spectator believes she would feel were she in the agent's place, has its own difficulties. If she takes on the character of the agent, as Smith wants, she expects to feel just what the agent does, and so again impropriety is impossible. If she interjects her own character, the extent of virtuous self-command may become too little rather than too great. I might know how I would behave under torture – but find propriety in much more self-command.[33] Requiring actual reproduction, along with noting our reproductive inabilities, lets Smith avoid this dilemma.

One conclusion is that it is harder than expected to find an attractive account of propriety and virtue that turns on correspondence between spectator and agent.[34] When Smith's difficulties with normative utilitarianism are added, it is easier to see why *The Theory of Moral Sentiments* grew obscure while normative utilitarianism and its intuitionist critics prospered. The field in which Smith surpasses the intuitionists and perhaps the utilitarians – the explanation of moral judgment – had by Sidgwick's time come to be the province of psychologists rather than philosophers. Unlike Hume, whose moral psychology was until recently equally ignored, Smith gave few meta-ethical arguments to keep the twentieth century attentive. Perhaps the current boom in

---

[33] For a similar point, see Reid's lectures on Smith, printed in J. C. Stewart-Robertson and David Fate Norton, "Thomas Reid on Adam Smith's Moral Theory," *Journal of the History of Ideas* 45 (1984): 314. Reid also argues that passions are reproduced by mimicking rather than by imaginary transport and that Smith requires a separate moral faculty, unexplained by sympathy, to generate reactions in the spectator (311, 312–17).

[34] One might try to avoid Smith's difficulties by decreasing his stress on our insensibility. Or one might impose a distinction between the moral and the nonmoral, or between the public and the private, to make the spectator's reactions sometimes irrelevant (in, say, cases of hunger or sexual passion when one cannot reasonably expect a real spectator and no harm to others is done).

Kantian ethics, virtue ethics, and particularism will call more attention to *The Theory of Moral Sentiments*, for in its stress on character, duty, and context, it answers, in one theory, to some of the motivations underlying all three.[35]

[35] Thanks to Bob Bright, Michael Feld, Kavita Joshi, Rhonda Martens, Carl Matheson, Tim Schroeder, Leah Steele, Jeff Verman, Sandra Vettese, and, especially, Joyce Jenkins for discussion of or comments on this chapter.

8 Adam Smith on Justice, Rights, and Law

I. THE UNEXECUTED ACCOUNT OF LAW AND GOVERNMENT

"I shall in another discourse," Adam Smith reported in the final paragraph of *The Theory of Moral Sentiments*, "endeavour to give an account of the general principles of law and government, and of the different revolutions they have undergone in the different ages and periods of society" (TMS, VII.iv.37). Smith's announcement of this future volume on the general principles of law and government – originally presented in the 1759 first edition of his moral treatise – was then reissued over the next three decades in all the subsequent editions of *The Theory of Moral Sentiments* published in Smith's own lifetime. Even the heavily revised sixth edition of 1790, published in the year of Smith's death, retained the passage; although by this time, Smith acknowledged that his "very advanced age" left him "very little expectation" of completing "this great work," which some thirty years earlier he "entertained no doubt of being able to execute" in its entirety (TMS, "Advertisement," p. 3).[1]

As in the case of Smith's two most famous publications, the projected work on "the general principles of law and government" took shape as part of Smith's duties as a professor at Glasgow University. He had, in fact, first lectured on law and jurisprudence even before he received election in 1751 to the first of his two Glasgow chairs.

---

[1] Several years earlier, in a letter of 1785 to Rouchefoucauld, Smith acknowledged that "the indolence of old age" rendered completion of the work "extremely uncertain," even though the "materials...are in a great measure collected"; *Correspondence*, no. 248.

Indeed, according to the testimony of one of his Glasgow students, it was the success of these earlier Edinburgh-based law lectures that secured Smith his appointment at Glasgow.[2] Smith's Glasgow teaching in moral philosophy, as described in the well-known summary John Millar furnished for Dugald Stewart's *Account of the Life and Writings of Adam Smith, LL.D.* (1794), was organized into four parts. The first was devoted to "Natural Theology." The second part "comprehended Ethics" and "consisted chiefly of the doctrines which he afterwards published in his Theory of Moral Sentiments." The third part treated at greater length "that branch of morality which relates to *justice*," and following the approach of Montesquieu, traced "the gradual progress of jurisprudence" and the attendant developments of "law and government" from "the rudest to the most advanced ages." The fourth and final part examined "those political regulations" designed to increase the riches, the power, and the prosperity of a State," and "contained the substance of the work" he later published as "An Inquiry into the Nature and Causes of the Wealth of Nations" (EPS, 274–5).

Although Smith himself failed to realize the long-projected volume on "law and government," two substantial manuscript reports of the third and fourth parts of his Glasgow teaching have survived, and are now published in the Glasgow Edition as Smith's *Lectures on Jurisprudence*.[3] While these notes of lectures cannot be treated as simple substitutes for the "great work" Smith never executed, they provide the fullest evidence we have for a major component of his moral philosophy. In biographical terms, the *Lectures on Jurisprudence* disclose the contours and principal elements of subjects that commanded Smith's philosophical attention throughout his adult career. In their content, the *Lectures* provided the setting

---

[2] The lectures on law were one of a series of freelance lectures Smith delivered in Edinburgh between 1748 and 1751. The content and biographical details concerning these lectures are described in Ross (1995, pp. 84–108).

[3] The two reports, referred to as LJ(A) and LJ(B), are identified as "Report of 1762–3" and "Report dated 1766," and comprise material from Smith's final years at Glasgow University. The editorial introduction to the Glasgow volume supplies a full account of the dating and condition of the two reports, and of the differences between them. A quite fragmentary report of an earlier version of the lectures is described in Meek (1976a). These lectures first became available to Smith scholarship in the edition of LJ(B) published by Edwin Cannan in 1896. In quoting from the *Lectures on Jurisprudence*, I have occasionally modernized spelling and corrected syntax.

for Smith's explorations of many of the major themes developed in *The Wealth of Nations*, including the account of the historical progress of civil society, which served to structure so much of the Smithian understanding of commercial society. Perhaps of most importance, these *Lectures on Jurisprudence* supply the illuminating connective tissue between Smith's two great and enduring published contributions to moral and social theory. As such, in recent years, these materials have come to figure critically in the general interpretation of Smith's science of man and of the broad jurisprudential orientation suggested by his placement of political economy within the "science of a legislator" (WN, IV.ii.39).[4]

II. JUSTICE AND NATURAL JURISPRUDENCE

The starting point for Smith's treatment of "the general principles of law and government" is the account of justice contained in the second part of *The Theory of Moral Sentiments*. The discussion turned on the several important respects in which the virtue of justice differed from other moral virtues.[5] In the operation of the moral sentiments, the failure to perform most virtues stimulated, in actual and ideal spectators, reactions of disapproval and disappointment. However, in the case of failures of justice, the moral response proved sharper and more potent. Violations of justice involved readily perceived "injury" to its victims (or, "real and positive hurt to some particular persons"); and in these cases, actual and ideal spectators were moved to "resentment," and even more, to the positive support for "punishment" (or "the violence

---

[4] See Meek and Skinner (1973), for a leading example of the use of the *Lectures on Jurisprudence* to chart Smith's development as an economic theorist. The scholarship of Winch and Haakonssen has proved the most critical and influential in indicating the importance of the *Lectures on Jurisprudence* for general interpretation of Smith's moral and social theory; see especially, Haakonssen (1981; 1982; 1996, chapter 4); and Winch (1978, chapters 3–4; 1996, chapters 4 and 6). My interpretation in this chapter is throughout heavily indebted to Winch's and Haakonssen's contributions.

[5] Smith's position here corresponds to the approach adopted by other contemporary Scottish moralists with whom he had direct contact: Kames (to whom Smith appears to refer at TMS, II.ii.1.5), and Hume (to whom Smith appears to refer at TMS, II.ii.3.6). Haakonssen (1981) places particular emphasis on the impact of Hume's theory of justice on Smith's legal theory.

employed to avenge the hurt") for those committing such acts of injustice (TMS, II.ii.1.3–5).

If violations of justice thus prompted a particular and atypically forceful moral reaction, the conduct required by the virtue of justice could likewise be differentiated from the rest of moral life. In contrast to the frequently open-ended and active performances attending the fulfillment of other social virtues, the virtue of justice was conspicuous for its largely "negative" orientation.

Mere justice is, upon most occasions, but a negative virtue, and only hinders us from hurting our neighbour. The man who barely abstains from violating either the person, or the estate, or the reputation of his neighbours, has surely very little positive merit. He fulfils, however, all the rules of what is peculiarly called justice.... We may often fulfil all the rules of justice by sitting still and doing nothing. (TMS, II.ii.1.9)

Justice was further distinguished on account of its unique societal impacts. Whereas some form of society might exist in the absence of the practice of other moral virtues, no society could "subsist among those who are at all times ready to hurt and injure one another." On this basis, justice was displayed as "the main pillar" supporting social life. Remove justice, Smith maintained, and "the immense fabric of human society...must in a moment crumble into atoms" (TMS, II.ii.3.3–4). It was this distinctive feature, Smith went on to carefully explain, which laid the foundation for the mistaken theory that identified the origins and obligations of justice in terms of its utility. This rival approach (such as that Smith found in Hume's account of justice) confused "efficient" and "final" causes. In cases of injustice, the distinctive moral response of resentment and punishment concerned the particular injury directly suffered, and not the general social interest ultimately served by this moral response (see TMS, II.ii.3.5–10).

In later sections of his moral treatise, Smith pursued further implications of what he had identified to be the distinguishing properties of justice. Because what was required by justice in a given situation could be identified with unique precision and specificity, it was possible to formulate the requirements of justice as a body of "general rules" whose operation admitted few "exceptions or modifications." In contrast, the "general rules" of all other virtues – in the case of (say) "the offices of prudence, of charity, of generosity, of gratitude, of friendship" – necessarily would "admit of many exceptions, and require so many modifications," as to make it impossible to regulate moral conduct in this way (TMS, III.6.9–10).

This contrast later came into particular prominence when Smith, in the final section of the final part of *The Theory of Moral Sentiments*, examined "the Manner in which different Authors have treated of the practical Rules of Morality" (TMS, VII.iv). There he condemned the tradition of Christian casuistry for its effort "to lay down exact and precise rules for the direction of every circumstance of our behaviour" (TMS, VII.iv.7). The approach rested on the foundational error of treating the whole of morality in terms of those kinds of general rules which could successfully regulate moral practice only in the case of the virtue of justice. "Books of casuistry," Smith accordingly noted, "are generally as useless as they are commonly tiresome" (TMS, VII.iv.33). On the other hand, it remained possible and entirely useful to treat systematically those general rules that properly obtained in the case of justice; such was the conventional program for jurisprudence, designed "to prescribe rules for the decisions of judges and arbiters" (TMS, VII.iv.8). In its usual manifestations, jurisprudence considered the particular versions of the rules of justice contained in actual systems of positive law. However, in its most ambitious and systematic form, this branch of moral philosophy aimed to construct "what might properly be called natural jurisprudence, or a theory of the general principles which ought to run through and be the foundation of the laws of all nations." Here the work of the Dutch jurist, Hugo Grotius, proved both seminal and exemplary. He was the first, Smith reported, to attempt a system of natural jurisprudence, and "his treatise of the laws of war and peace, with all its imperfections, is perhaps at this day the most complete work that has yet been given upon this subject" (TMS, VII.iv.37).

III. NATURAL JURISPRUDENCE

There was much that was quite conventional in Smith's identification of natural jurisprudence as a distinct and important branch of moral philosophy, and in his acknowledgment of Grotius's achievement in launching the field through his celebrated 1625 treatise,

On the Law of War and Peace.[6] His review of previous treatments
of moral rules echoed several of the claims advanced earlier in the
eighteenth century by several of the influential proponents of the
Grotian project – most notably, by Grotius's erudite translator and
propagandist, Jean Barbeyrac. Barbeyrac's An Historical and Critical Account of the Science of Morality, which first appeared as
the preface to his 1706 French translation of Pufendorf's The Law
of Nature and Nations (1672), lauded Grotius for helping rescue
moral science from the calamitous grip of scholasticism. It also
centered the subsequent history of morals on the reception and
critical recastings of Grotius's rights theory at the hands of such figures as Selden, Hobbes, and Locke – a process that reached its most
comprehensive and commanding expression in Pufendorf's natural jurisprudence. Smith joined Barbeyrac not only in emphasizing
the foundational nature of Grotius' jurisprudence, but also, more
generally, in finding an important point of unity between Grotius
and classical Stoicism in their shared repudiation of scholastic and
casuistical approaches (see TMS, VII.iv.3–6, 34–5). At the same
time, it is less clear that Smith viewed the post-Grotian development of the science in the same triumphalist terms mapped by
Barbeyrac. In the Lectures on Jurisprudence, Smith singled out
for praise Hobbes (the "next writer of note" after Grotius) and
reported the "very ingenious and distinct" publications of the Prus-
sian jurists, Henry von Cocceji and his son, Samuel (LJ[B], 1–4).[7]
Pufendorf, in contrast, was noticed glancingly and somewhat unen-
thusiastically as a critic of Hobbes; thus suggesting that the insistence in The Theory of Moral Sentiments on Grotius's continued
preeminence reflected Smith's reservations over the contributions
of his most famous successor.

One important dimension of this jurisprudential tradition,
directly relevant to Smith's own experience, was its impact on

---

[6] Recent scholarship in early modern and eighteenth-century intellectual history has
produced several important studies of the theory of natural rights and natural law
that Smith and his contemporaries termed natural jurisprudence. Among a rich literature, see the valuable surveys presented in Tuck (1979; 1987); Haakonssen (1996);
and Schneewind (1998, chapters 1–8). The more specifically Scottish engagement
with this and related forms of legal speculation are valuably surveyed and examined
by John Cairns (1993; 2003) and Haakonssen (2003).
[7] The notice of Cocceji's publications is unusual. The appeal of this material for Smith
is helpfully examined by Haakonssen (1996, chapter 4).

the teaching of moral philosophy at the Protestant universities of northern Europe. Pufendorf's natural law theory, especially in the form of his conveniently compact redaction, *On the Duty of Man and Citizen* (*De officio hominis et civis juxta legem naturalem*) (1673), became a standard and extensively used text of ethical pedagogy.[8] In the case of Scotland, Pufendorf's treatise entered the curriculum of Glasgow University in the 1690s, under the reforming initiative of Gershom Carmichael, whose innovation was soon copied at Edinburgh and elsewhere. Carmichael published an influential edition and commentary on Pufendorf's *De Officio* in 1718, and this remained the set text in moral philosophy at Glasgow during the period of Smith's studentship in the 1730s.[9] Smith's "never to be forgotten" teacher, Francis Hutcheson, praised Carmichael as "by far the best commentator" on Pufendorf's brief compendium of natural jurisprudence.[10] Hutcheson's own textbook, *A Short Introduction to Moral Philosophy . . . Containing the Elements of Ethicks and the Law of Nature*, largely conformed in structure and approach to the model of Pufendorf as mediated by Carmichael.

Accordingly, Smith's own entry into the science of jurisprudence can be thought of in terms of two powerful and largely complementary frames. There was first the argument of *The Theory of Moral Sentiments*, explaining the subject matter of natural jurisprudence and indicating the still imperfect state of the science.[11] Second was the established pedagogy of Glasgow University, with the writing of Grotius's successors firmly in place in the teaching of moral

---

[8] The reception and impact of Pufendorf's moral and legal philosophy is considered in Othmer (1970), Medick (1973), and Hochstrasser (2000).

[9] Carmichael's editorial material is included in Carmichael (2002). See also Moore and Silverthorne (1983; 1984).

[10] Hutcheson (1747, pp. i, iii–iv). The *Short Introduction* comprised a translation of the second edition of *Philosophiae moralis institutio compendiaria* (1745; first ed. 1742). In 1755, Hutcheson's son published a fuller work covering the same ground, the two-volume *A System of Moral Philosophy*. For contrasting commentary on these works, see Moore (1990) and Haakonssen (1996, pp. 65–85).

[11] Smith's judgment that the field still required further development was indicated in a passage in *The Theory of Moral Sentiments* that first described the project of natural jurisprudence: "The principles upon which those rules [of "the civil and criminal law of each particular state"] either are, or ought to be founded, are the subject of a particular science, of all sciences by far the most important, but hitherto, perhaps, the least cultivated, that of natural jurisprudence" (TMS, VI.ii.intro.2).

philosophy. The two frames clarify the importance Smith ascribed to the study of "the general principles of law and government," and they can usefully guide our initial consideration of the content of Smith's *Lectures on Jurisprudence*.

IV. LECTURES ON JURISPRUDENCE

The earlier of the two reports of Smith's lectures best reveals the more conventional elements of his teaching and the manner in which he developed his moral theory to accommodate the established categories of natural jurisprudence. The discussion of justice in *The Theory of Moral Sentiments* (as in the case of Hume's discussion in the *Treatise* and the *Enquiry*) contained no explicit theory or mention of rights. Rather, situations of justice were revealed and elucidated on the basis of the kind of spectatorial moral reaction which involved "resentment" and support for the "punishment" of those responsible for the misdeed in question. In the *Lectures*, Smith reformulated his theory, such that the kinds of "injury" which prompted this resentment involved the violation of another's right. "Justice is violated," Smith maintained, "whenever one is deprived of what he had a right to and could justly demand from others, or rather, when we do him any injury or hurt without a cause" (LJ[A], i.9). Having thus arrived at the key category of rights, Smith next navigated the established taxonomies and distinctions attending the jurisprudential analysis of rights.[12] He organized the exposition of rights in terms of the threefold classification used by Pufendorf in *De officio* and Hutcheson in the *Short Introduction*, distinguishing among the rights exercised "as a man," rights "as a member of a family," and rights "as a citizen or member of a state." His discussion again followed both predecessors by first taking up the class of rights "that belong to a man as a man." This category of rights enabled Smith quickly to cover and explicate a series of no less familiar taxonomies and classifications: the difference between "what Puffendorff calls natural rights" and "those which they call adventitious"; "the distinction which Mr. Hutchinson, after Baron

---

[12] Haakonssen (1981, pp. 99–114) provides the fullest commentary on Smith's utilization of the conventional categories of natural law and the older, Roman law tradition.

Puffendorf, has made" between "perfect and imperfect rights"[13]; and between "real" and "personal" rights (see LJ[A], i.12–16).

In addition to these occasions when Smith readily assimilated the analytical categories of natural jurisprudence (and the civilian tradition more generally), he proved in the *Lectures* no less adept at using the distinctive materials of his own moral theory to help resolve established controversies over the content of legal rights. In introducing the personal rights derived from contract, Smith referred to what "an impartial spectator would readily go along with" to explain the kinds of agreements that gave rise to legally valid obligations (LJ[A], ii.42–5). The same spectatorial perspective clarified that the grounds of contractual obligation rested on the expectation of performance (and the recognizable "injury" caused by non-performance), an insight which Smith next used to reject the rival interpretations (embraced by other "writers on the law of nature and nations") that derived contractual obligation "from the will of the person to be obliged" or the duty "of veracity" (LJ[A], ii.56–9).

In examining the personal rights created "by delinquency" (*ex delicto*) of another and the related issue of the appropriate severity of the sanction imposed by law on the offending party, Smith again returned to the ordering logic of the moral sentiments. Rehearsing themes fully explored in the account of justice in *The Theory of Moral Sentiments* (see TMS, II.ii.3.6–11), he insisted that "the measure of the punishment to be inflicted on the delinquent is the concurrence of the impartial spectator with the resentment of the injured" (LJ[A], ii.89). This perspective, Smith went on to explain, repudiated the alternative thesis, "which Grotius and other writers commonly alledge," that the original "measure of punishments" derived from utilitarian considerations "of the publick good" (LJ[A], ii.90–1).[14]

---

[13] Smith's discussion of justice in the *Lectures on Jurisprudence* was confined to the analysis of perfect rights. Smith's distinction between perfect and imperfect rights tracked the distinction between commutative and distributive justice developed in *The Theory of Moral Sentiments*. In *The Theory of Moral Sentiments*, however, Smith's treatment (again) did not employ the language or concept of rights; compare TMS, VII.ii.i.10 with LJ(A), i.14–15.

[14] The case of legal punishment figured prominently in Smith's general discussion of the relationship between justice and utility; see the commentary by Raphael (1972–3) and Haakonssen (1981, pp. 120–3).

Such instances, which might easily be expanded, provide useful indication of the relative ease with which Smith adapted his moral teaching to the established structures and controversies of natural jurisprudence (even though his published works gave scant indication of this potential). At the same time, they contrast with many important counterexamples, where Smith's discussion involved a more striking repudiation of major elements in the writing on the laws of nature and nations. Thus, to cite two well-known cases, his treatment of natural rights (which referred chiefly to rights of "our person" or "our reputation") proceeded without any recourse to the idea of a state of nature (LJ[A], ii.93). It "serves no purpose to treat of the laws which would take place in a state of nature," Smith curtly noted in criticism of Pufendorf, "as there is no such state existing" (LJ[B], 3). His treatment of rights relative to the sources and limits of political obligation included an explicit rejection of the proposition embraced by "the generality of writers" that "government owes its origins to a voluntary contract" (LJ[A], v.114–19).[15] Smith's discussion in these cases obviously involved more substantial revisions than the kind of discrete, doctrinal adjustments advanced in his treatment of contracts or punishment. They invite further scrutiny of the manner in which Smith's jurisprudence recast the intellectual and pedagogic traditions to which it contributed.

V. THE NATURAL HISTORY OF LEGAL ESTABLISHMENTS

In the course of a chapter-length survey of the recent "progress of science relative to law and government," Smith's most famous student, John Millar, rehearsed (what we have seen to be) familiar points concerning the novelty and achievements of "Grotius and other speculative lawyers." These jurists had aimed to construct "systems of jurisprudence" that contained those general principles of law which might ideally govern the administration of justice in particular states. Millar then turned to the succeeding, eighteenth-century contributions "by President Montesquieu, by Lord Kames and by Dr. Smith." Their studies of law and government had

---

[15] The rejection by Smith and other of the Scottish philosophes of the idea of a state of nature is routinely noted as a significant element in their historical or sociological approach to the science of human nature. See, for example, the influential discussion in Forbes (1954).

focused less on the Grotian effort to identify "a system of law" embodying "our views of absolute perfection," and instead scrutinized "the circumstances which occasioned various and opposite imperfections in the law of different countries" and which prevented human laws achieving the excellence "we find no difficulty in conceiving." To this end, they had emphasized "the first formation and subsequent advancement of civil society," the rise and development of "arts and sciences," the "acquisition and extension of property" in all its forms, and the combined impact of these and other social forces on "the institutions and laws of any people." The result was the construction of a "natural history of legal establishments" that constituted Smith's most distinctive contribution to the science of law.[16]

Millar's account probably served better to characterize his own conception of jurisprudence than to capture some uniform program contained in the writings of Montesquieu, Kames, and Smith. Nonetheless, the terms of the discussion plainly echoed Smith's own published description of jurisprudence, which similarly identified two complementary tasks for this field of moral speculation. First, natural jurisprudence had an explicitly normative and universalistic orientation: "a theory of the general principles which *ought* to run through and be the foundation of the laws of *all* nations" (TMS, VII.iv.37; emphasis added). As such, it stood in critical relationship to "systems of positive law," which were instituted to "enforce the practice" of justice, but whose operation never achieved the envisaged perfection of "a system of natural jurisprudence." Second was the effort to understand and elucidate the various circumstances that so prevented positive law from fully achieving the dictates of "natural justice." Here Smith noted such forces as the corrupting influences of "the interest of the government," "the interest of particular orders of men who tyrannize the government," or "the rudeness and barbarism of the people" (TMS, VII.iv.36). Accordingly, Smith's projected "discourse" on "the general principles of law and government" was designed to take up both questions: the established, normative goals of natural

[16] Millar (1818, vol. 4, pp. 282–5). See also his comments at vol. 2, pp. 429–30n, where Smith is identified as "the Newton" of these historical inquiries.

jurisprudence, as well as the more sociological discussion "of the different revolutions" positive law and government "have undergone in the different ages and periods of society" (TMS, VII.iv.37).

This orientation helps explain the major and most striking feature of the *Lectures on Jurisprudence*, which was the enormous amount of historical detail in terms of which Smith elucidated the established catalogue of legal rights, as "a man," a "member of a family," and "a member of a state." Indeed, as the cumulative weight of discussion makes clear, aside from the relatively narrow range of rules Smith treated under the category of "natural rights," the vast bulk of jurisprudence concerned materials that, for Smith, only could be understood in terms of the specific historical circumstances of their emergence and subsequent development. As Smith characteristically reported at the start of his discussion of the five conventional foundations of property rights (occupation, accession, prescription, succession, tradition): "Before we consider exactly this or any of the other methods by which property is acquired it will be proper to observe that the regulations concerning them must vary considerably according to the state or age society is in at that time" (LJ[A], i.26–7).

It was in this precise setting that Smith went on to identify the "four distinct states" (or "ages") through which "mankind pass" – "1st, the Age of Hunters; 2dly, the Age of Shepherds; 3dly, the Age of Agriculture; and 4thly, the Age of Commerce" (LJ[A], i.27).[17] This four-stage taxonomy of societal development became a central (and, in recent scholarship, a much studied) fixture of the historical writing of the Scottish philosophers, and there are strong reasons to think that Smith's jurisprudence lectures were the vehicle through which the theory first gained currency.[18] In the lectures

---

[17] In the second report of the lectures, the terminology is simplified: "The four stages of society are hunting, pasturage, farming, and commerce"; LJ(B), 149.

[18] The first published usages of the "four-stages theory" in Scotland appear in two historical legal studies of the 1750s: Dalrymple (1758) and Kames (1758). Meek proposes that Smith's Edinburgh law lectures were the likely source for both authors; see Meek (1976b, pp. 111–12). There is also evidence that the account of societal progress in the introductory section of William Robertson's (1769) *History of the Reign of Charles V* likewise was taken from the same source; see the discussion in Ross (1995, p. 105). Meek (1976b) remains the fullest survey of the use of the "four-stages theory" among the Scottish writers.

themselves, Smith used the "four stages of society" to explain the varied nature and especially the extent of rights of property under distinct social formations. Thus, in "the age of hunters" the objects of property generally were limited to goods of immediate possession so property rights themselves were largely confined to the juridical category of "occupation." In "the age of shepherds," inequalities of property grew dramatically (a development having profound consequence for the structure of authority in these communities). The most important objects of property were the animals under pasturage. This form of property gave rise to a wider range of property forms ("from herds and flocks to the land itself" LJ[A], ii.97) and to new grounds of property title (as, for example, property by "accession" in the case of the milk and offspring of the cattle under "occupation" LJ[A], i.64). However, it was not until the "age of agriculture" that rights of property attained their full juridical elaboration. It was not until this stage of social development that "property of land" became paramount, and it was this specific "species of property" which historically received "the greatest extension it has undergone" (LJ[A], i.52–3).

The four-stage theory again explicitly appeared when Smith came to consider the principal forms and functions of government, as part of his exposition of the individual's rights "as a member of a state." As in the case of property rights, Smith made it clear that the analysis of both the basic forms and the main functions of political society needed to be framed in terms of the broader progress of civil society. Government, which for Smith always presupposed "property" and an "inequality of . . . goods," did not arise until "the age of shepherds," when increasing inequalities of wealth first rendered it "absolutely necessary" (LJ[A], iv.22–3). In these societies, the earliest institutionalizations of judicial and executive power emerged (LJ[A], iv.34). However, as in the case of property rights, it was not until the age of agriculture that the organization of states and their characteristic functions assumed the shapes recognizable in the categories of modern jurisprudence. It was the governments of agrarian societies which routinely practiced the principal attributes of sovereignty (legislative, judicial, and federative [or executive] power) and which were organized historically as democracies, aristocracies, or monarchies (LJ[A], iv.1–3).

VI. HISTORICAL JURISPRUDENCE

The established jurisprudence on natural law and natural right had no difficulty recognizing the idea (as here voiced by Pufendorf) that "the laws or usages" of any particular state needed to be judged in terms of the specific "character of the people or of the territory" over which they governed.[19] Nonetheless, in its extensive historical detail and in its broader historical orientation, Smith's *Lectures on Jurisprudence* differed markedly from its immediate pedagogic predecessors. The contrast with Hutcheson's *Short Introduction to Moral Philosophy* occurs over many topics and can be illustrated in their treatments of chattel slavery, which both moralists considered conventionally as part of the rights of "masters and servants." Hutcheson's brief and critical survey of chattel slavery began with a firm condemnation of some of the standard justifications for the institution. Considering the case of slavery as a form of legal punishment, he warned, "no cause whatsoever can degrade a rational creature from the class of men into that of brutes or inanimate things, so as to become wholly the property of another, without any rights of his own."[20]

Smith, in his treatment, likewise drew attention to the moral outrages that attended chattel slavery. In his account of Roman slavery, for example, he was concerned to report not only those "hardships which are commonly taken notice of by writers," but also the "severall others which are not so generally attended to" (LJ[A], iii.94). However, the moral censure was counter-balanced and qualified by a no less forthright acknowledgment of the historical pervasiveness of slavery and of the near impossibility of its full abolition (LJ[A], iii.101–2). Smith devoted special attention to a more sociological discussion of the manner in which the condition of the slave worsened under social conditions of "opulence and refinement" or under the political conditions of democracy (LJ[A], iii.110–11). He then explained the quite exceptional political

---

[19] Pufendorf (1991, p. 143). The use of historical materials in Pufendorf's moral and legal philosophy is examined in Hont (1987) and Dufour (1991, pp. 579–86); and see Forbes (1982).

[20] Hutcheson (1747, p. 274). See also the longer and somewhat clearer discussion in Hutcheson (1755, vol. 2, pp. 201–12).

dynamics that had led to slavery's otherwise unlikely elimination "in only a small part of Europe" (see LJ[A], iii.101, 117–22).

The discussion of chattel slavery also illustrates the manner in which Smith standardly combined the normative goal of natural jurisprudence with the dense explanatory narrative of social and political history. The critical, normative argument served to identify institutionalized failures of "natural justice," whereas the historical material served to illuminate the explanatory contexts for these failures. To return to the formulation of *The Theory of Moral Sentiments*, much of this historical elucidation turned directly on "the rudeness and barbarism of the people" or "the interest of particular orders of men who tyrannize the government" (TMS, VII.iv.36). Thus, in the case of slavery, the institution arose among "poor and barbarous people," where it proved "more tollerable" owing to the shared poverty of slave and master (LJ[A], iii.105). Elsewhere, the institution's survival was effectively shaped by the imperatives of social and political power. Under democratic government, slavery's perpetuation was virtually certain since most often in such communities "the persons who make all the laws" were the "persons who have slaves themselves" (LJ[A], iii.102). Correspondingly, its atypical abolition in western Europe was owing to the manner in which two powerful elites – the church and the king – used their authority to promote the emancipation of the slaves ("the villains"), as part of their shared efforts to weaken the rival power of the slave-masters ("the nobles and their vassalls") (LJ[A], iii.118–20).[21]

Much the same logic appeared when Smith considered the manifest abuses attending the rights of private property, such as the law of entails or other rules of succession that supported the concentration of large landed estates under a single proprietor. The "right of primogeniture," he maintained, required careful explanation because "this method of succession" proved "so contrary to nature, to reason, and to justice" (LJ[A], i.116). The origins of primogeniture were to be found in the particular character of allodial and

---

[21] This historical analysis also points to the importance of Smith's efforts to convince the contemporary "masters" of slaves that the institution in fact violated their economic interests; see LJ[A], iii.126–30 and LJ[B], 290–1, 299–300. See also the better-known discussion of the institution in *The Wealth of Nations*; WN, III.ii.8–12.

feudal government, which tied together landed property, military capacity, and government authority. Both systems historically had emerged in conditions of weak and unstable government authority, in which the allodial and feudal lords functioned "as little princes," responsible for the security of themselves and their vassals. In such circumstances, the division of landed estates among all heirs threatened the sources of political authority, much as the division of a kingdom among all the royal heirs would undermine the power of the feudal monarchy (LJ[A], i.129–33).[22]

The example of primogeniture displays another critical dimension of Smith's historical jurisprudence. This was the manner in which his historical research frequently complemented the purposes of normative criticism by making clear the antiquated or anachronistic character of many of those positive laws which most glaringly violated natural justice. Thus, in the case of primogeniture, whatever justification this rule of succession might once have enjoyed under the circumstances of allodial and feudal government had completely eroded under the conditions of modern politics, where law and the public administration of justice secured "the smallest property" as effectively as "the greatest" (LJ[A], i.131).[23] In discussing the European game laws (which contrary "to reason" secured exclusive property rights in "wild animalls"), Smith explained how the rules derived from the "tyranny of the feudal government," when "the king and his nobles appropriated to themselves everything they could, without great hazard of giving umbrage to an enslaved people." Feudal government, of course, was now obsolete. However, the game laws furnished evidence of the manner in which elements of feudal institutions "still prevails in some measure in all the governments of Europe" (LJ[A], i.54–5). Similarly, in treating the various laws granting exclusive monopolies and corporate privileges in the exercise of particular trades and manufactures (whose pernicious economic effects were explored at length), Smith emphasized that such regulations might appear "very reasonable" at the time of their historical introduction, when they helped "to bring about . . . the separation of trades

---

[22] The law of entails, not discussed here, is considered at LJ(A), i.160–7.
[23] A more familiar rendering of this argument appears in *The Wealth of Nations*; see WN, III.ii.1–7.

sooner than the progress of society would naturally effect." The recovery of this historical rationale, however, plainly disclosed the moral failure of their anachronistic survival. "But as this end is now fully answered," Smith concluded, "it were much to be wished that these as well as many other remains of the old jurisprudence should be removed" (LJ[A], ii.40–1).[24]

VII. JURISPRUDENCE AND THE PROGRESS OF SOCIETY

In the case of several of the examples noticed previously – the eradication of slavery in western Europe, the introduction of primogeniture, and the legislation establishing corporate monopolies – Smith's discussion highlighted the impact of relatively specific and even idiosyncratic political dynamics on the legal institutions under examination. These accounts of legal change supply useful insight into Smith's broader understanding and utilization of the four-stage theory of society's progress, with which he introduced his jurisprudence of property and public rights. Some scholars have treated the four-stage theory as offering a fixed scheme of social evolution, in which societal change is ultimately determined by successive economies or "modes of subsistence."[25] The specific examples scrutinized in the Lectures on Jurisprudence give little indication that the theory operated either to reduce legal development to a single, overarching scheme of society's progress or to give final priority to modes of subsistence in the explanation of legal rules and legal change. Too much of the detailed discussion in the lectures concerned rules and practices which were specific to agrarian society for there to be much need for Smith to turn routinely to

---

[24] This form of historical criticism later figured routinely in the condemnation of unjust laws in The Wealth of Nations. See, for example, the discussion of primogeniture: "Laws frequently continue in force long after the circumstances, which first gave occasion to them, and which could alone render them reasonable, are no more" (WN, III.ii.4).

[25] This alternative characterization of the four-stages theory appears most emphatically in the scholarly attempts to compare Smith's historical theory with that of Marx; see Pascal (1938); Skinner (1967; 1975); and Meek's (1954) early (and subsequently revised) treatment. Salter (1992) offers an important survey of and contribution to the subsequent debate over the interpretation of Smith's theory of history. Salter's article was prompted, in part, by the revised interpretation of the historical orientation of Smith's Lectures on Jurisprudence presented by Winch and Haakonssen, which I chiefly follow here.

the larger pattern of societal development in the stages before and after agriculture. Also, too many of the instances of legal history which most interested Smith turned on the idiosyncratic political arrangements of feudal government for there to be much insight provided by the general features of agrarian society as such. Indeed, when in the *Lectures on Jurisprudence* Smith explored comparatively the pattern of development in particular agrarian communities such as Greece and Rome, his history suggested as much a cyclical pattern of growth and decline as it did a stadial scheme from rudeness to refinement.[26]

The critical appraisal of these historical examples also reveals the scope Smith allowed in matters of positive law for human purpose and normative reflection, as well as for political contingency and the machinations of social elites. This, perhaps, helps further explain why he viewed the history of jurisprudence as a complement and extension of the normative program of natural jurisprudence, rather than as an alternative to it. Legal history furnished insight and clarification as to why, in a particular historical setting, the institutions of law failed to achieve the standards of "natural justice," but it left in place (and, indeed, presupposed) the moral reality of natural justice itself.[27] At the same time, it must be acknowledged that the combining of natural jurisprudence and historical jurisprudence was never entirely seamless. One important fault line concerned the manner in which Smith's lectures accommodated two distinct organizing schemes for the analysis of a legal system. The first, supplied by natural jurisprudence, distributed the legal materials into three discrete categories according to the legal status of an individual legal subject: rights as "a man," rights as "a member of a family," and rights as "a member of a state." The second, supplied by the taxonomy of the four-stages theory, ordered the legal materials according to relevant "stage" of society, but in a manner that emphasized the interdependence of those legal rights and legal practices which the classification of natural jurisprudence separated. As heuristic devices, the two schemes thus pointed in different directions.

---

[26] See Winch (1978, pp. 63–4), and Haakonssen (1981, pp. 178–81), for a further exploration of this point.

[27] Again, my reading follows the interpretation advanced in Winch and Haakonssen; see especially, Haakonssen (1981, chapter 8).

The place in his jurisprudence where Smith made explicit something of this tension was in the second reported series of lectures, where he addressed the issue of where to begin his account of justice in terms of the standard, threefold division of rights in natural jurisprudence. In his earlier lectures, he had followed Hutcheson and Pufendorf in beginning with the individual's rights "as a man," which led him to present his historical jurisprudence of property rights before he came to his historical discussion of government (under the third category of the individual's rights as "a member of a state"). The problem, as Smith acknowledged it, was that "property and civil government very much depend on one another. The preservation of property and the inequality of possession first formed it, and the state of property must always vary with the form of government" (LJ[B], 11). The problem, in other words, was that the categories of natural jurisprudence analytically separated just those institutions whose *interdependence* Smith's historical jurisprudence sought to elucidate.

Smith's solution, as reported in the second lecture series, was to abandon Hutcheson's and his own earlier practice, and embrace the method of the "civilians" by beginning his discussion with "government and then [to] treat of property and other rights" (LJ[B], 11). One major result of this reordering of materials was that it enabled Smith to reach far more quickly, and thus give greater prominence to, one of the most original and powerful elements of his historical jurisprudence: his account of the emergence of the modern European system of public justice and regular government.

Smith's history of the transformation of European government and society under the impact of commerce and manufactures received its best-known and most confident formulation in the third book of *The Wealth of Nations*, on "the different Progress of Opulence in different Nations." The basic features of the account, however, received their first elaboration in the discussion of government in the *Lectures on Jurisprudence*. There, as in the later political economy, Smith explained how the introduction of "commerce and manufactures" came to destroy the feudal order. The great lords undermined their own social power by directing their surplus wealth away from the maintenance of retainers and tenants and on to the consumption of the refined and costly goods of the "tradesman or artificer." This, in turn, freed their tenants and retainers from their former positions of dependency, helped pacify the countryside, served to enrich and strengthen the social power of urban and mercantile orders, and made possible the extension throughout the society of that more ordered and stable administration of justice which earlier developed in the European towns and urban centers. Among the cumulative effect of these transformations, as Smith put it in *The Wealth of Nations*, was the gradual introduction of "order and good government, and with them, the liberty and security of individuals" (WN, III.iv.4).[28]

In the climactic, concluding passages of Book III of *The Wealth of Nations*, Smith coolly observed the profound ironies revealed by this historical transformation. "A revolution of the greatest importance to the publick happiness" had been produced by those "who had not the least intention to serve the publick." The "great proprietors," in their new expenditures, merely sought to "gratify the most childish vanity," whereas the "merchants and artificers" merely had pursued "their own pedlar principle of turning a penny wherever a penny was to be got" (WN, III.iv.17). The fuller and more detailed rehearsal of this history in the *Lectures on Jurisprudence* lacked these splendid ironies, although there, too, Smith's was a narrative of contingency and unintended consequences. What, however, the framework of the *Lectures* helpfully displays was the extent to which Smith's historical sociology mobilized and recombined in novel fashion its basic jurisprudential elements. The historical treatment neatly wove together a narrative of changes in the *objects* of property right (from land and retainers to the luxuries of commerce and manufactures), in the *practice* of property rights (from feudal dependency to security of tenancy and personal independence), and in the *government structures* preserving property rights and justice (from feudal instability to regular government and personal liberty). Here, as elsewhere in *The Wealth of Nations*, the synthetic achievement of Smithian political economy rested firmly on the pedagogic experience of the Glasgow professorship.

---

[28] The fuller discussion in the *Lectures on Jurisprudence* helpfully clarifies Smith's understanding of the particular features of England and English politics, which prevented it from conforming to the common pattern on the Continent, where the decline of the power of the feudal aristocracy led to the rise of royal absolutism; see LJ(A), iv.164–79 and LJ(A), v.1–15.

VIII. POLICE, REVENUE, AND ARMS

In the second and briefer part of the *Lectures on Jurisprudence*, Smith turned to "the general principles of law and government" as they related to "Police, Revenue, and Arms." The first topic addressed "the cheapness of commodities, public security and cleanliness"; "revenue" referred to the measures adopted "for defraying the expences of government"; and "arms" concerned the steps taken by government to defend the community "from foreign injuries and attacks" (LJ[B], 5–6). As in the case of the prior and more extensive discussion of the principles of law and government relating to justice, Smith's subject matter was taken from the established pedagogy of natural jurisprudence. Pufendorf, in *De officio*, had briefly identified each topic in chapters on "the functions" and "the duty" of the sovereign. These included, among other tasks, measures "to ensure the growth of the citizens' personal prosperity," authority "to compel the citizens to defray" the expenses of the state, and responsibilities "to ensure safety against outsiders" by organizing "as many men as may seem necessary for the common defence."[29] Hutcheson, in his Glasgow teaching, had raised several of the specific issues Smith explored in this part of his lectures, such as the discussion of "values or prices of goods," and the arguments identifying the sources of "wealth and power" in "diligence and industry."[30]

Nonetheless, Smith's treatment, and above all the extreme selectivity with which he focused on particular topics, clearly differed from the earlier pedagogic materials. The manner in which the lectures involved an innovative traversal of the established jurisprudential field is perhaps most clearly found in his coverage of "police." The term, as Smith clarified it, denoted a large and heterogeneous body of regulations, most often relating to urban spaces, covering such matters as the prevention of crimes, the safety of roads and the maintenance of public order, and the cheapness and supply of goods and staples.[31] Yet, while fully acknowledging

---

[29] Pufendorf (1991, pp. 154, 140).

[30] Hutcheson (1747, pp. 209–13, 322–3). Cannon (1896, pp. xxvi–xxvii) proposed that this material provided the initial stimulation for Smith's engagement with political economy.

[31] Smith at several points characterizes what he understands by "police, revenue and arms"; see LJ(A), i.1–4, vi.1–2; LJ(B), 5, 203–5. See also the surveys of

the capacious area of law conventionally covered under "police," Smith at the very outset of his lectures emphasized that many of these subjects were too "mean and trifling" to be included "in a system of jurisprudence." In contrast, those regulations devoted to "the cheapness of provisions" and "having the market well supplied" were identified as "the most important branch of police," and these, accordingly, warranted special attention (LJ[A], 2–4). Hence, when Smith later in his lectures came to this material following the more lengthy treatment "of Justice," he swiftly focused on the matter of "cheapness or plenty." The exploration of the topic, he no less swiftly explained, properly centered on the foundation question of "wherein opulence consists" (LJ[B], 203–6). Then followed, in summary form, a line of argument later made famous in the pages of *The Wealth of Nations* – that "the division of labour" was the source of "the opulence of a country" (a point already illustrated with the example of the manufacture of pins); that the cause of such division of labour was to be found in the "propensity in human nature" to "barter and exchange"; and that this analysis revealed that most of the government policies aimed at securing "cheapness and plenty" were, in fact, counter-productive contributors to "the slow progress of opulence" in "modern times" (LJ[B], 212–15, 218–20, 223, 235).

Smith's account of "taxes and revenue" – the second main topic of this part of the *Lectures on Jurisprudence* – immediately followed on the preceding analysis of those misguided government measures retarding "the progress of opulence." Indeed, the treatment effectively continued the same discussion, since it was in terms of the specific matter of "opulence" that Smith assessed at length the relative merits of the two principal sources of government revenue, "taxes upon possessions" and "taxes upon consumptions" (LJ[B], 307, 310). This was succeeded by another extended commentary devoted to what Smith identified as "the last division of police" (LJ[B], 326). This division concerned "the influence of commerce on the manners of a people," the setting in which Smith sketched many of the themes to which again he returned in *The Wealth of Nations*, particularly Book V's arguments in support of

eighteenth-century discussions of "police" and *"polizeiwissenschaft"* in Small (1909) and Walker (1978).

"institutions for the education of youth" under conditions of extensive division of labour (see LJ[B], 328–33, and WN, V.i.f.50–61).

In comparison with these extensive explorations of the nature, sources, progress, and moral impacts of opulence, Smith's coverage of the final title of this part of the lectures, "of Arms," was proportionately brief and routine. His closing remarks on the laws of war and peace – a topic which had received such lavish exposition in the mainstream literature on "law of nature and nations"– was perhaps most remarkable for its comparative lack of novelty. In contrast to so much of the preceding jurisprudence, this part of Smith's instruction boasted the less momentous qualities of balance, judiciousness, and predictability.

IX. JUSTICE AND POLICE

In his report of Smith's Glasgow teaching (to which reference was made previously[32]), John Millar distinguished the second part of the *Lectures on Jurisprudence* from the earlier material in two ways. The second part – "on police, revenue, and arms" – had largely reached publication through the vehicle of Smith's *The Wealth of Nations*.[33] The second part addressed laws and regulations founded on "*expediency*," whereas the first and larger part examined those laws and institutions founded "upon the principle of *justice*" (EPS, 275).

In so differentiating the moral principles animating the two parts of Smith's jurisprudence, Millar seemed eager to honor Smith's own insistence on the need in moral philosophy to keep distinct the special properties of justice as a moral virtue. As we have seen, only the practice of justice could be specified as a system of exact rules, and the failure to observe this peculiarity had led earlier moralists into casuistry (an error which seventeenth-century writers on natural jurisprudence had not entirely avoided; see TMS, VII.iv.7). Accordingly, the form of normative guidance to be expected in the treatment of justice and perfect rights did not set the model for the form of normative guidance to be expected in the treatment of police.

---

[32] See, Section i.

[33] Millar here followed Smith's own statement in the "Advertisement" to the sixth edition of *The Theory of Moral Sentiments*.

At the same time, however, Millar's juxtaposing of "justice" and "expediency" in Smith's moral teaching is, potentially at least, quite misleading. The risk lies in supposing that the laws and regulations founded on what Millar termed the principle of "expediency" were simply independent of, or unconnected with, the laws and regulations founded on the principle of justice. In fact, justice was relevant to the consideration of virtually all the practices and topics Smith covered under "police, revenue, and arms." The distinction between "justice" and "expediency" served to distinguish two distinct moral perspectives on law and government. However, it emphatically did not carve out two separate and autonomous regions of social life, each exclusively shaped by a single and different moral virtue.

The *Lectures on Jurisprudence* supplied ample testimony to the manner in which the virtue of justice saturated the varied laws and policies covered under the headings, "police, revenue, and arms." Thus, Smith reported that one of the principal branches of "police" concerned the general measures taken by government to ensure the security of the community by preventing crime or by bringing to justice those who committed crime. These materials Smith termed "the justice of police," and accordingly chose to discuss in "the former part of jurisprudence" covering justice and perfect rights (LJ[A], i.3). Again, in considering the established issues concerning "a just cause of war" – which appeared within the section on the laws of nations that Smith attached to the discussion "of Arms" – he promptly explained that "whatever is the foundation of a proper law suit before a court of justice may be a just occasion of war" (LJ[B], 340). The same direct appeal to "the rule of justice" featured routinely as Smith went on to consider what was lawful in the conduct of war and the obligations on belligerent states in their dealings with neutral nations.

In the case of "plenty or opulence" – the topic which dominated Smith discussion of "police" – the relationship to justice requires more careful elaboration. The "first and chief design of every system of government," he explained at the start of his lectures, was "to maintain justice" by securing to the members of the community their property and "what are called their perfect rights." The further measures government adopted "with respect to the trade, commerce, agriculture, [and] manufactures of the country" were secondary to, and presupposed the achievement of, government's primary goal of maintaining justice (LJ[A], i.1–2).

This initial formulation of the interconnection between "justice" and "opulence" was then given greater specificity when Smith examined at length "the causes of the slow progress of opulence," which implicated the operation of law and government (LJ[B], 285). First and foremost among these was the failure of government, particularly frequent "in the infancy of society," to secure its primary goal of establishing a stable structure of justice. Without the background security of rights and property, people had "no motive to be industrious," and no other political defect could "be more an obstacle to the progress of opulence" (LJ[B], 287–8). Smith next turned to a second and different way in which government might frustrate the advance of opulence, through the positive (and frequent) adoption of "oppressive measures" which damaged either "agriculture" or "commerce." The examination of this issue led Smith into several subjects he had scarcely noticed earlier in the lectures, such as the discussion of the relative merits of rival approaches to taxation. However, no less frequently, the examination led Smith back to topics he already had considered in terms of justice. Thus, to cite a leading example, his survey of "oppressive" government measures began with the various laws which threw "great tracts of land into the hands of single persons." This account naturally focused on the "right of primogeniture" and the "institution of entails," which Smith had previously analyzed at length in his treatment of property rights, and which he again related to "the tyranny of the feudal aristocracy." However, whereas in the first part of the lectures (on justice), these institutions were condemned as the unjust remnants of an earlier and oppressive political order, now they were condemned as "extremely prejudicial to the public interest" on account of their "great hindrance to the progress of agriculture" (LJ[B], 289–95). In this example, as elsewhere, the "principles of law and government" as applied to "justice" and to "police" offered two complementary frameworks for the assessment on the same body of positive law.[34]

---

[34] See also the similar example of Smith's treatment of slavery under the heading of police, LJ(B), 290–1, 299–300.

In the *Lectures on Jurisprudence*, the manner in which Smith's treatment of "opulence" thus extended and presupposed the jurisprudence of justice would have been readily apparent given the manner in which the two discussions appeared as successive parts of a single body of moral instruction. However, Smith's ultimate failure to execute his general work on "law and government," coupled with his celebrated triumph in publishing *The Wealth of Nations*, worked to sever this immediate thematic connection. As the work of a recent generation of Smith scholars has rightly emphasized, the special significance of the *Lectures on Jurisprudence* is to indicate just how much of Smith's mature political economy remained linked to his earlier study of justice and law.

X. CONCLUSION: JUSTICE AND *THE WEALTH OF NATIONS*

Justice, of course, was not Smith's subject in *The Wealth of Nations*. Nonetheless, his expansive exploration of the virtue of justice, and its place in the history of law and government, exercised a pervasive impact on his treatment of the political economy of commercial society. In the final book of *The Wealth of Nations*, Smith turned directly to one such dimension of his understanding of justice, first articulated in *The Theory of Moral Sentiments* and then chronicled in detail in the *Lectures on Jurisprudence*. This was the virtue's unique standing as a necessary prerequisite for the maintenance of any social order. Among the "duties of great importance" placed on the sovereign was "the duty of protecting, as far as possible, every member of the society from the injustice or oppression of every other member of it, or the duty of establishing an exact administration of justice" (WN, IV.ix.51, V.i.b.1).

Smith's discussion in Book V of "the Expence of Justice" reintroduced many of the themes of his earlier lectures. Government historically emerged and developed with the growing inequality of property. Its chief objective then was to preserve justice by securing the rights of property, which was to say that it was "instituted for the defence of the rich against the poor, or of those who have some property against those who have none at all" (WN, V.i.b.12). In this setting, though, Smith's special concern was with another, more particular historical development, again first charted in his history of law. This was the process by which the political institutions charged with the administration of justice – courts and judges – had come in the European states, and especially in England, to be detached from the other branches of public power. As ever for Smith, this was a history of unintended consequences, prompted by the immediate self-interest of the socially powerful (in this case, sovereigns lacking the financial incentives to dispense justice directly). However, the eventually resulting consequence of this dynamic was the separation and increasing independence of "judicial" from "executive power," an institutional structure that greatly enhanced opportunities for "the impartial administration of justice." This distinctive feature of modern British politics, moreover, was specifically responsible for "the liberty of every individual" and "the sense which he has of his own security" (WN, V.i.b.25).[35]

In these concluding remarks, Smith joined an important body of contemporary political speculation which emphasized the extent to which modern liberty in Britain owed more to the integrity and independence of the law and the courts than it did to the structures of parliamentary representation.[36] However, he also returned to the larger themes of his own political economy and to the manner in which the achievement of personal liberty and personal independence had been the product of the social and political transformations introduced by commerce and the progress of opulence. The "impartial administration of justice" treated in Book V, in this sense, was but a particular (although politically momentous) institutional manifestation of the historical sociology presented in Book III. Under the impact of commerce, the destruction of the feudal order and the power of the feudal aristocracy had created the opportunity for relations of justice to succeed the previous conditions of personal dependency. The historically parallel separation of judicial and executive power further served to realize this opportunity for justice. As Smith first explained in his jurisprudence "of

---

[35] For the parallel and fuller discussion of this legal history in the *Lectures on Jurisprudence*, see LJ(A), v.1–43, and LJ(B), 64–75.

[36] For a summary and introduction to this argument in eighteenth-century political theory, see D. Lieberman, "The Mixed Constitution and the Common Law," in eds. Goldie and Wokler (in press). Smith's own position is further illuminated in Winch (1996, chapter 4).

police," and then later elaborated in his political economy, this stable structure of rights and justice had done most to secure economic prosperity. As he put it in identifying the true sources for the success of Britain's colonial trade against that of other European states, "above all, that equal and impartial administration of justice which renders the rights of the meanest British subject respectable to the greatest" served to provide "the greatest and most effectual encouragement to every sort of industry" (WN, IV.vii.c.54).

To say that commercial society offered new opportunities for the practice of justice, however, was not to say that commercial society was in any sense inherently or effortlessly just. All systems of positive law, Smith maintained in his *The Theory of Moral Sentiments*, remained imperfect approximations of the rules of natural justice, and, as we have seen, among the objectives Smith assigned to natural jurisprudence was the task of revealing and elucidating such practical failures of justice. In scrutinizing in *The Wealth of Nations* the network of laws and institutions he synthesized into a unified system of "commercial or mercantile" regulation, Smith's primary concern was to explain the actual damage these rules caused to the economic prosperity they were alleged to promote. However, Smith was no less concerned to assess or to censure this mercantilist system from the perspective of justice. Such laws, he observed in examining the restraints governing the trade in corn, were "evident violations of natural liberty, and therefore unjust" and "as impolitick as they were unjust" (WN, IV.v.b.16). Or, as he more summarily expressed it in a set of concluding criticisms on the complex and counter-productive structure of bounties, subsidies, and monopolies: "It is unnecessary, I imagine, to observe, how contrary such regulations are to the boasted liberty of the subject, of which we affect to be so very jealous" (IV.viii.47).

Smith's jurisprudence had been concerned not only with identifying the imperfections of justice, but also with accounting for such failures historically – most often in terms of the distortions occasioned by "the interest of the government" or by "the interest of particular orders of men who tyrannize the government" (TMS, VII.iv.36). Here, too, the analysis of the law and justice in commercial society conformed to the logic of Smith's more general jurisprudence. The mercantilist system, Smith was eager to show, worked its injustices by serving the interests of one privileged social order against the interests of weaker social groups.[37] Indeed, this background framework perhaps helps explain the urgency and sheer repetition with which Smith insisted in identifying "our merchants and manufactures" as "the principal architects" of "this whole mercantile system" (WN, IV.viii.54).

Thus, "the greater part of the regulations concerning the colony trade" had been designed by the merchants conducting that trade, whose "interest" thereby had "been more considered than either that of the colonies or that of the mother country" (WN, IV.vii.b.49). "To found a great empire for the sole purpose of raising up a people of customers," Smith ironically noted of the legal monopolies governing colonial trade, was "a project altogether unfit for a nation of shopkeepers; but extremely fit for a nation whose government is influenced by shopkeepers" (IV.vii.c.63). The great linen manufactures had "extort(ed) from the legislature" the current system of protective bounties on exports and tariffs on competitive imports (IV.viii.4). The "woollen manufactures" had outpaced "any other class of workman" in persuading "the legislature that the prosperity of the nation depended upon the success ... of their particular business." The "cruellest of our revenue laws" proved "mild and gentle, in comparison of some of those which the clamour of our merchants and manufactures" had "extorted from the legislature" (IV.viii.17). "It is the industry which is carried on for the benefit of the rich and the powerful," Smith scathingly concluded, "that is principally encouraged by our mercantile system. That which is carried on for the benefit of the poor and the indigent, is too often, either neglected, or oppressed" (IV.viii.4).

In so distorting the operation of natural justice, the law of the modern commercial state, for all its distinctive features, recognizably conformed to the general patterns of legal imperfection expansively detailed in Smith's *Lectures on Jurisprudence*. As in earlier eras, the failures of justice could be identified in the political handiwork of the rich and the powerful. Natural justice thus provided

---

[37] See, for example, Smith's formulation at WN, IV.viii.30: "To hurt in any degree the interest of any one order of citizens, for no other purpose but to promote that of some other, is evidently contrary to that justice and equality of treatment which the sovereign owes to all the different orders of his subjects."

an appropriate template for delineating the defects, no less than the remarkable achievements of modern commercial society. In these respects, Smith's instruction in *The Wealth of Nations* proved a fitting testimony to his protracted and partially realized engagement with "the general principles of law and government."

REFERENCES

Cairns, John. 1993. "Adam Smith's lectures on jurisprudence: Their influence on legal education." In *Adam Smith: International Perspectives*, eds. Hiroshi Mizuta and Chuhei Sugiyama. New York, NY, pp. 63–83.

Cairns, John. 2003. "Legal theory." In *The Cambridge Companion to the Scottish Enlightenment*, ed. Alexander Broadie. Cambridge, pp. 222–42.

Cannan, Edwin. 1896. (ed. and intro.). *Lectures on Justice, Police, Revenue and Arms . . . by Adam Smith*. Oxford.

Carmichael, Gershom. 2002. *Natural Rights on the Threshold of the Scottish Enlightenment. The Writings of Gershom Carmichael*, eds. James Moore and Michael Silverthorne. Indianapolis, IN.

Dalrymple, John. 1758. *An Essay Towards a General History of Feudal Property in Great Britain* (1757), 2nd ed. London.

Forbes, Duncan. 1954. "Scientific whiggism – Adam Smith and John Millar." *Cambridge Journal.* (6): 643–70.

Forbes, Duncan. 1982. "Natural law and the Scottish enlightenment." In *The Origins and Nature of the Scottish Enlightenment*, eds. R. H. Campbell and Andrew Skinner. Edinburgh, pp. 186–204.

Goldie, Mark and Wokler, Robert. In Press. *The Cambridge History of Eighteenth-Century Political Thought*. Cambridge.

Haakonssen, Knud. 1981. *The Science of a Legislator: The Natural Jurisprudence of David Hume and Adam Smith*. Cambridge.

Haakonssen, Knud. 1982. "What might properly be called natural jurisprudence." In *The Origins and Nature of the Scottish Enlightenment*, eds. R. H. Campbell and Andrew Skinner. Edinburgh, pp. 205–25.

Haakonssen, Knud. 1996. *Natural Law and Moral Philosophy. From Grotius to the Scottish Enlightenment*. Cambridge.

Haakonssen, Knud. 2003. "Natural jurisprudence and the theory of justice." In *The Cambridge Companion to the Scottish Enlightenment*, ed. Alexander Broadie. Cambridge, pp. 205–21.

Hochstrasser, T. J. 2000. *Natural Law Theories in the Early Enlightenment*. Cambridge.

Hont, Istvan. 1987. "The language of sociability and commerce: Samuel Pufendorf and the theoretical foundations of the 'Four-Stages Theory'." In

The Languages of Political Theory in Early-Modern Europe, ed. Anthony Pagden. Cambridge, pp. 253–76.

Hutcheson, Francis. 1747. *A Short Introduction to Moral Philosophy*. Glasgow. [vol. 4 of Francis Hutcheson, *Collected Works*; facsimile reprint prepared by Bernhard Fabian, 7 vols. 1969–71. Hildesheim.]

Hutcheson, Francis. 1755. *A System of Moral Philosophy*, 2 vols. Glasgow. [vols. 5–6 of Francis Hutcheson, *Collected Works*; facsimile reprint prepared by Bernhard Fabian, 7 vols. 1969–71. Hildesheim.]

Kames, Henry Home, Lord. 1758. *Historical Law Tracts*, 2 vols. Edinburgh.

Medick, Hans. 1973. *Naturzustand und Naturgeschichte der burgerlichen Gesellschaft*. Göttingen.

Meek, R. L. 1954. "The Scottish contribution to Marxist sociology." In *Democracy and the Labour Movement*, ed. John Saville. London, pp. 84–102.

Meek, R. L. 1976(a). "New light on Adam Smith's Glasgow lectures on jurisprudence." *History of Political Economy*. (8): 439–77.

Meek, R. L. 1976(b). *Social Science and the Ignoble Savage*. Cambridge.

Meek, R. L. and Skinner, A. S. 1973. "The development of Adam Smith's ideas on the division of labour." *Economic Journal*. (83): 1094–116.

Millar, John. 1818. *An Historical View of English Government* (1803), 4 vols. London.

Moore, James. 1990. "The two systems of Francis Hutcheson: On the origins of the Scottish enlightenment." In *Studies in the Philosophy of the Scottish Enlightenment*, ed. M. A. Stewart. Oxford, pp. 37–59.

Moore, James and Silverthorne, Michael. 1983. "Gershom Carmichael and the natural jurisprudence tradition in eighteenth-century Scotland." In *Wealth and Virtue. The Shaping of Political Economy in the Scottish Enlightenment*, eds. Istvan Hont and Michael Ignatieff. Cambridge, pp. 73–87.

Moore, James and Silverthorne, Michael. 1984. "Natural sociability and natural rights in the moral philosophy of Gershom Carmichael." In *Philosophers of the Scottish Enlightenment*, ed. V. Hope. Edinburgh, pp. 1–12.

Othmer, Sieglinde. 1970. *Berlin und die Verbreitung des Naturrechts in Europa*. Berlin.

Pascal, Roy. 1938. "Property and society: The Scottish contribution of the eighteenth century." *Modern Quarterly*. (1): 167–79.

Pufendorf, Samuel. 1991. *On the Duty of Man and Citizen According to Natural Law [De officio hominis et civis juxta legem naturalem (1673)]*, ed. James Tully, trans. Michael Silverthorne. Cambridge.

Raphael, D. D. 1972–3. "Hume and Adam Smith on justice and utility." *Proceedings of the Aristotelian Society*. [new series]. (72): 87–103.

Ross, Ian Simpson. 1995. *The Life of Adam Smith*. Oxford.

Salter, John. 1992. "Adam Smith on feudalism, commerce and slavery." *History of Political Thought.* (13): 219–41.

Schneewind, J. B. 1998. *The Invention of Autonomy: A History of Modern Moral Philosophy.* Cambridge.

Skinner, A. S. 1967. "Natural history in the age of Adam Smith." *Political Studies.* (15): 32–48.

Skinner, A. S. 1975. "Adam Smith: An economic interpretation of history." In *Essays on Adam Smith,* eds. A. S. Skinner and T. Wilson. Oxford, pp. 154–78.

Small, Albion W. 1909. *The Cameralists, The Pioneers of German Social Polity.* Chicago, IL.

Tuck, Richard. 1979. *Natural Rights Theories. Their Origin and Development.* Cambridge.

Tuck, Richard. 1987. "The 'modern' theory of natural law." In *The Languages of Political Theory in Early-Modern Europe,* ed. Anthony Pagden. Cambridge, pp. 99–119.

Walker, M. 1978. "Rights and functions: The social categories of eighteenth-century German jurists and cameralists." *Journal of Modern History.* (50): 234–51.

Winch, Donald. 1978. *Adam Smith's Politics. An Essay in Historiographic Revision.* Cambridge.

Winch, Donald. 1996. *Riches and Poverty. An Intellectual History of Political Economy in Britain, 1750–1834.* Cambridge.

9   Self-Interest and Other Interests

Any discussion of Adam Smith's conception of self-interest labors under the shadow of Smith's encrusted reputation, summarized in George Stigler's claim that *"The Wealth of Nations* is a stupendous palace erected upon the granite of self interest."[1] Many puzzles of Smith interpretation, including the so-called "Adam Smith Problem" take this claim as a starting axiom. The Adam Smith Problem referred to the alleged inconsistency between *The Wealth of Nations*, which seemed to be premised on the claim that every individual was essentially self-interested, and *The Theory of Moral Sentiments*, which was based on a psychological principle of sympathy. This charge of inconsistency rests on a gross misunderstanding. Sympathy, for Smith, was not a principle of benevolence. It was rather a mechanism for moral judgment that allowed the agent to judge the appropriateness of all behavior. Within the judgments generated by the impartial spectator, there would be room for the proper pursuit of self-interest.

However, laying a simple version of the Adam Smith Problem to rest does not quite answer the question. Just what is the role of "self-interest" in Smith's account of motivation? What is the relationship of "self-interest" to other motivations and interests? This chapter does not intend to alleviate the various tensions that mark Smith's thought, but rather it is meant to work out the complicated ways in which conceptions of self-interest function in his major writings.

---

[1] George Stigler, "Smith's Travels on the Ship of the State," *History of Political Economy* 3 (1971): 265.

The first step of this enterprise requires that we put aside a persistent assumption about the way self-interest operates in *The Wealth of Nations*. It is often suggested, for instance, that there is an absence of ethical or moral concerns from this work. Many canonical interpretations argue that Smith's whole enterprise was to liberate economics from the reign of virtue or ethical concerns. Despite the efforts of numerous scholars, references to self-interest in *The Wealth of Nations* continue to be read in ways that disembed that notion from its *own* wider moral and historical concerns.[2] Accordingly, I begin by arguing that self-interest functions in a complicated way even within *The Wealth of Nations* and that it is a term suffused with moral connotations throughout. I then consider the way in which *The Theory of Moral Sentiments* makes room for a proper pursuit of self-love and the virtues appropriate to it, and conclude by arguing that for Smith our imagination, rather than our self-interest, is a more fundamental spring of human action. His theory of the imagination helps him overcome a puzzle left by previous moral theories. Why do people toil and labor? What is the conception of interest involved in such activity?

Any writing on Smith's account of human nature ought to begin by taking Smith's own methodological injunctions seriously. From his earliest lectures, Smith is hostile to the idea that human nature, especially human motivation, can be treated like an object in the physical world whose qualities could be exhaustively described:

The different passions all proceed from different states of mind and outward circumstances. But it would be both endless and useless to go thro' all these different affections and passions in this manner. It would be endless, because tho the simple passions are of no great number, yet these are so compounded in different manners as to make the number of mixt ones almost infinite. It would be useless, for tho we had gone thro all the different affections yet the difference of character and age and circumstances of the person would so vary the affects that our rules would not be at all applicable. (LRBL, i.165–6)

---

[2] For refutations of this view, see Knud Haakonssen, *The Science of a Legislator: The Natural Jurisprudence of David Hume and Adam Smith* (Cambridge, 1981); Emma Rothschild, *Economic Sentiments* (Cambridge, MA, 2001); Samuel Fleischacker, *A Third Conception of Liberty* (Princeton, NJ, 1999).

Even the most exhaustive description of human nature will, although it might set certain limits, *underdetermine* any conclusions we may draw from it. Smith's inquiry into human nature is not therefore essentialist. He is not asking: is human nature benevolent or malign?, or is human nature self-interested or benevolent? Smith's questions are rather, what in human nature makes virtue possible?, what in human nature makes morality possible?, and what in human nature makes the pursuit of wealth and honor possible? This inquiry does not yield a description of human nature in terms of a singular motive but charts some of its complex movements. Smith never erases the distinction between the ways in which human agents *usually* act in a variety of settings and the ways in which they are *capable* of acting – between what they *actually* do and what they *could* do.

One of the lessons that Smith learned from Stoicism against Hutcheson and Plato was that our psychology is not hierarchically ordered so that some part, say reason or benevolence, rules over others. The sources of human motivation are heterogenous and cannot be easily reduced to a few principles. There could be no virtuous action without passion; without fear, it would be impossible to explain the urge for self-defense and thus prudence; without resentment one could not explain the urge to punish; without pride there could be no sense of self-esteem; without wonder there would be no knowledge; and so on. It was implausible to suppose that these passions could be hierarchically ordered, or extirpated, without emptying human life of its most characteristic colors and depriving society of essential springs of action. Smith's avowed intention is to show that nature causes us to seek our good in terms of *all* these passions, and no account of our good can be given apart from them. Besides, all natural passions and psychological traits are, from a moral point of view, ambiguous and mixed. Some virtues or affections, such as benevolence, may come close to being considered an unqualified good, but others, equally natural, although not an unqualified good, are equally necessary. The worth of any of these passions, principally what Smith calls the unsocial and selfish passions, such as resentment, indignation, and self-love, cannot be determined simply from a description of the passions themselves but only from an account of their appropriateness to specific occasions. For Smith, each passion was distinct, and to redescribe the vast range of human motivation in terms of self-interest obscures its nature. Self-interest is just one among a whole range of motives, and it varies in its applications.

SELF-INTEREST IN *THE WEALTH OF NATIONS*

Stigler's exhortation that we admire the "granite of self interest" on which the palace of economics is built, captures the canonical view that self-interest is the central human motivation in *The Wealth of Nations*. This is true in a certain sense. It would be difficult to deny that for Smith the flow of economic life depends on self-interest. Consumers respond to prices, labor to changes in wages, and entrepreneurs to opportunities because they are guided by self-interest. For Smith, drive for self-betterment provides a basis for a perpetually expanding system of commerce and manufacture. It fosters the division of labor, gives dynamism to social life, and generates the energy to provide the resources to sustain the desideratum of social welfare for the least well off. This principle is at the center of the equilibrium of economic life. Capital rushes where profit margins are high and competition restores prices to their "natural repose and continuance." The impulse for self-betterment thus works to sustain the natural progress of things toward improvement. Smith's aim was to show that removing arbitrary restrictions on labor, prices, and supply would give self-interest free reign and bring about universal opulence. However, to present this view as implying that Smith emancipated economics from the restraints of morality is to miss the complex moral valences of self-interest. The pursuit of self-interest functions as a moral category in its own right in *The Wealth of Nations*.

THE MORALITY OF SELF-INTEREST

The moral undertones of Smith's conception of self-interest can be seen in what has probably become the single most famous passage in Smith's works:

But man has almost constant occasion for the help of his brethren, and it is in vain for him to expect it from their benevolence only.... It is not from the benevolence of the butcher, the brewer, or the baker, that we expect our dinner, but from their regard to their own interest. We address ourselves, not to their humanity but to their self-love, and never talk to them of our own necessities but of their advantages. Nobody but a beggar chuses to depend chiefly upon the benevolence of his fellow-citizens. (WN, I.ii.2)

Rather than an endorsement of the "granite of self interest" on which a "stupendous palace" could be erected, this passage is a platitude about the kind of motives one appeals to in a specific kind of transaction. As Fleischacker has argued, in transactions between us and the butcher what else are we supposed to appeal to but *their* self-love?[3] There is no claim here of the sort Bernard Mandeville espoused that all instances of benevolence really turn out to be, on close inspection, self-interested. The passage exhibits a dual movement characteristic of Smith. On the one hand, there are no motives, even benevolence, of which we can say that an appeal to them is an unqualified good. On the other hand, even self-love, may under certain circumstances be not only appropriate, but may signify moral qualities. An appeal to benevolence in such transactions would be a moral failing because it would be an insidious form of dependence. Would anybody but a beggar choose to depend on the benevolence of others? At the same time, moral qualities may attach to self-love. What would be more appropriate than to address the butcher and the baker by offering them something in return for what they might have to give? This passage focuses at least as much on the way in which these commercial exchanges prompt us to focus on *other* people's interests and the *mutuality* involved in doing so.

Furthermore, the problematic of *The Wealth of Nations* is not to establish the legitimacy of self-interest as the predominant human motivation at the expense of other forms of motivation. Smith takes it for granted that human beings act on a variety of motives, of which an important class is self-interest. The question is how can one ensure that acting on self-interest has beneficial outcomes for oneself and society as a whole?[4] Smith is committed to the thought that we ought to give those whose interest is in question more authority over its fulfillment. He sought to replace

[3] Fleischacker, *A Third Concept of Liberty*, chapter 6.
[4] Cf. similarly Fleischacker, p. 139.

the interests of those who exercise power over others with the interests of those over whom such power is exercised:

> The law which prohibited the manufacturer from exercising the trade of a shopkeeper, endeavoured to force this division in the employment of stock to go on faster than it might otherwise have done. . . . It is the interest of every society, that things of this kind should never either be forced or obstructed. The man who employs either his labour or his stock in a greater variety of ways than his situation renders necessary, can never hurt his neighbour by underselling him. He may hurt himself, and he generally does so. . . . But the law ought always to trust people with the care of their own interest, as in their local situations they must generally be able to judge better of it than the legislator can do. (WN, IV.v.b.16)

As we see from these reflections, *The Wealth of Nations* is not concerned with replacing other motives with self-interest. Rather, the issue is this: in economic transactions, such as choice of occupation, the employment of capital, or the selling of corn, where self-interest is the motive in any case, who is the best judge of that interest? Smith presumes that the person whose interest is in question must be regarded as the best judge. He is making room for the right kind of judgment to be exercised in those domains where our self-interest is at stake. Too often, legislators or others presume to know best how interests are to be served. In attacking that presumption, Smith is not replacing a public-spirited motive with a self-interested one. Rather, he is arguing that relevant agents be allowed to judge their own interests rather than having them judged by the powerful who, in any case, are likely to be guided by *their* interests.

It is also safer to trust people to pursue their own interests. Even if they judge their interests incorrectly, as many are apt to, the consequences will be less deleterious for society than if legislators, or those in positions of power, misjudge the interests of those over whom power is exercised.

Furthermore, when someone claims to act on behalf of others, there are usually competing interests at stake. *The Wealth of Nations* has an uncanny eye for the ways in which "systems of preference and restraint," whether advocated by legislators, merchants, mercantilists, or employers, usually privilege the interests of some over others and in reality mask the interests of the powerful about whom Smith rarely has anything good to say. Kings, ministers, clergy, educationists, monopolists, and merchants all thwart our interests with their own. Smith's point is clearly not to replace public spirit with self-interest but to ensure that an *equality* of interests prevails. "To hurt in any degree the interest of any one order of citizens, for no other purpose but to promote that of some other, is evidently contrary to that justice *and equality of treatment* which the sovereign owes to all the different orders of his subjects" (WN, IV.viii.30; italics added). The purpose of the *Wealth of Nations* is to redefine the public good so that it reflects the *equality* of interests:

It is the highest impertinence and presumption, therefore, in kings and ministers, to pretend to watch over the œconomy of private people.... They are themselves always, and without any exception, the greatest spendthrifts in the society. Let them look well after their own expence, and they may safely trust private people with theirs. If their own extravagance does not ruin the state, that of their subjects never will. (WN, II.iii.36)

THE SHAPING OF INTERESTS

To say that self-interest is an important human motivation would not be to say much. The brilliance of *The Wealth of Nations* is its analysis of what an adequate account of interest has to consider. First, what are the impediments to the pursuit of our interests? Not only powerful agents, but also our own passions, frequently impede our interests. In tune with his time, Smith thought self-love was far more benign than a range of other passions that were usually mistaken for it. For him the principal antonym of self-interest is not benevolence, although that is certainly one. As Stephen Holmes has pointed out, pride, an overestimation of one's own power and worth, vanity, possessiveness, domination, envy, and avarice can all impede the exercise of our interests.[5] The moral of *The Wealth of Nations* is that pride is the cause of injustice, irrationality, and folly. War is harmful but sustained by pride; colonies are detrimental but held onto because of pride; slavery is economically irrational but sustained by the love of domination; and primogeniture and entails,

[5] Stephen Holmes, "The Secret History of Self Interest," in *Beyond Self Interest*, ed. Jane Mansbridge (Chicago, IL, 1990).

even though unjust and against the *"real interest* of a numerous family," are sustained by the "pride of family distinctions." *The Wealth of Nations* is a virtual catalogue of the passions and rival motivations that impede the pursuit of self-interest.

Smith was part of a trajectory of thinkers, including Montesquieu, Hume, and Madison, who placed great stress on the fact that institutions, by structuring incentives, can alter the consequences of our pursuing our interests. Example after example in *The Wealth of Nations* is devoted to this thought. Smith traces carefully the relationship between the passions and the institutional contexts in which they operate. The motives on which we characteristically act depend on two things. Our behavior will often depend on the structure of incentives, to use the language of economics. However, more importantly, our sense of self, and therefore of our self-interest, is crucially shaped by the structure of our relationships with others. By placing motives in an institutional context, Smith redefines the debate over character and corruption by giving something like an institutional history of character. Consider, for example, his assessment of the difference between Roman and Greek justice.

Smith preferred Roman law over Greek because the former was more orderly and scientific. Furthermore, the

superiority of character in the Romans over that of the Greeks, so much remarked by Polybius and Dionysius of Halicarnassus, was probably more owing to the better constitution of their courts of justice, than to any of the circumstances to which those authors ascribe it. (WN, V.i.f.44)

In Greece, "the ordinary courts of justice consisted of numerous and, therefore, disorderly bodies of people, who frequently decided almost at random, or as clamour, faction and party spirit happened to determine." There was a less of a concern with rectitude because the "ignominy of an unjust decision, when it was to be divided among five hundred, a thousand, or fifteen hundred people..., could not fall very heavy upon any individual" (WN, V.i.f.44).

In Rome, by contrast, there was either a single judge or a small number who had to deliberate in public and, to avoid blame, sought shelter under some example or precedent. It was this attention to practice and precedent that made their courts more orderly. This is of direct relevance to Smith's emphasis on the separation of the executive and judicial branches of government in advanced societies where "the liberty of each individual" depends "upon the impartial administration of justice" (WN, V.i.b.25). The principle of this separation had to be made effective by devising institutional means that made judges less dependent on the patronage of the executive branch.

The "institutions" that form our characters, and hence modify and shape our interests, are much broader than those of the state. Consider his wonderful discussion of the differences in crime between Paris and London:

[I]n cities where there is most police and the greatest number of regulations concerning it, there is not always the greatest security. In Paris the regulations concerning police are so numerous as not to be comprehended in several volumes. In London there are only two or three simple regulations. Yet in Paris scarce a night passes without somebody being killed, while in London, which is a larger city, there are scarce three or four in a year. (LJ[B], 203–4)

However, ultimately, the difference was due to the "remains of feudal manners" in France, where the nobility continued to keep a large body of retainers who were responsible to their lords but not to themselves:

Nothing tends so much to corrupt mankind as dependencey, while independencey still encreases the honesty of the people. The establishment of commerce and manufactures, which brings about this independencey, is the best police for preventing crimes. The common people have better wages in this way than in any other, and in consequence of this a general probity of manners takes place thro' the whole country. (LJ[B], 204–5)

This passage illustrates both Smith's general method when talking about human motivations and his substantive position. Our motivations and dispositions are thoroughly shaped by our social and institutional contexts.[6] A condition of abject dependency of the kind that characterizes feudal relations prevents all sense of self-worth, which in turn obviates the need for any self-discipline. However, alter the structure of social relations by making individuals

---

[6] The best exposition of this view is still Nathan Rosenberg, "Some Institutional Aspects of the *Wealth of Nations*," *Journal of Political Economy* 68 (1960): 361–74.

independent, and we will find their natures transformed. It was this recognition that made Smith's writings free of easy moralism. Attempts to form human behavior through state regulation were likely to deal only with symptoms; the proper way was to cultivate a commercial society whose citizens would be free and responsible only to themselves.

Finally, Smith is, as I have alluded to previously, deeply aware of the presence of conflict in almost all societies. The common image of Smith is that he believed that a society of unfettered individuals, pursuing their own gain, without the perversions of false ideas or ill constituted governments, would form a harmonious whole. However, the bulk of *The Wealth of Nations* is devoted to the thought that for much of their history human beings have not acted on their interests; at least, they have set up systems of regulation and restraints such that only the interests of a few were served. Most important, and as mentioned already, the interests of humans are in conflict. For Smith, there is, in a sense, nothing natural about the "system of natural liberty." If mankind had, by degrees, unevenly and uncertainly, emerged from tutelage, it was less a testament to the power of interest than to unanticipated consequences of actions or to fortuitous combinations of interests.

His discussion of slavery captures many of the elements of his historical imagination in these matters. Smith was convinced that in republican governments there was scarcely any chance that slavery would ever be abolished because those who made laws owned slaves and therefore legislation had a view to the subjection of slaves. "The freedom of the free was the cause of the great oppression of the slaves," he declared, thus suggesting that those who did not know how to be governed would govern their slaves more insolently; after all, Smith was quite convinced that there was *no* economic rationale in that institution (LJ[A], iii.103, 114). Yet

the love of domination and authority and the pleasure men take in having every thing done by their express orders, rather than to condescend to bargain and treat with those whom they look upon as their inferiors and are inclined to use in a haughty way; this love of domination and tyrannizing, I say, will make it impossible for the slaves in a free country ever to recover their liberty. (LJ[A], iii.114)

Republican governments were generally condemned by Smith for this reason; and the more prosperous the republican government, the more so[7]:

The greater the freedom of the free, the more intollerable is the slavery of the slaves. Opulence and freedom, the two greatest blessings men can possess, tend greatly to the misery of this body of men, which in most countries where slavery is allowed makes by far the greatest part. A humane man would wish therefore if slavery has to be generally established that these greatest blessings, being incompatible with the happiness of the greatest part of mankind, were never to take place. (LJ[A], iii.111)

Slavery had been abolished in Europe because of the fortuitous coincidence of two circumstances that were unlikely to be replicated elsewhere.[8] The church and clergy saw that their influence would greatly increase on account of the emancipation of slaves, and relatively strong monarchs saw in their emancipation an opportunity to weaken the power of the nobles. However, in some instances the power of the monarchy or of the clergy was not sufficient to bring about the abolition of slavery. In Germany, Bohemia, and Poland, the authority of kings was not strong enough; in the case of Russia, the Russian Church was not as strong as the Roman Catholic Church in Europe.[9]

In Smith's reflections on slavery, one can see an example of the complicated ways in which conflicts of interest operate. By acting on their passions, the slave owners went against both their own economic interests and the interests of the slaves. The freedom of some enhanced the oppression of others. It was the interests of the clergy and the monarchy against the feudal lords that led the former two to combine against slavery, and the strength of the absolutist state needed to be mobilized to undercut the power of the nobles and emancipate the slaves.

---

[7] "We may observe here that the state of slavery is much more tollerable in a poor and barbarous people than in a rich and polished one" LJ(A), iii.105. The reason is that slaves are more abundant in a prosperous nation which can therefore afford to treat them with greater severity.

[8] "It is indeed allmost impossible that it should ever be totally or generally abolished" LJ(A), iii.101.

[9] Note, however, that Smith's assessment of the role of the clergy was rather less benign in the WN.

Conflicts of interest are ubiquitous in Smith's analysis. Even an established, well-constituted system of natural liberty contains deep conflicts of interest and inequities of power; inequality is a form of oppression, and low wages are iniquitous (Early Draft, 5–7). Humans, organized in groups, are constantly opposing each other's interests, and Smith had no illusion that the interests of laborers and employers would automatically harmonize. In contrast, Edmund Burke vehemently denied that the interests of two parties contracting for wages could conflict since "it is absolutely impossible that their free contracts can be onerous to either party."[10] For Smith, too, it was the case that the worker was as necessary to the master as the master to him, but only in the long run, and that had no bearing on any actual instance of wage negotiation, which, for Smith, was a matter of relative *power*. The masters had the edge in a context where there were "no acts of parliament against combining to lower the price of work; but many against combining to raise it" (WN, I.viii.12). "Whenever the law has attempted to regulate the wages of workmen, it has always been rather to lower them than to raise them" (WN, I.x.c.34). Given that the balance of power in this pursuit of interests was manifestly in favor of the employers, Smith remarked that "[w]hen the regulation...is in favour of the workmen, it is always just and equitable; but it is sometimes otherwise when in favour of the masters" (WN, I.x.c.61).

Establishing the "system of natural liberty" under which everyman is "left perfectly free to pursue his own interest his own way" is thus for Smith a *task*, rather than something that comes naturally (WN, IV.ix.51). The paradox is that the very motive, self-interest, that allows that system to produce the beneficial consequences it does, constantly threatens to undermine it. It is the pursuit of their interests that leads merchants to demand monopolies and privileges that harm society; yet, those very same interests can, under right institutional conditions, produce beneficial outcomes. *The Wealth of Nations* is an account of how the interests of all might be harmonized, not a claim that they are always, or naturally, in harmony.

---

[10] Edmund Burke, "Thoughts and Details on Scarcity," in *The Works of the Right Honorable Edmund Burke*, 12 vols. (Boston, MA, 1865–71), vol. 5, pp. 135–6.

The previous section outlined the complicated operations of self-interest within *The Wealth of Nations*. However, philosophically, the idea that self-love had its proper place required a defense, and Smith's defense was directed against two contemporaries in particular. At one extreme, Francis Hutcheson had insisted that all virtue could be understood in terms of benevolence, thus, in Smith's eyes, suggesting that that "[s]elf-love was a principle which could never be virtuous in any degree or in any direction" (TMS, VII.ii.3.12). Smith, in contrast, insisted that a "[r]egard to our own private happiness and interest . . . appear upon many occasions very laudable principles of action" (VII.ii.3.16):

> Benevolence may, perhaps, be the sole principle of action in the Deity. . . . But whatever may be the case with the Deity, so imperfect a creature as man, the support of whose existence requires so many things external to him, must often act from many other motives. The condition of human nature were peculiarly hard, if those affections, which, by the very nature of our being, ought frequently to influence our conduct, could upon no occasion appear virtuous, or deserve esteem and commendation from any body. (TMS, VII.ii.3.18)

For Smith, self-love thus had an appropriate place in the catalogue of human dispositions. The question was how it expressed itself and how it was limited. The need was met by the impartial spectator. There are two limits on self-love. First, it must be exercised within the bounds of justice and "fair play" (TMS, II.ii.2.1). Secondly, self-love has strong moral undertones in its own right: it refers to a wider range of concerns than simply material self-interest, namely something like a *proper* care of the self. This stoic notion of self-love is concerned not only with a being's existence, but with "all the different parts of its nature, in the best and most perfect state of which they were capable" (VII.ii.1.15).

Smith's relationship to Mandeville is altogether more complicated. Mandeville was notorious for the claim that all instances of virtue were simply self-interest in disguise. Mandeville acknowledged that our self-love was shaped and modified in response to imagining how others viewed us, but he insisted that this involved dissimulation and masquerade, albeit of a complex kind. For Smith,

Mandeville had simply failed to acknowledge the fact that not only do we desire praise, we desire to be praiseworthy:

[T]his desire of the approbation, and this aversion to the disapprobation of his brethren, would not alone have rendered man fit for that society for which he was made. Nature, accordingly, has endowed him, not only with a desire of being approved of, but with a desire of being what ought to be approved of; or of being what he himself approves of in other men. The first desire could only have made him wish to appear to be fit for society. The second was necessary in order to render him anxious to be really fit. The first could only have prompted him to the affectation of virtue, and to the concealment of vice. The second was necessary in order to inspire him with the real love of virtue, and with the real abhorrence of vice. In every well-formed mind this second desire seems to be the strongest of the two. It is only the weakest and most superficial of mankind who can be much delighted with that praise which they themselves know to be altogether unmerited. (TMS, III.ii.7)

However, there were important respects in which Mandeville's claim "bordered upon the truth" (VII.ii.4.14). Smith had few doubts that self-interest could be taken for granted as a reliable motive for action: "We are not ready to suspect any person of being defective in selfishness. This is by no means the weak side of human nature, or the failing of which we are apt to be suspicious" (VII.ii.3.16). However, this empirical fact was no warrant for effacing, as Mandeville had done, the distinction between virtue and vice altogether.

PRUDENCE AS A VIRTUE

Smith insisted, against Hutcheson, that a prudential regard for one's own affairs could be a virtue and that it was possible to distinguish a self-regarding prudence from unmitigated selfishness or unalloyed vice. Prudence was the virtue that directed us to care for the self.

To understand Smith's account of the virtue of prudence it is necessary to remember that Smith's theory is spectatorial; the primary ethical standpoint is that of the spectators. Hence, his account of morality is at odds with the inside-out conception of morality that understands the rightness of action in terms of the good character of the agent. Smith argues that this is a mistake because even though it is character and affections that are judged, such judgment requires a prior standard of "right." This standard is derived from the fittingness of the motive to the circumstances as tested by the *spectator*'s sympathy, or lack of sympathy, with the agent's sentiment. The impartial spectator is the measure of propriety. This provides an independent place for the virtues among moral reasons. Virtue is not a question of what is good for man, or of the obedience to laws or the satisfaction of desires. It is a matter of what the impartial spectator would approve of.

Smith added a whole new section "On the Character of Virtue" to the sixth edition of *The Theory of Moral Sentiments*, and it is interesting that he describes this as a system of "practical philosophy," a term clearly intended to contrast with the "theory" in the title of the book.[11] This section gives a detailed and vivid picture of the virtues and the agents who practice it.

The character of the individual, he suggests, may be considered under two aspects, as it concerns the happiness of oneself and the happiness of others.

Prudence is the virtue whose cultivation is instrumental to our own happiness, benevolence to that of others. Prudence is twofold:

[F]irst of all, superior reason and understanding, by which we are capable of discerning the remote consequences of all our actions, and of foreseeing the advantage or detriment which is likely to result from them: and secondly, self-command by which we are enabled to abstain from present pleasure or to endure present pain, in order to obtain a greater pleasure or to avoid a greater pain in some future time. (TMS, IV.2.6)

The spectator approves of prudence because from an impartial point of view our future pleasure is as important as the present, and the spectator would therefore disapprove of our sacrificing the future for the present. What the spectator really approves of is not the gain itself but the deferment of pleasure, the physical and mental labor that deferment expresses:

Hence arises that eminent esteem with which all men naturally regard a steady perseverance in the practice of frugality, industry, and application, though directed to no other purpose than the acquisition of fortune. The

---

[11] Smith must have decided to add Section IV between March 1788 and March 1789, as we see from correspondence with his publisher; Corr., pp. 310 and 320. The quoted words are on p. 320.

resolute firmness of the person who acts in this manner, and in order to obtain a great though remote advantage, not only gives up all present pleasures, but endures the greatest labour both of mind and body, necessarily commands our approbation. (TMS, IV.2.8)

Two aspects of the relationship between prudence and self-love are worth highlighting. First, as many commentators have noted, aspects of prudence form an important link between *The Theory of Moral Sentiments* and *The Wealth of Nations*. Not only does prudence more securely sustain one's own advancement; in doing so, it also contributes to economic growth. The impartial spectator approves of it, not on account of its success or failure in obtaining goods but because of the self-command that frugality and industry are thought to imply:

In the steadiness of his industry and frugality, in his steadily sacrificing the ease and enjoyment of the present moment for the probable expectation of the still greater ease and enjoyment of a more distant but more lasting period of time, the prudent man is always both supported and rewarded by the entire approbation of the impartial spectator. (TMS, VI.i.11)

Smith is concerned to point out that "selfish" and "prodigal" people foolishly spend their economic assets on their present enjoyment rather than employing them in productive investment. It is not selfish individuals, engaged in extravagant expenditure, who increase public wealth; it is rather frugal private individuals, with a capacity to defer their own desires, who create a fund of capital that can be employed for productive investment. Even the causes of economic growth are not served, as Mandeville had maintained, by selfishness and prodigality. Rather, economic growth requires a steady if less exalted virtue of its own, namely, prudence rightly understood. Prudence is the link between *The Theory of Moral Sentiments* and Book II of *The Wealth of Nations*, where Smith singles out frugality as an important factor in economic growth.

Prudence, however, is clearly a "private" virtue and does not command ardent love or admiration. In his privacy, the prudent man is conscientious, circumspect, industrious, persevering, sincere but not always frank, consciously inoffensive, and, on the whole, averse to public affairs (TMS, VI.i.7–13):

Prudence, in short, when directed merely to the care of health, of the fortune, and of the rank and reputation of the individual, though it is regarded as a most respectable and even, in some degree, as an amiable and agreeable quality, yet is never considered as one, either of the most endearing, or of the most ennobling of the virtues. It commands a certain *cold esteem*, but seems not entitled to any very ardent love or admiration. (TMS, VI.i.14; emphasis added)

SELF-LOVE AND INDUSTRIOUSNESS

It was a common question in the eighteenth century how industriousness could be promoted, given the pain and toil involved in labor. Why would self-interested individuals yield their labor instead of being indolent? These worries can clearly be seen in Smith's predecessors, Mandeville and Hutcheson. Mandeville's great virtue was to have exposed so starkly the violence inherent in civil society which was cloaked only by the dexterous management of a few artful politicians. Social harmony might be achieved only through violence: "All sound Politicks, and the whole Art of governing, are entirely built upon the Knowledge of human Nature. The great Business in general of a Politician is to promote, and, if he can, reward all good and useful Actions on the one hand; and on the other, to *punish, or at least discourage,* every thing that is destructive or hurtful to Society."[12] Mandeville's paradox was meant not only to show that private vice, in the Christian sense, led to public benefit, but also that the wealth of some was born out of the poverty of others. There was a sense in which all the talk of virtue disguised a form of violence that was at the core of the economy. The only way to sustain production was to make it *necessary* for the mass of mankind to labor. In a passage which Marx frequently quoted, Mandeville wrote:

From what has been said it is manifest, that in a free Nation where Slaves are not allow'd of, the surest Wealth consists in a Multitude of laborious Poor; for besides that they are the never-failing Nursery of Fleets and Armies, without them there could be no Enjoyment, and no Product of any Country could be valuable. To make the Society happy and People easy under the meanest Circumstances, it is requisite that great Numbers of them should be Ignorant as well as Poor.[13]

[12] Mandeville, *The Fable of the Bees: or Private Vices, Publick Benefits,* 2 vols., ed. F. B. Kaye (Oxford, 1924), vol. 2, pp. 320–1, emphasis added.
[13] Mandeville, *Fable,* vol. 1, pp. 287–8. For commentary and Marx's citations of Mandeville, see L. Colletti, *From Rousseau to Lenin* (London, 1972), p. 205.

Mandeville's explosion of the link between virtue and commerce was not merely a satirical episode in the history of moral philosophy. It formed the basis of the extended critique of civilization that Rousseau would so anxiously undertake. The juxtaposition of Mandeville and Rousseau was one that Smith himself made in his *Letter to The Edinburgh Review*, a poignant encounter between the principal defender of modernity and its fiercest critic.

Just how much the question of production was part of moral theory can be gleaned from the last pages of Hutcheson's *Inquiry*. The ultimate contradiction between the pleasure we derive from a beatific state of the soul and the pain of labor, between a state of virtue and hard work, was one that Hutcheson valiantly tried to overcome, but one which strained his account considerably. In Hutcheson, the passive pleasures of beauty and virtue were severed from material life and industry. Benevolence, the core of virtue, was not a strong enough motive to "bear Labour and Toil, and many other Difficultys which we are averse to from Self-love."[14]

The general good requires labor, but labor is not secured through the pleasures of the moral sense and has to be compelled by necessity and even physical force. The reluctance of the individual to volunteer his labor for the good of the whole is attributed by Hutcheson, not to the contradiction between the pleasures of the moral sense and labor, but to the inimical influence of the passions of self-love. Hence, if the poor are reluctant to yield their labor, the wrath of the wise and the wealthy would be justified. In fact,

perhaps no law could be more effectual to promote a general industry, and restrain sloth and idleness in the lower conditions, than making perpetual slavery... the ordinary punishment of such idle vagrants as, after proper admonitions and tryals of temporary servitude, cannot be engaged to support themselves and their families by any useful labours.[15]

The association of self-love and idleness led ineluctably to the conclusion that labor could only be procured through necessity. This involved keeping wages low. Smith, in contrast, having broken the association of self-love and idleness in *The Theory of*

---

[14] Francis Hutcheson, *An Inquiry into the Original of Our Ideas of Beauty and Virtue*, ed. W. Leidhold (Indianapolis, IN, 2004), II.7.8, p. 186.
[15] Francis Hutcheson, *A System of Moral Philosophy*, 2 vols. (London, 1755), vol. 2, p. 202.

Moral Sentiments, argued against the necessity of low wages in *The Wealth of Nations*. Labor and industriousness did not require coercion for they were produced by our moral psychology, namely the highly active and nervous operations of the imagination. Because it is beyond the scope of this chapter to give a detailed account of the imagination,[16] suffice it to say that the imagination is a great motivator of industry in many respects.

For Smith, our capacity to enjoy means in abstraction from their ends is the basis for the sentiment of beauty and, indeed, for the development of civilization. Smith attributed to Hume the argument that "[t]he utility of any object . . . pleases the master by perpetually suggesting to him the pleasure or conveniency which it is fitted to promote" (TMS, IV.1.2). Smith, on the contrary, argued "that the exact adjustment of the means for attaining any conveniency or pleasure, should frequently be more regarded, than that very conveniency or pleasure, in the attainment of which their whole merit would seem to consist" (IV.1.3). For Smith, action is not motivated necessarily by the desire to attain any particular end or by considerations of utility. Rather, we are motivated by the pleasure arising from the employment of the means to that end. More effort is exerted in pursuing the means than in the "rational" attainment of the end. Smith illustrates this claim with an example:

When a person comes into his chamber, and finds the chairs all standing in the middle of the room, he is angry with his servant, and rather than see them continue in that disorder, perhaps takes the trouble himself to set them all in their places with their backs to the wall. The whole propriety of this new situation arises from its superior conveniency in leaving the floor free and disengaged. To attain this conveniency he *voluntarily* puts himself to more trouble than all he could have suffered from the want of it; since nothing was more easy, than to have set himself down upon one of them, which is probably what he does when his labour is over. What he wanted therefore, it seems, was *not so much this conveniency, as that arrangement of things that promotes it.* (TMS, IV.1.4; emphasis added)

The desired end of pleasure or happiness is "naturally confound[ed] in our imagination with the order, the regular and harmonious movement of the system, the machine or the oeconomy by means of which it is produced" (IV.1.9). It is this confounding of ends and

---

[16] See Chapter 1, in this volume.

means that encourages the expenditure of more effort than is necessary for satisfying our needs.

The alliance of desire and imagination makes it impossible to define our interests in terms of a limited or antecedently individuated set of needs. For Smith, a consideration of mere needs is a state we attain only in sickness when we confront mortality. If mankind had aimed at "real happiness," society would have been bereft of any kind of complexity; it would have been devoid of all the sciences and the arts. Aiming at real happiness, in the sense of the simple satisfaction of our needs, would lead to a considerable impoverishment. Is it an accident, Smith seems to be suggesting, that in Rousseau's *Discourse on Inequality*, the savage is described as the figure who lost all desire once his needs were satisfied, given that his imagination did not operate?

It is the confounding in our imagination of the desired end of pleasure with the order that is supposed to bring it about which encourages the expenditure of more effort and the production of more goods than is necessary for the satisfaction of immediate desire. The confounding of the means and ends transforms "natural indolence" into "civilized industry":

It is this deception which rouses and keeps in continual motion the industry of mankind. It is this which first prompted them to cultivate the ground, to build houses, to found cities and commonwealths, to invent and improve all the sciences and arts, which ennoble and embellish human life; which have entirely changed the whole face of the globe, have turned the rude forests of nature into agreeable and fertile plains, and made the trackless and barren ocean a new fund of subsistence, and the great high road of communication to the different nations of the earth. (TMS, IV.1.10)

The alliance of the desire with imagination induces us to accumulate means beyond any particular end they serve and, in doing so, drives the economy toward complexity.

HAPPINESS AND THE IMAGINATION

The realization that goods are produced and consumed not because they serve fixed needs makes the relationship between happiness and our interests more obscure, according to Smith. Happiness is not defined as it is in Aristotle, as arising out of the possession of a certain character or the possession of objective qualities, but as a state of psychological ease. It is not connected to any one mode of being or, even, the possession of a certain form of knowledge. It is identified as a certain psychic repose, a state of "tranquillity and enjoyment" (TMS, III.3.30). Smith's conception of happiness reflects the Stoic idea of the will in the sense that it is not a consequence of our station or capacities, but something we can attain by attuning the will.

In the most glittering and exalted situation that our idle fancy can hold out to us, the pleasures from which we propose to derive our real happiness, are almost always the same with those which, in our actual, though humble station, we have at all times at hand, and in our power. (III.3.31)

This account of happiness does two things at once. First, it claims that the ordinary state of mankind is such that they are in a position to be happy. In a sense, it dignifies their lives by arguing that there is, as far as happiness goes, no qualitative difference between lives lead according to ordinary canons of practical wisdom and those lead according to special or rarified forms of insight. It rules out the exclusive identification of happiness with a unique kind of life, such as the contemplative life, or with particular ideals. In line with much of eighteenth-century thought, Smith never discusses the "art of living" in this way.

The source of misery is not that people are in different situations, but their tendency to overrate the difference between such situations. "Avarice over-rates the difference between poverty and riches" (TMS, III.3.31). The objective situation of the bulk of mankind is such that an act of will can make them happy. "What can be added to the happiness of the man who is in health, who is out of debt, and has a clear conscience?" (I.iii.1.7). Happiness, in this sense, depends on such objects chiefly as depend on ourselves.

There is something deeply odd about Smith's discussion of happiness which makes its connection to self-interest more obscure than might immediately appear. Neither the pursuit of virtue nor the pursuit of wealth has any necessary connection with our happiness. Although the reference to a clear conscience suggests that there is an internal connection between morality and happiness in the sense that a tormented conscience is unlikely to be happy, this connection is more distant than it appears. However, Smith also presents the individual who constantly strives to assimilate him- or herself to the archetype of perfection as being plagued by a sense of anxiety. The pursuit of virtue does not necessarily lead to tranquility for it catches us in the conflicting perspectives of our own partiality and the impartiality of the spectator:

> The different views of both characters exist in his mind separate and distinct from one another, and each directing him to a behaviour different from that to which the other directs him. When he follows that view which honour and dignity point out to him, Nature does not, indeed, leave him without a recompense. He enjoys his own complete self-approbation, and the applause of every candid and impartial spectator. By her unalterable laws, however, he still suffers; and the recompense which she bestows, though very considerable, is not sufficient completely to compensate the sufferings which those laws inflict. ... He suffers, therefore, and though, in the agony of the paroxysm, he maintains, not only the manhood of his countenance, but the sedateness and sobriety of judgement, it requires his utmost and most fatiguing exertions, to do so. (TMS, III.3.28)

If the pursuit of virtue is not necessarily connected with ease and tranquility, the pursuit of wealth is even less so. In addition to the familiar argument that the pursuit of wealth has no intrinsic connection with happiness, Smith makes the stronger argument that we pursue riches in full knowledge that these external goods do not bring happiness. Smith emphasizes that we distinguish the condition of the rich, but not on account of the superior ease or pleasure that they enjoy; that is, we do not imagine that they are happier, rather that they have more *means* to happiness.

Our relentless, compulsive, and overpowering ambition tends to induce anxiety, sorrow, and fear:

> Power and riches appear then to be, what they are, enormous and operose machines contrived to produce a few trifling conveniences to the body, consisting of springs the most nice and delicate, which must be kept in order with the most anxious attention, and which in spite of all our care are ready every moment to burst into pieces. ... They are immense fabrics, which it requires the labour of a life to raise, which threaten every moment to overwhelm the person that dwells in them. (TMS, IV.1.8)

There is a tension here analogous to Smith's account of the impartial spectator. It is a disquieting portrayal of the human condition in which "ease," "pleasure," and "happiness" seem to disappear as objects of desire because replaced by anxiety and the restless striving of the imagination. If happiness is within everyone's reach, why does ambition arise? Because mankind is apt to sympathize more with joy than with sorrow.

The rich man glories in his riches, because he feels that they naturally draw upon him the attention of the world, and that mankind are disposed to go along with him in all those agreeable emotions with which the advantages of his situation so readily inspire him.

In contrast, the poor man is all but invisible; he "goes out and comes in unheeded, and when in the midst of a crowd is in the same obscurity as if shut up in his own hovel" (TMS, I.iii.2.1). Rather than showing "hardheartedness" toward poverty, as has been suggested,[17] Smith is trying to explain its humiliation.

For Smith, the desire for the means to happiness, even a bohemian craving for wealth is, like morality itself, in league with the romantic ethic of imagination, if not self-illusion. Craving for "ease and pleasure" only *appears* to be the motive for our love of riches. Instead, what drives us to pursue wealth and worldly greatness is regard for "the sentiments of mankind," the intensified sensation of sympathy that the great receive from others. Thus to be rich is, above all, to be "the object of the observation and fellow-feeling of every body" (ibid). It is not ease of pleasure, but always honor, although frequently an honor ill understood, that the ambitious man pursues:

From whence, then, arises that emulation which runs through all the different ranks of men, and what are the advantages which we propose by that great purpose of human life which we call bettering our condition? To be observed, to be attended to, to be taken notice of with sympathy, complacency, and approbation, are all the advantages which we can propose to derive from it. (TMS, I.iii.2.1)

The accumulation of the means to happiness, although distinct from happiness and possibly inversely related to it, leads to the general benefit of society. The pursuit of imaginary desires and

---

[17] Robert Heilbroner, *The Worldly Philosophers* (New York, NY, 1979), p. 437. Cf. J. A. Farrer, *Adam Smith* (New York, NY, 1881), pp. 132ff.

sympathy contributes to the wealth of nations, for the rich

are led by an invisible hand to make nearly the same distribution of the necessaries of life, which would have been made, had the earth been divided into equal portions among all its inhabitants, and thus without intending it, without knowing it, advance the interest of the society, and afford means to the multiplication of the species. (TMS, IV.1.10)

This is the language of consolation. Most human endeavor is not aimed at procuring real satisfaction or a secure happiness, but, in transcending ourselves through our imaginations, we embark on the toil that keeps industry in motion and makes opulence a possibility.

CONCLUSION

The aim of this chapter has been to demonstrate the complexity of Smith's account of self-interest. Although Smith had no doubt that the pursuit of virtue would receive the highest approbation from the impartial spectator, he was less sanguine that the highest virtues are in fact the object of most human exertion. Most people pursue wealth, a less exalted aim. However, the deceptions that drive us to seek riches, contemptible as this on occasion may be, will produce great effects. Opulence, the sciences, the arts, and the flourishing of human ingenuity all result from the way in which our interests are refracted through our imaginations. What is the self-interest of creatures who are endowed with a restlessly expansive imagination? Only our imagination can determine that.

10   Adam Smith and History

Adam Smith was not a historian, in the sense that he wrote nothing that could be described as "a history." Nevertheless, he thought a great deal about history; he was deeply conscious of the history he was living in; it is probable that he saw the human species as immersed in history at all moments of its existence; and it is certain that he contributed to the development of historical thought in new directions and the acquisition of new meanings by the term "history." For these reasons, it would be easy for us to describe Smith as a "historian" in all these latter and innovative senses, and to dismiss as archaic and evanescent all the senses in which he is not one. This, however, would be to distort the ways in which the terms "history" and "historian" were used by Smith himself and understood by his contemporaries. Edward Gibbon, who knew him and his work well and looked on him with respect and affection, is the author of two statements which may be taken together as illustrating this point. The first is found in Gibbon's autobiography and runs:

The candour of Dr Robertson embraced his disciple; a letter from Mr Hume overpaid the labour of ten years; but I have never aspired to a place in the triumvirate of British historians.[1]

The second, probably written earlier, occurs in a late chapter of the *Decline and Fall*:

[1] Georges A. Bonnard, ed., *Edward Gibbon: Memoirs of My Life* (New York, NY, 1969), p. 158. Cf. J. E. Norton, ed., *The Letters of Edward Gibbon* (London, 1956), II, p. 361.

On this interesting subject, the progress of society in Europe, a strong ray of philosophic light has broke from Scotland in our own times; and it is with private, as well as public regard that I repeat the names of Hume, Robertson and Adam Smith.[2]

The second triumvirate does not complete the first. Hume and Robertson are historians because they have written histories, of England, Scotland, the reign of Charles V, and America. In the course of doing so, they have shed philosophic light on the progress of society in Europe. The same may be said of Gibbon himself, as of Adam Ferguson who qualifies as a historian because, as well as an *Essay on the History of Civil Society* – a work of philosophy – he has written a *History of the Rise, Progress and Termination of the Roman Republic*. However, Smith is not named as a historian because nothing he has written is a history of anyone or anything. To comment philosophically on the progress, or the history, of society is not in Gibbon's mind the same as to write history, although it may be of value to the latter and may even change our understanding of it. With the great figures of the later British Enlightenment, we are still at a point where the several components of historiography are coming together to create our modern understanding of the term and endow it with problems that continue to engage our attention.

From Arnaldo Momigliano, and those who have commented on his pioneer generalisations,[3] we have learned to think of eighteenth-century historiography as compounded of three elements: narrative, erudition, and philosophy. By the first of these is denoted a new-classical art form still of great authority in Smith's lifetime: the narration of exemplary actions, chiefly of war and statecraft – the exemplary including the negative exemplars of actions to be avoided – by ruling figures, normally male, in political

---

[2] Edward Gibbon, *The History of the Decline and Fall of the Roman Empire*, 3 vols., ed. David Wormersley (London, 1994), Book VI, chapter 61, note 69, vol. 3, p. 728.

[3] Arnaldo Momigliano, "Gibbon's Contributions to Historical Method," in *Contributo alla Storia degli Studi Classici* (Rome, 1955), pp. 195–211; Mark S. Phillips, "Reconsiderations on History and Antiquarianism: Arnaldo Momigliano and the Historiography of Eighteenth-century Britain," *Journal of the History of Ideas* 56 (1996): 297–316; J. G. A. Pocock, *Barbarism and Religion*, vol. 2: *Narratives of Civil Government* (Cambridge, 1999), pp. 4–6.

systems.[4] Since the actor was not to be divorced from the system he acted, the classical narrative had become one of the rise and termination of political systems: the city states and empires of antiquity, the ecclesiastical and feudal states of medieval Europe, and the multi-national and national kingdoms and confederations of modernity. While the classical narrative generated its own contexts, and these changed the ways in which it was understood, it remained the authoritative norm that defined the meaning of "history," and Smith is to be found so treating it in his *Lectures on Rhetoric and Belles Lettres* delivered at Glasgow University. He treats history as a genre arising within the practice of rhetoric and, originally, oratory, and defines it as follows:

The facts which are most commonly narrated and will be most adapted to the taste of the generality of men will be those that are interesting and important. Now these must be the actions of men; The most interesting and important of these are such as have contributed to great revolutions and changes in State and Governments...

The accidents that befall irrationall objects affect us merely by their externall appearance, their Novelty, Grandeur, etc., but those which affect the human Species interest us greatly by the Sympatheticall affections they raise in us. When we enter into their misfortunes, grieve when they grieve, rejoice when they rejoice, and in a word feel for them in some respect as if we ourselves were in the same condition.

The design of historicall writing is not merely to entertain: (this perhaps is the intention of an epic poem); besides that it has in view the instruction of the reader. It sets before us the more interesting and important events of human life, points out the cause by which these events were brought about and by this means points out to us by what manner and method we may produce similar good effects or avoid similar bad ones. (LRBL, ii.15–16)

Smith's doctrine of sympathy is here wholly in accord with the exemplary, moral and prudential function of the classical narrative. This function could in principle be served by resolving history into axioms and general laws, but it is more economical, and better stimulates the imagination, to leave it in the form of narrative appealing to our sympathies and intelligence. The lectures proceed to consider how narrative is best set forth, and to examine its chief ancient and modern practitioners. Tacitus is a leading figure among

---

[4] Philip S. Hicks, *Neo-Classical History and English Culture: Clarendon to Hume* (New York, NY, 1996).

the former of these. Because he deals with a time when public actions were in a particular way determined by secret emotions, Smith seems to consider him as appealing more to the sentiments than to the intelligence in search of *exempla* (LRBL, ii.63–9).

When Smith lectured on rhetoric and belles lettres – which he did concurrently with his lectures on jurisprudence, regarding both as contributions to the science of sociable morality – he thus retained the classical narrative in a central and authoritative role, as one of the genres into which human expressive capacity was organised. It is a different matter as erudition and philosophy, the second and third terms in Momigliano's formula, come into view and as we move from rhetoric to jurisprudence. The phenomena constituting erudition are not exhaustively discussed by Smith but are very much present to his mind. By erudition, or the study of "antiquities," was and is meant the study of all recorded information concerning the past, without immediate reference to its organisation into genres or modes of inquiry.[5] With regard to classical antiquity, it spilled across the borders defining history, poetry and philosophy, bringing light to information derived from all kinds of text and commentary, as well as from coins, medals, and inscriptions belonging to no recognised genre. The humanists and grammarians of Renaissance scholarship, who had devoted themselves to amassing this information, were much derided as "antiquaries" whose "curiosity" was disciplined neither by rhetorical elegance nor by systematic inquiry. They could, however, in some cases allege their connections with non-literary and non-classical disciplines, among which that of Roman and barbaric law was of peculiar importance because of the wealth of information about social behaviour and cultural values which it contained. As the archive of ancient literature was enlarged to include that laid down by medieval churches, kingdoms, and corporations, and then by modern bureaucratic and commercial states, its historical character changed, and "erudition" became a major source of information

---

[5] Momigliano, "Ancient History and the Antiquarian," *Contributo*, pp. 67–106; D. R. Kelley, *Foundations of Modern Historical Scholarship: Language, Law and History in the French Renaissance* (New York, NY, 1970), and *The Human Measure: Social Thought in the Western Legal Tradition* (Cambridge, MA, 1990); B. Barret-Kriegel, *Les Historiens et la monarchie*, vol. 2: *La Défaite de l'érudition* (Paris, 1988); C. Grell, *L'Histoire entre erudition et philosophie: étude sur la connaissance historique à l'âge des lumières* (Paris, 1993); J. M. Levine, *Humanism and History: Origins of Modern English Historiography* (Ithaca, NY, 1987).

regarding historical change itself. This is a principal route along which the word "history" came to mean the reconstruction of past states of society and culture, and the study of processes by which these states had been replaced by others, including those constituting the present as known to the "historian" defined as student of these matters. The problem we face is that of situating Smith in this history of "history."

In the LRBL we find Smith aware that the growth of erudition has been accompanied by the growth of criticism, meaning the discipline by which the authenticity of sources of information is established, and they are used to authenticate the statements made by historians in the course of the narratives the latter construct. He points out that this was not a preoccupation of ancient historians, who were rhetoricians but not archival researchers, and suggests that the change is due to the invasion of the field of historiography by actors of a new kind:

Long demonstrations as they are no part of the historian's province are seldom made use of by the ancients. The modern authors have often brought them in. Historicall truths are now in much greater request than they ever were in ancient times. One thing that has contributed to the increase of this curiosity is that there are now severall sects in Religion and politicall disputes which are greatly dependent on the truth of certain facts. This it is that has induced almost all historians for some time past to be at great pains in the proof of those facts on which the claims of the parties they favoured depended. (LRBL, ii.40)

History, Smith is telling his students, has become disputatious and forensic: a series of competitions for authority between jurisdictions spiritual and secular, which make claims of priority and original intent, and develop narratives supportive of their pretensions. Since these claims will be contested, they require to be substantiated; since they must be documented, their sources must be authenticated. This is a principal reason why history as a narrative art has come to be invaded by erudition and criticism, as well as by dispute, bias, faction, and special pleading. We see the process as vastly enhancing the historian's claim to be a searcher after verifiability, but this is not how it appears to Smith as lecturer on the belles lettres:

These proofs however besides that they are inconsistent with the historicall stile, are likewise of bad consequence as they interrupt the thread of the narration, and that most commonly in the parts that are most interesting. They withdraw our attention from the main facts, and before we can get thro them they have so far weakened our concern for the issue of the affair that was broke off that we are never again so much interested in them [it?]...

Besides no fact that is called in question interests us so much or makes so lasting impression, as those of whose truth we are altogether satisfied. Now all proofs of this sort show that the matter is somewhat dubious; so that on the whole it would be more proper to narrate these facts without mentioning the doubt, than to bring in any long proof. (LRBL, ii.40–1, ii.v.40).

Smith – if correctly reported – is at this point the inhabitant of a moral and exemplary universe, where a fact's edificatory value outweighs the tedious question of its actuality; he is not living in a Lockean universe of probability, or a Mabillonian universe of source criticism. As a professor of rhetoric, he is not going to bridge the gap between narrative and erudition. At the same moment, however, he is making what we unhesitatingly recognise as a historical statement: a statement about the history of historiography, showing how it changed from an activity of one kind into an activity of another, in consequence of changes in the historical circumstances surrounding it. The question is whether he came to see that the nature of the historical narrative was itself changing so it became a narrative of contingent cultural change. To approach this problem, we must turn from Smith as professor of logic and rhetoric to Smith as professor of moral philosophy; and we must continue our Momiglianan enquiry by considering the relations of narrative and erudition with philosophy.

An understanding of how the words "philosophy" and "philosopher" were used in the later eighteenth century is of course vital to the study of both Smith and Momigliano's formula. We may take them as denoting an enterprise of persuading Europeans that they lived, both as perceptual and as moral beings, in a universe defined by sociability and civil society, the latter being both a natural and a historical condition. "Human nature" furnished the philosopher with certain fixed propensities of behaviour, which might be used in clarifying and explaining the extraordinary diversities of conduct in which humans found themselves engaging. However, this did not mean that these propensities were often, or perhaps ever, to be observed operating unmodified by the contingent and contextual circumstances furnishing one of the meanings of the word "history." Given that this word retained both the meaning of "enquiry" and that of "narrative," it was possible to speak of a "natural history" of inanimate or animate objects – a systematic enquiry aimed at classification, systematisation, and explanation – and at the same time of a "civil," "ecclesiastical," or even a "sacred history," aimed at narrating events in their sequential order and presenting them in terms of their causes and consequences. When John Millar and Dugald Stewart speak of Smith and other philosophers employing a "conjectural history," in which events or past states of existence are explained by appealing to those propensities of "human nature" most likely to have operated in producing them, it is something akin to "natural history" that they have in mind.[6] We should note, however, that the phenomena being explained exist in sequential time, and are thus capable of being narrated, and that "conjectural history" comes into play only in the absence of what may be (and often was) termed a "civil history," capable of mobilising and presenting the particular, timebound, and contingent circumstances in which things actually happen. "Civil history" is the art of presenting the contingent in narrative form. "Conjectural history" operates when it is absent, assists in explaining it when it is operative, but in no case replaces or even controls it. An important reason for this is that in "civil history," or in "history" for short, things happen which are aberrant, deviant, and even inexplicable by the operations of nature alone.

There is an art of narrating human actions seen as arcane and enigmatic. In the neo-classical culture inhabited by Smith, this art was pre-eminently associated with the name of Tacitus, whose exceptional powers of uncovering the springs of enigmatic behaviour won him the name of the most "philosophical" of historians. Tacitean narrative, however, fits uncomfortably into the exemplary classicism that Smith expounded in his lectures on rhetoric, and perhaps this is why he depicts Tacitus as an artist of the extraordinary and says that most of his admirers have failed to appreciate this point. Hume and Robertson – we may add Gibbon – wrote histories in which the strangeness of human behaviour is not

---

[6] Dugald Stewart, *Account of the Life and Writings of Adam Smith, LL. D.*, in EPS, pp. 292–3; John Craig, "Life of John Millar, Esq.," in John Millar, *The Origin of the Distinction of Ranks* (1806), ed. A. Garrett (Indianapolis, IN, 2006), p. xlv.

concealed, and Smith without doubt understood what they were doing. He chose not to write narratives of this kind and pursued enquiries in which he was not called on to do so. This is one reason we have for saying that he was not a historian; however, there are other ways of dealing with the contingent and the peculiar when they present themselves in the course of history.

D'Alembert, in his *Discours préliminaire à l'Encyclopédie* – which Smith certainly knew – had presented two histories of the human mind unfolding its faculties in order.[7] The first was a natural history, in which the faculties appeared in the order they would have followed if the operations of nature had been undisturbed by contingency. The second may be termed a civil history, in which they were shown appearing in the order actually followed in the history of Europe. This narrative turned on two circumstances: the huge weight of classical literature, surviving as a damaged inheritance after the breakdown of ancient civilisation, and the long night of Christian barbarism, during which ancient philosophy had combined with Christian theology to distort all memory of the classical inheritance and render Europeans incapable of dealing with it. The recovery of ancient literature had in turn been distorted when it came, and in consequence the faculties productive of philosophy, poetry, and erudition had appeared in an order and relationship not of that nature. Smith did not follow up d'Alembert's analysis, but he shared with him the perception that natural and civil history were discrepant, and that there was a history of Europe consisting in part of the loss and recovery of philosophic capability.

There is, then, a necessary interaction between "conjectural" or "natural" history, on the one hand, and "civil" (not to mention "ecclesiastical") history, on the other; the former is found in the pure state only when evidence (mainly documentary) for the latter is lacking. Civil history may distort the course which natural history would have taken if left to itself, but natural history is of immense value in furnishing explanations for civil history. The "history" of human nature may, as we shall see, take a

---

[7] Jean le Rond D'Alembert, "Discours préliminaire des editeurs," in *Encyclopédie ou dictionnaire raisonnée des sciences, des arts et des métiers* (Paris, 1751); English translation, R. N. Schwab, *D'Alembert: Preliminary Discourse to the Encyclopedia of Diderot* (Chicago, IL, 1995); Pocock, *Barbarism and Religion*, vol. I: *The Enlightenments of Edward Gibbon* (Cambridge, 1999), chapter 8, pp. 169–207.

sequential form; however, it need not do so, and when it does not, "history" moves away from meaning "narrative," and toward its equally ancient meaning of "systematic enquiry." Smith's uses of the word may be explored for all these shades of meaning. We look, then, for the interactions between "natural" and "civil" history in his lectures and writings; these will supply our understanding of what was and is meant by calling him a "philosophical" historian, completing a synthesis of Momigliano's three terms.

It is important to realise, however, that "civil history," at the moment when the "philosopher" approached it, already contained "narratives" not limited to the classical sense in which Smith expounded the term in the *Lectures on Rhetoric and Belles Lettres*. These were narratives of systemic change, recounting the passage in the European past from one state of language, worship, law, government, and (increasingly, as Smith wrote) commerce, to another. They had been built up from many sources, from which "philosophy" itself cannot be excluded but among which it is one of several. "Erudition" includes many of these, since it denotes the labours of grammarians and philologists since the re-energisation of humane learning in the fourteenth and fifteenth centuries. These had reconstructed the ancient languages in such detail that they were seen to be articulations of an "ancient" culture which might still be imitated and revered, but could not be restored to contemporary existence. Here was a source of the *querelles des anciens et modernes* and "battle of the books" which figure in the intellectual life of the generations preceding Smith's own. The *érudits* in this sense had not confined themselves to the study of the belles lettres. They had investigated through the language the "antiquities" of ancient government, war, and religion, and as their studies moved forward through past time, they had investigated the tensions between pagan and Christian religion; between ancient, feudal, and modern law and government; and between ancient, scholastic, and enlightened philosophy. All these had furnished the literate and learned with a variety of past states of culture, and with the problems of how these had given way to one another and which of them retained authority in the present. "Philosophy" denoted both a renewed attempt to deal with these problems and a post-humanist attempt to dismiss some of them from consideration. However, "history" had acquired some new meanings, in addition to those considered in Smith's lectures on rhetoric. His observations that verification got in the way of narrative was the beginning, not the end, of a new set of problems.

Smith approached the problems of "history" in the previous senses through the study of jurisprudence. His lectures at Glasgow on this subject were delivered concurrently with his lectures on rhetoric, but from his chair as professor of moral philosophy. They develop the proposition that philosophy is the science of moral existence in society, organised under the four headings of justice (pre-eminently), police, revenue, and arms. They might have been, but are not, confined to the study of natural jurisprudence, of the principles of justice brought to light by the principles of human nature, exemplified and rendered actual in the practice of actual societies. In fact, they deal at great length with the content of actual legal systems, Roman, English, and occasionally Scottish, and with the complex historical situations which past and present legal practises reveal. Smith's subject matter as professor of moral philosophy must have overlapped considerably with that being treated by his younger contemporary John Millar as professor of law. Millar apparently lectured extemporaneously from notes, and we do not have detailed knowledge of how these courses were related to each other. However, the two professors, on excellent personal terms, were philosophical historians of law and saw law as a key to philosophical history. Did Millar have the same problems in the use of the term "history" as those arising from Smith's dual professorship of rhetoric and philosophy?

From the reports of Smith's lectures, *The Wealth of Nations*, and the writings of Hume, Robertson, Ferguson, and Millar, it is possible to reconstruct that philosophically illuminated account of the "progress of society in Europe" which Gibbon thought the major contribution of Scottish philosophy to contemporary European historiography (this does not mean that it was exclusively a Scottish creation or that Gibbon learned it only from Scottish sources). It was a general scheme of Eurasian and Euro-American history, leading to the advent of modern commercial Europe and the American Revolution, with which philosophical jurisprudence interacted and which the latter helped create. Although not fully integrated with "history" in the narrative sense of the word, it had begun to alter the word's usage. Smith spoke of it as "a pretty generall account of the history of government in Europe" to an audience some of whom must have heard him condemn demonstration as interruptive of narrative two months previously.[8]

We encounter the major interactions between "conjectural" and "civil" history when we find this scheme growing out of the stadial sequence of four states – hunting, herding, tillage, and commerce – into which the "progress" of civil society is distributed.[9] This scheme was not a Scottish invention, although Smith did much to promote it and made important contributions to it; it seems to have arisen from diverse sources and been assembled in scientific form through the work of a diversity of authors; and its principal value had been to moderate and civilise earlier accounts of the emergence of civil society from the state of nature.[10] It was thus "philosophical" in the sense most fully "conjectural"; in Smith's writings we meet it first as a desert island thought experiment designed to show how an ideal society would invent the means of substance and distribution in a purely "natural situation (LJ[A], i.27). However, the interaction of philosophical with civil history is the interaction of such conjectural devices with systemic schemes narrated and discovered by erudition and experience. There are two decisive, and in many ways disastrous, points of contact between the stadial sequence invented by natural jurisprudence and the discovery of non-European societies set going by west European maritime expansion and the overland expansion of the Russian state. These gave rise to an account of the progress of civil society which reinterpreted European history at the expense of non-European cultures. It made the extension of the concept "history" to these difficult and even deniable.

Smith's chief contribution to the four-stage theory was his insistence that the shepherd stage was dynamic and creative,[11] whereas previous theorists had tended to group the shepherd with the

---

[8] LJ(A) v.45, dated "March 14, 1763"; LRBL ii.31, gives the date "January 7, 1763" for the passages from ii.41 quoted previously.

[9] First set out in LJ(A), i.27–32.

[10] The pioneer study by R. L. Meek, *Social Science and the Ignoble Savage* (Cambridge, 1976), now needs revision. See Istvan Hont, "The Language of Sociability and Commerce: Samuel Pufendorf and the Theoretical Foundations of the Four Stages Theory," in *The Languages of Political Theory in Early Modern Europe*, ed. A. Pagden (Cambridge, 1987), pp. 227–99.

[11] LJ(A), ii.97, iv.7, iv.21; LJ(B), 20–1; WN, V.i.a.3–5, V.i.b.12.

hunting savage,[12] reserving progress until agriculture gave rise to commerce. There appears – and might be further investigated – an association between this move on Smith's part and a more general tendency to identify the shepherd stage with the nomadic pastoralisms of Central Asia and Arabia. We find Smith, as we do Ferguson, carrying on earlier (and largely Bibliocentric)[13] insistence that the European peninsula had been settled by successive waves of shepherds moving west out of Asia and had never passed through the hunter-gatherer or "savage" condition. As these shepherds – Cimmerians, Hellenes, Celts, and Germans – had penetrated the fertile soils and complicated inner seas and estuaries of the western peninsula, they had developed a capacity for corn growing and coastal trading more complex and creative than that of the Asian and African river valleys. As pastoral clans turned to agriculture and commerce, they had developed independent city republics which rendered the history of government in Europe unique.[14] Even the Roman Empire had differed from those of Persia, India, and China in being the fruit of one republic's conquest of the world to which it had access, and its consequent perversion by the weight of its own conquests. Contained in this was the premise that ancient Mediterranean culture, although set in motion partly by the growth of commerce, had remained a war-making society engaged in the capture of slaves to work lands, and had therefore failed to sustain or even tolerate its own expansion.

Europe had therefore a barbaric but not a savage origin, and the crucial developments from pasture through agriculture to commerce had occurred pre-eminently at that extreme of the Eurasian continent. Here westward-moving shepherds had discovered both agriculture and political freedom. It could be argued – although Smith does not seem to say so – that similar peoples moving into river valley cultures elsewhere in Asia had been trapped in the creation of palace-centred despotisms. At all events, the "progress of society" takes place "in Europe." The Gothic invaders, however,

---

12 Pocock, "Gibbon and the Shepherds: The Stages of Society in the *Decline and Fall*," *History of European Ideas* 2 (1981): pp. 193–202.

13 Colin Kidd, *British Identities Before Nationalism: Ethnicity and Nationhood in the Atlantic World, 1600–1800* (Cambridge, 1999).

14 LJ(A), iv.56–74 (republics); WN, I.iii.3–6 (water transport and configuration of Europe).

unlike the Huns forcing them on from behind, had discovered the rudiments of agriculture (LJ[A], iv.114), and their contribution to the history of freedom had been the allodial system of land tenure, of which the feudal kingdom had been a late formation and perhaps deformation.[15] From this point Smith can be seen going on, in both the *Lectures on Jurisprudence* and *The Wealth of Nations* to the "history of government in Europe," which is also a study of the replacement of feudal society by commerce.

This history, often mentioned and several times recapitulated,[16] is closely akin to those recounted by Hume in his *History of England* and Robertson in his *View of the Progress of Society in Europe* prefixed to his *History of the Reign of Charles V*. Smith's attention is focussed on, although not confined to, the French and English monarchies, which it was then usual to contrast. He has less to say about the government of Spain or the Netherlands, still less about Germany, and nothing about Bohemia, Hungary, or Poland. It may also be noted that he thinks Scotsmen should acquaint themselves with English history and has little interest in that of Scotland. The reason may be less the strength or weakness of his patriotic sensibility than his conviction that English history displays in depth and detail the principles on which that of Europe has proceeded.[17] The republics of medieval Italy and the Low Countries play an important part, both as furthering the growth of commerce and as exemplifying the differences between ancient and modern liberty, whereas the Greek or Roman city was an assembly of slave-holding warrior citizens, intent on the government of the self and the conquest of the other, and Venice or Amsterdam were corporations of merchants, supplying their inhabitants with economic and cultural activities far more satisfying than the pursuit of politics. For this reason, they had delegated government to oligarchies; democracy was imaginable only among slaveholders and no democracy was likely to emancipate its slaves.[18]

---

[15] LJ(A), iv.114–48; LJ(B), 50–7; WN, III.iv.8–9.

[16] E.g., LJ (A), v.44–5; LJ(B), 50–7; WN, III.ii–iii.

[17] This is part of a larger subject: Colin Kidd, *Subverting Scotland's Past: Scottish Whig Historians and the Creation of an Anglo-British Identity, 1689–c.1830* (Cambridge, 1993); Pocock, *Barbarism and Religion*, vol. 2, chapters 11 and 16.

[18] For modern republics, see LJ(A), v.45–50; LJ(B), 77–9; WN, III.iii.6–11. For slavery and democracy, LJ(A), iii.101–5; LJ(B), 36–9.

Smith's account of the history of feudalism displays the same concern with the history of commerce and productivity. Like Hume – with whom he was exchanging ideas from early in the 1750s as both men shaped their major writings[19] – he recorded a displacement of the feudal estate proper, with its vassals and tenants, by the great household and its retainers in what came later to be called bastard feudalism. Under certain historical circumstances, he contended, power over land and over men through land became less magnificent and effective than power over men fed at the lord's own table or otherwise dependent on his hospitality. This conspicuous consumption, however, like that of the later Roman aristocracy, had in the end proved self-destructive, and a significant step in the transition to modernity had been the conversion of retainers and servants into craftsmen and labourers, the wealth of nations replacing the unproductive power of the few.[20] It may fairly be asked whether this is more than a rhetorical contrast, whether, that is, Smith supplies an account of the actual process by which it took place.

The rhetoric of Protestant and enlightened historiography usually turned at this point to the dissolution of monasteries and nunneries and the abolition of clerical celibacy, measures which – in those happy countries where they had taken place – had turned many useless lives toward production, consumption, and philoprogenitiveness, all beneficial to the commercial economy and its workforce. Smith does not tell this story, less (in all probability) because he did not believe or approve of it than in consequence of the massive absence from all his accounts of the progress of society of either a natural or a civil history of religion. Hume and Robertson could not be accused of neglecting either, and it would have been possible for Smith to have considered the forms of belief and worship appropriate to all four of the stages of society. On the whole, however, he does not do so; nor are the rise, dominance, and disruption of ecclesiastical authority as salient in his accounts of late antique and medieval history as they are in the writings of his friends and equals. It is conceivable that an explanation may be

---

[19] Corr., 12 (from Hume, 24 September 1752), p. 8.

[20] LJ(A), iv.119, 124–5; iv.157–60; v.4–7; LJ(B), 59–60; WN, III.iv.5–15. For Hume, see *History of England* (Indianapolis, IN, 1983), vol. 2, pp. 281–2, 428.

found in the difficulty he had in including within his system those activities of a culture which did not reduce easily to the exchange of profitable goods in an economy. The longest account to be found in *The Wealth of Nations* of the diverse ecclesiastical structures of Christian history occurs during a discussion of whether university professors should be paid salaries or maintained by fee-paying students.[21] Here Smith presents Hume's argument that it is better that clergy should be salaried by the state than supported by congregations, since this will make them lazy and boring, rather than competitive and interesting, in propounding the pernicious nonsense they teach.[22] The offerings of philosophers and professors are salutary in comparison with theology but are not commodities to be exchanged in the pursuit of wealth. It may be better that professors are supported by the fees of their students, but education, like warfare, is an activity which may require the support of the state.[23] Smith's history is that of the progress of society toward commerce, and it is a question how far it needs to include a history of high culture. The growth of poetry is a feature of the shepherd stage, but his very remarkable histories of physics and metaphysics[24] are not aspects of the history of society. They concern themselves with how the mind generates systems of explanation which satisfy the imagination, and are to that extent closer to the natural history of ideas.

The progress of society toward commerce could in Smith's day be written only as a history arising from the tensions within European civilisation: ancient and modern, allodial and feudal, and rural and urban. (It may of course be asked how far we have escaped this unilinearity.) The civilisations of Asia were supposed to possess an internal but not an external commerce. Their ships did not sail to Europe in search of trade, and they had not remodelled their societies around its pursuit. This had not kept them from opulence, but it had kept them from progress.[25] As for the Americas,

---

[21] At large, WN, IV.i.f–g; for ecclesiastical history, V.i.g.1.39.

[22] WN, V.i.g.4–6, quoting Hume, *History of England*, vol. 3, p. 136.

[23] WN, V.i.f.54–8 (education and military training of the common people).

[24] In EPS. Cf. the history of ancient philosophy given in WN, V.i.f.23–7, which has more to do with the history of society.

[25] WN, III.i.7. For the longer point about the absence of an Asian navigation, see the 1780 edition of Raynal's *Histoire philosophique et politique du commerce et des établissements des Européans dans les deux Indes*, I, p. 704.

it was a consequence of the four-stage system that in their pre-Columbian condition they could generate no history of their own. While shepherd peoples had moved west into the European peninsulas, hunting peoples had moved east over the Kamchatka-Alaska landbridge into the American continents. Here, for whatever reasons – Smith did not engage in the climate-centred debates over American degeneracy – the decisive moves into the domestication of herds and cultivation by the plough had not taken place.[26] Smith followed Robertson and Raynal (that "eloquent and, sometimes, well-informed author")[27] in supposing that native Americans had uniformly lived in the hunting or "savage" condition, and that the cities of Mexico and Peru – whose economy and culture were indeed hard for Europeans to understand – were mostly a Spanish myth (WN, I.xi.g.26).

He did not excuse the rapacity and hunger for gold and extractive slave labour of the European conquests which had destroyed so many native American peoples – on the contrary, it was the foundation of everything he desired to eliminate from the European world economy – but he saw the original Americans only as victims and in no way as actors in history. The same is probably his view of Africans as a source of New World labour. The colonies[28] of North America, with their predominantly European and even British populations, had become European economies, heirs to European postfeudal history, and extensions of Europe to form a world system. Publishing *The Wealth of Nations* in the year of the Declaration of Independence, Smith was living in, and desired to explain, a revolution which he saw as a revolt of commerce, and its attendant social structures against obsolete structures of empire. Although he certainly saw an independent English America as an empire of a new kind (WN, IV.vii.c.75). Here, we may want to say that his history

---

[26] Smith is silent on why Americans have not advanced beyond the hunting stage. For the thesis that shepherds moved west and hunters east out of Asia, cf. Ferguson's *Essay on the History of Civil Society* and Pocock, *Barbarism and Religion*, vol. 2, chapter 22. For the broad questions of American savagery and degeneracy, Anthony Pagden, *The Fall of Natural Man: The American Indian and the Origins of Comparative Ethnology* (Cambridge, 1986) and *European Encounters with the New World* (New Haven, CT, 1993); Antonello Gerbi, *The Dispute of the New World*, trans. J. Moyle (Pittsburgh, PA, 1973).

[27] WN, I.xi.g.32.

[28] For the differences between "colonies" in the ancient and the modern senses, see WN, IV.vii, at length.

of Europe has also become a history of America, although it may be better to say that English America has become part of his account of "the progress of society in Europe," in whose history alone that progress can be seen as taking place. About American history as that of a chain of slave-based creole cultures extending south from the Caribbean to the Amazon and the Andes Smith (unlike Raynal) does not have much to say, and he does not follow Josiah Tucker in presenting the American Revolution as the response of backward slave economies south of the Delaware.[29]

Smith engaged in extensive historical research – we should say that he wrote much economic history – in the sense that he studied and used many "histories" and statistical accounts of commerce, taxation, and population in the era of European enterprise and American colonisation. They are to be found chiefly in Books I, IV, and V of *The Wealth of Nations*, and a study of Smith as statistician would call for a separate chapter. These are of course intended to buttress his arguments in favour of freedom of commerce, but they are at the same time productive of narratives which both continue the grand narrative of the progress of commercial society and point to its continuing problems: the persistence of mercantilism, the problems of military organisation, the menace of national debt, and the impact of commerce on public and personal virtue. Edward Gibbon, with whose praise of Smith this article began, admired *The Wealth of Nations* as a "science" and a "system."[30] He did not allow his perception that "philosophy" had become an account of "the progress of society" to lead him into calling Smith a "historian," and he probably would not have done so had he known that Smith mediated a grand synthesis in which all the phenomena of organised society would be philosophically mobilised and historically explained. This we know was never completed, possibly because it would have entailed the construction of more narratives than could be systematised into a "philosophy"; Millar's belief that

[29] Josiah Tucker, *A Letter to Edmund Burke, Esq...on His Late Printed Speech...* (Gloucester, 1775); Pocock, *Virtue, Commerce and History: Essays on Political Thought and History, Chiefly in the Eighteenth Century* (Cambridge, 1985), chapter 9.

[30] Norton, *Letters of Edward Gibbon*, vol. 2, pp. 166 ("the most profound and systematic treatise"), 335 ("an extensive science in a single book").

Smith would prove a Newton to Montesquieu's Bacon[31] was not in fact fulfilled. He wrote history to isolate and illustrate general principles, but this enterprise generated a wealth of narratives great and small, which are more than mere footnotes to his system. What subsequently became of his narratives of the progress of society, and how political economy became an activity other than history, are topics for a separate inquiry.

[31] John Millar, *A Historical View of the English Government* (London, 1818), vol. 2, pp. 429–30n.

11 Adam Smith's Politics

I. THE POLITICS OF "PUBLIC SPIRIT"

Adam Smith did not write any single comprehensive treatise on politics as such. He belonged to no particular established "school" of political thought. He espoused no specific political system. Yet, he was an enormously important and innovative political thinker, and it should never be overlooked that he was involved in politics or was in the employ of government for a significant portion of his mature years. Smith's political thought and his political activities deserve more attention than they have generally received from authors who have tried to take the measure of his contribution to modernity.

Smith was a systematic man, both a critic and a constructor of systems in thought. He was sharply critical, however, of the sort of reductive enthusiasm that enslaves thinkers to their systems. He *specifically* attacked the "man of system" whose love of the beauty of his own conceptual constructs blinds him to their limitations.[1] In political practice, he was a methodical and conscientious bureaucrat and a typically civic-minded member of that extraordinary intelligentsia which gave meaning and force to the idea of the "Scottish Enlightenment." In the area of theory, his legacy to posterity includes a radically innovative conception of a system of political economy whose significance for modernity can hardly be overstated, and systems of morals and jurisprudence which must be taken into account in any complete assessment of his political

---

[1] "The man of system ... is apt to be very wise in his own conceit; and is often so enamoured with the supposed beauty of his own ideal plan of government, that he cannot suffer the smallest deviation from any part of it" TMS, VI.ii.2.17, p. 234.

thought. None of them, however, should be seen as coextensive with it.

Smith gave a distinctive, highly significant and thoroughly self-conscious account of the idea of a system in his essay, "The Principles Which Lead and Direct Philosophical Enquiries; Illustrated by the History of Astronomy":

Systems in many respects resemble machines. A machine is a little system, created to perform, as well as to connect together, in reality, those different movements which the artist has occasion for. A system is an imaginary machine invented to connect together in the fancy those different movements and effects which are already in reality performed.[2]

He characterised philosophy in the same essay as "the science of the connecting principles of nature" (IV.12). The more sophisticated the system, he believed, the fewer and the more general its connecting principles would be. His essay on the history of astronomy was a brilliantly innovative review of the successive systems which had over preceding centuries been employed, as he put it, to "allay [the] tumult of the imagination, and to restore it, when it surveys the great revolutions of the universe, to that tone of tranquillity and composure, which is both most agreeable in itself, and most suitable to its nature" (II.12). It was in this spirit of critical and imaginative investigation of the connecting principles postulated in systematic philosophical and scientific inquiries that Smith developed his system of political economy, his system of morals, and his system of jurisprudence. Each system can be said to have employed one particularly striking "connecting principle" to "connect together in the fancy those different movements and effects which are already in reality performed." In Smith's system of political economy the remarkable imaginative construct of the "invisible hand"[3] served to impress on the reader both the power and the novel logic of the operation of the market mechanism in exchange relations in commercial society. In Smith's moral system

[2] "Astronomy," IV.19. The dating of this essay is conjectural. It was published posthumously in 1795, but can only be said with certainty to have been written sometime between 1746 and 1758.
[3] The phrase "invisible hand" occurs three times in Smith's writings: in WN at IV.ii.9, p. 456, in TMS at IV.i.10, p. 184, and in "Astronomy" at III.2, p. 49. In the WN, it is said to maximize aggregate production; in the TMS, it is said to produce an equal distribution of necessities, as opposed to luxury goods.

the imaginative construct of the "impartial spectator"[4] was used to exemplify moral sensibility and to illuminate the process of moral deliberation in a model citizen of commercial society. In Smith's system of jurisprudence the imaginative methodological device of a "conjectural history"[5] of forms of government and society was used to provide a retrospective rationale for the basic structures and functions of government in commercial society. It is from a balanced examination of these three Smithian systems and their respective connecting principles, not from any single abstract governing political principle, that a plausible picture of Adam Smith's political views must be derived.

In a recent book S. E. Gallagher has argued that, when Smith set forth his "system of natural liberty," he "rejected authority itself," marginalizing wisdom and virtue as principles of political leadership and social order, and reducing politics to "comparative insignificance."[6] This line of interpretation can be maintained only by mistaking the "system of natural liberty" referred to in *The Wealth of Nations* for Smith's entire system of moral and political thought. Smith's student John Millar wrote that Smith's course of lectures on moral philosophy at Glasgow had four parts: the first part dealt with natural theology; the second (which became Smith's *Theory of Moral Sentiments*) with ethics; the third with "that branch of morality which relates to *justice*" (Part I of the *Lectures on Jurisprudence*); and the fourth with "those political regulations which are founded, not upon the principle of *justice*, but that of *expediency*, and which are calculated to increase the riches, the power and the prosperity of a State."[7] *The Wealth of Nations* constitutes only the fourth part, not the whole of this

---

[4] The index to the TMS gives many locations for references to this "man within the breast." A good example is at III.2.32, pp. 130–1.

[5] See H. M. Hopfl, "From Savage to Scotsman: Conjectural History in the Scottish Enlightenment," *Journal of British Studies* 16 (1978): 20–40; and R. M. Meek, "Smith, Turgot and the 'Four Stages' Theory," in *Adam Smith: Critical Assessments*, 4 vols., ed. J. C. Wood (London, 1982), vol. 4, pp. 142–55.

[6] S. E. Gallagher, *The Rule of the Rich? Adam Smith's Argument Against Political Power* (University Park, PA, 1998), pp. 105, 98. Cf. WN, vol. 2, IV.ix.51, p. 687: "All systems either of preference or of restraint, therefore, being thus completely taken away, the obvious and simple system of natural liberty establishes itself of its own accord."

[7] Quoted in the editors' Introduction to LJ, p. 3.

immense project. It is to this project as a whole that we should look for the outlines of Adam Smith's politics.

Of the three "connecting principles" which hold in Smith's systems of political economy, morals, and jurisprudence, the most famous is a principle whose political implications are predominantly negative. The "obvious and simple system of natural liberty" over which the "invisible hand" presides is a system of market exchange. Within the boundaries of that system, political authority and political rules are required only to "hold the ring." The system, in Smith's famous phrase, "establishes itself of its own accord." This is to say that politics and politicians ought not to attempt to control exchange relations in the sense of manipulating them with political ends in view. This was surely at least one of the ends Smith had in mind in his critique of the political "man of system." He argued that "[s]ome general, and even systematical, idea of the perfection of policy and law, may no doubt be necessary for directing the views of the statesman," but held that "sovereign princes" in particular tend to attempt to actualize some "ideal plan of government...completely and in all its parts, without any regard either to the great interests, or to the strong prejudices which may oppose it." They mistake human society for a chessboard. This analogy, he warns, is false and even dangerous:

the pieces upon the chess-board have no other principle of motion besides that which the hand impresses upon them; but...in the great chess-board of human society, every single piece has a principle of motion of its own, altogether different from that which the legislature might chuse to impress upon it.[8]

Smith does not conclude from this discussion that there is in politics a system of natural liberty which naturally establishes itself if governments do not impede its flowering. He valued the "security of liberty"[9] as one of the chief achievements of the British constitution, but his defence of political liberty in his *Lectures on Jurisprudence* was conventionally Whiggish. From a brief review

[8] TMS, VI.ii.2.17–18, pp. 233–4.
[9] LJ(B), 62, p. 420: "We have now shewn how the government of England turned absolute; we shall next consider how liberty was restored, and what security the British have for the possession of it."

of the operations of the Civil List, Parliamentary control over key sources of tax revenue, and the use of the sinking fund to pay the public debt, he concluded that "the nation is quite secure in the management of the public revenue, and in this manner a rational system of liberty has been introduced into Brittain [sic]." The essence of this system of political liberty lay in its balancing of arrangements "securing the government in the present [royal] family" against others making it impossible for the king to "hurt the liberty of the subject" (LJ[B], 62–3). Add to these arrangements the "security to liberty" afforded by an independent judiciary, and Smith is moved to conclude that "Here is a happy mixture of all the different forms of government properly restrained and a perfect security to liberty and property" (LJ[B], 63–4). He makes a sharp and explicit contrast between the "spirit of system," which animates the ideal designs of the political despot, and the "public spirit," which embodies in the citizen the promptings of "humanity and benevolence." The public-spirited citizen will always respect the principles of motion of the pieces which move about on the great chessboard of human society:

[he] will respect the established powers and privileges even of individuals, and still more those of the great orders and societies, into which the state is divided... he will content himself with moderating, what he often cannot annihilate without great violence. When he cannot conquer the rooted prejudices of the people by reason and persuasion, he will not attempt to subdue them by force.... He will accommodate, as well as he can, his public arrangements to the confirmed habits and prejudices of the people; and will remedy as well as he can, the "inconveniencies" which may flow from the want of those regulations which the people are averse to submit to. When he cannot establish the right, he will not disdain to ameliorate the wrong; but like Solon, when he cannot establish the best system of laws, he will endeavour to establish the best that the people can bear. (TMS, VI.ii.2.16)

If "public spirit" is not a spirit of "system," Smith is equally clear that it is not a spirit of party. In a section of LJ, strikingly reminiscent of Hume's essay "Of the Original Contract,"[10] Smith identifies two competing principles on which the duty of political allegiance (and therefore the legitimacy of political authority) "seems to be founded": "[The] 1st we may call the principle of authority, and the

[10] See LJ(A), v.116 and fn. 71; v. 117 and fn. 74.

2d the principall of common or generall interest." Acceptance of the principle of authority reflects a natural human disposition to obey one's perceived superiors and a habit of obedience. The subject

born and bred up under the authority of the magistrates...sees they expect his obedience and he sees also the propriety of obeying and the unreasonableness of [dis]obeying....There is the same propriety in submitting to them as to a father, as all of those in authority are either naturally or by the will of the state who lend them their power placed far above you. (LJ[A], v.120)

Smith's other name for the principle of common or general interest is the principle of utility (sometimes "public utility"). As this second name suggests, this principle reflects the general shared sense, in a republican or "democraticall" polity, of the fundamental utility of government:

every one sees that the magistrates not only support the government in generall but the security and independency of each individual, and they see that this security can not be attained without a regular government. Every one therefore thinks it most advisable to submitt to the established government, tho perhaps he may think that it is not disposed in the best manner possible. (LJ[A], v.121)

The disposition to obey is here mitigated by a sense of calculation and critical distance from the regime on the part of the citizens. Still, what Smith calls "the naturall modesty of mankind" combines in this instance with a utilitarian judgment as to costs and benefits to ensure good order.

It is interesting to note that Smith began the lecture immediately following his introduction of these two political principles with a warning against seeing either of them as pervasive or total in its domination of politics. "In yesterday's lecture I showed you that whatever be the principle of allegiance and obedienc[e] of the sovereign, it must have some limits. I endeavoured also to shew that the commonly received one of a tacit contract can not be the just one" (LJ[A], v.128). Smith had indeed argued in his original lecture that "each of these principles takes place in some degree in every government, tho one is generally predominant." The principle of authority, he asserted, is predominant in monarchy. In aristocracy, it is "the leading one, tho there is no doubt but the other has also some effect." Finally "in a republican government, particularly in a democraticall one, [utility] is that which chiefly, nay almost entirely, occasions the obedience of the subject" (LJ[A], v.121). Where does the actual constitution of Britain fit into this taxonomy of regimes?

In Britain the sovereign power is partly entrusted to the king, partly to the people, and partly to the nobles. As it is therefore partly monarchical the principle of authority takes place in a considerable degree, as also because there is some small part of the government aristocraticall. But as the government is in great part democraticall, by the influence of the House of Commons, the principle of utility is also found in it. (LJ (A), v.123)

The fact that Smith's contrasting principles of authority and utility are balanced and interwoven in the fabric of the British constitution, neither ever entirely extirpating the other, accounts for the emergence and persistence of political parties:

Some persons are more directed by the one and others by the other. And to these different principles were owing the distinctions betwixt Whig and Tory. The principle of authority is that of the Tories, as that of utility is followd by the Whigs.[11]

It is important to notice that neither in Smith's own political thought nor in the British political system as he sees it are persons in their political behaviour driven by the force of abstract ideological principles. The case, as Smith presents it, is rather that principles reflect character. Whigs and Tories are simply different sorts of "folks":

The bustling, spirited, active folks, who can't brook oppression and are constantly endeavouring to advance themselves, naturally join in with the democraticall part of the constitution and favour the principle of utility only, that is the Whig interest. The calm, contented folks of no great spirit and abundant fortunes which they want to enjoy at their own ease, and dont want to be disturbed nor to disturb others, as naturally join with the Tories and found their obedience on the less generous principle of [authority]. (LJ[A], v.124)

If there is a pervasive or all-encompassing principle at work here, it is neither that of utility nor that of authority; nor, Smith points out

---

[11] Ibid, v.123, p. 319. The Whigs, Smith adds, "do not explain [their principle] very distinctly, endeavouring to reconcile it to the notion of a contract."

in another context, is it that of "national character": "It is far more reducible to self interest, that general principle which regulates the actions of every man, and which leads men to act in a certain manner from views of advantage, and is as deeply implanted in an Englishman as a Dutchman" (LJ[B], 327). Given this inescapable proclivity in every man to seek "advantage," the highest service that a party leader can render to his country is to use his political *influence* to "prevail upon his own friends to act with proper temper and moderation." In such a spirit of moderation, and only in such a spirit,

He may re-establish and improve the constitution, and from the very doubtful and ambiguous character of the leader of a party, he may assume the greatest and noblest of all characters, that of the reformer and legislator of a great state. (TMS, VI.ii.2.14)

Smith's politics, then, are neither the politics of party nor the politics of system. They are the politics of character and of public spirit. They echo in some respects the anti-enthusiasm and anti-dogmatism of the politics of David Hume, and it is perhaps this resemblance that has led some scholars to label Smith a "contemplative utilitarian" in matters of public policy.[12] I have illustrated this quality by reference to just a few of many passages in Smith's *Theory of Moral Sentiments* which speak eloquently of a politics of moderation and constructively cautious pragmatism. *The Theory of Moral Sentiments* highlights a principle, or at least a human sentiment, suitable to govern such a politics. It is the sentiment of propriety.

II. PROPRIETY, PROPERTY, AND POLICE

A brief excursion into the etymology of "propriety" will serve to underline the fact that Smith's usage of the term was carefully crafted, distinctive, and strategically important in the development of his social and political thought. In the works of Thomas Hobbes, the term "property" does not occur. "Propriety" is employed by

---

[12] See T. D. Campbell and I. S. Ross, "The Utilitarianism of Adam Smith's Policy Advice," *Journal of the History of Ideas* 42 (1981): 73–92.

Hobbes to convey the legal and economic idea of proprietorship as ownership:

Justice is the constant Will of giving to every man his own. And therefore where there is no *Own,* that is, no Propriety, there is no Injustice; and where there is no coërceive Power erected, that is, where there is no Commonwealth, there is no Propriety; all men having Right to all things.[13]

Clearly Hobbes's "propriety" is Smith's "property." What Smith refers to as "propriety," Hobbes deals with under the name of "manners."[14] The name employed is different, but the importance attached to the concept is similar. Both authors make a crucial distinction between "small manners," or insignificant matters of taste and style, and those qualities that enable humans to live together in peace and security. "Propriety" is as important to Smith's understanding of justice as "manners" are to Hobbes's account of sovereignty, commonwealth, and peace.

By the time of John Locke, the situation with regard to "propriety" seems to be etymologically inverted. In Locke the term "propriety" does not occur. "Property" in Locke conveys an idea of legal entitlement to objects of occupation and possession. However, in Locke's particular account, entitlement is a moral conception, based on his conceptualization of labour as both an expression of natural human capacities and the fulfillment of a duty to God.[15] The ideas of proprietorship and appropriate social behaviour, clearly separated and each carefully developed in Smith, are to an important degree merged in Locke, but merged in a way which leaves Locke's account of property both incomplete, in terms of what it sets out to explain, and unclear.[16] Locke's account lacks a sense of the tension between self-interested proprietorship and

---

[13] *Leviathan,* ed. C. B. Macpherson (Harmondsworth, 1968), chapter 15, p. 202.

[14] "By Manners, I mean not here, Decency of behaviour; as how one man should salute another, or how a man should wash his mouth, or pick his teeth before company, and such other points of the *Small Moralls;* But those qualities of man-kind, that concern their living together in Peace, and Unity." Ibid, chapter 11, p. 160.

[15] See Locke, *Two Treatises of Government,* ed. P. Laslett (Cambridge, 1988), 2nd Treatise, para. 34 at p. 291 and para. 45 at p. 299. See also editor's Introduction, pp. 101–8.

[16] Laslett, who is generally appreciative of the novelty and importance of Locke's idea of property, nevertheless finds it neither "wholly developed" nor "coherent." Ibid, p. 107.

the socially oriented sentiment of propriety that becomes strong
and clear in Smith's thought, perhaps because Locke is willing to
invoke a *deus ex machina* to resolve this tension, whereas Smith's
portrait of human nature perforce left it unresolved.

The idea of property played an enormously important role in
the political, social, and economic theories of David Hume. "A
man's property," says Hume, "is some object related to him. This
relation is not natural, but moral, and founded upon justice."[17]
Hume makes the stabilization of this relationship between person
and property the first and foremost objective of a system of justice (*Treatise*, 487–9). On the other hand, Selby-Bigge's "analytical
index" to Hume's *Treatise of Human Nature* has no entry at all
for "propriety." No vestige remains, in Hume's picture of property,
of the Thomistic view in which property was a matter of ethical stewardship, such that the rich were under a clear obligation of
natural law to share their superabundance with the poor.[18] In other
words, "propriety" disappears from Hume's analysis, functionally
replaced by "selfishness and limited generosity" (*Treatise*, 494). In
Smith the emphasis on property as a perfect legal right encased in
an essentially commutative legal carapace is carried forward from
Hume. However, the concept of "propriety" re-emerges in Smith's
moral theory, largely because, unlike Hume, he believed the property relationship had a significant moral dimension and that the
(necessarily) moral context of property relations was explicable by
reference not only to artifice, but also to our moral nature. Smith's
political writings, therefore, had to deal both with proprietorship
and with propriety. In Smith's writings in general, and in his writings on justice specifically, the tension between moral "propriety" and economic proprietorship is addressed and even in some
degree resolved. The ideal is that the economic proprietor will also
be a man of propriety. Failing this, the society may still flourish
in the absence of moral excellence provided that property is sta-
bilised, respected, and protected. The direction of Smith's movement in thought is important: Hume had already taken the theory,
and specifically the jurisprudence, of property as far as Smith felt

---

[17] Hume, *A Treatise of Human Nature*, ed. L. A. Selby-Bigge (Oxford, 1973), III.ii.2,
p. 491.
[18] See *St. Thomas Aquinas on Politics and Ethics*, ed. P. E. Sigmund, (New York, NY,
1988), p. 72.

it should go in the direction of purely utilitarian and commutative legality.[19] Smith strengthened, rather than weakened, the place of moral theory in the broad context of his thinking about the politics and jurisprudence of property by putting "propriety" in the foreground of his *Theory of Moral Sentiments*.

Smith's theory of justice thus focussed on two key concerns: one economic, and the other moral in nature. Economically, it was concerned with justice as protector of the perfect (commutative) right to proprietorship. Morally, it was concerned with propriety and the maintenance of a moral "sense of justice" in commercial society. Hume had argued that "the sense of justice and injustice is not deriv'd from nature, but arises artificially, tho' necessarily from education, and human conventions" (*Treatise*, 483). Smith signalled his discomfort with this position in an important letter to Gilbert Elliott in which he was at pains to distinguish his view of "sympathy" from Hume's. There he spoke of:

my Doctrine that our judgements concerning our own conduct have always a reference to the sentiments of some other being, . . . [but] that, notwithstanding this, real magnanimity and conscious virtue can support itselfe [sic] under the disapprobation of all mankind.[20]

The propriety of a human action, for Smith, is its appropriateness. All the complexities of his moral theory are necessary to establish the context and criteria for the measurement of this appropriateness. The first 57 pages of the *The Theory of Moral Sentiments* are explicitly dedicated to this task. We shall have occasion to refer again to this text further along in this argument, but it will be helpful at this point simply to establish that Smith introduced his readers to his moral theory by passing it through the lens, so to speak, of propriety. Smith's concept of sympathy, and by extension his pivotal moral metaphor of the "impartial spectator," are simply extensions and embodiments of the basic principle that

[19] See especially *Treatise*, III.2.3, pp. 501–13, "Of the rules, which determine property."

[20] Correspondence, letter 40, 10 October 1759, p. 49. This principle is clearly reflected in Smith's explanation of the impartial spectator at p. 55, where he says that people unaccustomed to consulting "the judge within" are "in consequence necessarily the Slaves of the world," while the individual who has recourse to "this impartial Spectator" will not be morally ruled by "what the world approves or disapproves of."

appropriateness is the criterion of excellence in moral sentiments, moral judgments, and moral actions. Adherence to a principle of propriety was to Smith's way of thinking an expression of basic human sociability. The essence of sociability, he felt, resides in the fact that humans take pleasure in their capacity for "fellow-feeling," or what Hume and Smith both called "sympathy."[21] "I wish that you had more particularly and fully prov'd, that all kinds of Sympathy are necessarily Agreeable," Hume wrote to Smith, "This is the Hinge of your System, and yet you only mention the Matter cursorily...."[22] Hume held that sympathy could be pleasurable or painful, depending on the nature of the stimuli thus vicariously experienced. Smith wrote to Gilbert Elliott that he had worked out a response that "entirely discomfitted" Hume.[23] It is always "agreable [sic] and delightful," Smith asserted, when we find that our sympathetic sentiments match those of the party whose behaviour we are witnessing. The experience, surely, strengthens our sense of the propriety (appropriateness) of our own sentiments. Hume knew that this connecting of sociability with a natural sense of appropriateness or propriety was a step which distanced Smith's moral theory from his own; he knew that a great deal hinged on it. Smith knew that it was important to establish it. Why so? The answer is given in the opening words of *The Theory of Moral Sentiments*:

How selfish soever man may be supposed, there are evidently some principles in his nature, which interest him in the fortune of others, and render their happiness necessary to him, though he derives nothing from it except the pleasure of seeing it. Of this kind is pity or compassion... this sentiment, like all the other original passions of human nature, is by no means confined to the virtuous and humane, though they perhaps feel it with the most exquisite sensibility. The greatest ruffian, the most hardened violator of the laws of society, is not altogether without it. (TMS, I.ii.1.1)

Thus, at the very outset of *The Theory of Moral Sentiments*, Adam Smith made it clear that his system of morals rested on a positive

---

[21] TMS, I.ii.1 and 2, pp. 9–16. For fellow-feeling, see I.ii.1.3 at p. 10.

[22] Correspondence, letter 36, 28 July 1759, p. 43.

[23] Correspondence, letter 40, 10 October 1759, p. 49. The resulting draft amendment to *The Theory of Moral Sentiments*, arguing that there is always something "agreable and delightful" in the sense of "coincidence" between the sentiments of observer and observed, is attached to this letter; see p. 51.

sentiment of sociability possessed by even the most antisocial members of a civil society. He connected this sentiment explicitly with the issue of violation of the laws of society. This sentiment, as we shall see, was to reappear at a crucial point in the argument of *The Theory of Moral Sentiments* as the basis for a sense of justice. We shall also see that a sense of justice, a sense, as Smith was to put it, of "guilt and ill-desert," was an integral and indispensable part of Smith's theories of justice and politics.

Stable and peaceful relations of interaction and exchange in commercial society require a supporting framework of both legality and civility. Smith's political writings provide such a framework. They offer a secure structure of laws, institutions, and morals to protect and stabilize private property and contractual exchange. They do so by elaborating 1) an ethic of propriety and 2) a jurisprudence combining economic attention to "police" with a distinctive and nuanced theory of justice:

Police, the word, has been borrowed by the English immediately from the French, tho it is originally derived from the Greek *politeia*, signifying policy, politicks, or the regulation of a government in generall. It is now however generally confind to the regulation of the inferior parts of it. (LJ[A], vi.1)

We will be misled, then, if we look to Smith's account of "police" for the nucleus of his account of politics. "Police" refers only to the *oikonome* of the state, its "household management" in Aristotle's sense of that expression. Smith is very much interested in "the regulation of a government in generall," and not merely in "the regulation of the inferior parts of it." We have already seen that he is passionately concerned both with the quality of the *politeia*, or the constitution, and the character of the *politeuma*, or citizen body. He seeks to identify and cultivate the characteristics of that type of citizen who can draw on true public spirit to contribute to the improvement and re-establishment of the constitution. This is the "greatest and noblest of all characters, that of the reformer and legislator of a great state." Smith's most important political principles, then, are not the straightforward and "inferior" principles of "police" but the more complex, general, and at times elusive principles of property and propriety. The conceptual arena, so to speak, for his thinking about property and propriety, and their inter-relationship in civil and commercial society, is justice. The unique character of Smith's understanding of justice derives from his belief that it must pursue in a balanced way two distinctly different objectives: on the one hand, the protection of proprietorship and the promotion of exchange; and on the other, the preservation of that sense of justice without which "a man would enter an assembly of men as he enters a den of lions" (TMS, II.iii.3.4).

"The first and chief design of every system of government," Smith held, "is to maintain justice" – justice in the sense of the peaceful maintenance of the citizens' perfect rights to property (LJ[A], i.1). Like Hume, Smith maintained that the protection of property was the first necessity of every system of government worthy of the name. This should not be mistaken for the very different claim that it is the *only* appropriate objective of government, or that superior systems do not pursue something more. In the same passage of the *Lectures*, Smith described "jurisprudence" as "the theory of the rules by which civil governments ought to be directed." Must these rules be confined to the protection of perfect rights to property? Neither Smith's text at this point nor a consideration of his enterprise as a whole suggests that they need, or even can, be so limited. Section IV of the seventh book of *The Theory of Moral Sentiments* deals with "the rules of justice" as a special subset of the "practical rules of morality": "the rules of justice are the only rules of morality which are precise and accurate; ... those of the other virtues are loose, vague, and indeterminate" (TMS, VII.iv.1). Aristotelian Ethics, for example, Smith sees as a "science ... both highly useful and agreeable" but incorrigibly imprecise, able to "correct and ascertain our natural sentiments with regard to the propriety of conduct," and to "form us to a more exact justness of behaviour, than what, without such instruction, we should have been apt to think of," but unable to generate precise, justiciable rules. He observes that two more modern groups of authors have attempted to lay down "exact and precise rules for the direction of every circumstance of our behaviour" and thus to articulate rules of justice. These groups are the late medieval casuists and the partisans of "natural jurisprudence":

It is the end of jurisprudence to prescribe rules for the decisions of judges and arbiters. It is the end of casuistry to prescribe rules for the conduct of a good man. By observing all the rules of jurisprudence, supposing them ever so perfect, we should deserve nothing but to be free from external punishment. By observing those of casuistry...we should be entitled to considerable praise by the exact and scrupulous delicacy of our behaviour. (TMS, VII.iv. 6–7)

The rules of justice according to natural jurisprudence are, at least in some cases, as precise – and as limited in scope and application – as those of strict commutative justice: where a wrong can be measured precisely, compensatory penalties can be specified fairly exactly. The keeping of promises and the paying of debts, for example, would seem to be unconditionally enjoined by the rules of justice. However, on closer examination Smith readily sees that the case is not so simple. What if the promise was extorted? What, if any, effect does the size of the payment promised have on the strength of the legal obligation to make it (TMS, VII.iv.12)? There is, he concedes, some validity to the casuists' claim that there are "general rules of justice" which make demands on us that are not just prudential but moral (ibid, 16). Despite his assertion that "casuistry ought to be rejected altogether" (ibid, 34), his sense of the important grain of truth in the casuists' basic contention leads him to reformulate the relationship between the laws of particular polities and the principles of jurisprudence. His new formulation differs significantly from the one (quoted previously) with which he had begun his *Lectures on Jurisprudence*. In Smith's new articulation, "positive laws" are evaluated not against the simple criterion of the absolute protection of perfect rights to property but against the prescriptions of "the natural sense of justice":

Every system of positive law may be regarded as a more or less imperfect attempt towards a system of natural jurisprudence, or towards an enumeration of the particular rules of justice....To prevent the confusion which would attend upon every man's doing justice to himself, the magistrate, in all governments that have acquired any considerable authority, undertakes to do justice to all...rules are prescribed for regulating the decisions of...judges; and these rules are, in general, intended to coincide with those of natural justice....In no country do the decisions of positive law coincide exactly, in every case, with the rules which the natural sense of justice would dictate. (TMS, VII.iv.36)

Here the rules dictated by the "natural sense of justice" have become second-order rules, moral criteria never fully instantiated in any specific and concrete body of positive laws. Justice, then, is no longer the matter of internal administration of prudential rules of property that it seemed to be according to Smith's students' notes on his lectures on jurisprudence. In relation to the principles and practice of politics, the "sense of justice" is not vestigial or merely decorative. It is constitutive.

III. THE NATURAL *SENSE* OF JUSTICE

In my view, Smith's theory of justice is a comprehensive and consistent whole – there is no "Adam Smith Problem" concerning justice. However, it is a complex and highly differentiated whole which resists monolithic characterisation. The economic aspect of justice is clearly and powerfully captured in the idea of a complete set of rules of commutative justice defining and protecting property. The moral aspect of justice is no less real or important for being more elusive, but it seems to be expressed in Smith's persistent adherence to the belief that there is such a thing as a "sense of justice," which is crucial to (and in some sense prior to) the operation of law, even commutative law, in civil society. The political aspect of the theory of justice is best understood as the attempt to arrive at principles by which governments and governors may adjudicate between the competing claims of the perfect right to property, on the one hand, and the moral sense of justice, on the other. To be sustainable, however, this view of Smith's theory of justice must support plausible readings of a variety of Smithian texts. So much of Smith's foreground discussion of justice seems to treat it as purely commutative that the claim that Smith's justice has an irreducible moral aspect may at first glance seem implausible.

In *The Wealth of Nations*, Smith situates "justice" in the context of a system of political economy. The key human traits in the analysis are the propensity to truck and barter and the desire to better one's condition in life. The systemic context within which these traits are highlighted is portrayed most memorably in the metaphor of the "invisible hand," but it is also captured in Smith's vivid image of a "simple and obvious system of natural liberty." The basic jurisprudential issue raised within this scenario is that of the security of individual persons and their property. This same concern most prominently shapes the treatment of justice in Smith's

Lectures on Jurisprudence, where the view that the jurisprudence of commercial society is essentially commutative and not distributive is clearly stated. Smith discusses the distinction made by "Mr. Hutchinson, following Baron Puffendorf" between "*jura perfecta* and *imperfecta*":

A beggar is an object of our charity and may be said to have a right to demand it; but when we use the word right in this way it is not in a proper but in a metaphorical sense. The common way in which we understand the word right, is the same as what we have called a perfect right, and is that which relates to commutative justice. Imperfect rights, again, refer to distributive justice. The former are the rights which we are to consider, the latter not belonging properly to jurisprudence, but rather to a system of morals as they do not fall under the jurisdiction of the laws. We are therefore in what follows to confine ourselves entirely to the perfect rights and what is called commutative justice. (LJ[A], i.15)

"Imperfect rights," claims made in the name of virtue or fairness, and matters of distributive justice are said to belong to the field of morals. The lectures on jurisprudence need not deal with them. It remains to be seen whether in fact Smith was able thus completely to compartmentalise his moral theory. When in *The Wealth of Nations* (IV.viii.30) Smith refers to "that justice and equality of treatment which the sovereign owes to all the different orders of his subjects," this may be read, in the light of the passage just quoted, as a guarantee of *jura perfecta* only. Yet it is surely arguable, as Haakonssen has suggested, that it involves something more. "Smith's legal criticism obviously presupposes that the negative and precise virtue of justice is "natural" in the sense that it is somehow outside the grip of social change."[24] Haakonssen seeks to avoid what he sees as the parochial consensualism of Campbell[25] and the deterministic post-Marxist perspective of Meek, while clarifying the sense in which "spectatorial" moral judgments must be "impartial," and therefore, as I have shown previously, not entirely contingent on external circumstances. Smith seems consciously to have struggled with this same problem. Indeed, his letter to Gilbert Elliott suggests that he thought he had solved it by recognizing both

[24] Knud Haakonssen, *The Science of a Legislator: The Natural Jurisprudence of David Hume and Adam Smith* (Cambridge, 1981), p. 147.
[25] Ibid, p. 150.

the social "reference" and the stubborn interiority of qualities such as magnanimity and virtue. When Haakonssen interprets Smith's assertion that natural justice and equity are antecedent to "the institution of civil government" as meaning that Smith finds them to be "independent of civil society," he may go too far.[26] However, it seems clear that Smith himself was unwilling to ground natural justice entirely on either political expediency or social contingency. If John Millar's account of how Smith described his body of work and thought to his students is at all accurate, Smith promised them an analysis of "that branch of morality which relates to justice" and, in a separate but related installment of his teaching, of "those political regulations which are founded, not upon the principle of justice, but that of expediency."[27] Justice and expediency are clearly contrasted in this summary statement, but equally clearly neither is subsumed under the other. Justice is distinguished not by its separation from morality, but by its connection with it.

Hume, in distinguishing between natural and artificial virtues, asserted that, on the one hand, artificial virtues were not "arbitrary" simply by virtue of being artificial, while, on the other hand, when we say that a principle (say a principle of human nature) is "natural" or "immutable," all we can possibly mean by this is that neither experience nor imagination can enable us to envisage a human social context in which it fails to hold.[28] This is as much as naturalness or universality could mean for Hume or Smith. This is the specific sense in which the principles of natural justice or equity were raised above dependence on the contingencies of social life for both authors. It is in the light of these reflections that we should read passages such as the following one from *The Theory of Moral Sentiments*:

Sometimes what is called the constitution of the state, that is the interest of the government; sometimes the interest of particular orders of men who tyrannize the government, warp the positive laws of the country from

---

[26] Ibid, p. 149.

[27] Quoted previously at footnote 7.

[28] "Tho' the rules of justice be *artificial*, they are not *arbitrary*. Nor is the expression improper to call them *Laws of Nature*, if by natural we understand what is common to any species, or even if we confine it to mean what is inseparable from the species." Hume, *Treatise*, III.II.I, "Justice, whether a natural or artificial virtue?," p. 484.

what natural justice would prescribe. In some countries, the rudeness and barbarism of the people hinder *the natural sentiments of justice* from arriving at that accuracy and precision, which in more civilized nations, they naturally attain to. (TMS, VII.iv.36; emphasis added)

As long as we confine our investigation to *The Wealth of Nations* and the *Lectures*, it is quite possible to sustain the impression that with Smith's analysis of the dynamics of commercial society the connection between justice and virtue is irreparably severed. It is worth noting that this impression has been immensely influential in the intellectual iconography of the "New Right" in twentieth-century politics. However, we simply fail to comprehend Smith's view of justice if we forget that liberty, legality, and prosperity could exist according to his theory only within a framework of sociality, the acknowledgment of interdependence and mutual sympathy. In Smith's characterisation of humanity and politics, a sense of "natural justice" or "natural equity" is a necessary condition for the maintenance of even the most basic forms of commutative justice. Smith was no Hobbesian. For Smith, it is not just the fear of punishment that distinguishes an "association of men" from a "den of lions." Commutative justice itself presupposes that certain basic moral sentiments have been "emplanted" by nature in "the human breast":

In order to enforce the observation of justice, therefore, Nature has emplanted in the human breast that consciousness of ill-*desert*, those terrors of *merited* punishment which attend upon its violation, as the great safe-guards of the association of mankind, to protect the weak, to curb the violent, and to chastise the guilty. Men, though naturally sympathetic, feel so little for another, with whom they have no particular connection . . . ; they have it so much in their power to hurt him and may have so many temptations to do so, that *if this principle did not stand up within them in his defence,* and overawe them into a respect for his innocence, they would, like wild beasts, be at all times ready to fly upon him; *and a man would enter an assembly of men as he enters a den of lions.* (TMS, II.ii.3.4; emphasis added)

In declaring justice to be commutative within a certain specified context, Smith did not declare the sort of moral excellence that had been at the very centre of classical theories of justice to be a triviality. He did indeed find that it was "less essential to the existence of society than [commutative] justice"; "It is the ornament which embellishes, not the foundation which supports the building" (TMS, II.ii.3.3). Society "may subsist" without it. Nonetheless, Smith's ideal as a moralist was a society in which our need of mutual aid would be generously and freely acknowledged:

Where the necessary assistance is reciprocally afforded from love, from gratitude, from friendship, and esteem, the society flourishes and is happy. All the different members of it are bound together by the agreeable bands of love and affection, and are, as it were, drawn to one common centre of mutual good offices. (TMS, II.ii.3.1)

What Smith had to say about the treatment of virtue in Plato and Aristotle in his review of "Systems of Moral Philosophy" in the seventh book of *The Theory of Moral Sentiments* is helpful in connecting Smith's view of justice with its classical antecedents. His treatment of Plato's tripartite division of the soul exemplifies his strategy. Smith sets out not to reject Plato's analysis of our moral nature but to show that it is in fact essentially congruent with Smith's own propriety-centred theory. In short, Plato's just man is Smith's man of propriety. Plato's philosopher is Smith's citizen-patriot. The highest and "governing" element or "principle" in the soul for Plato, says Smith, is "the judging faculty." "Under this appellation, it is evident, he comprehended not only that faculty by which we judge of truth and falsehood, but that by which we judge of the propriety or impropriety of desires and affections." (VII.ii.1.3). His emphasis throughout his explanation of Plato's moral theory is on propriety and on the equanimity which accompanies a sense of propriety. Thus he emphasizes, in terms reminiscent of his "Essay on Astronomy," the "happy composure" of the harmonious soul. Then he arrives at the Platonic view of justice:

Justice, the last and greatest of the four cardinal virtues, took place ... when each of those three faculties of the mind confined itself to its proper office ... when reason directed and passion obeyed, and when each passion performed its proper duty, and exerted itself towards its proper object easily and without reluctance, and with that degree of force and energy, which was suitable to the value of what it pursued. In this consisted that complete virtue, that perfect propriety of conduct, which Plato, after some of the ancient Pythagoreans, denominated Justice. (VII.ii.1.9)

There is no reference here to episteme or to sophia – to knowledge or to wisdom in the Platonic sense. Plato's metaphysics and epistemology are quietly evaded. What is presented is a blending of neo-Stoic equanimity and composure with an emphasis on Smith's own key concept of propriety.

Smith goes on to notice the "several different meanings" which the term justice has in Greek and "all other languages," and finds that these "various significations" boil down to two senses, a negative and a positive one. In the negative sense, "we are said to do justice to our neighbour when we abstain from doing him any positive harm.... This is that justice which I have treated of above, the observance of which may be extorted by force, and the violation of which exposes to punishment." This, says Smith, is "what Aristotle and the Schoolmen call commutative justice, and ... what Grotius calls the *justitia expletrix*." There is also a "second sense of the word" which "coincides with what some have called distributive justice, and with the *justitia attributrix* of Grotius." This Smith equates, neatly replicating the duality of propriety and beneficence emphasized in Book I of *The Theory of Moral Sentiments*, with "proper beneficence, ... the becoming use of what is our own, and ... the applying it to those purposes either of charity or of generosity, to which it is most suitable, in our situation, that it should be applied." "In this sense," Smith concludes, "[distributive] justice comprehends all the social virtues" (VII.ii.1.10). Now it is true that distributive justice encompasses all the social virtues for Aristotle and for Plato. However, it is not true that for these two authors beneficence is the distilled essence of all these virtues. When Smith turns to a third and last sense of justice in Plato, we see still more clearly what Smith has in mind in his argument. Here it is especially clear that Smith wants to substitute propriety for philosophical knowledge as the foundation of all virtue:

There is yet another sense in which the word justice is sometimes taken, still more extensive than either of the former, though very much a-kin to the last and which runs too, so far as I know, through all languages. It is in this last sense that we are said to be unjust, when we do not seem to value any particular object with that degree of esteem, or to pursue it with that degree of ardour which to the impartial spectator it may appear to deserve or to be naturally fitted for exciting....It is in this last sense that Plato evidently understands what he calls justice....His account, it is evident, coincides in every respect with what we have said above concerning the propriety of conduct. (VII.ii.1.10–11).

From here Smith moves directly to a thumbnail sketch of the idea of moderation in Aristotle's *Ethics* and to the conclusion that "It is unnecessary to observe that this account of virtue corresponds too pretty exactly with what has been said above concerning the propriety and impropriety of conduct." (VII.ii.1.12).

Thus, Smith offered a heavily qualified endorsement of classical theories of justice, by arguing that the forms of moral knowledge they had identified could be contained without essential loss within his own governing idea of a sense of moral propriety.

IV. POLITICS AND JUSTICE

As a professor of moral philosophy and as a leading Scottish *literatus*, Smith was intimately acquainted with the theories of justice which had successively dominated moral and political thinking from the time of ancient Athenian philosophy to his own day. These theories were of three basic kinds: "classical" theories exemplified in the Platonic and Aristotelian texts we have just been discussing, Christian theories best exemplified in Saint Thomas Aquinas's synthesis of Aristotelian and Catholic ideas, and the more modern theories developed within the school of "natural jurisprudence," exemplified in the works of Hugo Grotius and Samuel Pufendorf. Among these authors, it was Aristotle who provided the broadest, most inclusive, and most flexible framework for examining justice in the fifth book of his *Nicomachean Ethics*. There he identified three different kinds of justice, each entailing a different theoretical approach to the subject, and each having a different relationship to the theory and practice of politics. Aristotle's most purely philosophic (and neo-Platonic) form of justice was "universal" or contemplative justice.[29] This was the form which Plato had made the ideal and criterion of all politics. In Plato's *Republic*, for example, there are only two kinds of political life:

[29] Aristotle, *Ethics* (Harmondsworth, 1980), 1129b30, p. 173.

the life driven by the appetitive aspect of the human soul and eventuating in endless conflict and instability, including the endless instability of corrupt political regimes, and the philosophical life of contemplation and actualization (if this be possible) of the ideal. When Adam Smith turned Plato's just man from a man of philosophy into a man of propriety, he transformed not only Platonic ethics, but also perforce Platonic politics. Smith placed at the centre of his theorizing about justice and politics a conception of moral agency that emphasized moderation and propriety, qualities more accessible to and characteristic of "bustling, spirited, active folks, who... are constantly endeavouring to advance themselves" (LJ[A], v.124) than the Platonic *eidos* or "forms" of wisdom, courage, temperance, and justice could ever be. Where Plato had expelled economic activity to the margins of the polis, Smith conceived of a sense of justice that could morally pervade, or at least enframe, commercial activity. Thus, in his re-expression of Plato's text, Smith embedded a radical transformation of his meaning, and shaped Plato's principles to his own moral and political ends.

Aristotle considered the "universal" or Platonic theory of justice to be essentially philosophical in nature, and only realizable in the context of the "practical science"[30] of politics in the sense in which moral ideals always have the potential to shape practise. Political justice, for Aristotle, was distributive justice: justice in the sense of "proportionate equality,"[31] the proper proportioning of political (which for Aristotle included social) rewards to citizens' respective contributions to the excellence of their polity. Political rewards for Aristotle were principally moral and social in nature. High honours and high office were his chief concern. He gave little weight to the question of the distribution of economic rewards because he assumed all citizens, as a qualification for their participation in political deliberation and office, had an economic sufficiency. Thus, Aristotle's third form of justice, one associated in his analysis with *oikonome* or household management rather than with politics, was commutative or rectificatory justice,[32] which guaranteed the equal value of things exchanged in economic transactions. This

[30] *Ethics*, editor's Intro., p. 17.
[31] Ibid, Book V, 1131a, pp. 177–8.
[32] Ibid, 1132–3, pp. 179–83.

form of justice pursued no normative moral principle directly – it merely returned matters in the wake of an economic transaction to the *status quo ante*. Aristotle's three models of justice were not placed in watertight compartments. Rectificatory justice, while not a sufficient condition for the achievement of political or distributive justice, might well be a necessary condition for it in so far as it underwrote the affluence which alone enabled the citizen body to engage in public deliberation in a leisured and reflective, and thus excellent, way. However, political justice, for Aristotle, was the specific form of justice which enabled *homo sapiens* to reach his natural end ("telos") of moral excellence as a *zoon politikon*. We have seen how Smith transformed the Platonic conceptions of justice and politics in an important way. To what degree, we must now ask, did he transform Aristotle's political or distributive justice? The answer comes in two parts: first, his reworking of the idea of distributive justice reflects in important ways the influence on him of Grotius, Pufendorf, and the school of natural jurisprudence; secondly, however, Smith added a key twist of his own to this reworking.

Aristotle had relegated questions of property to the periphery of political life on the ground that the distinctive end or *telos* of human life was moral and political, rather than economic, in nature. He had correspondingly treated rectificatory justice as inferior to the political kind. Saint Thomas Aquinas, the great reviver of Aristotelianism, nevertheless differed from Aristotle in treating the distribution of property as a central moral issue in social life. He held that ownership of property by persons was never unconditional: it was always a matter of stewardship. Only God's ownership of anything could be absolute. A proper and lawful distribution of resources in the world, he argued, should reflect the benevolent and nurturing relationship of Creator to Creation. Through conscience ("synderesis"), persons could have access to a sense of justice in these matters. The school of juristic thought known as natural jurisprudence reconsidered both of these arguments.

As James Tully has shown in his summary characterization of the natural jurisprudence tradition, Aristotelian teleology and Thomistic synderesis were supplanted in this modern school of natural law by the new concept of socialitas. This was a term well-known to Adam Smith, one usually translated into English as "sociability." Pufendorf had argued that natural law properly understood dealt with a "set of moral duties common to all mankind," essential to their social life together, and discoverable by reason.[33] Absent from these arguments was any claim that either teleology or theology could provide a basic pattern for the distribution of goods in civil society.

Smith concurred with some of the central presuppositions of Pufendorf's analysis. Like his predecessor, he felt the aim of natural jurisprudence was to show how individuals might become more useful members of society – a goal both men shared, in a sense, with Aristotle. Smith, like Pufendorf, took the subjects of the natural law to be self-loving and self-interested by nature. However, Smith did not, like Pufendorf, leave the inner thoughts, desires, and intentions of men to be governed by divine law alone. In fact, he intended them to be governed by a novel principle, one which by its nature removes his moral and political theory substantially from the domain of Pufendorf's natural law theory – a principle of accountability:

Man is considered as a moral, because he is regarded as an accountable being…a being that must give an account of its actions to some other, and that, consequently, must regulate them according to the good liking of this other. Man is accountable to God and his fellow creatures.

This accountability is essentially moral, and it is first learned in the bosom of society. That is, the sense of accountability to one's fellows precedes the recognition of accountability to God:

[T]ho' he is, no doubt, principally accountable to God, in the order of time, he must necessarily conceive himself as accountable to his fellow creatures, before he can form any idea of the Deity, or of the rules by which that Divine Being will judge of his conduct. (Corr., 52)

The effect of this "turn" in moral theory, a reshaping quite specific to Smith's work, is to moralize politics and to politicize morality. In Smith's thought, the political arena is the primary social arena of accountability. Character and judgment, public spirit and moderation are qualities which unite political acumen and contribution

---

[33] Tully, Introduction to Pufendorf, *On the Duty of Man and Citizen* (Cambridge, 1991), pp. xiv–xxxii, at pp. xxii–iii.

with moral excellence. Smith saw that if citizens and statesmen could not be induced to invoke the perspective of the "impartial spectator" in making social judgments of both a moral and a legal nature, interest and passion, unmitigated, would incline men to pounce on the weak among their fellows like a pride of marauding lions discovering easy prey. Smith's political morality, then, like Aristotle's political justice, distributes to citizens the honours and the offices they truly deserve and makes the excellence of their political arrangements depend on their accountability to each other for their outward actions as well as their inner intentions and motivations. In Smith's idea of "public spirit" the spirit of Aristotle's ancient alliance of politics with ethics lives on. Aristotle's "distributive justice" to an important degree lives on in Smith's political morality.

It was in the economic realm that Aristotle felt commutative or rectificatory justice ought to reign, and Smith agreed. Istvan Hont and Michael Ignatieff have argued that Smith "transpose[d] the question [of justice] from the terrain of jurisprudence and political theory to the terrain of political economy":

[Smith's] position effectively excluded "distributive justice" from the appropriate functions of government in a market society. Smith insisted that the only appropriate function of justice was "commutative"; it dealt with the attribution of responsibility and the punishment of injury among individuals. Distributive justice, which dealt with the allocation of superfluity according to claims of need, or desert, or merit, was not properly in the domain of law, but of morality.[34]

Thus, rectificatory justice was the proper principle by which to govern the "police," or policy making, of a commercial or market society, while distributive justice belonged in the domain of political morality.

Hont and Ignatieff pointed out that Smith himself identified Hugo Grotius, the founder of modern natural jurisprudence, as the first modern author to make a rigorous distinction between "the laws of police" and those rules of natural equity "which ought

---

[34] I. Hont and M. Ignatieff, "Needs and Justice in *The Wealth of Nations*: An Introductory Essay," in *Wealth and Virtue. The Shaping of Political Economy in the Scottish Enlightenment*, eds. I. Hont and M. Ignatieff (Cambridge, 1983), pp. 1–44, at pp. 24–5.

to run through, and be the foundation of the laws of all nations" (TMS, VII.iv.37). Saint Thomas had asserted that "whatever goods some have in superabundance are due, by natural law, to the sustenance of the poor." He had even insisted that, "if a man under stress of ... necessity takes from the property of another what is necessary to preserve his own life, he does not commit a theft."[35] Grotius replied that St. Thomas's moral principles for the distribution of goods held only in times of utmost necessity, when the otherwise absolute legal right to property was superseded by a prior communal right to the meeting of basic need. In Grotius's new story, the rich man could find himself under an absolute obligation to conform to principles of "natural equity," but only in the most extreme and extraordinary circumstances: "– rights of desert and claims of need – were theorized as exceptions rather than as rules, as they had been in Thomistic jurisprudence" (Hont and Ignatieff, p. 29). Justice as now understood was properly concerned not with need or desert, but with *suum cuique* – "to each his own" – the definitive domain of "rectificatory justice" in Aristotle. This new justice, Hont and Ignatieff tell us, was "expletive," not "distributive":

Expletive justice was about "perfect rights," the chief of which were rights of property. Distributive or attributive justice was about "imperfect rights," such as "generosity, compassion, and foresight in matters of government". [These] were commanded by humanity, not by law.... Here is the seed-bed of Smith's treatment of distributive justice. (ibid)

For the operation of Smith's "invisible hand," together with the specialization of labour in commercial society, will eliminate, within any successful commercial system, scenarios in which the perfect right to private property need be superseded by the needs of the disadvantaged. Thus, the moral dilemma which was St. Thomas's central concern is marginalized. Grotius's juridical arguments, unaided by principles of equity, suffice to validate the idea of a "city of merchants" built on "the mercenary exchange of good offices," although not on any real "mutual love or affection" among citizens. (TMS, II.ii.3.2)

---

[35] W. P. Baumgarth, and R. J. Regan, eds., *Saint Thomas Aquinas: On Law, Morality and Politics* (Indianapolis, IN, 1988), p. 186: "Seventh Article: Is It Lawful to Steal Through Stress of Need?"

For Smith, however, civil society is neither coextensive with its system of commutative justice nor reducible merely to a matrix of morally indeterminate mercenary interactions. The individuals who create and sustain commerce and justice in Smith's theory are "men," not beasts. They are indeed persons possessed of a specific kind of moral capacity. Without such capacity neither commerce nor justice could flourish in security. They are not merely accountants. They are morally and politically accountable citizens.

V. SMITH AS ANTI-IDEOLOGUE: PUBLIC SPIRIT AND POLITICAL JUDGMENT

Adam Smith was not an ideologue. Historically, the term and its accompanying ideological categories were not available for use in his day. More important, though, Smith was not by temperament or intention an ideological thinker. Ideological thinking is inherently reductive. It simplifies complexity in order to facilitate commitment and a sense of efficacy in those faithful to its precepts. It is also, to borrow a postmodern term, totalizing. It naturally tends toward the deployment of a single system of thought, a single hierarchy of ideas, to include all the most important areas in economic, political, and even moral life. Smith's thought is the opposite of reductive and totalizing. It celebrates both complexity and differentiation. It is anti-ideological. His politics is not the partisan politics typically invoked in the promotion of an ideological system. We have seen that he rejected the "man of system" determined to push through some "ideal plan of government," without flexibility or compromise, as a dangerous extremist. Likewise, he rejected the man of party, counselling the wise political leader to "prevail upon his own friends to act with proper temper and moderation," while aspiring to "re-establish and improve the constitution" of his state (TMS, VI.ii.2.14). Smith was no political radical. The political characters he admired could have been taken from the pages of Aristotle or Cicero: the citizen, the patriot, and the statesman. Smith portrayed the good citizen as one whose love of his country enjoined him "to respect the laws and to obey the civil magistrate," and "to promote, by every means in his power, the welfare of the whole society of his fellow-citizens," by which Smith generally meant their tranquillity and their happiness. "In peaceable and quiet times" to do one of these was *ipso facto* to do the other. However, "in times of public discontent, faction and disorder," an urgent but painfully difficult political calculation must be made:

it often requires, perhaps, the highest effort of political wisdom to determine when a real patriot ought to support and endeavour to re-establish the authority of the old system, and when he ought to give way to the more daring, but often dangerous spirit of innovation. (TMS, VI.ii.2.11–12)

Politics is a matter of judgment, and political judgments are distinguished from others by the high stakes involved and the danger that the wrong spirit will animate the decision maker.[36] The context for political judgment is constituted, not by a simple system of liberty, but by the state, which Smith sees as a complex collage of "orders and societies":

Every independent state is divided into many different orders and societies, each of which has its own particular powers, privileges, and immunities. Every individual is naturally more attached to his own particular order or society, than to any other. (TMS, VI.ii.2.7)

The perspective, the criteria of judgment appropriate to the good citizen, will not, then, come easily to the self-interested man. Political judgment will need to be cultivated. Political studies will be essential. The study of politics will be anything but derivative or epiphenomenal, for on it will depend the capacity of the citizens to establish and sustain their constitution:

Upon the manner in which any state is divided into the different orders and societies which compose it, and upon the particular distribution which has been made of their respective powers, privileges, and immunities, depends, what is called, the constitution of that particular state. (TMS, VI.ii.2.8)

If a state or a constitution might be viewed in some sense as a system, it was certainly as a complex and arcane one, not at all obvious or simple. Smith saw constitutions and states much more in terms of conflicting interests than of natural liberty. If the polity was an "imaginary machine," it was an almost unfathomably intricate

---

[36] An important recent study brings the idea of judgment to the fore in the analysis of Smith's moral and political thought. See S. Fleischacker, *A Third Concept of Liberty: Judgment and Freedom in Kant and Adam Smith* (Princeton, NJ, 1999).

one. Better to view it as an overlapping or a coexistence of legal, moral, and economic systems. To equate Smith's political ideas, either in form or in content, with one of those constituent systems is to miss precisely what distinguishes his view of the study of politics from his moral, jurisprudential, and economic theories.

In his important study of Smith's politics, Donald Winch observes that Smith followed David Hume in taking a broad view of politics as comprising all fields of study concerned with "men as united in society, and dependent on each other."[37] He also points out that in standard works of interpretation in the past Smith's politics have been seen as having only "subordinate or derivative status," or even as being "enveloped" by his economic system (9, 7). Marxian scholars such as Meek have seen Smith as "treating law and government as epiphenomenal to the underlying social and economic forces producing progress" (20). At the other end of the ideological spectrum, Joseph Cropsey found Smith to be "of interest for his share in the deflection of political philosophy toward economics" (17), whereas from a position much closer to the middle of the spectrum Sheldon Wolin connected Smith with the "progressive sublimation of politics," converging with Cropsey in his ultimate judgment that Smith's politics involve an essentially "non-political model of society."[38] Like Winch, I think it wise to resist the judgment that Smith's politics must be vestigial or insubstantial because they are not ideological, programmatic, or easily categorizable in nineteenth- or twentieth-century terms. Smith spoke approvingly of the beauty and inspirational quality of a "great system public police," and he invited the public spirited man to lubricate "all the several wheels of the machine of government." However, he always conceived of the study of politics as a critical and comparative study:

the study of ... the several systems of civil government, their advantages and disadvantages, of the constitution of our own country, its situation, and interest with regard to foreign nations, its commerce, its defence, the disadvantages it labours under, the dangers to which it may be exposed, how to remove the one, and how to guard against the other. (TMS, IV.i.11)

[37] Hume, *Treatise*, introduction, p. xv; cited in D. Winch, *Adam Smith's Politics: An Essay in Historiographic Revision* (Cambridge, 1978), p. 13.
[38] Ibid; Cropsey's remarks are quoted at p. 17, Wolin's at p. 21.

This conception of political studies and the conception of political action which it entails are neither insubstantial nor derivative nor dated. In fact, a careful reading of the passage just quoted will surely discover in it qualities of moderation, pragmatism, and public spiritedness which stand the test of time very well indeed.

12   Adam Smith's Economics

I. A PRACTICAL AND POPULAR MANNER

Adam Smith's writings on economic subjects – to adapt the title that his closest friends gave to his posthumously published *Essays on Philosophical Subjects* – are diverse, discursive, and interspersed with almost everything else that he wrote. Economic life, for Smith, was intricately interconnected with the rest of life, or with the life of politics, sentiment, and imagination. Economic thought was interconnected with the rest of thought, or with legal, philosophical, and moral reflection. In the speculative thought of philosophers, as in the plans and projects of merchants, the economic and the political were virtually impossible to distinguish.

"I have begun to write a book in order to pass away the time," Smith wrote to David Hume from Toulouse, in 1764. He devoted some 12 years of his life to the composition of *The Wealth of Nations*, which was eventually published in 1776 ("finish your Work before Autumn; go to London; print it," Hume had written sternly in 1772) (Corr., pp. 102, 166). But *The Wealth of Nations* is not concerned only with wealth, and Smith's other writings and lectures were concerned in part with wealth, as well as with the emotional or moral lives of individuals (*The Theory of Moral Sentiments*), or with legal institutions (the lectures on jurisprudence).[1] In *The Wealth of Nations*, individuals seek amusement, attention, and conversation; they think about fear and oppression; they reflect on ontology; and they are interested

---

[1] On Smith's jurisprudence and *The Wealth of Nations*, see Knud Haakonssen, *The Science of a Legislator: The Natural Jurisprudence of David Hume and Adam Smith* (Cambridge, 1981), especially chapter 6.

in equity. In *The Theory of Moral Sentiments*, they desire trinkets and tweezer cases, they have theories about wealth and poverty, and they reflect on the commerce with China and on the precariousness of life. Smith says almost nothing about self-love in *The Wealth of Nations*; it is a principal theme of *The Theory of Moral Sentiments*. "[I]t is chiefly from this regard to the sentiments of mankind, that we pursue riches and avoid poverty," Smith wrote in *The Theory of Moral Sentiments* (I.iii.2.1), of the desire to be attended to, and taken notice of.

In this chapter, we will follow Smith's own "plan" or ordering of subjects, as outlined in the introduction to *The Wealth of Nations*. However, we will be concerned with *The Theory of Moral Sentiments* and the lectures on jurisprudence, as well as with *The Wealth of Nations*. We will look first at Smith's writings on the principles of human nature, on labour, and on "skill, dexterity, and judgment" (WN, Intro. 6), which are the principal subjects of Book One of *The Wealth of Nations*. We will look next at his descriptions of merchants and capital, the subject of Book Two. We then turn to Smith's views of the history of economic development and economic policy (of the progress of opulence), which is the subject of Book Three. The next section will be concerned with Smith's account of "theories of political œconomy" (ibid, 8), and especially of the "commercial system" or the system of international trade, which is the principal subject of Book Four. The following section, like Book Five of *The Wealth of Nations*, will be concerned with the revenues, expenditures, and designs of governments. In the concluding section, we will return to the great principles of which Smith is supposed to be in some sense the founding father. Each principle has some basis in Smith's thought, as will be seen; each is also a departure, in important respects, from Smith's system.

II. THE PRINCIPLES OF HUMAN NATURE

The Wealth of Nations begins with an extended description of the "universal opulence" which is characteristic of "civilized and thriving nations." This opulence extends to the lowest ranks of the people. It is the consequence, above all, of the productiveness of labour – of the "skill, dexterity, and judgement" with which labour is used – and its consequence, in turn, is a prodigious improvement in the conditions of even the poorest labourers. The day labourer in England has a woollen coat, a linen shirt, shoes, a bed, knives and forks, earthenware or pewter plates, bread and beer, and glass windows. The tools he uses, and his clothes and furniture, are brought, often, from distant parts of the country, and even from the remotest corners of the world. He is connected, in the details of his daily life, to a multitude of other workers and dependent upon the "assistance and co-operation of many thousands" (WN, Intro. 3–4; I.i.10, 11).

This idyll of universal comfort is ubiquitous in Smith's writings on economic subjects. The wages of the meanest labourer, he observes in *The Theory of Moral Sentiments*, are sufficient to buy conveniencies or superfluities, as well as necessities, and to "give something even to vanity and distinction" (TMS, I.iii.2.1). "[A] common day labourer in Britain or in Holland," he says in the "Early Draft" of *The Wealth of Nations*, is superior in luxury to "many an Indian prince." The civilized societies of modern times are characterised by a highly unequal distribution of wealth. However, "in the midst of so much oppressive inequality," even the poor are prosperous. Even the lowest and most despised members of civilised societies are possessed of "superior affluence and abundance." This is a circumstance, Smith says, which is not "so easily understood," and which is at the heart of his economic thought (Early Draft, 1, 5, 6, 4).

The division of labour, which is for Smith the principal source of universal opulence, is not in itself an uplifting spectacle. "I have seen several boys" who have never had any trade other than making nails, and who can make more than 2,300 nails per day, Smith says at the outset of *The Wealth of Nations*. It confines the views of men, he says in his lectures on jurisprudence, to bestow one's entire attention "on the 17th part of a pin or the 80th part of a button." One of the effects of the division of labour is indeed an epidemic of "gross ignorance and stupidity" in civilised societies. The country labourer is in Smith's description a person of judgment, understanding, and discretion. The mechanic, or the man whose "whole life is spent in performing a few simple operations," is by contrast at risk of psychological mutilation; of becoming incapable of "conversation," "sentiment," "judgement," and "courage." But these risks can be countered, in Smith's view, by an extensive system of education. It is possible, in a civilized and opulent society, that "almost the whole body of the people" should be instructed in reading, writing, counting, and even in the more "sublime" principles of science.[2]

The causes of opulence are to be found in the universal principles of the human mind. The source of the division of labour is thus the universal disposition to "truck, barter and exchange," which is a consequence of the faculties of reason and speech. In his lectures on jurisprudence, Smith describes exchange as a sort of oratory. "It is clearly the natural inclination everyone has to persuade," he says, which is "the principle in the human mind on which this disposition of trucking is founded": "the offering of a shilling, which to us appears to have so plain and simple a meaning, is in reality offering an argument to persuade one to do so and so as it is for his interest.... And in this manner every one is practising oratory on others through the whole of his life."[3]

This universal disposition or inclination is common to "the most dissimilar characters" (to "a philosopher and a common street porter, for example") (WN, I.ii.4). However, it is only in the circumstances of civilized societies that the general propensity to discursiveness gives rise to the division of labour, and thereby to universal opulence. One such circumstance is the existence and extent of markets. There is no point, that is to say, in producing hundreds of thousands of nails in a remote Highland village, with only expensive means of transport. In a seaside town, by contrast, one's market is as wide as the world. Smith generally uses the word "market" in a fairly concrete sense. A market is a collection of physical structures (a "fixed market") in which commodities are bought and sold. It is by extension the collection of locations, often widely dispersed, in which particular commodities are sold. London and Calcutta, Smith writes in The Wealth of Nations, carry on a considerable commerce with each other; they encourage each other's industry "by mutually affording a market" (WN, I.iii.3).

The other condition for the rise and flourishing of the division of labour is the use of money. It would not be convenient to transport muslins and spices by land from Calcutta to London, and it would be even less convenient to exchange muslins for oxen and spices for

---

[2] WN, I.i.6, I.x.c.23–4, V.i.f.50, 54–5; LJ(B), 329.
[3] WN, I.ii.1–2; LJ(A), vi.56.

sheep. Money, as a result, is the universal instrument of commerce. It makes possible the mutual exchange of services which is characteristic of commercial societies, and in which almost everyone is a customer, a merchant, or both at the same time. The improvement of communications – the reduction in the cost of transporting goods by land and sea, and the reduction in the cost of information – is a condition of the extension of markets. Money, too, is an instrument of communication. Smith indeed compares money, in one of his most elaborate figures of speech (a violent metaphor, he says), to an immense highway which circulates all the produce of a country. An efficient banking system is a "sort of waggonway through the air." Gold and silver constitute a solid ground on which commerce and industry can be transported from one location to another; commerce can with the help of banking institutions soar even higher, "suspended upon the Daedalian wings of paper money" (WN, II.ii.86; cf. LJ[A], vi.129, LJ[B], 245).

Labour, Smith writes, is the "real measure of the exchangeable value of all commodities" (WN, I.v.1). However, to estimate the value of goods in terms of labour would be almost as cumbersome as exchanging oxen and muslins. Value is usually therefore estimated in terms of money or in terms of its nominal price. This nominal price is in turn a market price, which may be larger or smaller than the natural price of the commodity in question, or the price to which market prices tend in the absence of extraordinary circumstances (the "center of repose and continuance").

These distinctions, Smith explains to his readers, can easily be thought of as "obscure," and even "tedious." However, they correspond to the ordinary life of the vast international society which Smith imagined or observed. If a merchant has imported a lot of expensive oranges, it becomes extremely important to him to "get immediately rid of the commodity," even at an unnaturally low price. If there is a public mourning, the price of black cloth rises, the price of coloured silk falls, and the wages of journeymen tailors rise.[4] Like the "man of humanity in Europe" in The Theory of Moral Sentiments, who is also a "man of speculation," Smith is intrigued by the details of trade and taste. On the news of a great earthquake in China, the man of speculation would be likely to

[4] WN, I.iv.18, I.vii.10–17, I.x.b.45–6.

express his sorrow, to reflect on the precariousness of life, and then to "enter into many reasonings concerning the effects which this disaster might produce upon the commerce of Europe, and the trade and business of the world in general" (TMS, III.3.4).

Smith identifies two universal dispositions or principles – the disposition to exchange goods or oratory, and the "desire of bettering our condition," which is "universal, continual, and uninterrupted" – as the sources of opulence. The trucking disposition is the source of the division of labour, and the disposition to self-improvement is the source of saving and investment (WN, II.iii.28–36). Both are common to all individuals, the rich and the poor, the Dutch and the Chinese, the sovereign, the philosopher and the porter. However, they are dispositions which can easily be discouraged or obstructed. The human constitution, in economic as in moral life, and in *The Wealth of Nations* as in *The Theory of Moral Sentiments*, is a theatre of conflicting and competing principles. The desire to better one's condition is counter-posed to the tendency to indolence. The desire to save is counter-posed to the passion for present enjoyment. The desire to exchange is counter-posed to the tendency to be servile and fawning. The passion for gain is counter-posed to sober reason and experience, and international trade is a source of golden dreams and strange delusions. The proprietor is afflicted by "anxiety" about the elegance of his dress, and the mason is plunged into "anxious and desponding moments" (WN, I.x.b.12, III.ii.7).

The progress of opulence can also be affected by political, legal, and religious institutions. Smith is resolute in his presumption of the natural equality of all individuals. The slaves of colonial planters, like the people of England or France, are more intelligent and more virtuous to the extent that they are considered "with more regard." They have notable virtues, including the virtue of self-command. ("There is not a negro from the coast of Africa who does not, in this respect, possess a degree of magnanimity which the soul of his sordid master is too often scarce capable of conceiving.") There is no monopoly of intelligence in the civilized or commercial societies of Europe; "in manufacturing art and industry, China and Indostan, though inferior, seem not to be much inferior to any part of Europe."[5] However, the effect of bad institutions is nonetheless such as to obstruct public opulence, and even to obstruct the dispositions on which opulence is founded.

China is thus in Smith's description a society which is rich and populous, but in which the "poverty of the lower ranks of people" is worse than in the "most beggarly nations in Europe." The situation of Bengal and the other "ruined countries" of India is even more miserable, under the tyranny of the "mercantile company which oppresses and domineers in the East Indies." There is superstition; there is insecurity, especially in respect of the property of the poor and of the "owners of small capitals" in China; there are very high rates of interest, sometimes as high as 40%, 50%, or 60% in rural Bengal. In Poland, which is one of the poorest countries in Europe, the feudal system still persists. In Spain and Portugal, it has been replaced by an "irregular and partial administration of justice," so uncertain that it inhibits the spirit of the "industrious part of the nation."[6]

The industrious disposition is easily discouraged even in the most commercial societies. One of Smith's most sustained diatribes, in *The Wealth of Nations*, is thus against the "corporation spirit" in respect to apprenticeship regulations and the English law of settlements. These regulations obstruct the free circulation of labour, the free competition of different manufacturers, the "sacred and inviolable" property which every man has in his own labour, and the "natural liberty and justice" whereby individuals can live where they want. It induces indolence, inattention, and jealousy of strangers (WN, I.x.c.). Giving bounties for one commodity and discouraging another, Smith says of the corporation spirit in his lectures on jurisprudence, "diminishes the concurrence of opulence and hurts the natural state of commerce" (LJ[B], 307).

One of Smith's other diatribes is concerned with the corn trade and the corn laws. The principal cause of famines was the denial to many people of adequate access to food, and the proximate causes of this can be one of many things: the interruption of communications between different regions, or a war, or the policies of an oppressive

[5] WN, i.xi.g.28, IV.vii.b.54; TMS, V.2.9.
[6] WN, I.viii.24–6, I.xi.n.1, I.ix.13–15, II.v.22, IV.vii.c.53.

or injudicious government. The Bengal drought of 1770, for example, was made far more dreadful by the policies of the East India Company. But regulations restricting the free commerce in corn can also contribute to scarcity and misery, even in commercial societies. Their effect is to obstruct the distribution of grain and the cultivation of land, to reduce the freedom and the security of industry, and to encumber the operations of even the universal principle of self-improvement. It is to discourage "people of character and fortune" from even entering the business of selling corn, and to abandon it to "wretched hucksters" (WN, IV.v.b.8).

"The liberal reward of labour" is for Smith the characteristic condition of commercial and civilized societies. "To complain of it is to lament over the necessary effect and cause of the greatest publick prosperity," he says in *The Wealth of Nations*, and it is "abundantly plain" that an "improvement in the circumstances of the lower ranks of the people" is of advantage "to the society." Such an improvement was a matter of justice: "No society can surely be flourishing and happy, of which the far greater part of the members are poor and miserable. It is but equity, besides, that they who feed, cloath and lodge the whole body of the people, should have such a share of the produce of their own labour as to be themselves tolerably well fed, cloathed and lodged." It was also a matter of prudence, in that it tends to make people more industrious: "The wages of labour are the encouragement of industry, which, like every other human quality, improves in proportion to the encouragement it receives."[7]

The real recompense of labour had increased substantially in England in the course of the eighteenth century, in Smith's observation. "We are more industrious than our forefathers," he says, and the "industrious poor" can afford an "agreeable and wholesome variety of food." (He mentions potatoes, turnips, carrots, and cabbages, as well as milk, cheese, butter, and oil; butcher's meat, he says, is not required for a "nourishing" and "invigorating" diet.)[8] The choices of the poor are concerned, in these circumstances, with their social position. They are depicted as prudent, reflective,

---

[7] WN, I.viii.27, 42, 36, 44.
[8] WN, I.viii.34–5, II.iii.12, V.iii.k.15.

civic beings, subject in particular to the emotion of shame. They understand leather shoes to be necessities in England: "the poorest creditable person of either sex would be ashamed to appear in public without them." In Scotland, shoes are necessities for men of the lowest order, "but not to the same order of women, who may, without any discredit, walk about bare-footed"; "in France, they are necessaries neither to men nor to women." The poor are concerned, too, with the future of their children and with their own future lives. The labourer is encouraged by the "comfortable hope of bettering his condition" – of changing his position in society – and of "ending his days perhaps in ease and plenty."[9]

III. MERCHANTS AND MANUFACTURERS

The second main theme in Smith's economic writings is capital or stock. There are three "great, original and constituent orders of every civilized society," Smith writes, who live respectively by the rent of land, by the wages of labour, and by the profits of stock (WN, I.xi.p.7). Each order has its own idiosyncratic way of life, its own interests, and its own way of thinking. Landlords are in Smith's description a somewhat foolish class of individuals. Their interests are closely connected to the general interest of the society. However, they are often ignorant of these interests. They are indolent because they can live comfortably without making plans or projects. They are often incapable, even, of "application of mind." There are agreeable landlords, mostly small proprietors, who improve their land and enjoy the tranquillity of mind which is characteristic of a country life. Great proprietors are much less admirable. In feudal times, as in eighteenth-century Poland, they surrounded themselves with dependents and retainers. In early commercial societies, they bartered their authority for "trinkets and baubles" ("diamond buckles, perhaps, or for something as frivolous and useless"). Their abiding shortcoming, which they share with the "richer clergy," is vanity, of the most childish and the most extravagant kind.[10] The "oeconomy of greatness"

[9] WN, V.ii.k.3; cf. I.viii.43–4.
[10] WN, I.xi.p.8, III.i.3, I.xi.n.1, III.iv.15, 10, V.i.g.25.

Smith says in *The Theory of Moral Sentiments*, is for the "proud and unfeeling landlord" a matter of "baubles and trinkets" (TMS, IV.1.10).

The second order, people who live by wages, are similar to the landlords in that their interests are closely connected to the interests of the society in which they live. They are similar, too, in that they are often incapable of understanding these larger interests. They are ignorant, not because they are indolent and excessively secure, but because they have "no time to receive the necessary information" and insufficient education with the help of which they can make judgments. They sometimes enter into (clamorous) combinations to increase or maintain wages, which are almost always crushed by the combined power of the masters or employers, the civil magistrate, and the parliament ("whenever the legislature attempts to regulate the differences between masters and their workmen, its counsellors are always the masters"). Their clamour is sometimes animated and supported by their employers to promote their own interests.[11] However, in their private lives, the people who live by wages are in general prudent and industrious. They are often "active, diligent, and expeditious," especially when wages are high. They are more diligent in England than in Scotland. They have a tendency to "over-work themselves," especially when they are paid piece rates. They tend to "strict frugality and parsimonious attention" in their expenditure, especially in comparison to the "disorders which generally prevail in the oeconomy of the rich" (WN, I.viii.40–4).

It is the third order, people who live by profit, who intrigue Smith the most. They are the heroes of *The Wealth of Nations* – of the epic of increasing opulence which is at the heart of Smith's economic thought – and they are at the same time its "sneaking" hypocrites. They are intelligent, and they have an acute knowledge of their own interests. The richest of them, the merchants and master manufacturers, are "during their whole lives . . . engaged in plans and projects." They often make pronouncements about the public interest. But their interests are not identical with, and are often opposed to, the interest of the society. They are an "order of men, whose interest is never exactly the same with that of the

---

[11] WN, I.xi.p. 9, I.viii.13, I.x.c.61.

public, who have generally an interest to deceive and even to oppress the public, and who accordingly have, upon many occasions, both deceived and oppressed it."[12]

The disposition of merchants and traders is generally to be bold. Their lives are tumultuous. They commit their fortunes, often, "not only to the winds and the waves, but to the more uncertain elements of human folly and injustice." They have "golden dreams" of the great profits to be gained in "vast and extensive projects," in banking, mining, or wartime procurement. Yet, men of business are also likely to be careful and orderly. The mercantile business induces habits of "order, oeconomy, and attention." Holland was in Smith's description "by far the richest country in Europe," and the way of thinking of the commercial order was in large part a Dutch model. "It is there unfashionable not to be a man of business," Smith wrote of Holland, or to "engage in some sort of trade." The "mercantile manners" of Amsterdam are "attentive and parsimonious," in part because the profits on stock are low. Nations which "like Holland and Hamburgh, are composed chiefly of merchants, artificers and manufacturers," have a tendency to "narrowness, meanness, and a selfish disposition." However, this common character, like the orderliness of merchants, is induced by circumstances. The credit of the trader depends on the way in which he is judged by other people; on "their opinion of his fortune, probity, and prudence."[13]

The "influence of commerce on the manners of a people," Smith said in his lectures on jurisprudence, is such that they turn to "probity and punctuality," as to the most fashionable of virtues. The Dutch are more reliable than the English, for example. Yet, in Smith's view "this is not at all to be imputed to national character, as some pretend." It is rather a consequence of self-interest, in the particular circumstances of a mercantile society. "A dealer is afraid of losing his character, and is scrupulous in observing every engagement," and when he makes a large number of contracts every day, he "does not expect to gain so much by any one contract as by probity and punctuality in the whole." There is no natural reason, that is to say, "why an Englishman or a Scotchman should not

---

[12] WN, I xi.p.10; cf. IV.iii.c.8–9.
[13] WN, I.ix.20, I.x.b.20, II.ii.69, II.v.35, III.i.3, III.iv.3, IV.ix.13.

be as punctual in performing agreements as a Dutchman" (LJ[B], 326–8).

Smith's account of capital and profit, like his account of labour, begins with an extended description of the subdivisions character-istic of commercial societies, "the Division of Stock." The accu-mulation of stock is for Smith anterior to the division of labour. It is only if a weaver, for example, has stored up an adequate stock of goods that he can devote himself entirely to his own peculiar business. He needs to have access to a supply of the things he con-sumes and of the materials he uses. In a more advanced stage of the division of labour, yet more stock is needed, as the operations of workmen become even simpler (or more specialized), and "a variety of new machines come to be invented for facilitating and abridging these operations." The progress of opulence is a consequence of the increase in the productive powers of labour, and the improvement in productiveness is in turn a consequence of the increase in cap-ital, "silently and gradually accumulated by the private frugality and good conduct of individuals."[14]

The principle or disposition which induces individuals to accu-mulate is the desire of bettering their condition. This is a universal yearning, which is related to a restlessness of spirit; there is never an instant in which the individual is "perfectly and completely satisfied with his situation." The object of all these aspirations, in the most profound sense, is to be looked at, respected, and sympa-thised with. The desire to be respected, Smith writes in *The Theory of Moral Sentiments*, is "perhaps, the strongest of all our desires." It is the purpose of "all the toil and bustle of this world," and the principal reason that "we pursue riches and avoid poverty."[15] However, the means to this elusive end is to be found, in general, in augmenting one's fortune. "It is the means the most vulgar and the most obvious," and the most obvious means to fortune is to be found, in turn, in savings and accumulation (WN, II.iii.28).

There are two main uses of the stock accumulated by individu-als, of which Smith has very different opinions. One part is used as capital and is expected to yield a revenue or profit. The other part is used for consumption. Smith appears to be extraordinarily sceptical

[14] WN, II.intro.3, II.iii.36.
[15] TMS, I.iii.2.1, VI.i.3.

about the joys of consumption. Individuals sometimes imagine the "pleasures of wealth and greatness" as beautiful and noble; at other times, or when they are in low spirits, they see "power and riches" as contemptible and even threatening conditions. It is a delusion, especially for individuals who are not born to riches, to imagine that they can find respect, or even satisfaction, by the consumption of goods and services. To use one's stock to buy consumer goods is a particularly futile exercise. Smith returns often to a distinctly splenetic enumeration of what he describes as "trinkets of frivolous utility." These include tweezer cases, toothpicks, ear pickers, and machines for cutting one's nails (in *The Theory of Moral Sentiments*); watch cases, snuff boxes, jewels, baubles, gewgaws, and diamond buckles (in *The Wealth of Nations*); and, in the lectures on jurisprudence, the productions of "architects, masons, carpenters, tailors, upholsterers, jewellers, cooks, and other ministers of luxury."[16]

Capital is the stock which is used for profit. Money is one of the constituents of capital, but only "a small part, and always the most unprofitable." It is the "great wheel of circulation, the great instrument of commerce," which is continually, at least in secure and commercial societies, being lent by one person to another, or running after goods. There are additional kinds of circulating capital, such as stocks of raw materials, which are also held for only short periods of time. The other constituent is fixed capital, which consists of machines, buildings, improvements in land (such as clearing and draining), and the "acquired and useful abilities of all the inhabitants or members of the society," or the "capital fixed and realised, as it were, in [the] person" of the individuals.[17]

The different branches of trade use these different kinds of capital in different ways. Agriculture, mining, manufacturing, wholesale trade and transportation, and retail trade have different needs and different relationships to the society. Fixed capital – the furnaces and forges of a great iron work, for example, or the "capital which the undertaker of a mine employs in sinking his shafts, in erecting engines for drawing out the water, in making roads and waggon-ways" or the machines used in "the new works at Sheffield,

---

[16] TMS, IV.i.8–9; WN, I.xi.h.5, II.iii.38, III.iv.10; LJ(A), i.117.
[17] WN, II.i.17, II.ii.23, IV.i.16–18.

Manchester, or Birmingham" – is most important to mining and manufacturing industries.[18] The capital of a merchant, in contrast, is composed entirely of circulating capital.

Capital used in agriculture and in retail trade is fixed in a particular place, in a particular society; it "must always reside within that society." Capital used in manufacturing is more restless; wool is sent from Spain to Britain, for example, and finished cloth is sent back to Spain. The capital of the wholesale merchant – whether in home trade, foreign trade, or carrying trade – is the most restless of all. It "seems to have no fixed or necessary residence anywhere, but may wander about from place to place, according as it can either buy cheap or sell dear." The merchant is "not necessarily the citizen of any particular country." Mercantile capital is thereby a "very precarious and uncertain possession" for the country, if not for the merchant; "it is in a great measure indifferent to him from what place he carries on his trade; and a very trifling disgust will make him remove his capital, and together with it all the industry which it supports, from one country to another."[19]

The different kinds of capital are associated with different ways of thinking. Smith is warm in his praise of the country gentleman. This figure is not particularly acute. He is a little timid, but he is generous and tranquil. He is free of the wretched spirit of monopoly which induces other men of property to combine and to conspire. The small proprietor is of all the owners of capital the most likely to improve his stock in a lasting and useful way. The owner of retail capital, too, is a generally agreeable character. The prejudices of political writers "against shopkeepers and tradesmen, are altogether without foundation"; the "little grocer" in a small seaport town is a tolerable judge of fifty or sixty different kinds of goods and provides a service to the poor (by dividing commodities into small parcels).[20]

The owner of industrial capital – the "undertaker" of large mining or manufacturing works – is also a diligent figure, although one in whom Smith takes rather little interest. He is not particularly industrious; indeed, he is "discharged of almost all labour," the

---

[18] WN, II.i.6–9, II.ii.64; LJ(A), vi.54.
[19] WN, II.i.7, II.ii.64, II.v.13–16, III.iv.24.
[20] WN, II.v.7, I.x.b.36.

work of "inspection and direction" having been handed over to a "principal clerk," and the improvement of production – the invention of new and ingenious machines – being the work either of the individuals who use the machines, or of the specialised makers of machines and instruments.[21]

The owners of smaller manufactures play a more substantial and a more insidious role. The word "manufacturer," in *The Wealth of Nations*, refers both to workmen ("manufacturers and artificers") and to employers ("master manufacturers"). Smith is admiring, in general, of the skill and dexterity of the workmen. His dislike of the output of artificing (the trinkets and postchaises and operose machines) is countered by a liking for the productive skills of the artificer (the "living instrument" of trade). However, the masters, or the owners of manufactures, are more foolish figures. They complain about the bad effects of high wages and attempt to make their employees overwork. They like their servants to be "humble and dependent." They are subject to the emotion of jealousy (in relation to strangers in their towns, manufacturers in other countries, and imports of painted calicoes). They seek monopolistic protection against foreigners, farmers, consumers, and their own workmen. In their political pronouncements, they are an adjunct of the merchants. Their characteristic discourse is to "clamour."[22]

It is the merchant, or the owner of mercantile capital, in whom Smith is most interested, and by whom he is most disturbed. The wholesale merchant, the restless, wandering man of capital, is the central figure of Smith's economic writings. *The Wealth of Nations* is in substantial part a work about seas and oceans. The progress of opulence is borne by water, as well as by impartial legal institutions. Seaports are places of conversation, risk, and adventure. Oceans are the source of commerce – of the inventiveness which makes "the trackless and barren ocean a new fund of subsistence, and the great high road of communication to the different nations of the earth" – and the source of civilization. They are a metaphor of prosperity; Smith describes one of the schemes of the East India Company as amounting to no more than "a drop of water in the

---

[21] On country gentlemen, see WN, I.xi.p.8, III.ii.20, III.iv.3, IV.ii.21; on shopkeepers and undertakers, I.i.8–9, I.vi.6, II.v.7.
[22] WN, I.viii.48, I.ix.24, I.x.c.25, IV.viii.17, 44, IV.ix.31–3.

vast ocean of Indian commerce." The whole globe of the earth is for Smith a scene of inlets, rivers, and oceans; the misfortune of the continent of Africa, he says, is that it has nothing like the "gulphs of Arabia, Persia, India, Bengal, and Siam, in Asia."[23]

Merchants are the masters of these vast extents, but they are as changeable as the oceans. "The speculative merchant exercises no one regular, established, or well-known branch of business. He is a corn merchant this year, and a wine merchant the next, and a sugar, tobacco, or tea merchant the year after," Smith writes. They are also complex and indecisive in their sentiments. They are bold, and they are at the same time in search of security and reassurance. They are indifferent citizens, and they at the same time seek political advantage from every government. They have an intelligent knowledge of their own interests, and they seek to promote these interests by the pursuit of monopolies. They are excited by risk, and they dread competition. They conspire with other merchants, and they also conspire against them. In one side of their lives, they wait endlessly, like Antonio in the *Merchant of Venice*, for news of their ships, or of fashions in Lyons or Sicily. In another side of their lives, they write disingenuous pamphlets about the balance of trade, or about the bribing and intimidation of officials. Their discourse, like that of the master manufacturers, is one of "clamour and sophistry."[24]

IV. INSTITUTIONS AND THE PROGRESS OF OPULENCE

The third of Smith's concerns, which is at the heart of all his writings on economic subjects, is with the course of economic progress or of economic history. It is an epic of what Dugald Stewart, Smith's biographer, described in 1793 as the "natural progress of the mind."[25] The mind, or the spirit, is depicted as becoming emancipated from obstructions of various sorts, and as being disturbed, again, by new obstructions. The subject of Books Three and Four of *The Wealth of Nations*, Smith says, is the "interests, prejudices, laws and customs" of Europe since the decline of the

[23] WN, I.iii.8, V.i.e.26; TMS, IV.1.10.

[24] WN, I.x.b.38, I.x.c.25.

[25] Dugald Stewart, *Account of the Life and Writings of Adam Smith, LL.D* (1793), in EPS, 271.

Roman Empire, which he will "endeavour to explain as fully and distinctly" as he can. It is the history of "human institutions" and of the "injustice of human laws," as they disturb the "natural course of things."[26]

The principal drama in Smith's account of the progress of opulence consists in the victory of the individual spirit, over the oppression of legal institutions. Institutions, as described in *The Wealth of Nations*, are largely deplorable. They impede the public opulence of China; they lead to the degradation of the value of silver in Spain and Portugal; they are discouraging and depressing, under the prejudiced administration of Colbert in France; and in England, they include such arrangements as duties on the import of corn and bounties on exports, promoted by "our country gentlemen" in a misguided imitation of the "conduct of our manufacturers."[27]

One discouraging set of legal institutions in early modern Europe – "barbarous institutions," Smith calls them – are the laws of inheritance. Primogeniture and entails, in particular, were fit only to "support the pride of family distinctions." They were contrary to the other interests of families, serving to enrich only one child, by making beggars of all the rest. Their consequence was to obstruct the improvement of land, either by landlords or by their dependent tenants and retainers. These effects were made far worse by what Smith described as "all the violence of the feudal institutions." The leases of tenant farmers were precarious and their security limited. They were obliged to provide arbitrary and irregular services to their landlords and to the state, a form of "servitude" and "oppression" which still persisted in France and Germany.[28]

Even the inhabitants of medieval towns were of "servile, or very nearly of servile condition." They lived in something close to villanage. They had only limited freedom to travel and inherit, to buy and sell. However, their condition was better than that of the inhabitants of the countryside, and it was in the towns of western Europe that the drama of "liberty and independency" began to unfold. The burghers were adept, in Smith's description, in establishing free jurisdictions, between the competing oppression of sovereigns and

[26] WN, I.x.c.26, III.i.3–4.
[27] WN, I.ix.15, IV.v.a.18, 23, IV.ix.3.
[28] WN, III.ii.4–6, III.ii.14–17, III.iv.9–10.

feudal lords. They became more secure, gradually, in respect of their property (their "stock") and of their personal liberty. They became more industrious as they became more confident that they would be able to enjoy the "fruits of their industry." In the unfortunate countries where individuals are "continually afraid of the violence of their superiors" – during the "violence of the feudal government" in Europe, much as in modern Turkey or India, Smith wrote – it is common to conceal one's stock, or to bury it in the ground. In countries where there is "tolerable security," individuals (or everyone who is not "perfectly crazy") will use their stock to improve their present circumstances and their future condition.[29]

"Order and good government, and along with them the liberty and security of individuals" were thus established in the cities of Europe. The commercial progress of the cities in turn helped to introduce liberty and security, even into the countryside. The essential transformation, in this process, was in the freedom and impartiality of judicial institutions. "Commerce and manufactures can seldom flourish long in any state which does not enjoy a regular administration of justice . . . in which there is not a certain degree of confidence in the justice of government." The commercial advantage of England consisted above all in the "equal and impartial administration of justice which renders the rights of the meanest British subject respectable to the greatest." Colonial monopolies, bounties on corn, the value of gold and silver in Poland, public debt, buried treasure, the history of early modern cities in Europe – Smith returns on the most disparate occasions in *The Wealth of Nations* to the judicial institutions which he considered to be the most important source of commerce and civilization.[30]

The progress of opulence can be seen, in these terms, as a virtuous circle, in which legal and political improvement leads to economic improvement, and economic improvement in turn leads to further improvement in political and legal institutions. "Commerce and manufactures gradually introduced order and good government, and with them, the liberty and security of individuals," into the "servile dependency" of the European countryside; "this, though it has been the least observed, is by far the most important of all their effects" (WN, III.iv.4).

[29] WN, III.iii.1, 3, 12, II.i.30–1.
[30] WN, III.iii.12, IV.vii.c.54, V.iii.7.

The distinction between the economic, the legal, and the political is indeed elusive in Smith's account of the history of commerce. It is not one which Smith put forward in any resolute sense. To be obstructed from crossing a bridge when one was carrying one's goods to market was an infringement of one's personal freedom, and not of a special and lesser condition, one's "economic freedom." To be able to seek redress in the courts, against the "violence" of one's landlord, or against the "violation" of the terms of one's lease, was an encouragement to commerce and industry, and it was also a form of personal freedom.

Even the freedom of the mind or the disposition, and the freedom of social relationships, are intimately connected with the progress of opulence. They are causes and effects of political freedom. Independency, together with security, is the condition to which civilized societies tend. Tenants become independent in relation to landlords, as a consequence of the regular administration of justice. Tradesmen become independent in relation to the rich because they depend on no single customer for their entire revenue. Only the country gentleman, or the North American planter, is truly "independent of all the world." (The planter in North America feels that even the artificer "is the servant of his customers.") However, to be independent is to be free to choose one's relationships, one's disposition, and one's trade. It is to be able to form what Smith described as the "reasonable hopes, imagination or expectation" that one can hold onto one's property without having to depend on one's master. It is to be like the tradesmen, the ministers of luxury, who are employed by a great proprietor, but who "do not think themselves in any way indebted to him." The money they receive is "equivalent" to the time and labour they provide, and a "tradesman to retain your custom may perhaps vote for you in an election, but you need not expect that he will attend you to battle."[31]

V. SYSTEMS OF POLITICAL ECONOMY

The fourth great theme of Smith's political economy is political economy itself, or the plans and theories by which the policy of Europe is directed. These theories are the outcome, in general, of the "private interests and prejudices of particular orders of men."

[31] WN, III.i.5, III.iv.12–14; LJ(A), i.118, 144–5.

However, they have been elaborated into vast systems of the "general welfare of the sociey." They have in turn had a considerable influence on the opinions and the conduct of sovereigns (WN, Intro.8). The "love of system," Smith suggested in *The Theory of Moral Sentiments*, is a universal condition, and one which can help explain the preferences of individuals (and even of sovereigns) for different public institutions, from premiums in the linen industry to political disquisitions on commerce (TMS, IV.i.11). The merchants of commercial societies, with their predilections for plans and projects, have a taste for systems of thought. Their sophistry is also such that they have been highly successful in persuading other people – legislators, princes, the endlessly imposed on country gentlemen – that their own private interests are identical with "the general interest of the whole" (WN, I.x.c.25).

There are three vast systems of political economy with which Smith is concerned. One is the "commercial, or mercantile system." The second is the agricultural system. The third, which is Smith's own, and which he describes only by indirection, is the "obvious and simple system of natural liberty," or the "liberal plan of equality, liberty and justice."[32] Of these, the system of commerce is Smith's principal concern. "It is the modern system, and is best understood in our own country and in our own times," he says; his explanation of it takes up a quarter of *The Wealth of Nations*. In a letter to his Danish correspondent Andreas Holt, Smith compares the abuse and "squibs" he had received in response to "my Book" with those in response to a "single, and as, I thought a very harmless Sheet of paper, which I happened to write concerning the death of our late friend Mr Hume." This famous description is indeed a metonymy, in which the part comes to stand for the whole; *The Wealth of Nations* is the "very violent attack I had made upon the whole commercial system of Great Britain" (Corr., p. 251).

Book IV of *The Wealth of Nations*, like large sections of Smith's lectures on jurisprudence, is a sequence of strong criticisms of different tenets of the commercial system. One such popular notion, promoted by the sophistry of merchants, is that wealth consists of money, or of gold and silver. Gold is in general, for Smith, associated with illusion and self-deception. The projectors of speculative

---

[32] WN, IV.i, ix (headings), IV.ix.3, 51.

banks have "golden dreams" of profit; Sir Walter Raleigh had "strange delusions" about the golden city of Eldorado; Britain's Atlantic empire, Smith writes in the peroration of *The Wealth of Nations*, is a "golden dream" of politicians, "not an empire, but the project of an empire; not a gold mine, but the project of a gold mine." To accumulate gold in order to increase the wealth of the country would be no less absurd than to try to "increase the good cheer of private families" by obliging them to accumulate ever more "kitchen utensils," "to the incredible augmentation of the pots and pans of the country."[33]

The doctrine of the balance of trade is for Smith even more absurd. It is the "most insignificant object of modern policy." To watch over the balance of a country's exports and imports was at least as foolish, for the government, as to watch over the export of gold and silver; "from one fruitless care it was turned away to another care much more intricate, much more embarrassing, and just equally fruitless." However, the doctrine is enshrined in theories of political economy, which are in turn promoted by the "interested sophistry of merchants and manufacturers." Its effect is to exacerbate national prejudice and animosity. The balance of trade has very little to do with national advantage, and it is in any case, Smith says, extraordinarily difficult to determine.[34]

Smith was in general unconvinced by the "books" and "registers" in which commerce was supposed to be measured. He refers in his description of the work of independent labourers to the "publick registers of which the records are sometimes published with so much parade, and from which our merchants and manufacturers would often vainly pretend to announce the prosperity or declension of the greatest empires" (WN, I.viii.51). However, he was particularly sceptical of the statistics of foreign trade. The "custom-house books" and the "course of exchange" provide only a "very uncertain criterion" of trade. It is in the interest of merchant importers, in a system of import duties and bounties on exports, to declare very little. It is in the interest of merchant exporters to declare a great deal, sometimes out of vanity and sometimes to gain bounties. The custom-house books are therefore likely to show

---

[33] WN, II.ii.69, IV.i.16–19, IV.vii.a.19–20, V.iii.92.
[34] WN, IV.i.10, IV.iii.c.10, IV.vi.13.

a balance of exports over imports, "to the unspeakable comfort of those politicians who measure the national prosperity by what they call the balance of trade." It is quite usual, meanwhile, in the complex seaborne commerce which Smith found so intriguing, that a merchant in England might pay for goods bought in Riga with "bills upon Holland." Nothing, in these circumstances, could be more unreasonable than to seek, by regulation, to establish an "exact equilibrium" of trade. Smith uses the word "equilibrium" only once in the entire *Wealth of Nations*; it is in the course of an explanation (one of many) that nothing "can be more absurd than this whole doctrine of the balance of trade."[35]

The obsession with gold and silver, in the commercial system, leads to an obsession with the balance of trade, and the obsession with the balance of trade leads in turn to an even more insidious obsession, with policies to discourage imports and encourage exports. Smith devotes an extended section of *The Wealth of Nations* to the restraints, duties, and prohibitions on imports, and the bounties, drawbacks, and premiums on exports, which had multiplied in British law since the reign of Charles II. It is in part an enumeration of petty restrictions, especially in relation to the seafaring and ocean-going society with which he was so concerned; double duties on saltfish, whale fins, whale bone, oil, and blubber; prohibitions on wrought silks, French cambrics, and painted calicoes; and bounties on the herring buss fishery, white herring fisheries, whale fisheries, and on "British-made sail-cloth."[36] However, it is also a sustained denunciation of the mentality of "merchants and manufacturers." In Dugald Stewart's description, it is "expressed in a tone of indignation, which he seldom assumes in his political writings."[37]

Merchants and manufacturers are associated, in *The Wealth of Nations*, with the "wretched spirit of monopoly" and with the "exclusive corporation spirit." Their voice is one of "clamourous complaint." The effect of their "interested sophistry" is to

---

[35] WN, I.viii.51, IV.iii.a.4–7, IV.iii.c.2, V.ii.k.29.

[36] WN, IV.ii.21, IV.iv–v.a.

[37] Stewart, *Account*, p. 316; this is a comment on Smith's remarks about the jealousy of commerce, in his consideration of restraints on imports and encouragements to exports.

confound common sense. The policies they support are inspired by "mean rapacity," by the "monopolizing spirit," and by "impertinent jealousy." The master manufacturers have increased in political power in England to the point where, "like an overgrown standing army, they have become formidable to the government, and upon many occasions intimidate the legislature." The member of Parliament who attempts to oppose them is subjected to the "most infamous abuse and detraction," arising from the "insolent outrage of furious and disappointed monopolists." The "sneaking arts of underling tradesmen" are expressed with "all the passionate confidence of interested falsehood." They are especially sinister to the extent that they influence relationships between countries and between peoples; "mercantile jealousy is excited, and both inflames, and is itself inflamed, by the violence of national animosity."[38]

Smith is even more indignant when he turns to colonial and imperial relations. The regulation of colonies and of exclusive mercantile companies is for Smith an integral part of the commercial or mercantile system. Gold, the balance of trade, the restriction of imports and the subsidy of exports, the establishment of colonies – one commercial illusion leads to the next, in a succession of ever more oppressive policies. "A great empire has been established for the sole purpose of raising up a nation of customers," Smith said of Britain's American and West Indian colonies, in his concluding diatribe against "this whole mercantile system" and its "contrivers," the merchants and manufacturers. Colonies and empires were in general, for Smith, a monument to unreason. The motives for their establishment, in modern times, were "avidity," "folly and injustice," and the "sacred thirst of gold." They brought injury to the "harmless natives" of the colonised countries.[39] They encouraged the slave trade, as a consequence of which, Smith said in his description of African virtues, a cruel fortune "subjected those nations of heroes to the refuse of the jails of Europe" (TMS, V.2.9).

The British were less "illiberal and oppressive" as colonialists than the Spanish or the Portugese. There was indeed an ordering

---

[38] WN, IV.ii.21, 31, 43, IV.iii.c.8, 13.
[39] WN, IV.vii.a.6, 17–20, IV.vii.b.6, 52–4, 59, IV.viii.53.

of tyranny, in which the government of Britain was less "arbitrary and violent" than that of France, which was in turn less arbitrary than that of Spain and Portugal. But the slaves in the French colonies were slightly more protected, and more gently treated, than in the British colonies.[40] The British, like the Dutch, were also peculiarly implicated in a system of exclusive companies for foreign trade, which Smith found both contemptible and characteristically mercantile. Some fifty-five such companies had been established in Europe since 1600, Smith wrote, citing the Abbé Morellet's polemics against the French East India Company. There was a Gothenburg East India Company, a Turkey Company, and a Royal African Company. Such companies were "nuisances in every respect." It was in India and the East Indies, and under governments inspired by the republican or democratical societies of Holland and England, that the "arts of oppression" had become most "perfectly destructive."[41]

There is something idiosyncratically disagreeable, Smith argues, in the circumstances whereby companies come to be "the sovereigns of the countries which they have conquered." They have the power of sovereigns. They are possessed by "the spirit of war and conquest." However, they continue to think of themselves as merchants, and they "regard the character of the sovereign as but an appendix to that of the merchant." The trading spirit makes them bad sovereigns, and the "spirit of sovereignty seems to have rendered them equally bad traders." The Dutch in the East Indian islands burn cloves and destroy trees, and use all the "oppressive genius of an exclusive company" to deprive the native population. The English in Bengal have exactly the same tendency. The members of the administration trade on their own account, and the superior servants of the company oppress the inferior servants. They are indifferent to the "happiness or misery of their subjects." The interest of the proprietors is to acquire a share in "the appointment of the plunderers of India." They are engaged in "the pleasure of wasting, or the profit of embezzling." Their successes are largely unintended. The East India Company's government in Bengal on

[40] WN, IV.vii.b.52, 63.
[41] WN, IV.vii.c.101, 108, V.i.e.31.

one occasion, in a "momentary fit of good conduct," accumulated large reserves in the treasury of Calcutta; soon afterward "all was wasted and destroyed."[42]

India is described as an innocent and industrious land, inhabited by the "mild and gentle people" of Indostan. Its "home market" is "very great," and Bengal, in particular, has been "remarkable for the exportation of a great variety of manufactures." The territories acquired by the East India Company are "represented as more fertile, more extensive; and, in proportion to their extent, much richer and more populous than Great Britain." The sovereigns of Bengal, "while under the Mahometan government," had been extremely attentive to roads, and canals, and to procuring the "most extensive market which their own dominions could afford." The "country trade of the East Indies" extends all the way from Indostan to China and Japan. Smith's view, as so often, is the view from the sea; Batavia is the "principal mart" of a great "frequented road," from Tonkin and Malacca to Cochin and Celebes, in which much of the trade "is carried on by the native Indians." However, the effect of the European mercantile system, in these societies, has been to bring destruction and misery. The population of the Dutch Moluccas has fallen sharply. In Bengal, the oppression and domineering of the mercantile company has led to "want, famine and mortality." During the drought of 1770, the policies of the company contributed to turn a "dearth into a famine"; in what had once been a fertile country, "three or four hundred thousand people die of hunger in one year."[43]

The commercial or mercantile system was of truly worldwide consequence. Smith had a lucid conception of the world as a unity – of the course of prosperity in "the whole globe of the earth, of which the wealth, population, and improvement may be either gradually increasing or gradually decaying" – and the modern system of Europe impinged on all countries. The opposing "agricultural systems" were in contrast of much more limited consequence. Systems of this sort had been implemented by the sovereigns of China, of ancient Egypt, and of Indostan under its "Gentoo government."

[42] WN, IV.vii.c.101–5, V.i.e.26, V.ii.a.7.
[43] WN, I.iii.26, IV.v.b.6, IV.vii.c.100–1, IV.ix.45, V.i.e.2, V.ii.d.5, V.iii.91.

However, their effect was subversive, in that they ended up by discouraging "their own favourite species of industry." The agricultural system of the French economists of the eigteenth century also tended to overvalue agriculture, just as the mercantile system of Colbert, to which it was a response, had tended to overvalue commerce. The French economists' scheme was a "liberal and generous system," in the sense that it proposed the "most perfect freedom of trade" to foreign manufacturers. It was indeed "the nearest approximation to the truth" that had yet been published on the science of political economy. (This was a less than resounding endorsement, in view of Smith's scepticism about the systems in question.) However, it was formulaic, in that it prescribed an implausibly exact regimen of "perfect liberty." It was purely speculative and thereby not worth refuting at any great length; it had not yet done any harm, and probably never would.[44]

Smith says even less in his account of systems of political economy about his own liberal system. The word "liberal," for Smith, had little to do with political positions. The liberal was the generous, or the ample: Smith speaks repeatedly of "the liberal reward of labour." To belong to the *species liberalis*, he said in the lectures on jurisprudence, is to have the behaviour and appearance of a gentleman, and in particular, to be free to involve oneself in public affairs (LJ[A], iv.70). The "liberal plan" of equality, liberty, and justice was by extension a system of generosity, in which individuals were allowed to pursue their own interests, in their own ways. However, Smith, in fact, says rather little about its implementation, except to insist on the importance of circumspection. A future, more judicious legislature would thus take care to establish no new monopolies, and to extend no further those already established. It would repeal the exclusive privileges of corporation, the statute of apprenticeship, and the laws of settlement. It might even attempt to repeal established restrictions on imports. Yet, humanity – the "more gentle public spirit" that consists of sympathy with the "inconveniencies and distresses" of others – would be likely to require "that the freedom of trade should be restored only by slow gradations, and with a good deal of reserve and circumspection." The sovereign, in the liberal system, or the system

---

[44] WN, IV.viii.c.16, IV.ix.24, 38, 42, 49.

of being unsystematic, would be "completely discharged" from the duty of "superintending the industry of private people." However, he would not be discharged from the duties of humanity, including the duty of proceeding, slowly and gradually, to the destruction of the established privileges of the commercial system.[45]

One of the most important elements, in Smith's depiction of the commercial or mercantile system, is the progress of laws and regulations. The lectures on jurisprudence are concerned in part with commerce, and *The Wealth of Nations* is concerned in large part with jurisprudence. Smith is fascinated by the administration of English justice; by the statutes and parish deeds which govern the settlements of the poor; by the celebrated compendium of English legal practice, Burn's *Justice of the Peace*; by the relationship between the "public law" of the country and the bylaws of particular corporations. He refers on nine separate occasions, in describing the commercial system, to statutes of the reign of Charles II; he describes the position in English law of copper and gun metal, glue and hares' wool, herrings and gum senega and gum arabic, boxes, barrels, casks, cases, chests, and other packages. These are matters which may well, as Jean-Baptiste Say surmised, be of interest only to the English. However, commercial law is also, in Smith's description, a matter of life and death, of blood and injustice. The laws governing the export of sheep are "all written in blood." They are contrary to the "national humanity." The laws governing the freedom of movement of artificers are contrary to the "boasted liberty of the subject." The commercial system is "futile," in Smith's opinion, and it impoverishes the countries in which it is imposed, or by which it is governed. It is also, and above all, a violation of justice.[46]

The other great element, in Smith's depiction of the commercial system, is the mentality of commercial life. All human existence, as has been seen, is for Smith a scene of conflicting and competing desires. However, the inner life of merchants is particularly tumultuous. They are pulled between the ordinary desire to better one's condition and the extreme desires of "avidity" and "avarice." They are sometimes long-sighted in their plans and projects, and

[45] TMS, VI.ii.2.15, WN, IV.ii.40, 42, IV.ix.3, 51.
[46] WN, IV.viii.17, 19, 47.

sometimes not at all long-sighted; "avarice and injustice are always short-sighted."[47] They are excited by the risks of long-distance trade, and they also yearn for the security of having their capital always within their sight. They seek the "good" security of information about the commodities in which they trade, or the individuals with whom they deal, or the laws by which they are governed. But they also seek the "bad" security of exclusive privileges, or of the power to influence regulations and laws. They know their own interests. But they pursue these interests by both political and commercial means.

Smith's single, fleeting use in *The Wealth of Nations* of the phrase "an invisible hand" comes in the course of his discussion of the restrictions on imports imposed by the commercial system, and it epitomises the conflicts of the commercial mind. In the midst of a discussion of monopoly, prohibition, and the clamourous importunity of partial interests, Smith introduces an oddly ingenuous merchant who determines that his own interests are better served by investing in domestic rather than in foreign industry, and who is thereby "led by an invisible hand to promote an end which is no part of his intention" (IV.ii.9).

Almost all the other merchants in Book IV of *The Wealth of Nations* are engaged, at least some of the time, in pursuing their own interests by seeking to influence government officials. Smith on one occasion refers to the "futile interests of merchants or manufacturers," and he certainly believes that the pursuit of these interests by political means is futile from the point of view of the society as a whole. However, he is also insistent on the capacity of all individuals, and of mercantile men in particular, to understand their own interests. In their arguments to Parliament about the benefits of foreign trade, the merchants "knew perfectly in what manner it enriched themselves. It was their business to know it." They derived the "greatest advantage" from monopoly. The commercial system, Smith concludes, "really and in the end encourages that species of industry which it means to promote."[48] The difficulty is that individuals are both knowledgeable and deluded; this is the conflict implicit in the image of the invisible hand. On the one

---

[47] WN, III.ii.16, IV.vii.a.19.
[48] WN, IV.i.10, IV.viii.47, IV.ix.49.

hand, they should be left to pursue their own interests as they themselves perceive them. On the other hand, they are likely to pursue these interests by political importunity. The "commercial system" is the characteristic objective of commercial societies, and it is at the same time subversive of commerce itself.

VI. THE SOVEREIGN OR COMMONWEALTH

Smith's final concern is with the activities of the sovereign, and with how they should be paid for. He was not in general an admirer of sovereigns and princes. They share the predilections of other great lords, in his description: vanity, gaudy finery, insignificant pageantry, frivolous passions, and costly trinkets. They are "unproductive labourers." They have power over the currency, and in their "avarice and injustice" they have everywhere debased it. They are "always, and without any exception, the greatest spendthrifts in the society." They even have some of the disagreeable propensities of merchants. They engage in mercantile projects, in which they are usually unsuccessful. They impose their own plans or systems; "of all political speculators, sovereign princes are by far the most dangerous," Smith wrote in the last additions he made to *The Theory of Moral Sentiments*.[49]

The "sovereign or commonwealth," who is the principal subject of Book V of *The Wealth of Nations*, is a more imposing and a more disembodied figure. The system of natural liberty assigns only three duties to this figure. The first is to protect the society from violence and invasion. The second is to protect "every member of the society from the injustice or oppression of every other member of it," which is equivalent to establishing an "exact administration of justice." The third is to be responsible for the public works and public institutions which are of substantial benefit to the society, but which are not of sufficient private benefit that rich individuals, or groups of individuals, will undertake them in their own interest (WN, IV.ix.51).

The sovereign is distinct, in this disembodied sense, from the person of the individual sovereign and may also be described as the "state or commonwealth." Smith thus says encouragingly,

---

[49] WN, I.iv.10, I.v.11, II.iii.2, 36, IV.i.30, V.ii.a.4–6, V.iii.2; TMS, VI.ii.2.18.

of the people of Great Britain, that "our state is not perfect, and might be mended; but it is as good or better than that of most of our neighbours."[50] However, in general he is unwilling to conceive of the state as abstract or disembodied. He returns, repeatedly, to the sentiments and the ways of thinking of the individuals of whom the state is constituted. The sovereign is attended by "all the officers both of justice and war who serve under him, the whole army and navy." The laws of settlement (the English Poor Laws) are implemented by parish officers, churchwardens, overseers of the poor, and justices of the peace. Taxes are collected by custom house officers, tax gatherers, officers of the excise, and officers who lurk outside one's house, counting one's windows.[51]

Smith is generous, in general, with respect to these armies of the inadvertently unproductive. While uniformly sceptical of the pretentions of individuals, in particular the powerful and the sanctimonious, he is convinced that their shortcomings often are a consequence of the circumstances in which they live. The Scots would be more punctilious if they were more occupied in making contracts. The "hardness of character" associated with officers of the excise is likely to have been created by the duties of their office. Even the officers of the East India Company are not individually odious: "it is the system of government, the situation in which they are placed, that I mean to censure; not the character of those who have acted in it."[52]

The first legitimate duty of the sovereign, to protect the society against invasion, is extremely expensive in civilized societies. It is "out of all proportion greater than the necessary expence of civil government." This is in part because of the effects of the division of labour on the "art of war," in part because of the new circumstances of countries which live under a "degree of liberty which approaches to licentiousness." The sovereigns of such countries require standing armies even in times of peace, such that even "the rudest, the most groundless, and the most licentious remonstrances can give little disturbance."[53] However, war has also become more expensive as a consequence of the mercantile or commercial system

[50] WN, IV.intro.1, V.ii.k.66.
[51] WN, I.x.c.46–9, II.iii.2, V.ii.e.17, V.ii.k.62–7.
[52] WN, IV.vii.c.107, V.ii.k.65.
[53] WN, IV.vii.b.20, V.i.a.41.

itself. The chapter in *The Wealth of Nations* on the duty of defense describes only ancient or far-flung conflicts, involving Scythia and Tartary, Hasdrubal and Scipio, the Russian Empire and the Swiss militia. But elsewhere Smith shows his awareness of writing at a time of widespread and virtually global war. The "late war" (the Seven Years War, in Europe, India, and America) had ended in 1763; the "present disturbances," or the "war in America," were raging in 1776.[54] These modern or civilized wars, as Smith suggests on several different occasions, have commercial causes and commercial effects.

"The whole expence of the late war," Smith writes, was incurred in support of the monopoly of colonial trade. Most of the expence took place in "distant countries; in Germany, Portugal, America, in the ports of the Mediterranean, in the East and West Indies." It was "altogether a colony quarrel," and its entire expence ought to be considered as a cost of the colonies and, therefore, of the mercantile system. It was a bounty to monopoly. The wars of the seventeenth and eighteenth centuries (the two Dutch wars, the war in Ireland, the "four expensive French wars") were for Smith the clearest illustration of the "profusion of government." They were also examples of the frivolity of British governments, who over more than a century, "amused the people with the imagination that they possessed a great empire on the west side of the Atlantic." This was not security but childishness. The people in the capital are not in danger of violence, but "enjoy, at their ease, the amusement of reading in the newspapers the exploits of their own fleets and armies.... They are commonly dissatisfied with the return of peace, which puts an end to their amusement, and to a thousand visionary hopes of conquest and national glory."[55]

The expence of justice is for Smith a very different and more solemn responsibility. The origins of justice were at the heart of Smith's interests, in *The Theory of Moral Sentiments*, in his lectures on jurisprudence, and in *The Wealth of Nations*. Justice is the "main pillar that upholds the whole edifice..., the great, the immense fabric of human society," he says in *The Theory of Moral*

---

[54] See Donald Winch, *Adam Smith's Politics: An Essay in Historiographic Revision* (Cambridge, 1978), chapter 7.

[55] WN, II.iii.35, IV.i.26, IV.vii.c.64, V.iii.37, 92.

Sentiments. It is a virtue which is represented more or less imperfectly in the legal institutions of different societies. The "natural sentiments of justice" change over time and become more civilized. Legal institutions are the record of these sentiments. However, institutions are sometimes, because of "the constitution of the state, that is, the interest of the government," or because of the "unfortunate constitution of [the] courts," less civilized than the sentiments of individuals.[56]

The institutions of justice are intimately connected with disputes over property or over economic relationships. They are also concerned with disputes over love, honour, and verbal injuries. Laws and government are in every case "a combination of the rich to oppress the poor," and to preserve the inequality with which goods are distributed; the civil government, which is instituted for the protection of property, is "in reality instituted for the defence of the rich against the poor."[57] The effect of these institutions, at least in societies with a reasonably impartial administration of justice, and with the "boasted liberty of the subject," is to protect the property of all, including the poor. This is for Smith the single most important condition, as has been seen, for the progress of opulence. However, the justification of justice – and of the expense of justice – is not only, or principally, a matter of expediency with respect to opulence or prosperity. Without justice, "civil society would become a scene of bloodshed and disorder." (This is one of Smith's extremely infrequent uses of the familiar eighteenth-century phrase "civil society.")[58] Justice is also an end in itself, or an essential constituent of the human spirit. It is part of the inner lives of all individuals. There is a "sense of justice"; "we feel ourselves to be in a peculiar manner tied, bound, and obliged to the observation of justice."[59]

---

[56] TMS, III.ii.3.4, VII.iv.36.

[57] LJ(A), vi.22–3; WN, V.i.b.12.

[58] TMS, VII.iv.36. The phrase occurs on one other occasion in *The Theory of Moral Sentiments*, when Smith is commenting on the tendency to think of the violently resentful as people who should, like wild beasts, be hunted out of civil society (I.ii.4.3); both uses are from the original 1759 edition. The single use in the entire *Wealth of Nations* is in the course of a discussion of disputes between sixteenth-century reformed churches over the distribution of ecclesiastical benefices, a subject of some interest "to the peace and welfare of civil society"; WN, V.i.g.33.

[59] TMS, II.ii.1.5, II.ii.2, heading.

The third duty of the sovereign is to do with public works and public institutions. In his discussion of institutions which might be thought necessary to facilitate commerce, Smith is principally concerned with the "mercantile system," as represented by the Royal African Company, the Turkey Company, and their assorted subscribers, enlarged monopolies, and "particular friends." He is opposed, not surprisingly, to government expenditure to help "particular branches of commerce"; this section of Book V of *The Wealth of Nations*, which was heavily revised and augmented in the *Additions and Corrections*, published by Smith in 1783, is the occasion, in fact, for some of his most pointed criticism of the British in India (their eagerness in the appointment of plunderers, their spirit of war and conquest, their negligence and profusion, their depredations, their misunderstanding of a mild and gentle people.)[60]

The expenses of facilitating "commerce in general" are for Smith less misguided. He believed communications to be a necessary condition for the progress of opulence; he approved of the policies of the Muslim sovereigns of Bengal for improving roads and canals. However, the expense of most public works (bridges, canals, harbours, roads) could be met, he argued, by the individuals and enterprises who make use of them. Smith was very attached to roads in a figurative sense, as we have seen; he was much less well disposed toward real, existing roads. The high roads of a country "produce nothing," just like unproductive labourers, such as churchmen, lawyers, physicians, musicians, and opera dancers. They facilitate the carriage of food and clothing, but they do not themselves produce food or clothing. In each of his series of lectures, and in his early draft of *The Wealth of Nations*, he indeed imagines a violent reform to "save the ground taken up by highways," without "interrupting the communication." Banks and banknotes, he says, "enable us, as it were, to plough up our high roads, by affording us a sort of communication through the air by which we do our business equally well."[61]

Smith's explanation of the economy of roads, as so often in his account of government, is distinctively personal. He imagines the

---

[60] WN, V.i.e.2, 7.
[61] LJ(A), vi.128–30; LJ(B), 244–5; Early Draft, 35–6; WN, II.iii.2.

individuals who build the roads and the individuals who make the decisions to build them. The obligation to make and maintain roads was a form of "servitude" imposed everywhere on the poor, with different degrees of "cruelty and oppression." The *corvées* by which individuals were obliged to work on road projects were "one of the principal instruments of tyranny" in rural France. The decisions to build roads were made, meanwhile, in the frivolous spirit which is characteristic of oppressive governments. In France, "the great roads, the great communications which are likely to be the subjects of conversation at the court and in the capital, are attended to, and all the rest neglected." Highways are built in locations where there is little or no commerce, but which happen to be on the way to "the country villa of the intendant of the province," whereas to "execute a great number of little works...[which] have nothing to recommend them but their extreme utility," would be beneath the dignity of the government. It is much better, therefore, that the expenses of roads be borne, wherever possible, by the people who will use them, just as the expenses of paving and lighting the streets of London should be borne by the people of London.[62]

The other public institutions which Smith describes are also suited, in general, to private support. Smith was favourable, as has been seen, to the establishment of an extensive system of schools whereby the "public can facilitate, can encourage, and can even impose upon almost the whole body of the people, the necessity of acquiring [the] most essential parts of education." This was important to counteract the stultifying effects of the division of labour or to "prevent the almost entire corruption and degeneracy of the great body of the people." It is interesting that Smith's principal justification for universal education had little to do with improving skills or diligence, but was rather a matter of the disposition of the people to make disinterested and reflective judgments about the government's own conduct. The new system would require little expense, namely a limited support to the established public teachers. Smith draws a parallel with the merchants of the commercial system. If public teachers have full salaries, the private teacher is put into "the same state with a merchant who attempts to trade without a bounty." The public role in the new system

---

[62] WN, III.ii.18, V.i.d.6, 16–19.

should consist, rather, of "establishing in every parish or district a little school"; of paying part, but not all, of the salary of the teacher; of giving prizes to children; and of setting public examinations.[63]

The public institutions for the support of instruction for people of all ages are "chiefly those for religious instruction." Smith takes issue, in his discussion of public expenditure on religion, with the policy, favoured by David Hume, of government support for an established church. He prefers the competition of "two or three hundred" or several thousand small sects, "of which no one could be considerable enough to disturb the public tranquillity." Established religion has several of the more distasteful characteristics of both the mercantile and the land-owning orders. The great clergy of medieval Europe were "like the great barons," in their "vanity, luxury, and expence." However, the church is also like an incorporation, which Smith describes in the language of mercantile plans: "the clergy of every established church constitute a great incorporation. They can act in concert, and pursue their interest upon one plan." The use of public money should be for instruction which is not religious. The intention is, indeed, to correct the excessively unsocial and rigourous morality of the religious sects by encouraging the "study of science and philosophy" through a system of public qualifications, and by securing the "frequency and gaiety of public diversions" through the "entire liberty" of the arts.[64]

Smith's final concern is with the sources of public revenue. Government becomes more expensive as countries become more opulent. It may even become more judicious, and more informed by "an extensive view of the general good" (WN, IV.ii.44). It is of the greatest importance, therefore, that its revenue should be secured in an equitable and encouraging way through observation of certain maxims. "Maxims" are in general, for Smith, repositories of prejudice ("the vile maxim of the masters of mankind," the maxims of the commercial system or of "underling tradesmen").[65] However, his own maxims of taxation are a matter of "justice and utility." The first is equality: that individuals should pay taxes in proportion

[63] WN, V.i.f.45–61; cf. Emma Rothschild, "Condorcet and Adam Smith on Education and Instruction," in *Philosophers on Education: New Historical Perspectives*, ed. Amélie Oksenberg Rorty (London, 1998), pp. 209–26.

[64] WN, V.i.g.1, 8, 13–17, 25.

[65] WN, III.iv.10, IV.iii.c.8–12.

to their income. The second is that the tax should be certain, not arbitrary. The third is convenience to the taxpayer. The fourth is economy, to the tax collector and to the public; that is to say, that the costs of taxes to the taxpayers should not exceed by too much their benefits to the sovereign (WN, V.ii.b.2–7).

British taxes, at the time of the publication of *The Wealth of Nations*, were of four principal sorts. There were taxes on land, stamp duties, duties of customs, and duties of excise (WN, V.iii.69). (William Pitt introduced the first, temporary income tax in Britain only in 1799.[66]) All were in varying degrees uneconomical. Some required a "great number of officers" to collect. Others created temptations of tax evasion, for example, by buying smuggled goods, especially when the regulations in question were widely perceived as unjust and scruples in their regard as "pedantic pieces of hypocrisy." Yet others were vexatious. The individual was subjected to the "mortifying and vexatious visits of the tax-gatherers," or to the "insolence and oppression of the officers, still more insupportable than any tax." Vexation is not, strictly speaking, expence, Smith says, but "it is certainly equivalent to the expence at which every man would be willing to redeem himself from it."[67]

As so often in *The Wealth of Nations*, Smith's description of the economy of taxation is extraordinarily concrete. He was intrigued by taxes and other charges on the use of luxuries. Taxes on "carriages of luxury," for example, were such that "the indolence and vanity of the rich is made to contribute in a very easy manner to the relief of the poor" (WN, V.i.d.5). Smith was generally in favour of taxes on luxuries, including the luxuries of the poor. However, he was opposed to taxes on necessities, and it is in the course of a discussion of fiscal policy that he identifies linen shirts and leather shoes as the requirements of a decent public life in England. Indeed, his earliest influence on policy seems to have been in relation to fiscal innovation, and he learnt in 1778 that he had "awaked some new Ideas about improving the Revenue," on the part of Lord North.[68]

---

[66] See P. K. O'Brien, "The Political Economy of British Taxation, 1660–1815," *Economic History Review* XLI (1988): 1–32.

[67] WN, V.ii.b.6–7, V.ii.k.64–5, V.iii.54–5; LJ(A), vi.34.

[68] Letter of November 1778, in Corr., p. 237.

Smith was at the same time preoccupied with the motives of taxpayers and of tax collectors. The "multitude of revenue officers" are odious, but they are also the victims of their duties. Window taxes are less oppressive than taxes on hearths because windows can be counted without going into every room in a house. To tax the spruce beer, which is the "common drink of the people in America" and is brewed at home, would be "to subject every private family to the odious visits and examination of the tax-gatherers."[69]

Smith even considers that the desire to flee from countries which impose high taxes – a widespread inclination among the great merchants of the commercial system, in his view – is inspired by the feeling of being vexed, as much as by the dislike of having to contribute. The proprietor of stock "is properly a citizen of the world," and he would "be apt to abandon the country in which he was exposed to a vexatious inquisition, in order to be assessed to a burdensome tax." Merchants are in general disposed to remove their capital from countries with high taxes. It is when they are "continually exposed to the mortifying and vexatious visits of the tax-gatherers" that their disposition is expressed in an actual departure. The motives of merchants, like the motives of the poor and creditable day labourer, reluctant to appear in public without leather shoes, are to be respected, to avoid vexation and mortification. The great merchants of Holland remain there, Smith says, even though they make low rates of profit on their capital and low rates of interest on the money they lend, and even though they are subject to high rates of taxation. They do so, in his opinion, because Holland is a country in which they are respected and important. A different form of government, dominated by nobles and soldiers, "would soon render it disagreeable to them to live in a country where they were no longer likely to be much respected."[70]

The peroration of *The Wealth of Nations* is concerned with public debt. This is the modern system of revenue for it is only possible in the circumstances of commercial countries. It is to be explained by a condition – "the operation of moral causes" – which is at the heart of all Smith's economic theories. Sovereigns have relatively little capital or treasure in commercial countries, in part because

---

[69] WN, V.ii.e.15, V.ii.k.67, V.iii.74.
[70] WN, V.ii.f.6, V.ii.k.80, V.iii.55.

they are captivated, like other rich men, by the "frivolous passions" associated with expensive luxuries. They have large expenditures, especially in times of war, and they are afraid of "offending the people by raising taxes." There are at the same time large sums of money available in a "country abounding with merchants and manufacturers." These merchants have confidence in the justice of the government; if this were not the case, commerce would not be flourishing. So they are confident, too, in the security of loans made to government. They are inclined to fund government expenditures, and the reluctance of sovereigns to save is matched by the willingness of their subjects to lend (WN, IV.iii.3–10).

This "pernicious system of funding" is for Smith a monument of modern delusion, defended with all the "sophistry of the mercantile system." War becomes an amusement. It is in the course of his account of the funding system, under which wars can be waged with only a modest increase in taxes, that Smith describes the virtual bellicosity of newspaper readers in times of distant war. Smith was cautious, in general, about predicting the ruin of societies. However, the funding system is in his description a source of "weakness or desolation" or both. The enormous debts of governments, he says, "at present oppress, and will in the long-run probably ruin, all the great nations of Europe."[71]

Smith's solution, as so often, is to be found in a combination of prudence and vast reform. Governments should do no more than they can pay for, and the costs of wars, in particular, should be defrayed out of current revenue. In future, the government of Britain should extend its system of taxation to the entire empire of countries (or "provinces") inhabited by people of "British or European extraction." To do so would require a vast zone of free trade and wide extension of "fair and equal" political representation; a "states-general of the British Empire." The seat of the empire would be likely to move, "in the course of little more than a century," to the other side of the Atlantic; it might even, as suggested by his use of the un-English phrase "states-general," move eventually to the other side of different seas. This is a "new Utopia," Smith says; it is no worse, at least, than the golden dreams of Britain's existing

[71] WN, V.iii.10, 37, 51–7.

rulers, which are "not an empire, but the project of an empire; not a gold mine, but the project of a gold mine."[72]

VII. RATIONALITY AND EXCHANGE

Smith's economic writings, in conclusion, present a subtle and diverse view of individual motivations. He argued for the importance of a plurality of motivations that may be relevant to and influence the behaviour of any individual. First, a narrowly defined self-interest, the only motive of the so-called "economic man," may feature in this along with others, including prudence, sympathy, generosity, and public spiritedness. However, self-interest cannot be sufficient for understanding human behaviour in society and even in the economy, except for very special cases such as the desire to exchange commodities to satisfy simple wants. Secondly, the overcoming of self-love may happen through moral or social reflection, but can also occur through imitative behaviour, the survival and flourishing of which may depend on their evolutionary role. While Smith does not pursue the evolutionary angle very explicitly, there is enough in Smith's writings on the emergence of social fashion to link comfortably with the recent literature on evolutionary behaviour.[73] Thirdly, Smith does not confine his motivational analysis to the listing of different motives. He also probes their implications and their causal consequences. One of the motives that figure prominently in *The Wealth of Nations* is the desire to be respected, which Smith sees as being part of the reason for the pursuit of wealth.

Fourthly, because of Smith's insistence on interpersonal variations in behavioural norms related particularly to different classes and occupation groups, the Smithian behavioural analysis never takes the mechanical form of finding a "reliable" mix of motivations and then applying that mix to explain the behaviour of all. Finally, in the Smithian perspective, rationality does not consist of falling into line with any pre-selected motivation, such as self-interest maximization which is often *defined* as rational behaviour

---

[72] WN, IV.vii.c.79, V.iii.68, 92.
[73] See, for example, Jörgen Weibull, *Evolutionary Game Theory* (Cambridge, MA, 1995).

in parts of modern economics, for example, in "rational choice theory." Rather, rationality is seen as reasoned reflection on the nature of the processes involved and the consequences generated, in the light of valuations one has reason to accept. Rationality is an exercise of reasoning, valuation, and choice, not a fixed formula with a pre-specified maximand.

Smith's analysis of trade and exchange is a central feature of his overall economic understanding. Potential gains from trade can arise for at least three distinct reasons. First, in a situation of pure exchange – involving no alteration of production – a bilateral or a multilateral exchange can help improve the situation of each, if each would rather have what he or she can obtain through exchange than what they happen to own to start with. If I have a banana and you have a mango, and I would rather have the mango and you the banana, then an exchange will benefit us both (even in the absence of any change of production of commodities). This basic point, for what it is worth (and it is by no means worthless), gets immediate recognition from Smith, and indeed even the famous butcher-brewer-baker case can be seen as something rather like this operation of mutually beneficial pure exchange (until of course we start considering the production effects of the new exchange, which will, then, take the analysis beyond one of pure exchange). This is a natural starting point for seeing the benefits of exchange since it also tends to be incorporated into more complex developments.

The second argument for trade relates to comparative costs and the gains from trade arising from differences in resource bases of different traders (individuals, groups, or countries). Production patterns adjust to accommodate the efficiency advantages of each producing what it is comparatively better suited to produce. This is an argument that came to full flowering in the analysis of David Ricardo. Even though traces of this argument are also present in a relatively rudimentary form in Smithian discussions, it is not to Smith that we look for a definitive statement of this "comparative costs" argument.

The third argument concerns economies of scale related to division of labour, as well as skill formation and the long-run gains of specialization. This is, in fact, the quintessentially Smithian case for free trade, and it gets plentiful exposition in *The Wealth of Nations*. Even if every country or every group of people had exactly the same resource endowments, they can all benefit from specialization and the exploitation of increasing returns to scale, as well as skill formation and the cultivation of distinctive dexterity. Despite getting an early start in Smith's writings, this argument for free trade has proved to be rather harder to accommodate formally within standard economic theory, to a great extent because of the difficulties of providing an adequately full analysis of increasing returns to scale in models of competitive equilibria. The needed reformulations of the standard price-based equilibria, with consideration of various forms of markets and different kinds of equilibria, have been pursued by a number of distinguished economists in recent years, and the implications of this "Smithian" model of trade is now much better understood.[74]

Smith's interest in market forms other than pure competition has also proved to be deeply insightful. Indeed, in assessing the market mechanism, it is important to take note of the nature of the markets and not to confine oneself to the analysis of pure competition, which much of standard trade theory has done until recent years. The model of pure competition, which is assumed explicitly or implicitly, tends to hide monopolistic competition, missing markets, and other complexities. Smith's interest in what are often considered "details" (to use J. B. Say's expression) provides the basis of a much richer overall theory of what trade does or does not achieve. In explaining the differential benefits obtained from trade by the newly industrializing countries, for example, in East and Southeast Asia and in Latin America, these more extensive formulations, ultimately traceable to Smith's interest in division of labour, economies of scale, the formation of skills, and the presence of market imperfections, have been particularly profound.

There are also other fields in which the sophistication of Smith's analysis has proved to be extremely rewarding, and its implications are still invoked in contemporary economics and social analysis. The conceptual connection between poverty and inequality is one such implication, and is related to Smith's penetrating analysis of poverty. There are two interconnected points here. First, Smith sees poverty in the form of certain basic "unfreedoms" – well

---

[74] See, for example, Paul R. Krugman, "Scale Economies, Product Differentiation, and the Pattern of Trade," *American Economic Review* 70 (1981): 950–9; Paul M. Romer, "Growth Based on Increasing Returns Due to Specialization," *American Economic Review* 77 (1987): 56–62; Robert E. Lucas, "On the Mechanics of Economic Development," *Journal of Monetary Economics* 22 (1988): 3–42.

illustrated by his interest in the ability (or lack of it) of someone
to appear in public without shame. (In England, even the poorest creditable people "would be ashamed to appear in publick"
without leather shoes.) Poverty, thus, consists of certain failures of
capabilities, rather than of lowness of income per se. A capability-
based approach of poverty and deprivation can draw substantially
on Smith's pioneering analysis.[75]

In Smith's analysis of poverty the pivotal role is played by deprivation of necessaries which in turn are determined by the consumption standards in the rest of the society. This clarifies why
poverty cannot be divorced from the existence of inequality. A person's ability to be clothed or to have other items of consumption
goods that are appropriate by the standards of the society in which
she lives may be crucial for her capability to mix with others in
that society. This relates directly to her relative income vis-à-vis
the general level of prosperity in that community and is well illustrated by Smith's interest in the ability or inability of someone to
appear in public without shame (WN, V.ii.k.3). A relative deprivation in terms of income can, thus, lead to an absolute deprivation in
terms of capabilities, and in this sense, the problems of poverty and
inequality are closely interlinked. Even if someone finds poverty
but not inequality offensive, he or she still may have to take an
interest in economic inequality as a determinant of poverty in the
form of basic capability deprivation. Whether a person's income
is critically low depends, in this analysis, on various contingent
circumstances, including the prevailing standards of consumption
in the society in which the person lives, for this determines the
minimum income a person may need to be capable of certain basic
functionings, such as taking part in the life of the community. That
insight of Smith has been important for contemporary investigations of poverty and inequality.

VIII. A HISTORY OF HUMAN MOTIVES

Walter Bagehot described *The Wealth of Nations* in 1876 as "a very
amusing book about old times," now "dropping out of immediate

---

[75] On this see Amartya Sen, *Poverty and Famines: An Essay on Entitlement and
Deprivation* (Oxford, 1981), and *Commodities and Capabilities* (Amsterdam,
1985).

use from change of times."[76] Even in its own times, *The Wealth of Nations* was in large part a book about history. In following Smith's own plan or order of subjects, we have been concerned with controversies (over the "corporation spirit" and the East India Company, over apprenticeships and the English Poor Laws, over the regulation of customs and excise) which were the subject of intense contemporary debate. Others of Smith's disquisitions, on Peruvian silver, on the Roman art of war, or on bullion policies in seventeenth-century Amsterdam, were of less than compelling concern, even to contemporaries. His historical descriptions of English laws and institutions were "lacking in interest for anyone other than the English," in Jean-Baptiste Say's words.[77]

The Wealth of Nations is in a profound sense a work of history. It is about the causes of economic progress, even more than about its nature. Smith's lifelong investigation, Dugald Stewart wrote in 1793, was of "human nature in all its branches, more particularly of the political history of mankind."[78] The two historical epics which are at the heart of *The Wealth of Nations* – the slow revolution in legal institutions and the progress of the human mind – unfolded over many centuries. This "increase in length of perspective" was itself one of the most important innovations of Smith's book, as Donald Winch has emphasised.[79] To explain the causal relations between freedom and commercial opulence was to contribute to contemporary political disputes. The greatly increased "request" for historical truths in recent times, Smith said in his lectures on rhetoric, was associated, in part, with the circumstance that "there are now severall sects in Religion and politicall disputes which are greatly dependent on the truth of certain facts" (LRBL, ii.40). However, historical explanation was also, and above all, the most important way to understand economic life.

---

[76] Walter Bagehot, "Adam Smith as a Person," in Walter Bagehot, *Biographical Studies* (London, 1881), p. 295.

[77] "Discours préliminaire," in Jean-Baptiste Say, *Traité d'Economie Politique, ou simple exposition de la manière dont se forment, se distribuent, et se consomment les richesses* (Paris, 1803), p. xxv.

[78] Stewart, *Account*, p. 271.

[79] The contrast was striking, in particular, with the "popular literature of jeremiad and mercantile panacea"; Donald Winch, "Adam Smith," *The New Dictionary of National Biography*.

Smith believed there are universal principles of human nature, including the desire to better one's condition and the disposition to conversation, or persuasion. However, the principles of political and commercial life are very different. They are influenced by historical circumstances; they are imprecise and incomplete. They are quite unlike the glittering principles – the "jewels" of thought, in Friedrich List's sardonic phrase – which have been identified, in Smith's work, by so many subsequent observers.[80] There is little in Smith's writings on economic subjects, for example, which corresponds to the timeless and universal dogma of self-interest, or of rational economic man.[81] Smith believed that people were sometimes, but not always, influenced by self-interest, and that their self-interest was fulfilled sometimes, but not always, by money and goods. The augmentation of fortune is simply "the means the most vulgar and the most obvious" by which individuals seek to better their condition (WN, II.iii.28). Commodities are means to other ends, and in particular to the end of being well regarded. "To be observed, to be attended to, to be taken notice of with sympathy, complacency, and approbation" – these are the advantages to be derived from "all the toil and bustle of this world" (TMS, I.iii.2.1). Exchange is sometimes an end in itself, as an agreeable form of traffic or oratory. It is founded on the principles, including justice (or fairness), reflection (or deliberation), and the desire to persuade, which distinguish men from spaniels: "nobody ever saw a dog make a fair and deliberate exchange" (WN, I.ii.2).

Rationality is in general, for Smith, a sociable and discursive condition. Reasoning and conversation are companions. To reason, Smith says in The Theory of Moral Sentiments, is to be able to evaluate means and also ends. It is a companionable activity, in which one seeks to justify one's actions, and is influenced by the opinions of one's friends. The objective of ordinary life is "decent and becoming actions, for which a plausible or probable reason could be assigned" (TMS, VII.ii.1.42). It is interesting that self-love or self-interest, for Smith, is often in conflict with reason; it is a characteristically warm and confusing sentiment. The self-interest

---

[80] Friedrich List, The National System of Political Economy, trans. Sampson S. Lloyd (1885) (Fairfield, CT, 1977), p. 135
[81] See Chapter 9 in this volume.

of merchants and traders, in *The Wealth of Nations*, is inimical to the cool evaluation of consequences, to reason, and even to truth. The deceptions of tradesmen are expressed with "all the passionate confidence of interested falsehood" (WN, IV.iii.c.13). Merchants have golden dreams of the great profits to be gained in vast and extensive projects. The whole mercantile system, with its colonies and empires, is a monument to unreason, the outcome of avidity, folly, and injustice.

The "principles of market" – the phrase was used by Edmund Burke in the 1790s – were for Smith similarly imprecise. Smith can be described as the discoverer of the market economy in the sense that *The Wealth of Nations* is an extended encomium to the interdependence of economic activities in different villages, cities, and continents. The more imposing idea of a general competitive equilibrium, in which the outcome of the self-interested actions of individuals is a system or order of maximal efficiency, is far less close to Smith's own conceptions. He was preoccupied, in all his economic writings, with the imperfections of markets, and with the obstructions to commerce imposed by insecurity, oppressive institutions, and imperfect communications. The longest book of *The Wealth of Nations* – and the one in which the invisible hand makes its fleeting appearance – is concerned with political influences on commerce, and with the self-interest of merchants, as expressed in their support for the regulations of the commercial or mercantile system. The image of the invisible hand was a minor and even, it has been suggested, an ironic element in Smith's own economic thought.[82] The principle of the invisible hand, in its twentieth-century sense, was quite un-Smithian.

The principle of non-interference, or of laissez-faire, was also, for Smith, a matter of historical circumstance. The obvious and simple system of natural liberty was no more than a guide to policy. It was to be implemented with the greatest circumspection. It endowed the sovereign with duties "of great importance," as has been seen.[83] One of these duties, of protecting every member of the society from injustice and oppression, was itself of potentially vast extent. It also

---

[82] See Emma Rothschild, *Economic Sentiments: Adam Smith, Condorcet and the Enlightenment* (Cambridge, MA, 2001), chapter 5.

[83] See Jacob Viner, "Adam Smith and Laissez Faire," in Jacob Viner, *The Long View and the Short* (Glencoe, IL, 1958).

required considerable interference with the interests of merchants. Monopolies are described as oppressive in *The Wealth of Nations*; Smith's principal example of "oppressive genius" is, as so often, the "exclusive company."[84] Even inequality, for Smith, could be a form of oppression. "Smith placed himself in all cases of conflict of interest between the poor and the rich, between the strong and the weak, *without exception* on the side of the latter," Carl Menger wrote in 1891.[85] This partiality was expressed in the policies that Smith recommended; in the principles (as distinct from the oppressive implementation) of the English Poor Laws, in certain regulations of wages, in his elaborate schemes for the taxation of luxuries.

The principle of the international division of labour, or of the connections over long distances which were eventually identified as "globalization," was for Smith a description of historical transformation. Smith wrote *The Wealth of Nations* at a time of euphoric excitement over the mid-eighteenth century expansion in worldwide commerce, investment, information, and influence. His conception of prosperity in "the whole globe of the earth" was a reflection of this excitement, and so was his conception of a large liberal system, in which "the different states into which a great continent was divided would so far resemble the different provinces of a great empire." But he was also suspicious, as so often, of great and global systems.[86] The restless, wandering proprietor of stock, the wholesale merchant, the "citizen of the world," is the central figure of *The Wealth of Nations*. Yet, its closest approximation to a hero is the proprietor of local agricultural land, the improver of the small estate, the tranquil man of civility and cultivation.

The Wealth of Nations is a great book – the greatest book ever written about economic life – in part because it is a book about old times. It is about the universal principles of the human spirit, and the circumstances of the human spirit in the sixteenth, seventeenth, and eighteenth centuries. These circumstances have a great deal in common with our own, at the outset of the twenty-first

---

[84] See WN, IV.vii.c.100; cf. I.x.c.17, IV.viii.17, V.i.e.8–12.

[85] Carl Menger, "Die Sozial-Theorien der classischen National-Oekonomie und die moderne Wirthschaftspolitik," (1891) in Carl Menger, *Kleinere Schriften zur Methode und Geschichte der Volkswirtschaftslehre* (London, 1935), p. 223.

[86] WN, IV.v.b.39.

century. Smith's continuing preoccupation with the relationship between the local and the global, in particular, is strikingly evocative in the new epoch of globalization and privatization. However, his economic writings, and his history of economic progress, are likely to be read long after our own historical moment has come to an end.

13   The Legacy of Adam Smith

David Hume, writing on his deathbed in 1776, congratulated Smith on the appearance of his long-awaited *Inquiry into the Nature and Causes of the Wealth of Nations*: he predicted that it would take time for the work to make an impression, was confident that its "depth and solidity and acuteness" would ensure that "it must at last take the public attention" (Corr., 186). Recent studies of the slow and uneven reception given to *Wealth of Nations* during the first decades after its appearance have proved Hume correct.[1] What Hume could not have known is for just how long the work would retain a hold on public attention and how potently diverse Smith's influence would become. In 1759, reporting to Smith on the London reception of *The Theory of Moral Sentiments*, Hume had taken the opposite tack; he had teasingly suggested that the signs of immediate popularity were cause for concern about the work's claims on philosophical posterity (Corr., 35). Here, too, Hume proved correct for reasons he could not have predicted. For whereas *Wealth of Nations* marks the beginning, or revitalisation, of a science of considerable significance to the conduct of public life, the apparent conformity of *The Theory of Moral Sentiments* with some conventional expectations of what a moral philosophy should be, has, we will argue, set limits on how that work has been perceived.

However, before embarking on what must inevitably be a highly selective treatment of Smith's legacy, it may be useful to distinguish such an inquiry from those other kinds of study often

---

[1] R. F. Teichgraeber, "'Less abused than I had reason to expect': The Reception of the *Wealth of Nations* in Britain, 1776–90," *Historical Journal* 30 (1991): 337–66.

collected together under *fortuna* – the reception, influence, diffusion, translation, and reputation enjoyed by Smith's writings as they have made their way in the world. Whereas *fortuna* invites an examination of the vicissitudes of opinion at various times and places, legacy entails a more analytical and judgmental position. *Fortuna* is essentially a matter of recorded history, a kind of diachronic stock market valuation that can be recaptured with more or less accuracy. Luckily for our purposes, Smith's iconic status has ensured that this type of inquiry has now been extensively undertaken.[2] Legacy, on the other hand, requires a verdict on the more fruitful lines of inquiry that spring from an interpretation of the meaning of Smith's intellectual enterprise taken as a whole, regardless of passing fashions. It poses such questions as where and how Smith's systematic vision has benefited those who have accepted and developed his methods and ideas; and it presumes that we can distinguish between what properly belongs to Smith and those accretions that reflect the preoccupations of his legatees.[3]

The general problem we face in assessing Smith's legacy is one of distinguishing – amid a crowd of enthusiastic claimants – between legitimate and illegitimate legatees, and between claims that have substance and those that are merely based on opportunism or caricature. We also confront the Adam Smith Problem in one of its various guises. Since Smith's death in 1790, the legacy of the author of *The Wealth of Nations* has dominated the legacy of the author of *The Theory of Moral Sentiments*. The two works have also, until fairly recently, led separate lives, only being regularly brought together for biographical or polemical purposes. In the case of *The Wealth of Nations*, we have a large number of claims to the legacy, an embarrassment of riches littering the surface. In the case of *The Theory of Moral Sentiments*, we have to uncover paths that

---

[2] See especially, *Adam Smith: International Perspectives*, eds. H. Mizuta and C. Sugiyama (Houndsmills, Hampshire, 1993); *On Moral Sentiments. Contemporary Responses to Adam Smith*, ed. J. Reeder (Bristol, 1997); *On the Wealth of Nations. Contemporary Responses to Adam Smith*, ed. I. S. Ross (Bristol, 1998); *A Critical Bibliography of Adam Smith*, ed. K. Tribe (London, 2002).

[3] For earlier suggestions, see K. Haakonssen, *Natural Law and Moral Philosophy. From Grotius to the Scottish Enlightenment* (Cambridge 1996); D. Winch, *Riches and Poverty. An Intellectual History of Political Economy in Britain, 1750–1834* (Cambridge, 1996).

have either been obscured or seem to have run into the sand. To a large extent, of course, this state of affairs is due to two related phenomena: the prominence of the economic dimension in the lives of European societies since 1776; and the way in which political economy developed rapidly during the nineteenth century as an autonomous branch of the moral or social sciences, resistant to reincorporation and prone to extend its boundaries by forms of economic imperialism. Comparative neglect of *The Theory of Moral Sentiments* can also be attributed to the importance attached to that pervasive nineteenth- and twentieth-century body of ideas that falls under some version or other of Liberalism, with or without its capital letter. While the relevance of *The Wealth of Nations* to economic liberalism has often seemed self-evident to Smith's disciples, it is not immediately apparent what political or normative label, if any, should be attached to the theories of morals and justice advanced in *The Theory of Moral Sentiments*.

Economists, when they give the subject any thought, are pleased to accept Smith as one of the founding fathers of their discipline. No comparable body of celebratory literature exists in the case of *The Theory of Moral Sentiments*. Only comparatively recently have Smith scholars had some success in convincing others that both of Smith's major works benefit from being treated as the outcome of a single ambitious intellectual project. Indeed, judging by those who have used *The Theory of Moral Sentiments* to supply a "moral" dimension to the "amoral" world depicted in *The Wealth of Nations*, they may have been too successful: another version of the Adam Smith Problem has come into existence. We can understand Smith's project better if we call on his "History of Astronomy" for testimony as to his methodological preferences, and the *Lectures on Jurisprudence* for evidence that helps bridge the gap between *The Theory of Moral Sentiments* and *The Wealth of Nations*. The *Lectures on Rhetoric and Belles Lettres*, instead of being a literary oddity, can now be used to aid interpretation of Smith's stylistic preferences, giving language use the central role he assigns to it when dealing with our moral and economic exchanges. As a further aid to comprehension, we can also call on improved understanding of the work of Smith's Scottish contemporaries, and more especially that of Hume, his closest intellectual ally.

SMITH'S SYSTEM

In view of the uneven and divided nature of the legacy sketched so far, it seems necessary once more to emphasize Smith's own view of the subject. His last communication with his readers was a reassertion of the systematic intent behind his works. In the Preface to the sixth edition of *The Theory of Moral Sentiments*, which appeared in the year of his death, Smith drew attention to the promise he had made in the concluding lines of the work when it first appeared in 1759. There he announced that he would complete his moral philosophy with "an account of the general principles of law and government, and of the different revolutions they have undergone in the different ages and periods of society, not only in what concerns justice, but in what concerns police, revenue, and arms, and whatever else is the object of law" (VII.iv.37). Presenting his last and major revision of the text, a clear sign in itself of Smith's desire that his posterity would not depend on *The Wealth of Nations* alone, he declared that *The Wealth of Nations* had fulfilled his promise so far as police, revenue, and arms were concerned, and that he still stood by his "design" for a major work on jurisprudence, even though he had little hope of being able to execute it to his satisfaction. Satisfactoriness weighed more heavily with Smith than most, and during his final illness he decided to take no further chances with posterity by destroying what he had written on the uncompleted parts of the system, thereby obscuring his design.

Despite these scruples, Smith could hardly have suspected that the question of systematic coherence and/or incompleteness in his intellectual endeavour would constitute an enduring part of his legacy. It is true that among his contemporaries and for many years afterward, the question hardly arose as a serious problem. It was placed in doubt by Henry Thomas Buckle's clumsy attempt at methodological reconciliation of *The Theory of Moral Sentiments* and *The Wealth of Nations* in 1861.[4] Buckle maintained that Smith had divided human motivation into two groups, altruism in *The Theory of Moral Sentiments*, and self-interest in *The Wealth of*

[4] Henry Thomas Buckle's *History of Civilization in England* (1857–61), 3 vols. (London, 1894), vol. 3, pp. 304–30.

Nations, but that this was a temporary and purely heuristic device. The latter part of the argument hardly persuaded anyone, but the former gave rise to an accusation of fundamental inconsistency and fuelled a major debate in Germany, where it was elevated to the status of "das Adam Smith Problem" that has been with us ever since. Originating in the polemics within German political economy against English "Manchestertum" and the latter's supposed Smithian ancestry, and continued by the German historical school of economics represented by Wilhelm Roscher, Bruno Hildebrand, Karl Knies, and Lujo Brentano, the issue was whether Smith himself "knew better" than to see all human motivation as self-interested.[5] That is to say, on the assumption that the grand socio-economic theory of *The Wealth of Nations* was based on a reductive self-interest theory, the supposed sympathy theory of motivation in *The Theory of Moral Sentiments* was evidence either that Smith was confused and incoherent or that he had changed his mind between the writing of the two books.[6]

There were formidable and obvious obstacles to such an interpretation. For instance, Smith continued to revise and re-issue the two works during his lifetime without ever hinting at any discrepancy between them. However, the effective break with "das Adam Smith Problem" and its pattern of argument was only made with the publication by Edwin Cannan in 1896 of a newly found set of students' notes on Smith's lectures at the University of Glasgow in the mid-1760s, toward the end of his professorship.[7] These notes showed how political economy was conceived by Smith as part of a comprehensive scheme of morals and politics that had the moral theory of *The Theory of Moral Sentiments* as its foundation. At the same time, scholars such as August Oncken and Walther Eckstein began to make sense of the relationship between

---

[5] See editors' Introduction in TMS, 20–4; and Keith Tribe, "The German Reception of Adam Smith," in *A Critical Bibliography of Adam Smith*, ed. K. Tribe (London, 2002), pp. 120–52, at 137–48; and L. Montes, *Adam Smith In Context. A Critical Reassessment of Some Central Components of His Thought* (Basingstoke, Hampshire, 2004), pp. 20–39.

[6] See especially the polemical work by Witold von Skarżyński, *Adam Smith als Moralphilosoph und Schoepfer der Nationaloekonomie* (Berlin, 1878).

[7] Adam Smith, *Lectures on Justice, Police, Revenue and Arms*, ed. E. Cannan (Oxford, 1896).

sympathy, self-interest, and the multiplicity of other motivations with which Smith operated.[8]

This appreciation of Smith's systematic intent was greatly strengthened and enriched through the publication in the 1960s and 1970s of additional student notes both from his lectures on moral philosophy and from his course on rhetoric and belles lettres at Glasgow.[9] Scholars such as D. D. Raphael and A. L. Macfie suggested that *The Theory of Moral Sentiments* provided a general theory of moral psychology in which self-interest was only one feature, and that in *The Wealth of Nations*, Smith developed the social and economic implications of this part of humanity's moral motivation.[10] This was underpinned by more detailed analysis of Smith's concept of sympathy, showing how it functions as a "value neutral" medium of social intercourse that has nothing to do with positive attitudes such as benevolence.[11] Even so, the Adam Smith Problem remains a feature of the literature.[12]

That Smith's intended system has had no other impact than that of becoming an object of controversial scholarly reconstruction has been decisive for the rest of his legacy, at least until very recently. During the first century after his death, no statement of systematic intent, other than the Preface to *The Theory of Moral Sentiments*, was commonly available, and when such statements were provided by the lectures, their status as arcane students' notes ensured that they would not readily disturb set patterns of interpretation. Outside a small circle of historical scholars, then, while *The Wealth of*

---

[8] August Oncken, "Das Adam Smith-Problem," *Zeitschrift für Socialwissenschaft* 1 (1898): 25–33, 101–8, 276–87; Walther Eckstein, "Einleitung," in Adam Smith, *Theorie der ethischen Gefühle*, ed. Walther Eckstein (Leipzig, 1926), pp. ix–lxxi, at lii–xvi.

[9] LJ and LRBL.

[10] See the editors' Introduction to TMS; A. L. Macfie, *The Individual in Society* (London, 1967), pp. 59–81; D. D. Raphael, *Adam Smith* (Oxford, 1985), pp. 88–90. Cf. also R. F. Teichgraeber, III, "Rethinking 'Das Adam Smith Problem,'" *Journal of British Studies* 20 (1981): 106–23 (reprint in *Adam Smith*, ed. K. Haakonssen [Brookfield, VT, 1998]).

[11] See T. D. Campbell, *Adam Smith's Science of Morals* (London, 1971); J. R. Lindgren, *The Social Philosophy of Adam Smith* (The Hague, 1973); and K. Haakonssen, *The Science of a Legislator. The Natural Jurisprudence of David Hume and Adam Smith* (Cambridge, 1981).

[12] See, e.g., V. Brown, *Adam Smith's Discourse: Canonicity, Commerce, and Conscience* (London, 1994), and J. R. Otteson, "The Recurring 'Adam Smith Problem,'" *History of Philosophy Quarterly* 17 (2000): 51–74.

Nations retained its place as the foundational text for economics, *The Theory of Moral Sentiments* remained a minor – very minor – classic in the history of moral philosophy. Since these disciplines preserve their identity by avoiding properly historical study of their own past, shaping instead their "history" according to the needs of their current self-perception, it has been difficult for newer scholarly readings to have much general impact. As a concession to the hold modern disciplines have over Smith's legacy, the discussion that follows is divided into separate considerations of his political economy, his moral philosophy, and other branches of modern inquiry. However, it must be borne in mind that much of Smith's originality lies in his transgression of the boundaries of modern divisions.

POLITICAL ECONOMY

Smith's legacy under this heading has been absorbed within a long sequence of developments in the science and art of economics, beginning with a succession of Scottish, English, and French disciples who created a body of thinking retrospectively labelled as "classical political economy." While there can be no doubt that for figures such as Robert Malthus, David Ricardo, and Jean-Baptiste Say, *The Wealth of Nations* was the single most important starting point for their own speculations, they adopted only part of Smith's legacy and transformed it into something different in the process of abridgement. Protests against the appropriation of *The Wealth of Nations* by these economists were registered in the nineteenth century, but their force was diffused by concentration on methodological polemics: whether Smith would have endorsed the "viciously" deductive methods of his followers or the sounder inductivist and historical methods of their critics.[13] The idea that Smith's legacy could be encapsulated, virtually without remainder, within a homogenized "classical" model has proved most attractive to

[13] These disputes, part of a larger *Methodenstreit*, were rehearsed during the centennial celebrations of the WN in 1876. One of the participants, T. E. Cliffe Leslie, went beyond methodology to grasp the idea that Smith's entire enterprise might not conform with later conceptions of economics. On this, see the discussion and the references cited in D. Winch, "An Amusing Book About Old Times," in *Contributions to the History of Economic Thought*, eds. A. E. Murphy and R. Prendergast (London, 2000), pp. 73–95.

economists and those who write the histories that occasionally accompany a training in that discipline. However, there have also been some significant demurrals from economists who have sought to recover elements of Smith's legacy that have been overlooked or distorted. Before considering some of these, it is first necessary to recall the ways in which most orthodox economists have appropriated the legacy.

To those neo-classical economists for whom general equilibrium theory of the Walras-Pareto type represents the highest achievement of modern economic theorising, Smith is remarkable for having posed the original problem: under what market conditions does the "invisible hand" generate the most efficient allocation of a society's scarce resources on the basis of decisions made by individual economic agents, acting as the buyers and sellers of productive resources and final goods and services? From this perspective it is possible to regard Smith as foreshadowing one of the central problems of economics, while recognising that his intuitions left much to be repaired by more sophisticated generations. Joseph Schumpeter set the patronising tone when discussing Smith's pioneering efforts in this field.[14] Others, notably Paul Samuelson, exercised great mathematical ingenuity in showing that the central core of Smith's economics, as found in Books I and II of *The Wealth of Nations*, can be accommodated within a sophisticated version of a "canonical" model of neo-classical growth theory.[15]

In recent decades, economists belonging to the Chicago school, as well as advocates of "public choice theory" or "constitutional economics," led by George Stigler, Gary Becker, James Buchanan, and others, have stressed Smith's credentials as the forerunner of another version of neo-classicism. They hold that by constructing his economics on the "granite" foundations of the self-interest principle, Smith was able to unify his subject matter, give penetrating analyses of market-oriented behaviour, and provide a powerful insight into the special-interest politics surrounding economic legislation and the "rent-seeking" activities of organised economic agencies. As an advocate of the explanatory power of

---

[14] See *History of Economic Analysis* (London, 1963), pp. 188–9.
[15] "The Canonical Classical Model of Political Economy," *Journal of Economic Literature* 16 (1978): 1415–34.

self-interest–based models, however, Stigler was disappointed to find how often Smith departs from the logic of rational, utility-maximising man when he deals with politics: why, asks Stigler, does Smith accord "a larger role to emotion, prejudice, and ignorance in political affairs than he ever allowed in economic affairs"?[16] The question is an interesting one but needs a different answer from the one given by Stigler and public choice theorists generally.

One could contest the contrast between economics and politics at the outset: prudential assessments of self-interest in *The Wealth of Nations* are not the only motives on display, and they are rarely long-sighted or characterized by a high degree of rational calculation. Honour, vanity, self-deception, love of ease, and love of domination play almost as much of a part in *The Wealth of Nations* as they do in *The Theory of Moral Sentiments*, where Smith is dealing with a larger range of possible types of social interaction. The ideal-type "legislator" to whom both of Smith's works are addressed is not presented with anything quite as simple as an economic model of politics to guide his actions and inactions. Unlike the "man of system" criticised in *The Theory of Moral Sentiments* for arrogance in adhering to a dogmatic plan of action and for treating a society composed of individuals with their own "principles of motion" as though they were the passive figures on a chess-board – unlike this, Smith's legislator is expected to be more sensitive to the "confirmed habits and prejudices of the people," framing his actions in the light of what the current state of opinion can bear.

Another economist with Chicago connections, but with deeper roots in Austrian economic thought, Friedrich Hayek, has seen virtue in what other Chicagoans regard as faint-heartedness on Smith's part – the short-sightedness and imperfect knowledge Smith attributes to economic agents and legislators. Instead of seeking to tighten the nuts and bolts of Smith's analysis of a market economy, Hayek concentrated on a feature of Smith's thinking that he shares with his Scottish compatriots, Hume and Adam Ferguson, as well as Bernard Mandeville – the methodology or epistemology that underlies the penchant of these authors for

---

[16] George J. Stigler, "Smith's Travels on the Ship of State," in *Essays on Adam Smith*, eds. A. S. Skinner and T. Wilson (Oxford, 1976), p. 241.

explaining complex social and historical outcomes as the unintended result of purposive behaviour undertaken by short-sighted individuals. In Hayek's hands this is part of a general attack on the kind of "constructivist" thinking he associates with the French *philosophes*, post-revolutionary French positivism, and, in the twentieth century, with interventionist forms of social democracy.

Since there are some genuine echoes here of Smith's criticism of the "man of system" and of the sceptical stance that Smith, following Hume, adopted toward rationalist and utopian political visions, it may be worth saying a little more about Hayek's appropriation of Smith's legacy. There are two dimensions to Hayek's position. The first relates to the information-discovering properties of the price mechanism operating in decentralised forms of capitalism. Markets become the means by which the "dispersed bits of incomplete and frequently contradictory knowledge which all separate individuals possess" are coordinated. They achieve this in a manner that could not be duplicated in any centrally planned society, if only because that knowledge is "tacit" and hence not capable of being articulated, let alone transmitted, except through participation in a system of market rewards and penalties.[17]

Confined in this manner to economics, Hayek's insight would merely be an Austrian variation on other economic theories of market efficiency. In giving it an Austrian twist, however, there are two features of Smith's economics that have to be overlooked or forgiven. Whatever else it might be, *The Wealth of Nations* is certainly a contribution to the theory of aggregate wealth generation or retardation. In an older formulation, it is a form of *plutology* rather than *catallactics* based on the free exchange of pre-existing forms of property. In addition, by separating exchange values from utility or use values, and by treating "natural price" in terms of labour effort and costs of production, Smith adopted what Austrians would call an "objectivist" as opposed to a "subjectivist" position. This is an unacceptable move to them because it implies that wants, instead of being the outcome of subjective and non-comparable individual choices, have an objective empirical dimension. The worrying

---

[17] The quotation comes from an early work, "The Use of Knowledge in Society," first published in 1945 as reprinted in *Individualism and the Social Order* (Chicago, IL, 1947), p. 77, which Hayek later developed with greater sophistication.

element here consists in the suggestion that if wants can be measured objectively, they provide a basis on which interventionist-minded bureaucrats could supplant or supplement the subjective choices made through market processes.

The second dimension of Hayek's appropriation of Smith contains an insight of broader significance to the social sciences. Hayek extended the idea of spontaneously generated order to the evolution of such crucial social institutions as language, law, and morality. Hayek's reading of Hume's theory of justice as the product of human artifice is crucial here and can be extended to Smith. One aspect of Hayek's formulation of the evolutionary thesis is its "functionalism": the idea that what has evolved through a process of natural selection must be presumed to serve a positive purpose in maintaining social order or in lending survival value to existing social institutions and customs. This runs the risk of reifying "tradition" in the manner adopted by Edmund Burke when faced with post-French revolutionary plans for the reformation of society. Or, to modify the comparison, it risks identifying what has happened "naturally" with normative qualities of "fitness" that we associate with some nineteenth-century forms of Social Darwinism.[18]

Smith has been accused of relying on optimistic teleological explanations of the social order and of supplying them with theistic or providentialist foundations. In more recent work on Smith, however, the role foisted on him as apologist for, and patron saint of, liberal capitalism has given way to one that stresses his capacity to supply the ingredients for a critical approach to the kind of society emerging in his own day and persisting into ours.[19] Much of *The Wealth of Nations* is devoted to analysing those cases where private interests conflict with public good, as Smith had redefined it; and his constructivist tendencies are revealed in the large number of practical legislative and institutional proposals he made for minimizing that conflict.[20] Since the balance sheet he used in judging

[18] For a discussion of "Hayek, the Scottish School, and Contemporary Economists," see John Gray's article under this title in *The Scottish Contribution to Modern Economic Thought*, ed. D. Mair (Aberdeen, 1990), pp. 249–62.

[19] For a survey article that stresses the "critical" dimension, see Keith Tribe's "Adam Smith: Critical Theorist?," *Journal of Economic Literature* 37 (1999): 609–32.

[20] One of the earliest students of this part of Smith's legacy was Nathan Rosenberg; see his "Some Institutional Aspects of the *Wealth of Nations*," *Journal of Political Economy* 18 (1960): 557–70.

the process known as civilisation contained debit items as well
as credits, there is no guarantee that spontaneous social evolution
will deliver the best outcome. One aspect of the scepticism that
Hume and Smith share reveals itself in their attitude to the part
played by wickedness, folly, and accident in human affairs. Unintended consequences are not uniformly beneficial, as is shown by
the famous case of Smith's diagnosis of the effects of the division of
labour in producing a form of "mental mutilation" that has serious
moral and social consequences. Just how seriously Smith regards
these consequences can only be fully appreciated by reference to
the mechanisms of mutual adjustment to moral norms expounded
in *The Theory of Moral Sentiments*.

Neo-liberalist attempts to monopolize Smith's legacy have naturally given rise to counter claims from the opposite end of the
current politico-economic spectrum. Deciding what is right or left
wing, or optimistic or pessimistic, about Smith could be a harmless sport, the modern equivalent of an older game of trying to
separate Cavaliers from Roundheads or Tories from Whigs. Of
more lasting significance, however, are those attempts to build on
Smithian intellectual foundations rather than imputed ideological
ones. Within economics there is now a large family of such models, the ancestry of which can be traced back to a classic article
on "Increasing Returns and Economic Progress" written by Allyn
Young in 1928.[21] Unlike the more conventional interpretations
advanced by neo-classical economists mentioned earlier, Young
used the famous chapters on the division of labour and the extent
of the market in Book I of *The Wealth of Nations* to construct a
model of self-sustaining growth in which cumulative movements
away from market equilibrium become the means by which internal and external economies of scale are harnessed. In other words,
Young made use of a distinction chiefly associated with the work of
Alfred Marshall to recover a dynamic dimension to Smith's thinking that had been overlaid by neo-classical concerns with static
allocation problems.

Young's work has now given rise to a variety of non-neo-
classical approaches to the economics of under-development,
international trade, and industrial growth in mature capitalist

[21] *Economic Journal* 38 (1928): 527–42.

economies.[22] The chief merit of these attempts to build on Smith's legacy is that they capture the exponential properties of his vision of growth, especially when compared with those asymptotic models that make Smith the precursor of "classical" ideas more readily associated with Malthus, Ricardo, and Marx, in which diminishing returns dominate the scene. Economists are now more inclined to turn to Smith's division-of-labour chapters for endogenous theories of growth, especially those parts of them that turn on the "skill, dexterity and judgement" mobilised by occupational specialisation. At the very least such approaches give a more convincing account of how growth is sustained in mature capitalist societies than can be found in conventional neo-classical economics, where an opaque appeal to technological change as an almost literal *deus ex machina* has to be made. There is also a link with Hayek, and one of Hayek's pupils, George Shackle, in the emphasis placed on how the division of labour develops "capabilities" (a key concept in this literature) and overcomes the partiality of the knowledge available to individuals or organisations. The models are endogenous in the sense that technological improvement is internal to the process; it *creates* the skills and capabilities of its human agents as much as it makes use of those that already exist. The process involves qualitative as well as quantitative improvement in a manner that imparts a genuinely Smithian feel to the business.

One can also find admirers of Smith's legacy among economic historians and those historical sociologists who seek to explain long-term economic change on a comparative basis. "Nations" in *The Wealth of Nations* is plural, and much of the book is concerned with the reasons for retardation as well as the circumstances that differentiate progressive, stationary, and declining states or nations. It was one of Smith's achievements to have lengthened the time scale according to which economic change should be

---

[22] Those most closely associated with the development of Young's position in the early stages were Nicholas Kaldor, Hla Myint, and George Richardson; see the references to their work in D. Winch, "Adam Smith's Problems and Ours," *Scottish Journal of Political Economy* 44 (1997): 384–402. Lauchlin Currie provides another conduit through which Young's ideas have been transmitted, with Roger J. Sandilands acting as editor and interpreter for both figures; see his, "Perspectives on Allyn Young in Theories of Endogenous Growth," *Journal of the History of Economic Thought* 22 (2000): 309–28. For a recent survey of the literature, see Ramesh Chandra, "Adam Smith, Allyn Young, and the Division of Labor," *Journal of Economic Issues* 38 (2004): 787–805.

assessed. He also provided a new set of criteria for measuring economic growth and judging the benefits of "opulence" as part of his antidote to the short-termism of much of the mercantile literature he attacked. One sees this in Book III, the shortest and oldest part of *The Wealth of Nations*, which deals with the mixture of legal, political, and economic factors that underlie the crucial transition from feudal to commercial society, the last two stages in Smith's four-stage taxonomy of types of society. Schematic though Book III may be, when taken in conjunction with the *Lectures on Jurisprudence* it is an important source for understanding what Smith shared with Hume as historian of civil society, and how Smith delineated those features of "modern" society that differentiate it from its predecessor. It is also possible to gauge from these chapters how Smith combined a cosmopolitan, or European-wide argument, with an appreciation of the accidental features that accounted for England's peculiarity.

Karl Marx's appreciation of the qualities of some of his bourgeois predecessors as historians of civil society later gave rise to the view that Smith's theory of four stages was a materialist interpretation of historical change, if not the full-blown version we associate with Marx and Engels.[23] After considerable debate, conducted in the light of the newer versions of the *Lectures on Jurisprudence*, this interpretation has been in retreat for some years now, not least because it requires giving economic causes a pre-eminence over legal and political variables that conflicts with Smith's priorities as legal-moral philosopher. The work of Max Weber has been suggested as a more promising approach to Smith, with a new term, "institutional individualism," being proposed as the link between both authors.[24] Custom, rationality, and religion do not play the same part in Smith that they do in Weber, which may mean that those who wish to combine the larger themes of sociological history with a proper regard for historical contingency in Smith's manner may have to accept Smithian rather than Marxian or Weberian as the label under which they operate.

---

[23] This was the view advanced by Ronald Meek, in "The Scottish Contribution to Marxist Sociology" as reprinted in *Economics and Ideology and Other Essays* (London, 1967), pp. 34–50.

[24] See Hyun-Ho Song, "Adam Smith as an Early Pioneer of Institutional Individualism," *History of Political Economy* 27 (1995): 425–48.

SMITH'S ETHICS

The legacy of Smith's moral philosophy is elusive in the extreme. In so far as there has been any coherence in this story, it is only at a high level of generality. For most of the two centuries since *The Theory of Moral Sentiments* stopped being read on the premises of Smith's contemporaries, the work has been seen as an exercise in normative moral psychology. As with such precursors as Francis Hutcheson and Joseph Butler, Smith is supposed to have put forward a theory according to which those features of the world which are subject to moral evaluation, namely actions or their intentions, are perceived by a moral faculty: when this moral faculty functions well, it approves and disapproves *correctly*. On such a reading of Smith, the morally correct action is approved sympathetically by an impartial spectator. This pattern of interpretation had already begun during Smith's lifetime, as instanced by the critical reception of *The Theory of Moral Sentiments* by the Common Sense philosophy of Thomas Reid and its development by Dugald Stewart, Thomas Brown, and James Mackintosh.[25] It was pursued during the nineteenth century both in specialised monographs by J. A. Farrer and R. B. Haldane, and in more general histories by Henry Sidgwick, James McCosh, and others.[26] Allowing for many variations and additions, the central concern has been twofold: whether Smith's theory of sympathy provided an adequate account of the moral powers, and whether the spectator could be a foundation for a normative ethics that avoided collapse into mere relativism. One of the most attractive and subtle readings in this vein is Charles Griswold's recent argument that while the impartial spectator is

[25] Dugald Stewart, *Account of the Life and Writings of Adam Smith, LL.D*, II.1–43, in EPS; and Stewart, "The Philosophy of the Active and Moral Powers of Man" (1828) in *Collected Works of Dugald Stewart*, 11 vols., ed. W. Hamilton, (Edinburgh, 1854–60), VI passim, but esp. pp. 328–33 and 407–14; Thomas Brown, *Lectures on the Philosophy of the Human Mind* (1820), 4 vols. (Edinburgh, 1896), vol. 4, pp. 77–100; James Mackintosh, *Dissertation on the Progress of Ethical Philosophy, Chiefly During the Seventeenth and Eighteenth Centuries* (1830) (London, 1836), pp. 232–42.

[26] J. A. Farrer, *Adam Smith* (London, 1881); Richard Burdon Haldane, *The Life of Adam Smith* (London, 1887); Henry Sidgwick, *Outlines of the History of Ethics for English Readers* (1886) (London, 1931), pp. 213–18; James McCosh, *The Scottish Philosophy, Biographical, Expository, Critical, from Hutcheson to Hamilton* (London, 1875), pp. 162–73.

rooted in particular contexts, this figment of the moral imagination will nevertheless transcend individual and otherwise parochial
values. There is an asymmetry between agent and spectator: when
people act, they will form their standpoint under the influence
of the spectator, showing that the latter has normative superiority.[27] There have been other variations on the normative reading of
Smith, for instance with an emphasis on the procedural criterion
of impartiality and of the "ideal observer."[28] Contrariwise, where
the interest centres on the substantive issue of right moral character, attempts have been made to enroll Smith in the newly re-
established camp of virtue ethics. What is more, Smith has repeatedly been measured and found wanting as a utilitarian theorist.
Thus, T. D. Campbell and Ian S. Ross have suggested that Smith
might be said to subscribe to a merely "contemplative utilitarianism," according to which what is good and right is ultimately what
has the best consequences for all concerned. Such interpretations
concede that Smith avoids giving a utilitarian account of human
behaviour, while maintaining that the overall meaning of his system, the God's-eye meaning, is best seen as a form of contemplative
utilitarianism.[29]

While often exercises in sharp analysis, these and many other
readings of Smith do not ask the basic question, whether in fact
he was attempting a normative theory of ethics comparable to
those contained in Kantianism or utilitarianism. When that question is asked, they seem to beg it. Taking the reading by Charles
Griswold indicated previously as the strongest recent representation of the normative approach, the influence of the impartial spectator on the formation of agents' standpoints does not, of itself,

---

[27] Charles L. Griswold, Jr., *Adam Smith and the Virtues of Enlightenment* (Cambridge, 1999).

[28] See J. C. Harsanyi, "Morality and the Theory of Rational Behaviour," in *Utilitarianism and Beyond*, eds. A. Sen and B. Williams (Cambridge, 1982), pp. 39–62. For
the "ideal observer" theory, see especially Roderick Firth, "Ethical Absolutism and
the Ideal Observer," *Philosophy and Phenomenological Research* 12 (1952): 317–
45, and the criticism in T. D. Campbell, *Adam Smith's Science of Morals* (London,
1971), pp. 128–34. This argument was conducted in terms of the *meaning* of moral
judgments, and it is difficult to see that this was Smith's concern.

[29] T. D. Campbell and I. S. Ross, "The Utilitarianism of Adam Smith's Policy Advice,"
Journal of the History of Ideas 42 (1981): 73–92 (reprint in *Adam Smith*, ed.
Haakonssen). However, Campbell's earlier account of Smith as a scientist of morals
is close in tenor to the reading to be sketched here.

make that "superiority" normative in any other sense than that particular individuals in given circumstances believe it to be so. There is, however, a completely different tradition of ethical theorising which takes its departure from Smith and which issues in a sharp rejection of normative ethics. The most interesting examples of this tradition can be found in the attempts within earlier anthropology to account for morality as the central feature of human life and as a decisive factor in human evolution. In his early notebooks, Charles Darwin pointed to Hume's and Smith's notion of natural (or instinctual) sympathy as central to an explanation of the formation of moral consciousness and, hence, as key to understanding the social evolution of morality.[30] In this form, Smith's legacy came to play a role in nineteenth-century social evolutionism's concern with "environmentalist" explanations of morality. The extent of this role remains little explored, but it was summed up by a sharp, and critical, contemporary observer, Noah Porter, President of Yale, as being a matter of fact:

That a strong current of thinking at the present day sets in the direction of deriving all moral relations from social forces, substantially after the theory of Adam Smith, is too well known to be denied or questioned (cf. Alexander Bain, *Mental and Moral Science*; Herbert Spencer, *Data of Ethics*; Charles Darwin, *Descent of Man*; G. H. Lewes, *Problems of Life and Mind*; Professor W. K. Clifford, *Essays and Lectures*; John Fiske, *Cosmical Philosophy*; Leslie Stephen, *The Science of Ethics*). The theory, in its fundamental principle, is the same whether "environment," "the tribal self," "social tissue," or Adam Smith's "abstract man within the breast," or any other phrase, is employed to designate this social conscience or standard of duty.[31]

The high point of this use of Smith was reached by the Finnish philosopher and anthropologist, Edvard Westermarck, who developed it into a detailed socio-psychological theory of morality that could account for all the major features of morality. Since this side

---

[30] P. Barrett et al., eds., *Charles Darwin's Notebooks, 1836–1844; Geology, Transmutation of Species, Metaphysical Enquiries* (Cambridge, 1987), pp. 558–9, 591–3. See also Charles Darwin, *The Descent of Man, and Selection in Relation to Sex*, 2 vols. (London, 1871), vol. 1, chapters 3 and 5. The most extensive treatment of this issue can be found in Robert J. Richards, *Darwin and the Emergence of Evolutionary Theories of Mind and Behavior* (Chicago, IL, 1987).

[31] Noah Porter, *The Elements of Moral Science, Theoretical and Practical* (1st ed., 1884) (New York, 1890).

of Smith's significance has been largely forgotten, it warrants a brief outline.[32]

In Smith, Westermarck found a much appreciated precursor: "I recognize with gratitude that of all moral philosophers or moral psychologists there is nobody from whom I have learnt anywhere near as much as from Adam Smith." This applies to Westermarck's own basic idea – for which he also invokes Hume – that morality ultimately derives from the passions, and that the moral life of the species and of the individual is a matter of the socialisation and acculturation of the passions.[33] The basis for all morality, according to Westermarck, is what he called "retributive" passions, which are either negatively or positively retributive; that is to say, they intend either the harm or the benefit of their object. These elementary passions are what we see as moral passions when they assume a set of qualities which Westermarck refers to as disinterestedness, impartiality, and a certain generality – that is, when they are not simply the particular, idiosyncratic, and self-serving responses of individuals but, rather, the sort of passions which, because of their impartiality and disinterestedness, are common in diverse types of situations in a moral community. This has nothing to do with the requirement of universalizability in normative ethical systems, such as that of Kant. It is simply an empirical hypothesis to the effect that people tend to give special status to commonly shared reactive passions and that this special status is what we have come to call morality.

[32] Westermarck is occasionally referred to in newer Smith literature but then always as an analyst of the meaning of moral judgments, something he adamantly rejected as a worthwhile pursuit. See, e.g., Campbell, *Adam Smith's Science of Morals*, 94; Lindgren, *Social Philosophy of Adam Smith*, 36. For a thorough exposition of Westermarck and his use of Smith, see T. Stroup, *Westermarck's Ethics* (Åbo [Turku], 1982), esp. pp. 138–47.

[33] The explicit references to Smith in Westermarck's published works are scattered, although highly appreciative, but the full significance of Smith's influence is seen in the basic structure of the Finn's theories, and it is made pleasantly explicit in his manuscript "Föreläsningar i filosofins historia vårterminen 1914" (Lectures on the History of Philosophy spring term 1914), Edvard Westermarks Handskriftsamling, Box 78, in Åbo Akademi Library. I (KH) have translated the quotation in the text from p. 21/217 of the lectures (they carry a double set of pagination). A useful and reliable account of the lectures is given by Stroup, op. cit. For Westermarck's main theory, see *The Origin and Development of the Moral Ideas*, 2 vols. (London, 1906–8), vol. 1, chapters 1–6.

Like the Scots he admired, Westermarck did not mean this as
an analysis of the meaning of moral judgments according to which
such judgments are expressions of the passions but, rather, as an
empirical account of the emergence of moral judgments as a practice among people. A central feature of this is that we tend to
objectivize our moral sentiments. That the members of a given
moral community tend to have the same moral passions causes
them to see their morality as an objective piece of the world's
furniture, as something independent of their individual feelings.
This objectivizing tendency is reinforced by our common use of
subject-predicate constructions in our moral judgment. Westermarck devotes considerable effort to tracing this process of objec-
tivization of our moral passions, something which he sees as comparable to the "correction" of ordinary optical illusions that are
commonly accepted features of human life. In his evolutionism,
too, Westermarck is close to Smith. The central point of the argument is that the drive to extend the circle of people with whom
one is able to sympathize or share (objectivize) moral passions confers an advantage in the struggle for survival and security. As in
Smith, there is no identification of evolution with progress in an
objectively moral sense.

The only significant modern philosopher to appreciate Westermarck's way of reading Smith was the Finnish thinker's contemporary, Samuel Alexander. In his late work, *Beauty and Other Forms
of Value* (1933), he attempted a "genealogy of morals" according
to which "[v]irtue is not so much adjustment to our natural sur-
roundings as it is adjustment to one another in the face of these sur-
roundings." In accounting for this mutual adjustment as an emergent order of the passions, he refined on Westermarck and went to
some length to explain that, "[it] is no new doctrine of ethics which
I have been suggesting, but in a different form that which was put
forward by Adam Smith."[34]

This way of reading Smith is entirely alien to recent moral philosophy. It does not ask whether the moral life that is analysed
and explained by Smith is in some sense "valid" – whether the

[34] Samuel Alexander, *Beauty and Other Forms of Value* (London, 1933), pp. 236, 240,
248–9.

ideal impartial spectator really is the criterion for "true" moral judgment. Morality is a feature of the world that has to be explained causally in exactly the same way as any other part of human nature and of nature in general. This applies to the standard or criterion of morals itself, the ideal impartial spectator or, in Westermarck, the objective standpoint which is an emergent phenomenon arising from social exchange between individuals. Whether, in addition to its varied roles in human lives, including failures to honour it, the objective point of view is valid was not a question Smith asked. This is not to say that Smith had no concepts of moral obligation, rightness, and goodness; it is simply to maintain that once we have an account of the origin and function of these moral concepts – their causes and effects – there is nothing more to say about them in philosophical or "scientific" terms. If we want guidance on how to live the good life, we should look elsewhere, namely to the complexities of life presented by Lucian and Jonathan Swift, who "together form a System of morality from whence more sound and just rules of life for all the various characters of men may be drawn than from most set systems of Morality."[35]

Most traditional moralists had of course been of the opinion that the origin and function of our moral concepts ultimately had to be explained and validated by reference to divine intention. What Smith thought on this point is a matter for conjecture, where he is commonly seen as unclear, if not downright confused. On the one hand, he often uses traditional deistic language that seems to be meant as a justification of the judgment of the impartial spectator. On the other hand, he clearly sees belief in the justificatory role of the deity as an object of explanation on par with the rest of morality. The latter consideration leads one to the conclusion that it is as mistaken to ask whether, for Smith, God licenses the objective validity of morality as it is to ask whether the judgment of the impartial spectator is objectively valid in some ultimate sense. As part of the empirical account of the moral life given by Smith, God and the impartial spectator must figure in that imagined life. The

---

[35] LRBL, i.125. Smith rounds off a further paragraph of praise thus: "In a word there is no author from whom more reall instruction and good sense can be found than Lucian." Ibid, 126.

empirical science of human nature – moral philosophy in Smith's sense – does not go beyond this, and Smith never indicates whether it would be meaningful to try to do so. Instead, he urges:

Let it be considered . . . , that the present inquiry is not concerning a matter of right, if I may say so, but concerning a matter of fact. We are not at present examining upon what principles a perfect being would approve of the punishment of bad actions; but upon what principles so weak and imperfect a creature as man actually and in fact approves of it. (TMS, II.i.5.10)

There is an exact parallel between his concept of morals and his view of the physical sciences. In his essay on the history of astronomy, he goes through the various theories that the world has seen, presenting them as if they were self-contained systems. When he nevertheless expresses the conventional enthusiasm for the Newtonian system, he draws back from endowing it with any privileged truth-claims:

Even we, while we have been endeavouring to represent all philosophical systems as mere inventions of the imagination, to connect together the otherwise disjointed and discordant phaenomena of nature, have insensibly been drawn in, to make use of language expressing the connecting principles of this one [Newton's], as if they were the real chains which Nature makes use of to bring together her several operations. ("Astronomy," IV.76)

Smith shows no discomfort with what we would call moral or cultural relativism. For him, this was not a metaphysical issue but, rather, a matter of empirical investigation of how much or how little was stable in morals. He certainly subscribed to the relativity of morals in the sense that he saw moral phenomena as objects of causal explanation (i.e., as understandable in relation to their generation and effect).[36] However, that is different from the metaphysical doctrine that values inherently or necessarily vary with their circumstances so that universal values are impossible, a doctrine with which Smith would have as little truck as with any other piece of metaphysics. For Smith, there were in fact three features of the moral life that seemed to have a high degree of stability across time and place – a conclusion reached by his empirical, especially historical, study of the species. First, the negative virtue of

---

[36] In this regard, too, Westermarck followed in Smith's footsteps with his *Ethical Relativity* (London, 1932).

justice – essentially the regulation of violence – is as close to universal as we are likely to get in human affairs, for without at least a guiding ideal of minimal justice, human togetherness, beyond momentary intimacy, seems impossible. Secondly, the positive virtues that regulate people's love of each other – broadly conceived – while varying so widely according to time and place that they cannot be made into a universal system, nevertheless have a more or less universal family resemblance that allows empirical comparison and enables us to establish trans-cultural understanding. Thirdly, there is what we may call the procedural "virtue" of impartiality. Wherever two or more persons are together, they will be observing each other, and this will, for reasons that seem to be common to the human mind, lead to impartiality as an ideal for the participants. Impartiality has a special status in as much as it entails explaining the other virtues and their rules. Put differently, the first two points – about justice and benevolence – indicate that, as a matter of empirical fact, human morality as hitherto known has had certain stable features. The third point, concerning impartiality, indicates that this is for a good reason, namely that the character traits which we know as the traditional virtues of justice, benevolence, and so on, have as a matter of fact been picked out for special recognition by an underlying pattern of reasoning, which, on the whole, groups of people have found it difficult to avoid if they are to have a chance of remaining as a community enjoying social communication, literal or metaphorical.[37] In other words, Smith posits impartiality as a selector of behaviour, and history shows that the resulting patterns are those of justice and benevolence in the sense indicated previously.

This reading of Smith's moral theory is confirmed by the fact that all his moral, legal, and political criticism is, as it were, internal to an historically given situation (e.g., country, period, institution). He explicitly rejects the idea that we can step outside history by means of a state of nature. The patterns he discerns in the record of

[37] One of us tried to provoke attention to this feature by saying that there is an elementary similarity with Kant here: given morality as we know it in any human circumstance, what must be assumed as its precondition, apart from the faculties of the human mind? But of course Smith has room only for empirical preconditions. See Haakonssen, *Natural Law and Moral Philosophy: From Grotius to the Scottish Enlightenment* (Cambridge, 1996), chapter 4.

humanity, namely the four stages, are not historical "laws" bridging past and future. In fact, he has virtually nothing to say about
what to expect of the future; and his prescriptions are all "inter-
nalist," piece-meal, and hedged with qualifying doubt on all sides.
For Smith, life is a matter of contingency and uncertainty which
we negotiate with varying degrees of success, as experience shows
and philosophy accounts for.

JURISPRUDENCE AND POLITICS

While such an interpretation can be built on *The Theory of Moral
Sentiments* alone, as the cases of Westermarck and, much less distinctly, Darwin show, it becomes particularly striking in Smith's
extension of his moral philosophy into jurisprudence and politics.
This is the part of his planned system for dealing with law and politics that was not published and which we only know in some detail
from lecture notes. Accordingly, these aspects of Smith's work have
played a limited role in the Smithian legacy until recent times. It
has been suggested, however, that we must see the matter very differently, namely that Smith's jurisprudence remained unwritten
and, hence, uninfluential, "because it could not be written." The
argument is that Smith's notion of justice was so historicized that
it could not possibly be a properly normative moral notion: "How
can history yield general normative principles that are always the
same? Is not the process either circular or inherently impossible?"[38]
Evidently, Smith himself remained convinced until the end of his
life that the trick could be performed; and at least one considerable
thinker actually undertook it, namely John Millar, Smith's most
important student and, later, his colleague as a professor in the
chair of law at Glasgow.

In common with law professors in the civil law cultures of continental Europe, Millar used his lectures on Roman law to present
what we would call his philosophy of law.[39] In Millar's case, this

---

[38] Griswold, *Adam Smith and the Virtues of Enlightenment*, p. 37, note 61, and p.
257. For a concurring opinion, see Samuel Fleischacker, *On Adam Smith's Wealth
of Nations. A Philosophical Commentary* (Princeton, NJ, 2004), pp. 146–7. Fleischacker goes on to distinguish subtly between several different notions of justice
in Smith.

[39] See Haakonssen, *Natural Law and Moral Philosophy*, chapter 5; John Cairns,
"'Famous as a School for Law, as Edinburgh . . . for Medicine': Legal Education in

was an elaboration of what he had learned from Smith. Based on a spectator theory of the moral sentiments, Millar followed Smith (and Hume) in drawing the clear distinction between justice and the other virtues mentioned previously. Justice is a "negative" virtue in that it tells us what not to do, and it stands out because it is generally more precise and because breaches of it tend to be met with much sharper reactions, from both victim and spectators, than infringements of other virtues. Resentment at injury when regulated by impartial spectators is the foundation for judicial settlement of disputes; and those areas of life which are protected by such resentment constitute our "perfect" rights. This Smithian division of jurisprudence into "actions" and "rights" was basic to all Millar's legal thought. It completely set aside traditional ideas of natural rights as metaphysical touchstones, a moral reality outside the forces of historical society. Instead, it was a scheme which invited historical explanation of how rights and actions had been formed and reformed in the life of the species. Millar excelled in developing this part of Smith's ideas, using the so-called four-stages theory of society as a general framework. Smith divided societies into four types according to their range of human needs and methods of satisfying them. Since need and need satisfaction are determining for the available concepts of injury (and thus in turn for rights), the result is a typology of societies according to their recognition of rights. Arguably, Millar went further than Smith in historicizing this scheme.[40]

Was Millar's attempt at a Smithian jurisprudence "circular or inherently impossible"? Could he meaningfully be said to have succeeded in establishing what Smith called the "general principles which ought to run through and be the foundation of the laws of all nations" (TMS, VII.iv.37)? If one is looking for universality in some absolute sense, Millar has failed as badly as Smith himself would have done. However, if reference to the known patterns of human reaction is a valid argument in deciding how to act, for

Glasgow, 1761–1801," in *The Glasgow Enlightenment*, eds. A. Hook and R. B. Sher (East Linton, 1995), pp. 133–59.

[40] See John Millar, *The Origin of the Distinction of Ranks; Or, An Inquiry into the Circumstances which give Rise to Influence and Authority in the Different Members of Society* (4th ed., 1806), ed. Aaron Garrett (Indianapolis, IN, 2006); see also Garrett's Introduction.

instance, how to make law, then both Smith and Millar may legiti-
mately be said to have a natural jurisprudence. Whether all known
reactions, for instance the various "rights," are "valid" for humanity in general is a matter of experience, varying according to what
people in hitherto unknown societies and circumstances will recognize. Smith's preference for the common law of England was
not casual; he considered it "formed on the naturall sentiments of
mankind" (LJ[A] ii.75). This makes his jurisprudential legacy different from that of Aquinas or Leibniz and that is not the least of its
attractions.

Millar's jurisprudence had a lasting influence on Scots law
through one of his pupils, David Hume, future Professor of Scots
Law in Edinburgh who had been sent to study with Millar by his
uncle, the philosopher David Hume.[41] The younger Hume was an
avid Tory, not at all sympathetic to Millar's politics and unin-
terested in philosophy. Nevertheless, Millar's Smithian teaching
pervades Hume's highly influential lectures on Scots Law, and is
modified only by the reversal of Millar's treatment of real rights
and personal rights. Beyond this specific impact, Smith and Millar
prepared the way for the relatively early and important reception
in Scottish jurisprudence of the German historical school of Carl
Friedrich von Savigny and Gustav Hugo. In fact, as John Cairns has
shown, there was a direct link through the work of James Reddie,
who had been Millar's student, and in that of Reddie's son, John.[42]
Any influence in the other direction seems to have been slight,
although Millar was certainly known in German legal history.[43]

Millar was not the last to take up the historical aspect of Smith.
Echoes of it can be found in the attempt by the historical economist,

---

[41] See John J. W. Cairns, "From 'Speculative' to 'Practical' Legal Education: The
Decline of the Glasgow Law School, 1801–1830," *Tijdschrift voor Rechtsgeschiede-
nis* 62 (1994): 331–56, at 341–2, 352–5.

[42] James Reddie, *Inquiries Elementary and Historical in the Science of Law* (London,
1840); John Reddie, *Historical Notices of the Roman Law, and of the Recent
Progress of Its Study in Germany* (Edinburgh, 1826); and id., *A Letter to the Lord
Chancellor of Great Britain, on the Expediency of the Proposal to Form a New
Civil Code for England* (London, 1828). John W. Cairns, "The Influence of the German Historical School in Early Nineteenth-Century Edinburgh," *Syracuse Journal
of International Law and Commerce* 20 (1994): 191–203.

[43] See, e.g., Johann Friedrich Reitemeier, *Geschichte und Zustand der Sklaverey und
Leibeigenschaft in Griechenland* (Berlin, 1789), p. 12.

Cliffe Leslie, to reunite jurisprudence and economics.[44] Karl Marx regarded the histories of civil society compiled by Smith, and more especially, Adam Ferguson, as one of the more advanced products of the bourgeois mind. From him, it went into the lore of historical materialism and eventually surfaced as an influential element in modern scholarly debates about Smith.[45]

POLITICAL LEGACY

Whereas lawyers, like economists, possess some clear, if some-times over-simplified, criteria for judging Smith's performance over their terrain, these are less easy to state in the case of politics. Are we, for example, talking of political theory, political philosophy, or political science? Where does Smith fit within the accepted genealogies and categories of these branches of academic inquiry? One prevalent view of Smith's significance for political theory maintains that in magnifying the anonymous aspects of our eco-nomic relationships – as one who, before Marx completed the pro-cess, had begun to identify civil society with economy – Smith was responsible for marginalizing or displacing politics in any signifi-cant sense of that term. Among political theorists, this argument has almost become a cliché. By contrast with such approaches, and following in the footsteps of Duncan Forbes, although working for the most part independently, we have been exploring the "science of politics," or as we prefer to call it, the "science of the legislator" cultivated by both Hume and Smith.[46] This science embraced the practical guidance offered to legislators in *The Wealth of Nations*, as well as the critical theory of natural jurisprudence expounded in *The Theory of Moral Sentiments* and illustrated historically in the *Lectures on Jurisprudence*. It also becomes possible to explain what Smith had in mind when describing his own system in *The Wealth*

---

[44] See especially "The Political Economy of Adam Smith" in T. E. Cliffe Leslie, *Essays in Political Economy*, 2nd ed. (1888), and footnote 13 in this chapter.

[45] For an overview of the historical-materialist debate from Roy Pascal to Ronald Meek and beyond, see Andrew S. Skinner, "A Scottish Contribution to Marxist Sociology?" in *Classical and Marxian Political Economy. Essays in Honour of Ronald L. Meek*, eds. I. Bradley and M. Howard (New York, NY, 1982), pp. 79–114.

[46] See D. Forbes, *Hume's Philosophical Politics* (Cambridge, 1975); and "Sceptical Whiggism, Commerce, and Liberty," in *Essays on Adam Smith*, eds. A. S. Skinner and T. Wilson (Oxford, 1976), pp. 179–201.

of Nations as the "system of natural liberty and perfect justice," and why he was so confident in describing many institutions and policies as unjust rather than merely inexpedient.

If we are to understand the shift of focus associated with Hume and Smith within what traditionally passed for the sciences of morals and politics in the eighteenth century, one way of doing so is to stress the secular, "experimental," or empirical side of their work. This emerges in their thoroughgoing efforts to provide naturalistic explanations for moral and political order that were free from prevailing religious treatments of these themes, and from self-serving defences or attacks on existing political institutions. In politics, for example, they attempted to shift debate away from the normative theories of obligation to be found in contractual accounts of the origin of civil government. In place of the rational individualistic fictions of a "state of nature," they put explorations of the actual historical and anthropological record based on the assumption that man was a natural social creature whose evolving institutions could best be understood as the outcome of harnessing or curbing persisting passions to be found in the everyday experience of "common life." Opposition to contractualism and a commitment to reconstructing the actual history of civil society, differentiated Hume and Smith from such figures as Hobbes and Locke in the seventeenth century and from Rousseau in their own century. Thus Smith could not endorse Rousseau's account of the origin of civil government because it was based on the assumption that man was not by nature a sociable creature. Hence Rousseau's belief that man could only be induced to enter into civil association by a kind of conspiracy or trick. Yes, historical evidence showed that governments have frequently been established on the basis of force and fraud. Elites or small groups have exercised a disproportionate influence on government: the rich and powerful have achieved laws favouring the protection of their forms of property, just as men have framed laws against women and merchants were capable of obtaining special privileges that did not consort with the public good. However, there is also a fundamental need for society, for basic rules for settling disputes over property in its widest sense. The capacity to work these out could not be attributed solely to conspiracy, as Rousseau, following Mandeville, had argued.

CONCLUSION

It is possible to appreciate those aspects of Smith's legacy we have mentioned without turning him into a hero for our times. Or rather, whether we seek to do so is a matter of personal taste. All that we have claimed here is that by comparison with other philosophers or social theorists who have tackled similar large-scale problems, there are some characteristics of Smith's approach that are still worthy of admiration and emulation. One group of these turns on tough-mindedness, scepticism, and cautiousness, his preference for the long view, the calm over the excited one. Another turns on what we have spoken of previously as his anti-utopianism: his assumption that while institutions and social practices could provide a measure of protection against the most destructive proclivities, there was little point in positing an inherent capacity for progressive improvement in the basic ingredients of human nature. Related to this was a preference for theorising on the basis of an assumption of imperfection in our knowledge. Smith's economics does not begin with an assumption of isolated and equal individuals possessing equal powers and engaged in catallactic-style exchanges on the basis of perfect information. It is a world of social emulation, a good deal of self-delusion, and marked inequality between individuals and groups judged by their wealth, incomes, opportunities, and power, but where the scope for exercising power malevolently is limited by other institutions and practices, some legal, some political and social, that lie beyond the control of the rich and powerful. As a practitioner of the art of advising legislators, Smith consistently takes account of the need to qualify the ideal solutions suggested by theory by having regard to what is feasible in existing, always imperfect, circumstances. We have to reconcile ourselves to partial evils, not out of complacency but out of regard for the social complexities of living in a world of "immediate sense and feeling" that is both willed and yet also will-less.

For a final word we return to our starting point: Hume's letter of congratulation in 1776. Hume was right in thinking that the success of *The Wealth of Nations* would be guaranteed by its copious illustrations derived from "curious facts," where this meant facts that excite our curiosity rather than mere curiosa. This might not seem to be as true of *The Theory of Moral Sentiments*, although we have argued that the appeal to the introspective knowledge we have as social actors, as well as the historical and anthropological record, provides equally curious facts that Smith was able to turn to his own systematic and impressive purposes.

BIBLIOGRAPHY

STANDARD EDITION

The Glasgow Edition of the Works and Correspondence of Adam Smith, 7 vols. (Oxford and Indianapolis, IN, 1976–2001).

BIBLIOGRAPHIES

James Bonar, *A Catalogue of the Library of Adam Smith*, 2nd ed. (London, 1932).

Vivienne Brown, "'Mere inventions of the imagination': A survey of recent literature on Adam Smith," *Economics and Philosophy* 13 (1997): 281–312.

Hiroshi Mizuta, *Adam Smith's Library: A Catalogue* (Oxford, 2000).

Keith Tribe, *A Critical Bibliography of Adam Smith* (London, 2002).

BIOGRAPHIES

R. H. Campbell and A. S. Skinner, *Adam Smith* (New York, NY, 1982).

Richard Burdon Haldane, *The Life of Adam Smith* (London, 1887).

John Rae, *Life of Adam Smith* (1895), with Introduction by Jacob Viner (New York, NY, 1965).

Ian S. Ross, *The Life of Adam Smith* (Oxford, 1995).

William Robert Scott, *Adam Smith as Student and Professor* (Glasgow, 1937).

Dugald Stewart, *Account of the Life and Writings of Adam Smith*, in EPS.

Donald Winch, "Adam Smith," in *The Oxford Dictionary of National Biography* (Oxford, 2004).

395

SELECTED MONOGRAPHS AND OTHER WORKS

James E. Alvey, *Adam Smith: Optimist or Pessimist? A New Problem Concerning the Teleological Basis of Commercial Society* (Aldershot, Hantshire; Burlington, VT, 2003).

Georg Johannes Andree, *Sympathie und Unparteilichkeit. Adam Smiths System der natürlichen Moralität* (Paderborn, 2003).

Luigi Bagolini, *La simpatia nella morale e nel diritto. Aspetti del pensiero di Adam Smith* (Turin, 1952).

Karl Graf Ballestrem, *Adam Smith* (Munich, 2001).

C. Berry, *Social Theory of the Scottish Enlightenment* (Edinburgh, 1997).

Michaël Biziou, *Adam Smith et l'origine de libéralisme* (Paris, 2003).

Michaël Biziou, ed., "Adam Smith et la Théorie des sentiments moraux," Special issue of *Revue philosophique de la France et de l'étranger* 4 (2000).

Maurice Brown, *Adam Smith's Economics: His Place in the Development of Economic Thought* (London, 1988).

Vivienne Brown, *Adam Smith's Discourse: Canonicity, Commerce, and Conscience* (London 1994).

Daniel Brühlmeier, *Die Rechts- und Staatslehre von Adam Smith und die Interessentheorie der Verfassung* (Berlin, 1988).

Henry Thomas Buckle, *History of Civilization in England* (1857–61), 3 vols. (London, 1894), III: 304–30.

Tom D. Campbell, *Adam Smith's Science of Morals* (London, 1971).

Kenneth E. Carpenter, *The Dissemination of the Wealth of Nations in French and in France, 1776–1843* (New York, NY, 2002).

J. M. Clark et al., *Adam Smith, 1776–1926. Lectures to Commemorate the Sesquicentennial of the Publication of the Wealth of Nations* (Chicago, IL, 1928).

Stefan Collini, Richard Whatmore, and Brian Young, eds., *Economy, Polity, and Society. British Intellectual History 1750–1950* (Cambridge, 2000), Part I.

S. Copley and K. Sutherland, eds., *Adam Smith's Wealth of Nations. New Interdisciplinary Essays* (Manchester, 1995).

S. Cremaschi, *Il systema della ricchezza. Economia politica e problema del metodo in Adam Smith* (Milan, 1984).

Joseph Cropsey, *Polity and Economy. An Interpretation of the Principles of Adam Smith* (The Hague, 1957; reprint Westport, CT, 1977).

F. Dermange, *Le Dieu du marché. Éthique, économie et théologie dans l'oeuvre d'Adam Smith* (Geneva, 2003).

John A. Dwyer, *The Age of the Passions. An Interpretation of Adam Smith and Scottish Enlightenment Culture* (East Linton, 1998).

Walther Eckstein, "Einleitung," in Adam Smith, *Theorie der ethischen Gefühle*, ed. Walther Eckstein (Leipzig, 1926).

J. A. Farrer, *Adam Smith* (New York, NY, 1881).

Athol Fitzgibbons, *Adam Smith's System of Liberty, Wealth and Virtue* (Oxford, 1995).

Samuel Fleischacker, *A Third Conception of Liberty. Judgment and Freedom in Kant and Adam Smith* (Princeton, NJ, 1999).

_____, *On Adam Smith's Wealth of Nations. A Philosophical Commentary* (Princeton, NJ, 2004).

V. Foley, *The Social Physics of Adam Smith* (West Lafayette, IN, 1976).

Pierre Force, *Self-Interest Before Adam Smith. A Genealogy of Economic Science* (Cambridge, 2003).

S. E. Gallagher, *The Rule of the Rich? Adam Smith's Argument Against Political Power* (University Park, PA, 1998).

Claude Gautier, *L'invention de la société civile. Lectures anglo-écossaises: Mandeville, Smith, Ferguson* (Paris, 1993).

F. R. Glahe, ed., *Adam Smith and the Wealth of Nations, 1776–1976. Bicentennial Essays* (Boulder, CO, 1978).

Charles L. Griswold, Jr., *Adam Smith and the Virtues of Enlightenment* (Cambridge, 1999).

Knud Haakonssen, *The Science of a Legislator: The Natural Jurisprudence of David Hume and Adam Smith* (Cambridge, 1981).

_____, ed., *Traditions of Liberalism. Essays on John Locke, Adam Smith, and John Stuart Mill* (Sydney, 1988).

_____, *Natural Law and Moral Philosophy: From Grotius to the Scottish Enlightenment* (Cambridge, 1996), chapter 4.

_____, ed., *Adam Smith* (Aldershot, Hantshire; Brookfield, VT, 1998).

_____, ed., "Introduction," in Adam Smith, *The Theory of Moral Sentiments* (Cambridge, 2002).

Samuel Hollander, *The Economics of Adam Smith* (London, 1973).

Vincent Hope, *Virtue by Consensus: The Moral Philosophy of Hutcheson, Hume and Adam Smith* (Oxford, 1989).

Michael Ignatieff, *The Need of Strangers* (London, 1984).

Peter Jones and Andrew S. Skinner, eds., *Adam Smith Reviewed* (Edinburgh, 1992).

Stuart Justman, *The Autonomous Male of Adam Smith* (Norman, OK, 1993).

Witold von Skarżyński, *Adam Smith als Moralphilosoph und Schoepfer der Nationaloekonomie* (Berlin, 1878).

Cheng-Chung Lai, ed., *Adam Smith Across Nations: Translations and Receptions of the Wealth of Nations* (Oxford, 2000).

J. Ralph Lindgren, *The Social Philosophy of Adam Smith* (The Hague, 1973).

A. L. Macfie, *The Individual in Society, Papers on Adam Smith* (London 1967).

Robin P. Malloy and Jerry Evensky, eds., *Adam Smith and the Philosophy of Law and Economics* (Dordrecht, 1994).

Reiner Manstetten, *Das Menschenbild der Ökonomie. Der homo oeconomicus und die Anthropologie von Adam Smith* (Freiburg, 2002).

C. Marouby, *L'économie de la nature. Essai sur Adam Smith et l'anthropologie de la croissance* (Paris, 2004).

Hans Medick, *Naturzustand und Naturgeschichte der bürgerlichen Gesellschaft* (Göttingen, 1973).

Ronald L. Meek, *Economics and Ideology and Other Essays* (London, 1967).

———, *Social Science and the Ignoble Savage* (Cambridge, 1976).

———, *Smith, Marx and After. Ten Essays in the Development of Economic Thought* (London, 1977).

Peter Minowitz, *Profits, Priests and Princes: Adam Smith's Emancipation of Economics from Politics and Religion* (Stanford, CA, 1993).

H. Mizuta and C. Sugiyama, eds., *Adam Smith: International Perspectives* (Houndmills, Hampshire, 1993).

Leonidas Montes, *Adam Smith in Context. A Critical Reassessment of Some Central Components of His Thought* (Houndmills, Basingstoke, Hampshire, 2004).

Glenn R. Morrow, *The Ethical and Economic Theories of Adam Smith* (New York, NY, 1923).

Jerry Z. Muller, *Adam Smith in His Time and Ours: Designing the Decent Society* (Princeton, NJ, 1993).

M. L. Myers, *The Soul of Modern Economic Man. Ideas of Self-Interest from Hobbes to Adam Smith* (Chicago, IL, 1983).

A. Oakley, *Classical Economic Man. Human Agency and Methodology in the Political Economy of Adam Smith and John Stuart Mill* (Cheltenham, 1994).

Rory O'Donnell, *Adam Smith's Theory of Value and Distribution* (London, 1990).

August Oncken, *Adam Smith und Immanuel Kant* (Leipzig, 1877).

James R. Otteson, *Adam Smith's Marketplace of Life* (Cambridge, 2002).

Spencer J. Pack, *Capitalism as a Moral System: Adam Smith's Critique of the Free Market Economy* (London, 1991).

E. Pesciarelli, *La jurisprudence economica di Adam Smith* (Turin, 1988).

Mark S. Phillips, *Society and Sentiment: Genres of Historical Writing in Britain, 1740–1820* (Princeton, NJ, 2000).

J. G. A. Pocock, *Virtue, Commerce, and History. Essays on Political Thought and History, Chiefly in the Eighteenth Century* (Cambridge, 1985).

———, *Barbarism and Religion*, vol. 2: *Narratives of Civil Government* (Cambridge, 1999), chapters, 20–1; vol. 3: *The First Decline and Fall* (Cambridge, 2003), chapter 16.

David D. Raphael, *Adam Smith* (Oxford, 1985).

John Reeder, *On Moral Sentiments. Contemporary Responses to Adam Smith* (Bristol, 1997).

David Reisman, *Adam Smith's Sociological Economics* (London, 1976).

Ian Simpson Ross, ed., *On the Wealth of Nations. Contemporary Responses to Adam Smith* (Bristol, 1998).

Emma Rothschild, *Economic Sentiments: Adam Smith, Condorcet and the Enlightenment* (Cambridge, MA, 2001).

A. S. Skinner's *A System of Social Science: Papers Relating to Adam Smith* (Oxford, 1979).

Andrew S. Skinner and T. Wilson, eds., *Essays on Adam Smith* (Oxford, 1975).

Richard F. Teichgraeber III, *'Free Trade' and Moral Philosophy. Rethinking the Sources of Adam Smith's Wealth of Nations* (Durham, NC, 1986).

Gloria Vivenza, *Adam Smith and the Classics. The Classical Heritage in Adam Smith's Thought* (Oxford, 2001).

Patricia H. Werhane, *Adam Smith and His Legacy for Modern Capitalism* (Oxford, 1991).

Edwin G. West, *Adam Smith and Modern Economics. From Market Behaviour to Public Choice* (London, 1990).

Donald Winch, *Adam Smith's Politics. An Essay in Historiographic Revision* (Cambridge, 1978).

———, *Riches and Poverty. An Intellectual History of Political Economy in Britain, 1750–1834* (Cambridge, 1996).

John C. Wood, ed., *Adam Smith. Critical Assessments*, 7 vols. (London, 1983–94).

J. Young, *Economics as a Moral Science: The Political Economy of Adam Smith* (Cheltenham, 1997).

A. Zanini, *Genesi imperfetta: il governo delle passioni in Adam Smith* (Turin, 1995).

———, *Adam Smith. Economia, morale, diritto* (Milan, 1997).

ARTICLES

Comprehensive selections from the extensive articles literature are to be found in the collections by Haakonssen, *Adam Smith*, and Wood, *Adam Smith. Critical Assessments*, listed previously. *The Adam Smith Review* surveys and reviews the new literature.

INDEX

accountability, 312–313, 315
action, 45, 74, 77
Adam Smith problem, the, 164–165,
    246, 303, 367, 368, 369–371
Addison, Joseph, 70, 75
aesthetics, 75–77, 86. *See also* arts; taste
agency, 5, 12
d'Alembert, Jean le Rond, 113, 277
Alexander the Great, 189, 191–192
Alexander, Samuel, 384
American Revolution, 279, 286, 349
animals, 82
anti-realism, 121–125
approbation, 43–45, 170, 173, 175, 176,
    177, 178–179, 185–186, 194–203,
    258–259, 380
Aquinas, Thomas, 297, 309, 311, 314,
    390
Aristotle, 60, 105, 113, 125, 134, 140,
    194, 196, 265, 300, 307, 308, 309,
    313, 314, 315
Arnauld, Antoine, 104
artifice and nature, 9, 22–50, 67, 93, 95,
    139, 143, 144, 145, 149, 297, 298,
    305–306, 376
arts
  imitative, Chapter 5
  and morality, 26
atheism, 86
authority, political, 292–294
autonomy, 30

Bacon, Francis, 68, 80, 95, 113,
    287
Bagehot, Walter, 360
Bain, Alexander, 382

Balliol College, 2, 114, 117
Barbeyrac, Jean, 219
barter, 178, 235, 303, 324
beauty/the beautiful, 23–46, 48, 105,
    139, 144, 155, 264
Becker, Gary, 373
belles lettres, Chapter 2
  concept of, 62
benevolence, 17
Bentham, Jeremy, 199
Berkeley, George, 38, 84n
Berlin Academy, 87
Black, Joseph, 4, 115–116, 137
Blair, Hugh, 57, 63
Boccalini, Trajano, 77
Boyle, Robert, 60
Brentano, Lujo, 370
Brown, Maurice, 120–121
Brown, Thomas, 380
Bryce, J. C., 58
Buchanan, James, 373
Buckle, Henry Thomas, 165, 166,
    369–370
Burke, Edmund, 86, 257, 363,
    376
Burn, Richard, 345
Butler, Joseph, 380
Butler, Samuel, 198

Cairns, John, 390
Calisthenes, 189, 191
Cambridge Platonists, 8
Cameron, of Lochiel, 131
Campbell, George, 57, 304
Campbell, T. D., 120–121, 180, 181, 198,
    381

401

Camus, Albert, 211
Cannan, Edwin, 370
capital, 330–332
Carmichael, Gershom, 220
Cassini, Giovanni, 121, 123
casuistry, 205–206, 218, 236
Cato, 192
cause/causality, 48, 54, 130–133, 135
    moral, 130–133, 134
    social, 51
character, 5, 36, 74, 75, 99–100, 208,
    348
    and institutions, 253–255
Charles II, 345
Charles V, 271
Chicago school, the, 373–374
Christie, John R. R., 120–121
church and state, 45
Cicero, 60, 89, 315
citizens, 300, 315–316
Clarke, Samuel, 8, 13, 194
classification, 117–118
Clifford, W. K., 382
Cocceji, Heinrich von, 219
Colbert, Jean-Baptiste, 335, 344
colonies, 3, 242, 252, 349
    and commerce, 341–343
commerce, 132, 232–233, 235–236, 281,
    282, 286–287, 327–334, 341–343
    history of, 283, 284–287
    and justice, 315
    and virtue, 286
common sense, 71
Common Sense philosophy, 2
commonwealth, the, 347–357
Condillac, Étienne Bonnot de, 82, 84–86,
    90, 94, 103
conscience, 13–14, 181–182, 186–187
consequences, unintended, 233, 240,
    375, 377
constitution, 300, 316
    British, 294
consumption, 330–331
contract theory, 222, 223, 293, 392
Copernicus, Nicolaus, 120, 121–122
corn laws, 325–326
corruption, 43–46
Crawford, James, 161
Crawford, Robert, 61, 62

Crebillon, Prosper Jolyot de, 77
Cremaschi, Sergio, 120–121, 122
Cropsey, Joseph, 317
Cudworth, Ralph, 8, 194, 198
Cullen, William, 115
curriculum, 113, 220
custom/habit, 36, 39, 117, 118, 131, 143,
    144, 193–194, 200, 379
    and morality, 133–134

Darwin, Charles, 382, 388
Darwinism, Social, 376
death, 28–30
debt, public, 286, 292, 355–357
democracy, 228, 282
dependence/independence, 254
Descartes, Réné, 82, 104, 113, 120, 121,
    123
description
    direct and indirect, 74–75
desires, 36, 330
determinism, 130–133
Dick, Robert, 114
Dionysius of Halicarnassus, 253
Dubos, Jean-Baptiste, 60, 63, 154
duty, 15, 30, 204, 207–208

East India Company, 326, 333, 342–343,
    348, 361
Eckstein, Walther, 370
economic(s), 249–257, 286, 370, 391,
    393, Chapter 12
    growth, 261, 377–378, 379
Edinburgh Review, 85–87
education, 20, 235–236, 321–322,
    352–353
    moral, 45–46
Elliott, Gilbert, 185, 298, 299, 304
emotions, See passions
Empedocles, 116
encyclopédistes, 84
Engels, Friedrich, 379
epicureanism, 1, 8–9, 16–17
Epicurus, 194, 196
equality/inequality, 19–20, 239, 252,
    256–257, 269, 310, 321, 324–325,
    338, 350, 353–354, 359–360, 364,
    393
ethics, See philosophy, moral

Euclid, 114
evolution/-ism, 357, 376–377, 382, 384
exchange, 357–359, 362. *See also* barter
explanation
  causal, 126–128, 130–133, 135, 386
  historical, 392

facts
  external and internal, 74
  historical, 274–275, 361
faculties, moral, 51
fanaticism, 43, 45
Farrer, J. A., 380
fellow-feeling, 25, 28, 168, 170, 268, 299
Ferguson, Adam, 271, 279, 281, 374, 391
feudalism, 131–132
Firth, Roderick, 184
Fiske, John, 382
Fleischacker, Samuel, 250
Forbes, Duncan, 391
Forty-five, the. *See* Jacobite rebellion of
  1745–6
Foucault, Michel, 96
Foulis School for the Art of Design, 141
freedom, *See* liberty

Galilei, Galileo, 120, 121
Gallagher, S. E., 290
Gassendi, Pierre, 8
Gibbard, Allan, 211
Gibbon, Edward, 270–271, 276, 279, 286
Girard, Gabriel, 96
Glasgow Literary Society, 115–116, 136
good, public, 199, 222
Gordon, Thomas, 77
Gothenburg East India Company, 342
government. Chapter 8, Chapter 11, *See*
    also sovereign
  origin of, 223, 392
  principles of, 292–294, 303
  purpose of, 301
Griswold, Charles, 380, 381
Grotius, Hugo, 218–219, 220, 222, 223,
    308, 309, 311, 313–314

habit, *See* custom
Haldane, R. B., 380
Halley's comet, 117
Hamann, Johann Georg, 84

hand, invisible, 20, 30, 45, 48, 132, 269,
    289, 291, 303, 314, 346, 363, 373
happiness, 43–45, 132, 199, 233, 256
  and God, 196–197
  and the imagination, 265–269
  and morality, 266
Harris, James, 86
Hayek, Friedrich, 374–376, 378
Herder, Johann Gottfried, 84, 87
Hetherington, Norris S., 125
Hildebrand, Bruno, 370
historical writing/narrative, 57–58, 63,
    67–68, 71–77, 272–279
historiography, 71–77, Chapter 10
history, 17, 361, 387, Chapter 10
  civil, 276–279, 280–282
  conjectural/natural, 107, 127, 276,
    277, 279, 280–282, 290
  of government, 281, 282–283
  literary, 69–70
  non-European, 280–281, 284–286
Hobbes, Thomas, 8, 44, 80, 82–83, 86,
    160, 194, 219, 306, 392
Holmes, Stephen, 252
Holt, Andreas, 338
Home, Henry, *See* Kames
Home, John, 59
honour, 268, 374
Hont, Istvan, 313–314
Howell, Wilbur, 60, 62
Hugo, Gustav, 390
humanism, civic, 64
human nature, 77, 114, 117–120,
    127–128, 131, 133–134, 135,
    247–249, 259, 275, 276, 312,
    320–327, 361–363, 393
  history of, 277
Hume, David (1711–76), 1, 2, 3, 4, 8–9,
    12, 13, 16, 22, 51, 53–54, 73, 86, 117,
    118, 124, 126, 130, 135, 154, 158,
    159–163, 165, 166, 167, 170, 171,
    172, 188, 194, 199, 201–202, 217,
    221, 253, 270–271, 276, 279, 282,
    283, 284, 292, 295, 297–298, 299,
    301, 305, 319, 338, 353, 366, 368,
    374, 375, 376, 377, 379, 382, 383,
    389, 390, 391, 392
Hume, David (1757–1838), 390
humour, 66, 70–71

Hutcheson, Francis, 1, 2, 8, 13, 70, 86,
    158–159, 194, 196, 199, 211, 220,
    221–222, 227, 232, 234, 248, 258,
    262, 304, 380
Hutton, James, 4, 116, 137

identity, national, 65
Ignatieff, Michael, 313–314
imagination, 9–14, 21, 63, 118, 247, 284,
    Chapter 1
  and corruption, 43–46
  and desire, 265
  and happiness, 265–269
  and the impartial spectator, 38–40,
    180–181
  and industry, 264
  and order, 23, 46–54
  and the passions, 26–28, 41–42,
    189–192
  and sympathy, 23, 24, 55, 163, 166,
    169
imitation, Chapter 5
impartiality, 387. See also spectator
industriousness, 262–265, 325–327,
    332–333, 336
infanticide, 134, 193, 196, 200
injury, 216, 217, 221, 313, 389
institutions, 253–255, 324–326,
    350–357, 393
  and character, 253–255
  and progress, 334–337
interests, 251–257, 316, 327, 328–329,
    346

Jacobite rebellion of 1745–6, 59
Johnson, Samuel, 87
Johnson Literary Club, 136
Jones, Peter, 154, 156
judge, ideal/disinterested, 13, 38,
    158
judgment
  moral, 14–16, 39–40, 45, 185–186, 246,
    384–385
  standards of, 55, 183, 384–385
jurisprudence, 6–7, 15, 196, 205–206,
    369, 388–391, Chapter 8
  and commerce, 345–347
  definition of, 301
  historical, 227–230, 231–233
  and history, 279

natural, 216–226, 231–233, 236, 241,
    279, 280, 302–303, 311–315, 390,
    391
justice, 5–7, 17–18, 42, 102, 131, 132,
    195–196, 204–208, 295–296,
    297–300, 349–350, Chapter 8
  and commerce, 325, 336
  commutative, 297, 302, 303–304,
    306–308, 310–311, 313–315
  distributive, 20, 304, 308, 310,
    311–315
  emergence of, 298, 376
  and expediency, 236–237, 290
  Greek vs. Roman, 253
  natural, 228, 242–243, 303–309
  negative, 308, 386–387, 389
  and politics, 309–315
  and propriety, 307–309
  and society, 217

Kames, Henry Home, Lord, 58, 59, 223,
    224
Kant, Immanuel, 5, 39, 84, 207–208,
    213, 383
Keill, John, 117, 124
Kepler, Johannes, 120, 121, 123
Knies, Karl, 370
knowledge, 134
Kuhn, Thomas Samuel, 123

labour
  division of, 19–20, 129–130, 149, 156,
    235–236, 249, 321–322, 330, 348,
    352, 358–359, 364, 377–378
  and morality, 262–265
  productive/unproductive, 147–148,
    155–157, 296, 323, 326–327, 351
  and value, 323
  wage, 328
laissez-faire, 363
Land, Stephen K., 104
Langton, Bennet, 136
language, 11, 38, 52, 66, 117–118,
    128–129, 368, Chapter 3
  and mind, 80–87, 90–97, 103–104,
    105–106
  and naturalism, 91, 93–97
  and system, 87–88
law and government, 303, 349–350, 369,
    Chapter 8

law(s), 2, Chapter 8
  and commerce, 345–347
  game, 229
  of nations, 223
  natural, 297, 312. *See also*
    jurisprudence, natural
  of nature, 223
  positive, 224, 231, 241, 302–303
  Roman, 273
legislator, 374, 391
Leibniz, Gottfried Wilhelm, 81–83, 88,
  390
Leslie, Cliff, 391
Lewes, G. H., 382
liberalism, 368
liberty
  and commerce, 325, 335–337,
    344–345
  and history, 282
  individual, 19–20, 233, 240–241, 325
  natural, 46, 48, 255–257, 290–292,
    303, 316, 338, 347, 363, 392
  political, 291–292, 316, 337, 344–345
Lindgren, J. Ralph, 120–121, 123
List, Friedrich, 362
Livy, 75, 76
Locke, John, 60, 80, 82, 84, 86, 87, 89,
  104, 114, 117, 128, 129, 219, 275,
  296–297, 392
logic, 65
Lothian, John, 58
Lucian, 70, 71, 385

McCosh, James, 380
Macfie, A. L., 371
Mackintosh, James, 380
Maclaurin, Colin, 124
Mabillon, Jean, 275
machine(s), 22–50, 55, 82, 97–98, 103,
  107, 289, 332–333
Madison, James, 253
Malthus, Thomas Robert, 108, 372, 378
Mandeville, Bernard, 8, 9, 250, 258–259,
  261, 262–263, 374, 392
manners, 295–296, 329–330
manufacturers, 333, 340–341
Marivaux, Pierre Carlet de Chamblain
  de, 77
markets, 322, 358–359, 361, 373–376,
  377

Marshall, Alfred, 377
Marx, Karl, 262, 378, 379, 391
materialism, 86
Maupertuis, Pierre-Louis Moreau de,
  123
Meek, Ronald L., 304, 317
Menger, Carl, 364
mercantilism, 241–242, 286
merchants, 327–334, 338, 340–341,
  345–347, 355, 356, 362–363
merit/demerit, 174–175, 178–180, 187,
  189–190, 193, 196, 198–199, 203
metaphysics, 284
Mill, John Stuart, 5
Millar, John, 2, 65–66, 125, 128, 215,
  223–224, 236–237, 276, 279, 286,
  290, 305, 388–390
mind, 9–14, 56, 66
  and language, 80–87, 90–97, 103–104,
    105–106
Momigliano, Arnaldo, 271, 273, 275,
  278
money, 322, 331
monks, 196
monopoly, 229–230, 241, 257, 340–341,
  346, 364
Montesquieu, Charles-Louis de
  Secondat, baron de, 215, 223, 224,
  253, 287
morality, 71, 133–134
  and God, 186–187, 312, 385–386
  and happiness, 266
  and reason, 39, 51
  and self-interest, 249–252, 258–269
moral luck, 183, 198–199
moral sense, 8, 194, 263, 303
Morellet, André, 342
motive/motivation, 77, 246–257,
  357–358, 360–363, 370–371, 374

naturalism, 66
  and language, 91, 93–97
nature, 47, 52, 55–56, 143. *See also*
  artifice
  and imagination, 48–50, 122
  principles of, 119
  state of, 9, 37, 223, 387, 392
Newton, Isaac/Newtonianism, 52, 83,
  89, 107, 113–114, 117, 120, 121,
  122–126, 140, 287, 386

norms/normativity, 5, 55, 195–201, 212,
    227–228, 231, 236, 381–385, 388,
    392
North, Frederick, Viscount of, 354

objects
    external and internal, 74
    simple and compound, 74
obligation, 222, 302, 392
    political, 223
Oncken, August, 370
opulence, 130, 235, 237–239, 240, 249,
    256, 320–325, 328, 330, 333, 350,
    351, 361, 379
    and institutions, 334–337
oratory, 67–68
    and barter, 322
orders, social, 327–330
order/system, 10–11, 13, 21, 23, 44,
    45–54, 264, 288–292. See also
    system
    social, 19–20, 124, 233, 239, 336,
    376–377

party/parties, 294–295
passions, 23, 25–26, 38, 64, 77, 202, 247,
    248, 252–253, 299, 382–384
    and imagination, 26–28, 41–42
    moral, 382–384
    and propriety, 189–194, 211–212, 248
    selfish/unsocial, 248
    social character of, 36
personality, moral, 18
persuasion, 77–78
philosophes, 375
philosophy, 119–120, 275, 278, 279, 289
philosophy, moral, 3, 4–9, 14–18, 24,
    100–103, 215–216, 236, 369,
    380–388. See also morality
    and political economy, 370
physics, 284
physiocrats, 2
Physiology Library (Edinburgh), 161
Piles, Roger de, 152
Pitt, William, 354
Plato/Platonism, 39, 40, 54, 116, 134,
    194, 196, 248, 307–312
pleasure, 137–140, 142–143, 146–147,
    148–151, 152–154, 155, 156–157,
    264–265
    and sympathy, 170–174

police, 234–239, 254, 300, 369
politeness, 64–65
political economy, 1, 4, 7, 17, 18–21, 23,
    239, 240, 303, 337–347, 368,
    372–379
    and justice, 313–315
    and moral philosophy, 370
politics, 20, 373–374, 388–392, 393,
    Chapter 11
    and commerce, 336–337
    and justice, 309–315
Polybius, 253
poor, the/poverty, 20, 130, 135, 228, 239,
    242, 262, 263, 266, 268, 297, 314,
    319–320, 321, 325, 326–327, 348,
    350, 352, 354, 359–360, 364
Poor Laws, 348, 361, 364
Porter, Noah, 382
Port Royal logicians, 82, 104
powers, separation of, 240, 253–254
Pownall, Thomas (Governor Pownall),
    126
praiseworthiness, 181, 186, 258–259
Price, Richard, 198
pricing, 152–154, 375
pride, 252–253
primogeniture, 228–229, 230, 238,
    335
progress, 45, 134, 230–233, 238, 240,
    270–271, 279, 280–282, 283,
    284–287, 330, 333, 334–337, 361
promises, 302
property, 129, 224, 225–226, 227–229,
    230, 232, 233, 237–239, 295–303,
    311–314, 315, 325, 350, 375, 392
    and morality, 297–303
propriety/impropriety, 14–18, 174–176,
    178–182, 183, 187, 189–194,
    196–197, 200, 203, 206, 246,
    295–303, 307–309
    and virtue, 208–212
prudence, 17–18, 259–262
Ptolemy, 120
Pufendorf, Samuel, 8, 219–222, 223, 227,
    232, 234, 304, 309, 311, 312
punishment, 194–196, 201, 216, 221,
    222, 306, 309, 313

querelles des anciens et modernes,
    278
Quesnay, François, 2

Raleigh, Walter, 339
Raphael, D. D., 125, 371
rationality, 357–358, 362–363, 379
Raynal, Guillaume Thomas François, 285, 286
reality, 51–54
reason
  and morality, 39, 47, 51
reasonable man, 39
Reddie, James, 390
Reddie, John, 390
Reid, Thomas, 2, 86, 96, 163, 198, 380
Reisman, David, 120–121
religion, 3, 13–14, 20, 40, 43, 119, 124–125, 353, 361, 379
  and history, 283–284
republicanism, 77
resentment, 191, 202, 221. See also punishment
revenue, See taxation
Reynolds, Joshua, 136
rhetoric, 98–101, 105, 272–273, Chapter 2
Ricardo, David, 108, 358, 372, 378
Richardson, William, 144
Richelieu, Armand Jean du Plessis, cardinal de, 152
rights, 221–223, 225–226, 231–232, 236, 237
  human and natural, 7, 18, 55, 223, 225, 368
  perfect/imperfect, 297, 298, 301, 302, 303, 304, 314, 389
  spectator theory of, 18, 388–390
Robertson, William, 270–271, 276, 279, 282, 283, 285
Rollin, Charles, 60, 63, 72
Romanticism, 63
Roscher, Wilhelm, 370
Ross, Ian S., 198, 381
Rousseau, Jean-Jacques, 37, 87, 89, 128, 263, 265, 392
Royal Africa Company, 342, 351
Royal Society of Edinburgh, 3, 66, 68
Royal Society of London, 60, 116
rule/rules, 15–16, 45, 208, 236, 301–303
  of criticism, 71
  emergence of, 93
  of justice, 102, 206, 217–218, 301–303

and language, 92, 102–103
  moral, 71, 102–103, 186, 203–208
Ryle, Gilbert, 95

Sallust, 143
Samuelson, Paul, 373
Sanchez de las Brozas, Francisco, 104
Savigny, Carl Friedrich von, 390
Say, Jean-Baptiste, 345, 359, 361, 372
scepticism, 1, 40, 86, 377
Schumpeter, Joseph, 373
science, 386, Chapter 4
  of human nature, 4
  of a legislator, 135, 216, 391
  of man, 135, 216
  and society, 113–114
Scottish Enlightenment, 3
Selby-Bigge, Lewis Amherst, 297
Selden, John, 219
self-command, 17, 192–193, 209–212, 260
self-delusion, 43
self-interest, 7–9, 357, 362, 363, 370–371, 373–376, Chapter 9
  and morality/virtue, 249–252, 258–269
  and politics, 294–295
  and sympathy, 24, 29–35, 163, 164–165
self-love, 38, 43, 180–182, 183, 320, 357. See also self-interest
Seneca, 143
sense(s)/sensation, 24, 25–26, 94
sentiments, 23, 25, 27, 29, 40, 41, 44, 51, 77, 101–102, 117
  moral, 138, 222, 306
  natural, 43
  and rhetoric, 67
Seven Years War, 349
Shackle, George, 378
Shaftesbury, Anthony Ashley Cooper, Earl of, 8, 41, 70, 86, 100, 105, 194
Sheridan, Thomas, 65
Sidgwick, Henry, 203, 212, 380
simplification, 97–98
Simson, Robert, 114
Skinner, Andrew, 121
slavery, 227–228, 230, 252, 255–256, 263, 264, 282, 285, 286, 341

Smith, Adam
  "Ancient Logics and Metaphysics,"
    116, 119
  "Ancient Physics," 116, 120
  as teacher, 214–216, 236–237
  "Considerations concerning the First
    Formation of Languages," 79,
    85–87, 88–98, 101, 103–108, 118,
    128–129, Chapter 3
  Correspondence, 88, 116, 126, 298,
    299, 319, 338, 354, 366
  education of, 114–115
  Essays on Philosophical Subjects, 4, 9,
    47, 48–49, 87–88, 116, 137, 319
  "Of the External Senses," 139, 146,
    150
  "History of Astronomy," 107, 115,
    116, 137, 138, 139–140, 142, 146,
    176–177, 289, 307, 368, 386
  Lectures on Jurisprudence, 4, 22,
    77–78, 129, 138, 150–151, 195,
    215–216, 219, 221–223, 225–239,
    242, 254, 255–256, 273, 279,
    280–283, 290, 291–295, 300, 301,
    303–304, 306, 310, 319, 320, 321,
    325, 329–330, 331, 338, 344, 345,
    349, 350, 368, 371, 379, 390, 391
  Lectures on Justice, Police, Revenue
    and Arms, 370
  Lectures on Rhetoric and Belles
    Lettres, 4, 10, 22, 98–101, 102, 105,
    125, 126, 139, 140, 144, 147, 164,
    176, 247, 272–273, 274–275, 278,
    361, 368, 371, Chapter 2, passim
  Letter to the Edinburgh Review, 123,
    263
  "On the Nature of that Imitation
    which takes place in what are called
    the Imitative Arts," Chapter 5
  The Theory of Moral Sentiments, 3, 4,
    7, 8, 9, 12, 13, 17, 20, 22, 24–56, 57,
    73, 75, 77, 79, 100–103, 114,
    133–135, 138, 143, 146, 147, 155,
    158, 163, 164–165, 166–167,
    168–172, 173, 175–176, 177, 181,
    182, 183–188, 189–213, 214, 215,
    219, 220, 221, 222, 224–225, 228,
    239, 241, 246, 247, 258–269, 290,
    291, 292, 295, 298–300, 301–303,
    305–306, 309, 314–316, 317,
      319–320, 321, 323–324, 327–328,
      330, 331, 338, 341, 347, 349–350,
      362, 363, 366, 367, 374, 377,
      380–388, 389, 391, 394
  The Wealth of Nations, 2, 3, 4, 7, 16,
      17, 18, 19, 22, 23, 35, 42, 43, 44, 45,
      50, 73, 77, 78, 117, 120, 129–133,
      134–135, 147–148, 149, 153,
      155–157, 164–165, 178, 216,
      232–233, 235–236, 239, 246–247,
      249–257, 261, 263, 264, 279, 282,
      284, 285, 286, 290, 303, 304, 306,
      319, 366, 367, 372–379, 391–392,
      393–394
  Works, Glasgow Edition, 137, 215
Smith, John, 8
sociability, 37, 127, 299–300, 311–312,
    392
societies, 115
society, 205, 206
  civil, 18–21, 224, 226, 275, 303, 312,
    315, 350, 379, 391, 392
  commercial, 18, 19–21, 45, 64, 132,
    239, 240–243, 286, 289, 298
  and justice, 217
  political, 226
  and sympathy, 36–38
sovereign, the, 347–357, 363
spectator, 12–13, 20, 23, 25, 26, 27–35,
    37–38, 42, 44, 75, 101–102, 203–205,
    206, 216, 259, Chapter 6
  impartial, 13, 14–15, 23, 30–31, 38–40,
    42, 45, 49, 50, 55, 75, 107, 141,
    193–194, 198, 200, 203–205, 208,
    211–212, 222, 246, 258, 260, 261,
    267, 269, 290, 298, 304, 308, 313,
    380–381, 384–385, Chapter 6 passim
Spencer, Herbert, 382
Sprat, Thomas, 60
stages theory, 18–19, 127, 129–130, 131,
    134, 225–226, 230–231, 280–282,
    283, 285, 379, 388, 389
state and church, 45
state of nature, 9, 37, 223, 387, 392
Stephen, Leslie, 382
Stewart, Dugald, 65, 79, 106–107, 108,
    114, 127–128, 132, 140, 215, 276,
    334, 340, 361, 380
Stewart, Matthew, 114
Stigler, George, 246, 249, 373–374

stock, 330–332
stoicism, 1, 8–9, 16–17, 161, 194, 196, 248, 258, 266
Struever, Nancy, 64, 65
suicide, 196, 200
Swift, Jonathan, 66, 69–71, 105, 385
Swiggers, Pierre, 96
sympathy, 11–14, 23, 101–102, 125, 145, 146, 194, 246, 260, 268, 272, 298–299, 306, 370–371, 382, Chapter 6
    artificial, 28
    illusive, 28–31, 34
    and imagination, 23, 24, 47, 55, 163
    and the passions, 41, 161, 190
    and rhetoric, 67, 69, 76, 100
    and society, 36–38, 169–170
    and will, 171
    with the dead, 28–30, 34, 168–169
    with lovers, 35
system, 10–11, 44, 45–54, 87–88, 102–103, 107–108, 288–292, 337–338, 386. See also classification of duties, 43, 47

Tacitus, 76–77, 143, 276
taste, 152–154
taxation/taxes, 235, 238, 348, 353–357, 364, 369
teleology, 47–49
Temple, William, 69, 70
Thomism, See Aquinas
Thomson, James, 70
Thucydides, 73, 75, 76
Tooke, Horne, 86, 104
trade, free, 358–359
trade balance, 339–340
Trajan, 77
tranquility, 16–17, 21, 49, 119, 138, 267, 315
trucking, See barter
truth, See facts
Tucker, Josiah, 286
Tully, James, 311
Turgot, Anne-Robert-Jacques, 2
Turkey Company, 342, 351

Turnbull, George, 126
Tytler, Alexander Fraser, 58, 59

understanding, 139–140, 142
universality
    and morality, 385–388
Universities
    Edinburgh, 59, 115
    Glasgow, 1, 2, 7, 58, 59, 113, 114–115, 136, 148, 160, 214–216, 220, 233, 236–237, 272, 279, 370
    Oxford, 58
utility/utilitarianism, 155, 194–203, 207, 212, 217, 222, 264–265, 298, 353, 375, 381, Chapter 7
    and government, 292–294

value, 323, 375
    and the arts, 152–154, 156–157
virtue, 5–7, 17–18, 25, 194, 196, 208–213
    natural and artificial, 305–306
    negative, 217, 304, 386–387, 389
    republican, 77
    and self-love, 258–269
Voltaire, François-Marie Arouet, 2

wages, 263, 264, 328
Walras-Pareto theory, 373
Ward, William, 88, 96
war and peace, 236, 237, 252, 348, 356–357
wealth, 43–45, 267–269
    distribution of, 19–20, 45
    productive, 156–157
Weber, Max, 379
Westermarck, Edvard, 382–384, 388
Whichcote, Benjamin, 8
Wightman, W. P. D., 137
Winch, Donald, 317, 361
Wolin, Sheldon, 317
Wollaston, William, 8, 13, 194
wonder, 117–120, 123, 134, 139, 142, 176–177
works, public, 350–352

Young, Allyn, 377

Printed in the United States
81339LV00002B/219